D0617295

NEW ENGLISHES

JOHN PRIDE, EDITOR

Victoria University of Wellington

NEWBURY HOUSE PUBLISHERS, INC.
ROWLEY, MASSACHUSETTS 01969

ROWLEY • LONDON •TOKYO

1982

Library of Congress Cataloging in Publication Data
Main entry under title:

New Englishes.

   Bibliography: p.
   1. English language--Study and teaching--Foreign
students--Addresses, essays, lectures.   2. Bi-
lingualism--Addresses, essays, lectures.   3. Socio-
linguistics--Addresses, essays, lectures.   I. Pride,
J. B.
PE1128.A2N38   420'.42   81-9625
ISBN 0-88377-204-3   AACR2

Cover design by Leslie Bartlett

NEWBURY HOUSE PUBLISHERS, INC.

Language Science
Language Teaching
Language Learning

ROWLEY, MASSACHUSETTS 01969
ROWLEY ● LONDON ● TOKYO

First printing: February 1982

Printed in the U.S.A.   5   4   3   2   1

LIST OF CONTRIBUTORS

John Pride   Professor of English Language, Victoria University of Wellington, Wellington, New Zealand.

Rodney Moag   Associate Professor in Linguistics, University of Michigan, Ann Arbor, Michigan, U.S.A.

Mary Tay   Associate Professor of English, University of Singapore, Republic of Singapore.

Munzali Jibril   Lecturer in English, Bayero University, Kano, Nigeria.

Funso Akere   Senior Lecturer in English, University of Lagos, Lagos, Nigeria.

Robert Serpell   Director, Institute for African Studies, University of Zambia, Lusaka, Zambia.

Loreto Todd   Senior Lecturer in English, University of Leeds, England.

Sisir Kumar Das   Reader in English, Calcutta University, Calcutta, India.

Raja Ram Mehrotra   Reader in Linguistics, Banaras Hindu University. Varanasi, India.

Shivendra Kishore Verma   Professor of Linguistics, Central Institute of English and Foreign Languages, Hyderabad, India.

Chitra Fernando   Senior Lecturer in English and Linguistics, Macquarie University, North Ryde, Australia.

Andrew Gonzalez   President, De la Salle University, Manila, Philippines.

Jack Richards   Professor of English as a Second Language, University of Hawaii, Honolulu, Hawaii.

John Augustin   Associate Professor of Linguistics, Universiti Pertanian Malaysia, Selangor, Malaysia.

Irene F.-H. Wong   Associate Professor of English, University of Malaya, Kuala Lumpur, Malaysia.

CONTENTS

NEW ENGLISHES

1 THE APPEAL OF THE NEW ENGLISHES

John Pride

In the present-day world English is the major international language. In Mediaeval Europe, Latin dominated the scene; it was the commonly shared language, right through to the seventeenth century. From then on, French took over, giving way eventually to English with the establishment of the British Empire. English spread far and wide in the world at large (it is now estimated to be spoken—that is to say, used outside of classrooms—by some three hundred million nonnative speakers alone), not for any purely linguistic or aesthetic quality it might possess, but rather as a result of political and economic factors. More recently, of course, the United States has kept up the pressure.

The story has not however been one of sheer linguistic imperialism: English has played a vital role for many countries in their achievement of independence. Mazrui (1976) for example brings out very clearly the wide range of audiences that had to be addressed in the years leading up to independence by politicians in countries like Nigeria, Kenya, Uganda, and so on. Quite different audiences all had to be reached somehow: local indigenous populations, local colonial authorities, European governments, the public at large in European countries, other black African populations, black Americans, the government and people of India, international organisations and agencies, and so forth. In all those African countries where the European language was English, as opposed to say French, English was the only possible language for this purpose. Much the same demands have been made on English in other parts of the once British colonial world.

At the same time, the language had to be politically neutralised, so far as possible. It could not have been easy for an African, or any other, politician struggling for independence if the language he used was shot through with associations of colonialism. Fortunately, in most parts of the world. this in itself

1

is no longer a problem: as Moag puts it, English in these contexts has largely come to be accepted as a fact of life.

Not that such acceptance resolves itself into any simple, straightforward state of mind. Serpell, for example, points out that at a very basic level, there are several polarised contrasts in what has been called the colonial ideology: superior vs. inferior, foreign vs. indigenous, cash vs. subsistence, urban vs. rural, modern vs. traditional, advanced vs. primitive, and so forth. If all such contrasts are accepted as somehow absolute and distinct, it might seem appropriate to conclude that English, and languages like English, should simply serve as languages of technology, as neutral instruments of modernisation, and no more. All other purposes would be served by other languages.

Yet for ordinary people everywhere these parallel oppositions represent conflicting interests and values; and the need is felt widely for some means of resolving these various conflicts. The sociolinguistic notion of triglossia, which recognises not only "high" and "low" but also "mid" languages, reflects a widespread and even popular awareness that certain languages, so-called mid languages, could serve to bridge the various gaps, thereby fulfilling (as some anthropologists have put it) an "overarching" role. Mid languages can seem not so much to stand in the middle, as astride, having a foot in both camps.

But the question soon arises: what language or languages should be adopted for this powerful role? Can any single language function in this way? The obvious solution is, of course, to regard an existing or potential national language as the new overarching mid language; perhaps it can be linguistically developed to fit it to take over, in time, some or all of the functions of some existent high language, while being promoted widely as the carrier of national identity, that is to say, as a language equally in touch with all the various low languages spoken by different ethnic groups. However, as we know, the selection and acceptance of national languages is not always a straightforward matter, nor is it always self-evident that such languages can be sufficiently developed, in the time available, to meet the society's needs for technological advancement, international communication, and the like.

There is in particular a recurring paradox to be faced, one that is well summed up in a statement made by President Kenyatta in 1969: "We are soon going to use Swahili in Parliament, whether people like it or not." For it is a fact that all over the world one finds that ordinary people are obstinate in this regard, that is to say, very likely to aspire to the use of English, or some other international language, while official policy dictates or encourages some other solution. "Kanu [the ruling party in Kenya in 1970 pronounced] will not tolerate homes where mothers and children talk to each other in English, forgetting their way of life." The same paradox can apply equally to French. In the British newspaper *The Guardian*, a French correspondent wrote, in 1976: "As the 'lingua del pane,' it remains the sole means for families and their children to emerge from anonymous poverty. In seeming to relegate French too quickly to the status of a foreign language governments may have acted contrary to what the public wants." Unesco, in 1951, urged that an "unwilling public" be persuaded to "accept education in the mother tongue" (Report of the Unesco Meeting of Specialists, 1951).

It is not difficult to multiply instances of this sort. It may indeed be very relevant to one's understanding of what English means to the people of some Third World country to investigate the changing habits of intergenerational code-switching between English and other languages, and the preferences that lie behind these, within the homes of ordinary people. English was, for example, the clear first choice of Kenyan children when Gorman asked them which language they would want to bring their own children up in (Gorman, 1971).

But mere neutrality, even an enriched kind of neutrality that goes deeper than the need for a utilitarian language of science, technology and so on, is not enough. The language will continue to grow, in the breadth of its uses and the number of its users, for just so long as those who use it feel it is their own possession, with its own range of uses, its own body of users, its own set of linguistic features. Nor should it aspire to political or social predominance over the indigenous languages close to home. The English language of the future must be accepted from within, rather than be felt as something imposed from outside. All the papers in the present volume underline this basic truth, bringing to it various emphases, and set against various regional, ethnic, political, and other backgrounds.

It it surprising, therefore, that in the study of language learning motivation most emphasis so far has been placed on a simple two-way contrast between integrative and instrumental motivation. Here is a representative quotation: "This thoery, in brief, maintains that the successful learner of a second language must be psychologically prepared to adopt various aspects of behavior which characterise members of another linguistic-cultural group. The learner's ethnocentric tendencies and his attitudes toward the members of the other group are believed to determine how successful he will be, relatively, in learning the new language. His motivation to learn is thought to be determined by his attitudes toward the other group in particular and toward foreign people in general and by his orientation toward the learning task itself. The orientation is said to be *instrumental* in form if the purposes of language study reflect the more utilitarian value of linguistic achievement, such as getting ahead in one's occupation. In contrast, the orientation is *integrative* if the student wishes to learn more about the other cultural community because he is interested in it in an open-minded way, to the point of eventually being accepted as a member of that other group" (Lambert and Gardner, 1972).

There has been much support for an integrative view of language learning motivation in recent pronouncements on the nature of bilingualism, and, in particular, on the requirement that dominant groups in society speaking a major language, should learn not only the language of a subordinate group but also, thereby, something of its culture, its way of life. It is in this special context that, for example, Haugen's pronouncements on bilingualism and biculturalism gain most of their force. He has written:

> Some have tried to distinguish biligualism from biculturalism. I wish to suggest that the two are indistinguishable except in detail. Only a linguist or an anthropologist operating with fictions can separate them; in practice they are inextricably inter-woven, and one is quite incomprehensible without the other. Any learning of a language for 'tool' purposes is to be excluded from the concept of bilingualism. . . . This is the reason we do not call our students who acquire a foreign language in school bilingual.   (Haugen, 1972)

With this, one should compare some stirring remarks from Bolinger (1971), who urges that students be brought into face-to-face communication, from the very beginning, with native speakers of the foreign language; that this language be that of the "most accessible ethnic group"; and that "we need a measure that will tell us whether our students are gaining insight and not just an alternative set of habits." In a similar vein, Gaarder (1970) asserts that "it is at the bastion of biculturalism rather than at the bastion of language alone that bilingual education will succeed or fail."

Practical solutions have taken two main forms. One is the adoption of monolingual instruction of the dominant group in the subordinate group's language in so-called immersion programmes. The other is that of bilingual education proper, applied, that is, to learners coming from the dominant group as well as to those from the subordinate group. In terms of language learning motivation, the aim in both cases is to engender an integrative outlook on the part of the dominant group who already speaks the major language, together with the added bonus of encouraging subordinate group learners who may witness or share in the process.

However, two points have to be borne in mind. One is that the birthplace of the integrative-instrumental theory was North America, where particular circumstances prevail. The other is that in spite of this the dichotomy itself has become more or less established lore in all sorts of quite different language learning contexts. When the group of learners is, or feels itself to be, subordinate in some way, the need for a basically integrative type of motivation comes into question. On the one side is the universal need to learn the language that offers most hope of "emerging from anonymous poverty." On the other is the need to acquire some other language to be able to communicate, probably for the first time, something about one's own culture, aspirations, experiences, and so on to those who do not already share or appreciate these. We should recognise the power that this third kind of "expressive" language learning motivation may have in helping to mould the special character of the new Englishes.

There are some interesting consequences. The late Professor Pandit, from Delhi, urged that English should be "just another Indian language," part of the traditional Indian situation of "grassroot multilingualism," where there would be no single dominant language: "A bilingual speaker who communicates in two or three languages in different contexts contributes to the development of the languages he uses; the competence of the bilingual speaker is spread over the languages he uses and will eventually result in easier and faster transfers from one to the other; language contact of this type is language development." For this reason, he wrote, "Removing English from the Indian scene at the moment would be disastrous for the *Indian* languages and literature." The papers by Das, Mehrotra, and Verma in Section 3 of this volume discuss the case of India itself, while the role of English in other multilingual societies is treated in all the remaining papers. The widespread habit of code-switching, which Pandit refers to, between English and other languages figures most prominently in Sections 3 and 4, while the associated process of mutual language transference (or code-mixing) is well explained and illustrated by Serpell, Mehrotra, Verma, Fernando, and Gonzalez.

Note that the scope of language transfer may at times extend far beyond the familiar nuts and bolts of syntax, morphology, and phonology as such. These latter tend to monopolise traditional studies of interference, just as they have in the past largely monopolised debates centred on the relative importance of language transfer, on the one hand, and developmental processes of second language learning, on the other. For his part, the language learner cannot help but transfer into his use of English certain of the more deep-seated culture-bound communicative competences which he has acquired and developed in his native language or languages, while at the same time having to learn new communicative competences appropriate to the target, nonnative language. The character of one such set of transferred communicative competences is brought to light by Akere for the case of Nigerian English, while the fundamental theme of biculturalism as an essential accompaniment to bilingualism is discussed at some length by Akere and Serpell.

In these contexts the question frequently arises as to whether the language must necessarily be in the process of diversifying, even to the point of fragmenting into ever more "nonstandard" varieties, each only partially comprehensible (if that) outside its own home territory. On the face of it, there may seem to be some danger of this. A. H. King, one-time head of the English Language Teaching Division of the British Council, wrote:

The situation in any country may be represented as a pyramid divided into three superimposed sections of which the uppermost indicates internationally-comprehensible English—in the universities of Africa, but not always of India and Pakistan, the middle indicates a local standard of English understood throughout the country (spoken by those who have been to secondary school), and the lowest (those whose education stopped during primary school) Pidgin, which is not intercomprehensible. With the spread of education, one would expect more speakers to come within the two upper sections, but I am not sure that this will be so. There are rival pressures working in the opposite direction. As education spreads, English spreads and becomes more lax as it does so. There is the danger that, as you get more English in a country, it may become less internationally comprehensible. There are two movements working against each other—which is going to win? The key to the impasse lies in the primary schools of Africa—the battle has already been lost in the primary schools of south Asia. (King, 1971)

Many others have expressed fears of this sort, hence one of the main purposes of the present volume is to throw some scholarly light on the whole issue of standards, intelligibility, and educational objectives.

That there *are* pidginised forms of English to take into account, often not properly described (or even their existence known of), in many parts of the world is illustrated from two continents by Todd and Mehrotra, the latter in particular relating these forms of speech to the general question of levels of intelligibility, both within the country and abroad. However, the great majority of the colloquial and indigenised (or nativised) forms of English found in so many parts of the world cannot be classified as pidgins. More exactly, they should be recognised as rule-governed stylistic variants of the more "standard" varieties in use in the speech communities in question, the latter in some cases differing in only minor details from what the native speaker would regard as correct, or standard, English.

In other words, linguists are now able to uncover some of the regular connections between different stylistic levels of nonnative varieties of English, revealing in the process how the users of the language acquire the ability to move from one level to another according to changes in the situational context. This ability is essentially no different from that of the native language user himself in his own everyday handling of the language, except that, as already mentioned, different types of communicative competence are called upon, features of native languages are likely to be transferred, and so forth. The linguistic levels in question may well be conceptualised, both by linguists who study them and by the speakers themselves, as scales of formality (from most formal or distant to most casual or intimate), and such scales may or may not be regarded in terms of unbroken continua, but rather of discrete levels. These and related questions are discussed under the general heading of "Variation within English" by Moag, and they form the main topic of all three papers in Section 4. The key role of formality in stylistic variation appears also in the papers by Serpell, Mehrotra, and Verma, while the factor of intelligibility is given special attention by Mehrotra, for India. Finally, consequential problems of educational policy are dealt with specifically by Tay, Serpell, Todd, and Wong.

The overall layout of the book needs little explanation. Section 1 opens with an unusually comprehensive paper by Moag, who succeeds admirably in his stated purposes of "looking at the full range of language situations within which English operates around the world" and doing so from a wide range of perspectives. Many interesting patterns emerge, and the whole volume benefits from his original approach. The only other paper in this section, by Tay, provides a perfect balance in focussing on one single society, and in its sociolinguistic breadth allied with exact linguistic detail.

Section 2 brings together four in-depth studies of the working relationships existing between English as a second language and the many indigenous languages of three countries in Africa. The fundamental lesson here is that bilingualism and biculturalism are two sides of the same coin, and that the wisdom of educational policy decisions will always, in the long run, be measured against this fact.

Section 3 contains four accounts of English in India and Sri Lanka, their intimate sociolinguistic detail forcing the reader to ask a very basic question: Whose language *is* English in these countries? Is Pandit's call for English to be "just another Indian language" being now realised? Is the "highly Anglicised life style" associated with one of the three patterns of bilingualism in Sri Lanka pointed to by Fernando yielding to something more regional in character, and if so, how is this affecting the shape of the language itself? Moag classifies English in India and Sri Lanka as "transitional" between second language and foreign language status. How controversial is such a view? What is meant by the now familiar labels Indian English and Lankan English?

Section 4 looks at the use of English in each of three Southeast Asian countries from the point of view of stylistic variation. What do the most standard, or formal, styles of the language, written as well as spoken, look like when set against the most nonstandard, or informal? How are the two extremes connected? What kinds of stylistic repertoire might various individuals and groups be expected to possess? What is meant by variable sociolinguistic rules? These and many more questions of related interest are explored in this section.

The paper by Wong which makes up the final section poses the ultimate question of the choice of a model of English for the Third World today. Should the goal for excellence necessarily be the acquisition of a native-like command of the language, or are there other viable alternatives? It is entirely fitting that the author of this paper is one of the few nonnative users of English who have acquired just such a native-like command. The question itself is a familiar one, but there are signs that new answers are in the air.

REFERENCES

Bolinger, D. Let's change our base of operations. *Modern Language Journal*. March 1971.

Gaarder, A. B. The first seventy-six bilingual education projects. *Georgetown University Monograph Series on Languages and Linguistics*. 1970, 23.

Gorman, T. P. Socio-linguistic implications of a choice of media of instruction. In W. H. Whiteley (ed.), *Language Use and Social Change*. London: Oxford University Press, 1971.

Haugen, E. On the meaning of bilingual competence. In A. S. Dil (ed.), *The Ecology of Language*. Stanford Calif: Stanford University Press, 1972.

King, A. H. Intercomprehensibiltiy—The humpty-dumpty problem of English as a world language. *The Incorporated Linguist*. 1971, 10: 1.

Lambert, W. E., and Gardner, R. C. *Attitudes and Motivations in Second Language Learning*. Rowley, Mass.: Newbury House, 1972.

Mazrui, A. *The Political Sociology of the English Language*. The Hague: Mouton and Co., 1976.

Report of the Unesco Meeting of Specialists, 1951. In J. A. Fishman (ed.), *Readings in the Sociology of Language*. The Hague: Mouton and Co., 1968.

Section *1*

SOCIOLINGUISTIC AND LINGUISTIC FEATURES

2 ENGLISH AS A FOREIGN, SECOND, NATIVE, AND BASAL LANGUAGE: A NEW TAXONOMY OF ENGLISH-USING SOCIETIES

Rodney Moag

GOALS

Sociolinguistic literature contains a number of attempts to classify societies or nations in terms of language situation as well as attempts to look at English in one or more societies from a particular perspective. This paper has the more comprehensive purposes of (1) looking at the full range of language situations within which English operates around the world, and (2) doing so from a sufficient range of perspectives to make the resultant taxonomy meaningful.

METHODS AND RESULTS

Reaching for these new goals seemed to require novelty of approach as well. A taxonomic instrument was developed employing the principles of distinctive feature analysis. The number of dimensions plotted in the matrix has risen from 11 in a preliminary version of the paper presented as a guest lecture at the University of Papua New Guinea, to 17 when delivered at the conference on Non-Native Englishes at the University of Illinois in July 1978, to 26 in the present version. The majority of the features plotted are trinary, while a few are binary; the specific terms chosen to represent the gradients along each scale are, in general, my own, selected on the basis of data in print, or on the basis of personal observations of English in one or more of the societal types.

The language situations in which English operates were organized into four classes for the purposes of Table 1. This permitted testing of the widely accepted distinction between EFL and ESL and also allowed for a comparison of these two types with two additional situations where English is a mother tongue. ENL (English as a native language) refers to the situation where English is the mother tongue of the dominant group and, hence, the dominant language in the society. The EBL (English as a basal language) category, used for the first time here, refers to a small group of societies where English is the mother tongue of a

TABLE 1   *Features of English-Using Societies*

Feature	EFL	ESL	ENL	EBL
SOCIOLINGUISTIC FEATURES				
Language Policy				
1. Degree of official recognition	low	high	high	low
Language Use				
2. Percentage of population using English	very low	3% or more	40% or more	less than 10%
3. Influence of English-using group in the society	minor	major	major	minor
4. Range of activities conducted in English	narrow	broad	full	broad
5. Use in formal domains	+	+	+	–
6. Use within informal domains	–	+	+	+
7. Learner/user ratio	high	moderate	inverse	inverse
Language Acquisition				
8. Dominant type of motivation	instrumental	integrative	expressive	expressive
9. Reference group for integrative component	external	internal	internal	internal
10. Secondary external reference group	–	+	–	+
11. Degree of informal learning	minimal	considerable	maximal	maximal
Language Attitude				
12. Prestige to speakers	+/–	+	+	+/–
13. Prestige in society at large	+/–	+	+	+/–
Bilingualism				
14. Individual versus societal	individual	societal	individual	societal
15. Type of English bilingualism	functional	coordinate	nil	coordinate
16. Language of higher proficiency	L1	L2	L1	L1
17. English skills attrition	high	moderate	low	low

minority group of a larger populace whose native tongue, often Spanish, is clearly the dominant language of the society as a whole.

A list of countries falling into each of the four categories appears in Table 2. The list for each class is intended to be broadly representative rather than exhaustive.[1] Wherever possible, countries were brought into the list which other writers had placed in the same category as that indicated by screening through

TABLE 1   (continued)

Feature	EFL	ESL	ENL	EBL
LINGUISTIC FEATURES				
Models				
18. Competence model	native	non-native	native	native
19. Performance model	non-native	non-native	native	native
Variation Within English				
20. Basis of lectal variation	dominant language	communal	regional & social	regional & social
21. Stylistic variation	minimal	moderate	maximal	moderate
22. Language distance between varieties	minimal	moderate	minimal	maximal
23. Range of registers	minimal	moderate	maximal	moderate
24. Rapid speech forms	nil	few	many	many
Interlanguage Features				
25. Transfer from other languages	maximal	moderate	minimal	moderate
26. Overgeneralization of rules	moderate	maximal	minimal	minimal

the feature matrix. Even greater pains were taken, however, to include cases where previous writers and our new taxonomic tool differed in the hope of promoting further debate and eventual resolution of the issues raised by the differences. Transitional societies have been put into the class toward which they are moving, rather than into that which they have been formerly considered to occupy. For both the preceding reasons, readers may find some surprising entries in the EFL column and some seeming glaring omissions in the ESL list. Problem and transitional cases are indicated in Table 2 and treated at appropriate points in the text.

The countries designated as ENL will be noncontroversial with the exception of South Africa which Conrad and Fishman (1977, p. 10) include among "non-English mother-tongue countries." I have preferred to treat ENL White South Africa and EFL Black South Africa separately, as this seems more in step with linguistic as well as political realities obtaining today and for the foreseeable future. Several Caribbean nations are included as a reminder that, though Caribbean English is often grouped among the New Englishes, the post-Creole continua there do represent native rather than second language varieties. The South Pacific island of Pitcairn with some 70 souls documents the full range of nations having English as their native tongue. The Falkland Islands, in the South Atlantic off Argentina, are populated almost entirely by citizens of Great Britain whose colony they still are and provide an added dimension in terms of the range of nations holding ENL status. The seven EBL societies listed are also

TABLE 2   *Example Societies in the Four Categories*

EFL	ESL	ENL	EBL
Afghanistan	Brunei	Australia	Argentina
Botswana*	Dominica	Bahamas	Costa Rica
	(Windwards)		(Jamaican Blacks)
China	Fiji	Barbados	Dominican Republic
(Peoples)			(Samaná)
Egypt	Gambia	Belize	Honduras (Coast and
			Bay Islands)
Ethiopia	Ghana	Bermuda	Mexico (Mormon
			Colonístas)
Europe	Kenya	Canada	Nicaragua (Meskito
(Continental)			Coast)
India†	Liberia	Falkland Is.	Panama
Indonesia	Nigeria	Grenada	San Andres (Columbia)
Japan	Sierra Leone	Guyana	St. Maarten (Netherlands
			Antilles)
Lesotho*	Singapore	Ireland	
Malaysia†	St. Lucia	Jamaica	
Malawi*	Uganda	Leeward Is.	
Mauritius*	Zambia	New Zealand	
Papua New	Zimbabwe	Pitcairn Island	
Guinea			
Paraguay		South Africa	
		(White)	
Philippines†		Trinidad and	
		Tobago	
Sri Lanka†		United Kingdom	
Somalia*		United States	
Swaziland*		Virgin Islands	
Tanzania†			
Tonga*			
USSR			
Western			
Samoa*			

*   Monolingual societies where English has some significant internal role during the period of decolonization and modernization.

†   Societies in transition from ESL to EFL status.

the result of migrations, but only one, Argentina, is based on immigration from Great Britain. All others are composed of descendants of migrants from Creole-speaking ENL areas in other parts of the Caribbean. Since these English mother-tongue enclaves have been relatively little studied, it was necessary to rely on very scant data in determining the feature designations for the newly proposed EBL class of society.

Plotting the four societal categories in terms of 26 dimensions yields a total of 104 feature designations in Table 1. Ideally, one would wish to have at least one documented source for the accuracy of each designation for one, and preferably several, nations within each class, but this is clearly impossible at this exploratory stage of the taxonomy. The rationale for including each dimension, and for the particular designations assigned in each of the four classes is given in the two sections that follow together with whatever documentation is available. With several of the features it was necessary to refine, or even to reshape, concepts used by previous writers, since, in most cases, the dimensions were being applied for the first time to the task of classifying the role of a given language in various contexts. Feature 10, secondary external reference group, and feature 24, rapid speech forms, grew out of my work on English in the South Pacific and are, I believe, completely my own.

Results obtained through the application of the distinctive feature approach include the following:

1. Individual feature designations are often shared by more than one class of society, but any two societal types taken together have more dissimilar designations than shared ones.
2. Contrasts and interdependencies of the different dimensions are brought into sharper focus. The final ordering of the subsets of dimensions within Table 1 and of individual dimensions within each subset, were arranged to exploit this capability of the matrix format.
3. Most importantly, the feature matrix is able to classify more definitively the position of English in several societies where classification was either uncertain or erroneous by previously employed measures. This was particularly true for transitional nations such as India, Malaysia, the Philippines, and Tanzania as well as for a group of small single vernacular nations in Africa and the Pacific all of which are moving toward EFL status.

To state the principal points, interrelationships, and contrasts in the somewhat lengthy and involved matrix more succinctly, a summary matrix (Table 3) was prepared in which the 26 separate features were reduced to eight composite ones. The reader may find it helpful to become familiar with this summary matrix before going on to the detailed matrix and the text relating to it in the following two sections.

SOCIOLINGUISTIC FEATURES OF THE FOUR SOCIETAL TYPES

The topics treated in this section, for the most part, fall within the generally accepted purview of sociolinguistics. Thus their inclusion here needs no particular justification. Language acquisition, however, is generally considered to be an area of psycholinguistics, but the features treated later in this paper's section on language acquisition demonstrate that it has sociolinguistic aspects definitely having a place here. Other features relating to the internal structure of English in the four societal types are grouped under linguistic features.

TABLE 3   *Composite Features of English-Using Societies*

Feature	EFL	ESL	ENL	EBL
1. Degree to which policies favor English	slight	extensive	full	slight
2. Use factor of English	slight	extensive	full	extensive
3. Index of factors favorable to English acquisition	slight	extensive	full	extensive
4. Favorable attitudes toward English	uncertain	certain	certain	uncertain
5. Bilinguality measures	slight	extensive	slight	extensive
6. Models	conflicting	nonnative	native	native
7. Language variation within English	slight	considerable	full	considerable
8. Interlanguage features	extensive	extensive	slight	extensive

Note: Shared composite features are:

EFL:ESL, 1	ESL:ENL, 1
EFL:ENL, 1	ESL:EBL, 5
EFL:EBL, 3	ENL:EBL, 1

Language Policy

Kloss (1966, p. 15) sets forth a scale of recognition along which the official status of languages can be measured. His five points are:

1. Status as an official national language,
2. Official status within a region only,
3. Official promotion through use in schools, notices, governmental activities, and so on,
4. Tolerance in the private sphere (newspapers, private schools, and cultural events), and
5. Proscription of the language.

Kloss's scale may be reorganized into four degrees of recognition—official status, encouragement, tolerance, and proscription—any of which may apply on a national or regional level. For purposes of this paper, a significant binary opposition may be assumed between "high degree of official status," Kloss's official status, and all lower degrees. Conrad and Fishman (1977, pp. 10–12) make a similar distinction between nations in which English is "designated as official language" and those where "there is some official status for English but in which English is not designated as an official language." A vital factor not amply treated in either of the works just cited is the distinction existing in quite a few nations between the official recognition which is de jure (by law) or that which is simply de facto. In fact, looking only at the official status of English can be very misleading. The co-official status of English in Singapore, for example (shared with Mandarin, Malay, and Tamil), and the fact that it is not designated as the principal language either of the nation or of its parliament (Conrad and Fishman, 1977, p. 10) completely belies the position of primacy it actually holds in the society attested by various writers on the subject including Platt (1977a, p. 377).

It may prove surprising that de jure official status for English is a poor index of its status in the society. Of the 11 nations having English as the sole designated official language in Conrad and Fishman's data (1977, p. 10), only nine are ESL. The special case of Mauritius will be discussed later, as well as that of Botswana. Further, of the 13 countries (after deleting South Africa) showing co-official status for English, only one, Singapore, actually has it as a second language, while three others—India, the Philippines, and Tanzania— are in transition (marked with a † in Table 2) from ESL to EFL status, and eight others (asterisked in Table 2) are in the group of very small monolingual nations making limited internal use of English as part of the concurrent processes of decolonization and development. On the other hand, Kenya, which may still be ESL judging from Conrad and Fishman's statement (1977, p. 8) that there has been little change in the use of English despite the 1974 designation of Swahili as national language, appears in those authors' list of countries "in which there is some official status for English but in which English is not designated as official."

Official status, in this taxonomy, therefore, is taken to mean the de facto official status of English as revealed by current governmental practice. Whereas Conrad and Fishman (1977, p. 8) broaden their definition of official status to include practice, the definition adopted here recognizes its supremacy over policy. Official legal status is, thus, included, but given secondary consideration only in the following discussion of the official status of English in the four societal types.

In ENL societies, in the main, the practice of using English at all levels is so much a fact of life that it often needs no supporting legislation. Only when one or more other languages play a significant role in the language situation, either at the national or regional level, does the need for legislative support for English arise. Thus Canada had to stipulate the use of English as well as that of French in its bilingualism act, and the South African Constitution must give official status to English as well as Afrikaans (Conrad and Fishman, 1977, p. 10). The most striking case of this, as well as of the disparity between de jure and de facto situations, is the position of "primary official language" given to Irish and the "secondary official language" status accorded English in the Constitution of Ireland (Conrad and Fishman, 1977, p. 9).

ESL societies are much more likely to have de jure official status of English, owing to their multilingual makeup, unless, as in the case of Fiji, the use of English was so much taken for granted that it was not deemed necessary to include it in the constitution. On the other hand, nonlinguistic factors can, as in the case of Singapore, beget a de jure status of equality with local languages for English entirely out of line with conditions or trends.

A high degree of official status for English is not possible in EFL societies, though in special cases, as already mentioned, a high degree of legal status and a moderate degree of status in practice can occur. In the more typical EFL countries of Europe, Latin-America, and Francophone Africa, policies to promote English tend to be localized within specific government departments, such as education, tourism, foreign affairs, and the like, and do not occur at the higher levels of executive or legislative authority.

Official status in EBL societies seems to cover a range. Edwards's (1974) description of San Andres bespeaks de facto, if not de jure, full official status for English. Stewart's description of the Netherlands Antilles (1968, p. 544) suggests a similar condition in St. Maarten. Such high status is, of course, regional rather than national. The English literacy figures for Creole speakers in Honduras (Reyburn, 1975, p. 102) suggest tolerance, if not encouragement, of English there.

Language Use

The type and degree of use that English enjoys in a given society occupies a pivotal position in the taxonomy as it not only correlates with the official status of English (as discussed in the preceding section) but in turn conditions the designations for the majority of dimensions plotted subsequently in Table 1. Language use is generally discussed in terms of domains, defined by Fishman (1971, p. 251) as "a higher order generalization" composed of clusters of congruent situations defined in turn as "situations in which individuals interact in appropriate role relationships with each other, in the appropriate locales for these relationships, and discuss topics appropriate to their role relationships." When two or more languages, or distinct varieties of the same language, are available in one's linguistic repertoire, the choice of which one is used under various conditions becomes potentially significant. Three of the most common conditioners of language choice—role, setting, and topic—are subsumed under Fishman's definition just cited. There is some variation from society to society as to which domains are significant, but there is a core of domains common to all including: family, informal social contacts, work, education, and religion

(Fishman, 1971, p. 248). To these, in most cases, one must add the media, shopping, and frequently, politics. The domains in which English finds use in the various societal types is discussed in later sections.

Other conditioners of language choice, such as age, sex, education, socio-economic status, and rural versus urban residence, are subsumed under the broader heading of the segment of the population using English treated in the next section and are mentioned individually where applicable to a particular type of English-using society there.

Sociolinguists have, in general, tended to step delicately around the question of degree of language use. In a very conherent theoretical model Mackey (1968, p. 559) suggests precise measures in terms of hours per week for spoken usage and pages per week for written usage but I know of no studies to date employing them. Language use in Fiji is described by Moag (1978b, p. 71) in terms of a three-point scale running from infrequent, through moderate, to extensive use. In the absence of data from more than one society, it seemed impractical to try to include this obviously important factor of the proportion of the total amount of time of an individual's or group's activities consumed by English and by other languages in the various societal types. The relative influence of the group who uses English has, however, thanks to a suggestion by Braj Kachru, been included as feature 3 in Table 1.

Percentage of the Population Using English

In most ENL nations, the overwhelming majority of the population uses English in all domains all the time. In 1960, 11 percent of the United States population had non-English mother tongues (Fishman, 1966, p. 392), though the figure is slightly higher now. Australia and New Zealand both have 91 percent native English speakers, while Ireland and the United Kingdom have 97 percent and 98 percent, respectively, with similar figures for Trinidad and Jamaica. Bilingual Canada with its 58% still falls well within the "over 50%" criterion set by Ferguson (1962, p. 11) for the dominant language in a bi- or multilingual nation. (Preceding percentages from Rustow, 1968, p. 100). White South Africa has only 40 percent native English speakers as opposed to 60 percent for Afrikaans (South Africa Statistics, 1976, 1.33). Here the numerical imbalance is offset by the relative socioeconomic dominance of the English-speaking community together with the international prestige of English with its richer and longer literary and cultural tradition. The dominance of English is evidenced by Kloss's report (1966, p. 11) "the users of Afrikaans are more often bilingual than those speaking English." Ferguson (1962, p. 11) has pointed out the significance in nations having two or more major languages of whether a language is learned by outgroup members. Indians in Natal also learn English to the growing abandonment of their mother tongues (Bughwan, 1972, p. 62). Thus, though it contains very large communities of ESL speakers, White South Africa is still English dominant, hence ENL. It is not clear how great a numerical imbalance can be overcome by the power and prestige of a local ENL group.[2] Ferguson (1962, p. 11) suggests that a minimum figure of 10 percent of the total population speaking a language natively is required to give that language major status in a multilingual setting. There appear to be no ENL nations with an ENL group on the 10 percent borderline to provide a clear test case, but I suspect that 25 percent would be a more realistic lower limit. Needless to say, the actual number of English users in any ENL society will exceed the number of native speakers, due to ESL use of many minority group members.

In an ESL society, English will be the mother tongue of a statistically insignificant percentage of the population but the second language of a much higher, though not always high, percentage. In Fiji, for example, part-Europeans (those of mixed Caucasian and Melanesian stock) account for less than 2 percent of the total populace (Parliament of Fiji, 1979, p. 71) and only a proportion of these claim English as a mother tongue (Simpson, 1974, p. 13.). Transitional India has an infinitesimal proportion with 191,595 native speakers out of 550 million (Sekhar, 1971, p. 72). Even the highly unusual case of Rhodesia finds only 260,000 whites (presumably nearly all English mother-tongue speakers) out of a total population of 6.9 million (Europa Yearbook, 1979, p. 1258), less than 3.8 percent.

The percentage of ESL speakers is not provided in the censuses of most ESL nations, and one must, therefore, rely on estimates. One factor that must be taken into account is that in some nations a greater number of people know the informal or pidginized variety than the standard one. This is reported for Nigerian Pidgin (Mafeni, 1971, p. 95), and for the so-called Singlish of Singapore (Platt, 1975, p. 16). India seems to provide a minimum for ESL users with 3 percent (Kachru, 1976, p. 229), where the importance of the relative influence of the English-using group within the society, plotted as feature 3 in Table 1 and discussed in the next section, may be seen. In the true ESL situation, the total of English users would have to exceed the number of secondary school pupils. The fact that the number of English users in India has not grown apace with the progress of secondary education is another index of that country's movement toward EFL status. However, the fact that until a few years ago India was an ESL society with 3 percent or less of English users indicates that a much lower minimum percentage of English users is required to make English a major language in an ESL society than is needed to make it the dominant language in an ENL situation. The 3 percent figure is the one set by Kloss (based on the number of Italian speakers in Switzerland) as the dividing line for languages that are not counted in the classification of a society as bi- or multilingual (1966, p. 7), and Ferguson sets a 10 percent breaking point between major and minor language status (1962, p. 11), but both of these figures are intended to apply to mother-tongue, not second language, speakers.

There is also an upper limit to the number of English users in an ESL society. I have written elsewhere (Moag and Moag, 1977) that significant areas of Fiji and other ESL nations use English as a foreign rather than a second language, particularly outlying rural areas. Cities play a very important role in the promotion of second languages, just as they do in the development of standardization within languages (Garvin and Mathiot, 1956). I suggest the rule of thumb that the percentage of the population using English in an ESL society will be no greater than the percentage of the population living in urban centers (figures on Fiji are given later in this section). This rough figure also takes account of a certain number of rural users, since there will always be a significant proportion of working-class citizens in urban centers who do not participate in the cosmopolitan lifestyle and continue to carry on all their activities, except school, in the vernacular (Platt, 1977a).

In EFL and EBL societies the upper limit of English users is very low, though a much higher number in the EFL case will be studying the language in school. This is due to the restricted and highly specialized domains in which English is used in the EFL situation (see next section). EBL societies range from 16,000 in San Andres out of Colombia's 25 million (Edwards, 1974) to 8 percent of the population in Panama (Rustow, 1968, p. 96).[3] The low status of their Creole English doubtless means their numbers would have to approach 25 percent to render that language a major force nationally, particularly given the high percentage of Spanish speakers in most EBL nations.

Influence of the English-Using Group in the Society

There can be little doubt of the overriding influence of the English-using group in the ENL society since they are usually numerically superior as well as being native speakers of the dominant language. On the other side of the coin, the minor role of the English-using group in EBL societies is equally clear, since they are not only numerically small, but have relatively low socioeconomic status and are native speakers of a variety of English (Creole) which is regarded as substandard by majority group members within their larger society for whom standard English is an FL.

English users in the ESL society, though they do not often form a majority of the total population are like those in the ENL society in that their major influence stems from the fact that they are habitual users of the dominant, and most prestigious, language in the society and, as such, form a reference group for many other members of the society. Thus their influence is disproportionate to their numbers. Kachru pointed out in the 1978 Illinois conference on English in nonnative contexts that some 45 percent of India's population knows Hindi, either as first or second language, but the 3 percent who know English have been far more influential in national life. This, of course, is beginning to change now with the rise of Hindi and the curtailment of English.

Those using English in EFL societies, though they constitute an elite or a subgroup within the nation's elite, do not constitute a reference group for large numbers of their countrymen. They are accessible to other members of the society through languages other than English. The activities for which they use English are limited, highly specialized, and largely keyed to external contacts,[4] all of which combine to give the language and its users a minor role and influence within the society, especially as compared with that in the other three types of English-using societies.

The Range of Activities Conducted in English

The core group of domains common to all societies has been listed and includes: family, work, informal social activities, school, religion, usually shopping, and politics, and in many cases, entertainment (subsuming the aural and print media). It need hardly be stated that in the ENL society English, and only English, is used in all of them by most of the population. Hence the designation "full" for ENL on feature 4. Since nearly all of these same domains are occupied by the local language in EFL societies, it can be seen that a very narrow range of activities remains for English. Specific domains may vary from one society to another (Fishman, 1976, p. 64); in the EFL case, they almost certainly occupy specialized subdomains within the two domains of work and education. In a workshop that my wife and I gave primarily to Mexican teachers of English at TESOL 1978, participants identified the subdomains of big business, tourism, and higher education as those in which English is used in their country. Fishman (1977, p. 167) specifies technology as the primary area in which English is used in many societies.

The range of activities in which English is used in both the ESL and EBL societies is broad, not full, since some functional territory is dominated by other languages in the situation. The specific formal and informal domains for the four societal types are dealt with in the following subsections.

Use in Formal Domains

Moag (forthcoming b) identifies three crucial domains into which English must move strongly in the transition of colonial nations from earlier EFL to subsequent ESL status—education, governmental activities, and the media—in order of chronological occurrence. These are the same three that Conrad and Fishman (1977) use to document the spread of English as an "additional language" throughout the world without specific reference to its foreign versus second language status in individual countries. The use of English in one or more formal domains occurs in all four classes save EBL. The three key domains are discussed in turn with special reference to the EFL-ESL distinction.

Education.   Education was an elitist privilege in many British and American colonies well into this century. English was the medium of instruction, but did not touch the bulk of the population who, if educated at all, received religious or traditional training in vernaculars or occasionally classical languages. The picture changed dramatically with the development of mass education and has set the stage in some nations for English to become a second language on a societal level. The typical ESL pattern has English as a school subject, often from the outset, with English-medium instruction beginning in upper primary or at junior secondary level for most subjects. Conversely, in the EFL case, the local or national language serves as sole medium of instruction, generally through university level. English is typically not even a subject until secondary level, and then often only in selected schools, and it serves as the medium of instruction only in specialized courses in the sciences or modern professions at the tertiary level. In fact, education seems to be the only domain in which English enjoys any significant role in many of the world's countries. Conrad and Fishman's (1977) data shows 112 nations in which English is a school subject for at least some percentage of secondary students, whereas English has at least a minor degree of recognition in governmental activities in only 33 nations and some representation in the media in 51 (pp. 37–40).

A few nations differ markedly from the typical EFL pattern just outlined. English is the medium of instruction for Mauritius, but its FL status is plain from the fact that Creole (French) is the language of the playground (Benedict, 1961, p. 34). Further, English remains the medium of instruction at the secondary level, at least, in several small African and Pacific nations exemplified by Lesotho and Tonga though this is declining as more local teachers become trained and curriculum development units produce more vernacular language materials for the higher grades. There is not enough data to suggest a clear trend in Mauritius. English has, of course, already been replaced by local languages in the former ESL nations of India, Malaysia, Tanzania, and, to a lesser extent, the Philippines (Sibayan, 1974) and Malaysia (Alisjabana, 1974) and more through popular pressure in India (Khubchandani, personal communication). It is simply that this latter group of nations, having more human or other resources to bring to bear on the task, underwent development somewhat earlier than the small African and Pacific nations previously cited. Thus they have already completed the transition from late colonial ESL status to the EFL situation, which is the natural corollary of the presence of a widespread and viable local language (see Moag, forthcoming b).

Language situations are not always stable and the role and function of a given language can change dramatically over time. Moag (forthcoming b) presents a "Life Cycle of Non-Native Varieties of English" showing how societies under the aegis of an Anglophone colonial power pass from initial EFL to subsequent ESL status (c.f. Fiji, Singapore, India, and nations of West Africa) and how some nations complete the cycle by returning to EFL status after independence. It is not clear whether policymakers in these former colonies foresee fully the long-term outcomes of their decisions to replace English-medium instruction with that of local languages and to keep English merely as a classroom subject in the mass education system. "Second language learning as a classroom subject is one thing, and being a bilingual person another and they often have little to do with each other" (Jakobovits, 1971, p. 22). It is impossible to maintain the second language role of English given such a restricted role in education. The lingua franca function is all important to second language status, and once people learn more Malay, Hindi, Swahili, or what have you, then English—the natural result of the shift in medium of education—they will use the national language rather than English to communicate with each other. At the same time, these new national languages are becoming more and more able to handle a full range of modern-day activities through their planned standardization and modernization. Thus ESL status was a temporary one for a number of former

British and American colonies having viable local languages, while it appears to be a more permanent development for a few nations in West Africa and the Pacific where there is no clearly contending local vernacular or language of wider communication.

Education in ENL nations is overwhelmingly English dominant. Even where there are growing numbers of bilingual education projects, as in the United States, they are mostly of the transitional type (Fishman, 1978, p. 407) where the goal is to enable the students to function fully in the English-medium system, rather than to make them fully bilingual. This same type of system, used in specialized cases in ENL societies, is generalized in most ESL societies. English appears to have some place in schools in EBL settings as well. The minus designation for EBL on feature 5 signifies that the degree of use in formal domains is small with respect to that in informal ones in EBL societies.

Governmental activities. Several important subdomains fall within the major domain of governmental activities including: legislation, high-level administration, low-level administration, law enforcement, the courts, and various institutionalized means of disseminating information and services in fields such as agriculture, health care, social welfare, and so forth. Despite the broad range of activities encompassed by it, the domain of governmental activities (which is itself only a subcomponent of the feature of the range of activities covered in English) is more limited than, and distinct from, the feature of the degree of official recognition discussed earlier. De facto recognition applies to actual governmental policies toward English, running the gamut from mandatory use through encouragement and tolerance, even to proscription of the use of English—in all areas of societal activity under their direct or indirect influence, be they public or private. The domain treated here relates to the actual use of English within activities under the direct control of the government, excluding education and, in many cases, the media.

Language use within governmental activities, as with education, shows a clear division between EFL and ESL societies. In the ESL case, one can expect to be able to carry out all business, both oral and documentary, in any governmental office in English. All official government publications, currency, and licenses will appear in English and government records and interoffice memoranda, at least at the higher level of administration, will be in English as well.

The foregoing pattern is quite unheard of in the EFL society where a local language serves all the functions just specified and English will be used only for communication with foreigners. In contrast, the ENL setting finds governmental activities at all levels operating solely in English, though some institutionalized arrangements may exist for linguistic minorities, such as election ballots and certain government forms now being available in Spanish in the United States, or for non-English speaking individuals, such as court interpreters. English speakers in the EBL society are in a comparable situation to non-English speakers in ENL countries. Being speakers of a minority language, participation in governmental activities or access to government services requires the use of the dominant language of the society, either through direct knowledge or through an interpreter.

The media. This is another domain where EFL and ESL societies differ markedly. English newspapers and broadcasts in Japan, for example, are for the consumption of American military forces and for resident and visiting foreigners. Imported English language films and television programs are, as a rule, shown with Japanese dialogue dubbed in. The same films and programs will be dubbed in German in Germany, Arabic in Egypt, Spanish or Portuguese in Latin America, and so forth, while a few nations, such as Indonesia, use subtitles, apparently for economic reasons.

Conversely in the ESL society, English language newspapers and broadcasts are directed at the educated local populace, not at foreigners, and dialogue is not dubbed in for movies and television shows. The assumption is that most viewers will be able to follow the English dialogue. In transitional societies, measures may be in force to promote the national language. In Malaysia, for instance, all films (English, Chinese, Tamil, and Hindi) must, by law, have subtitles in Malay (Paauw, 1980). English language films have neither subtitles nor dubbed-in dialogue in the Philippines, but this is explainable in terms of the time lag between the replacement of English by the national language in education and its assumption of dominance in other domains, as well as by the presence of a separate and thriving local language film industry that allows English films to remain as elitist fare.

Conrad and Fishman (1977, pp. 37–40) present a list of the English language press in 51 non-English mother-tongue countries. Though they acknowledge "a strong relation between official language countries and an English-language press with substantial circulation" and the fact that "in the absence of any governmental policy to promote English, there is little motive or purpose for English newspaper publishing" (p. 35), they have apparently missed the insight which their data reveals into the more basic correlation between the role of English in non-English mother-tongue societies and the type of English language press that it conditions. In fact these authors make no distinction between foreign and second language status at all, referring to English as a foreign language in Latin America in one place (p. 25) and as a "second language" in another (p. 35).

Conrad and Fishman took insufficient notice of two all-important factors: (1) the target audience of the English language press, and (2) the proportional role of the English language press in the country's press as a whole. The authors claim to have excluded publications produced "apparently only for foreigners or for the expatriate community" (p. 34), then go on to describe one of the entries in their table as "circulating primarily in the Canal Zone, presumably to Americans" (p. 35). Just about half of the entries in their tables have English newspapers aimed largely at resident or visiting foreigners. Venezuelan English teachers confirm that the English-using elite in their country look to overseas papers from ENL countries for their English periodical reading matter rather than to the local *Daily Journal* (see Conrad and Fishman, 1977, p. 40), though the latter is sometimes used as a source of assignments for local EFL classes. Paauw (1980) has shown through examples from EFL Indonesia and ESL Singapore how the expatriate versus local readership of an English language paper is reflected in its content.

There is an even more clearly discernable difference in EFL and ESL societies with respect to the role of English newspapers in the total press of the country. In 1977 Fiji, for example, had two English dailies with a combined circulation of just over 50,000 (personal research), while vernacular papers were weekly or fortnightly. Taking the combined total weekly circulations, at least 20 English papers are produced for each vernacular paper in a given week. The proportion would be even more lopsided if actual pages of newsprint were taken as the basis of comparison rather than copies, as vernacular papers normally comprise less than a dozen pages. The balance is skewed in the opposite direction in the EFL society with the vernacular press holding a position of overwhelming dominance. In 1975 Indonesia had a total daily newspaper circulation of 2.171 million with the three small English papers (exact figures unavailable) accounting for only a few thousand (Paauw, 1980). Conrad and Fishman (1977, p. 52) have given percentages of the total production for English book titles, but not for newspapers, save for a set of figures in a footnote for daily English newspaper readership in India (p. 41), where the daily English circulation of 1.3 million is just under half of the 2.82 million total.

Newspaper circulations in societies in which the role of English is in a state of flux may be misleading as they tend to lag behind the trend, since they reflect the reading habits of the former generation as well as those of the present one. Broadcasting, on the other hand, tends to lead the trend, since radio and television in many countries are controlled by the government and, hence, can be directly influenced to implement its newest language policies. Films and newspapers, being part of the private sector in most nations, can hold out so long as the former generation of English-educated patronizes them.

The crucial part the media plays in determining the role of English in a society is borne out by Mauritius. There English is the official language, used in government and as medium of instruction, but French and Creole (French) have remained the languages of formal and informal intergroup contact, respectively. Each of the seven daily newspapers is not only bilingual but apparently French-dominant, judging from the names (see Conrad and Fishman, 1977, p. 37).[5] Thus it is not necessary after leaving school for the average citizen to use English in any daily activities. A bilingual press is typical, in fact, of a subgroup of nations differing only temporarily from the normal EFL pattern, including: Botswana, Bhutan, Lesotho, Malawi, Swaziland, Tonga, and Western Samoa (see Conrad and Fishman, 1977, pp. 37–40). These are all small nations with a single clearly dominant vernacular. Moag (forthcoming b) points out that the temporary internal use of English in these countries stems from the need to employ expatriates, usually from the former colonial power, to serve at the higher levels of government and education, while locals are being trained for the jobs. In the long run, their press will become vernacular dominant like that of other EFL societies, whereas the vernacular press will remain secondary to the English language press in ESL societies.

A particularly equivocal case is that of Papua New Guinea where there is strong competition between languages in two of the three key domains. Wurm (1977, p. 342) reports that New Guinea Pidgin in the 1970s became the "main debate language in the Papua New Guinea House of Assembly, was more and more used in the media, and began to be used again in primary education." My own observations during a brief trip in 1978 were that (1) education was still overwhelmingly English-dominant, (2) the media was a stand-off, with Pidgin, and, to a lesser extent, Hiri Motu dominating broadcasting but having a long way to go before taking over creative writing and the print media, and (3) government services were also a mixed picture with oral activities not involving expatriates largely in Pidgin, and English beginning to lose ground in the written sphere.

In terms of long-range trends, the role of English seems destined to even further decline. Wurm (1977, p. 353) concludes his treatment by citing Mühlhäusler's 1977 evaluation that most experts agree that New Guinea Pidgin and Hiri Motu are likely to be given official language status, with English remaining the language of higher education and special pursuits, such as the nation's dealings with the outside world. For these reasons, and because of the very limited use of English in informal domains (see the next section), Papua New Guinea has been placed in the EFL column.

Use in Informal Domains

The domains discussed in detail in the preceding section are basically formal in nature, although a certain amount of informal activity also takes place within them including playground activities at school, comic strips in the press, and popular music shows on the radio. It has been shown that English is used in formal domains in EFL, ESL, and ENL societies. EBL societies apparently vary considerably according to situation. San Andres and St. Maarten, doubtless due to their geographic discontiguity, are microcosms of the larger Creole-speaking nations of Jamaica and Guyana with a full range of styles between the pure Creole basilect and the standard Caribbean English acrolect (DeCamp, 1971a, and Bickerton, 1973). The standard variety is heard over the radio in St. Maarten and apparently learned in school on both islands. Holm (1979), on the other hand, makes no mention of a standard variety in his treatment of Meskito Coast Creole from Nicaragua and Honduras. In the four Central American EBL societies, it seems reasonable to assume that education, government activities, and perhaps the print media would be largely Spanish dominated (this is attested for Panama by Cedergren, personal communication), while in the insular EBL societies these would be mainly English dominant.

Of the core domains listed earlier, home, informal social activities, and shopping are basically informal in nature. Activities within them take place in English in the ENL societies, and are at least dominantly English in the native-speaking EBL ones. In these domains, the major distinction is between the EFL and ESL patterns. English is, for all intents and purposes, excluded from them in the EFL situation. Occasional individuals might use a bit of English with family members at home now and then, but this would be conditioned by personal whim, not by sociolinguistic factors. When porters, bartenders, and others chat informally with foreign tourists in English this falls within the domain of work for them rather than that of social activity. In the ESL situation, however, English shares these domains with local languages, the choice of language being conditioned by such factors as role and topic. The use of English in informal domains in Fiji is documented by Moag (1978b) and by Moag and Moag (1978) and for Singapore and Malaysia by Platt (1977a), including the important domain of shopping. Naturally it is the informal variety of English that finds use in such activities. Banjo (1975) attests the same functions for Nigerian Pidgin.

Factors Blocking the Spread of English

Now that the four types of society have been discussed with respect to specific domains, it's an appropriate point to recapitulate the factors that have a significant effect on the kinds of use patterns that can develop and, hence, the role that English can play in a society. English cannot achieve the role of lingua franca and, hence, second language status in a society with a single vernacular. I have written elsewhere (Moag, 1978b and forthcoming b) on the situation in the supposedly bilingual South Pacific nations of Tonga and Samoa. English has greater use in education, government services, and the media than is typical for EFL situations, but less than that for ESL ones. Its greater use is related to the fact that the independent governments of these nations have found it necessary to employ a fair number of civil servants and teachers from ENL nations, particularly Australia and New Zealand. Government records and the portions of the newspapers in both countries that are in English are, therefore, for the benefit of foreigners, just as they would be in an EFL nation; there is simply a larger than normal proportion of them in these small nations and probably will be for some time to come. A somewhat expanded role for English is only a necessary concomitant of socioeconomic development in Samoa and Tonga. The same seems to be true also for a few small monolingual former British colonies in Africa, such as Lesotho, Swaziland, and others (listed earlier). In fact the four nations just mentioned accord English co-official status (along with the vernacular) in their constitutions (Conrad and Fishman, 1977, p. 10). A similar limitation on the role of English exists in multilingual nations according co-official or primary official status to another former colonial language (c.f. French in the Cameroons).

I have written elsewhere (Moag, forthcoming b) that the role of English is also affected by the presence of a more indigenous lingua franca. One of the most unlikely, but striking, cases is that of Pidgin in the Southwest Pacific which, since it is English-based, might seem to typify the outside colonial rule. Mihalic however reports that Papua New Guineans "feel that Pidgin is their own in a way in which English never can be" (1971, p. xv). Although Pidgin is a very recent development, many other multilingual areas of the world had fairly well-developed lingue franche used for purposes of trade and, occasionally, government before the time of the first European colonial contact. Chatterji (1972, pp. 209–210) describes how Hindi was made a language of intergroup contact in Bengal by businessmen from various parts of North India and by military officers from Delhi who used it in administration of this far-flung part of the Mughal Empire, despite the fact that Persian was the official court language. It became so widespread that "they [the British] had to take into account not only Persian and Bengali, in dealing with the government and people of Bengal, but also Hindustani, to communicate directly with the Mohammadan officialdom of Bengal" (Chatterji, 1972, p. 210). Being learned informally and not being written down, the language underwent some simplification along with its diffusion which resulted in the Bazaar Hindustani which Chatterji describes as having such wide use in Calcutta and throughout North India in the present century. Swahili in East Africa has a longer history than Hindustani, and the use of Bazaar Malay across a wide area has been documented since the early Christian era (Alisjabana, 1974, p. 392). The British capitalized on local lingue franche in all parts of the Empire. Hausa was used for low-level administration in Northern Nigeria (Brosnahan, 1963, p. 57) and Urdu (the same as Hindi on the spoken level) was the language of colonial administration at the district level in nineteenth century India (Gumperz and Naim, 1960, p. 97). Their primary use in the highly informal domain of trade gave most of these languages low status. In preserving and expanding their functional territory, the British not only enhanced their status, but unwittingly provided a handy tool and rallying point for popular independence movements. The use of these languages in primary education lent them further status and paved the way for an anticolonial press in them. More importantly for our purposes here, this also served to block the expansion of English to a broad enough range of activities by a large enough segment of the population to achieve true second language status.

It is not usually the case, however, that the local language used in schools, in political tracts, and so on is the lineal descendant of the pidginized lingua franca. It has been widely, though erroneously claimed that Bazaar Malay was developed into the standard national languages of Malaysia and Indonesia (Kahin, 1952; Hall, 1962, 1972; Stewart, 1968; among others). There were never any newspapers in the reduced second language varieties such as Bush Swahili, Bazaar Hindustani, or Bazaar Malay. In seeking a suitable medium for written expression, creative writers, as well as political and local leaders, and more recently, language planners, turned to the related but distinct, and more highly developed, native-speaker models, sometimes with minor modification. (See Alisjabana, 1974, for a participant linguist's account of the modern development of Bahasa Indonesia.) The principal exception is, of course, Neo-melanesian Pidgin which is an expanded form of the original lingua franca. In this case, there was no indigenous native or literary form of the language to switch to, since the parallel high tradition was that of the foreign colonials and, hence, poorly suited for motivating national allegiances. The lack of such a tradition has clearly retarded the progress of Pidgin, particularly into more formal domains where English tends to dominate. Nevertheless, Pidgin is making inroads, though at different rates in Papua New Guinea, the Solomons, and the New Hebrides, and has certainly effectively blocked the movement of English into informal domains (see Moag, forthcoming b). Societies with a strong indigenous contact language, like those with a dominant single vernacular, can never develop ESL in the full or true sense, though English may play some significant internal role during periods of colonization and post-independence economic development. If the local lingua franca is only regional, however, it may even assure the status of English at the national level, as with Hausa in Nigeria, whereas competition from a second lingua franca, such as Hiri Motu in Papua New Guinea, seems to have a much more temporary effect.

Learner-User Ratio

"It has been shown for Southeast Asia [Noss, 1965] and assumed to be the case for the rest of the world that English-medium schools in non-English mother-tongue countries will produce a higher proportion of students than will schools in which English is merely taught as a subject of instruction" (Conrad and Fishman, 1977, p. 17). This reinforces the Jakobovits quote cited earlier that "second language learning as a classroom subject is one thing and being a bilingual person is another thing, and these two things have very little to do with one another" (1971, p. 22). For purposes of this discussion, learner is defined as one who seeks to gain or improve competence in a non-mother-tongue language through formal, usually classroom, study. In EFL countries, the total number of English learners will be a subset of the total number of all those attending school, since there seems to be no EFL society in which pupils are introduced to English in the first year of schooling. Israel, for example, is fairly typical, beginning compulsory English instruction in public schools in fifth grade (Rosenbaum et al., 1977, p. 180). The number of learners will be very low in Francophone nations like Zaire, Senegal, and Morocco where English instruction is offered late in the education process and only to those training for certain specialized occupations, while it can be great in nations like Japan, Indonesia, and Israel where English is a required subject for all students from upper primary onward.

Whatever the number of learners, a much smaller number of English users is guaranteed by the inevitably low effectiveness of the instructional process. In speaking of FL learners in the United States, where conditions are admittedly anything but favorable toward high success in learning, Jakobovits (1972, p. 23) says, "the proportion of students who develop sufficient competence in their second language to make it possible for them to use it outside the classroom is extremely small." Even in EFL societies where economic and other incentives may be high, it is hard to imagine a learner-user ratio of less than four to one, with ten to one being a much more likely figure.

A lower ratio obtains in the ESL society, even though the actual relative number of learners will be higher than in any EFL society, constituting all or nearly all of those attending school. In Fiji, for example, where ESL instruction begins in class one and English medium in class four, 27 percent of the total population is in school (Parliament of Fiji, 1979, p. 280). Recall that the total urban population was suggested as a rough approximation of the segment of the population using English in ESL societies. With 37 percent of Fiji's population living in urban centers (Parliament of Fiji, 1979, p. 182), this yields a ratio of less than 1:1. The ratio must vary according to differing conditions within various ESL societies, but a learner-user ratio of 2:1 seems high, and a 3:1 ratio quite improbable.

This lower ratio is accounted for by two factors. First, Jakobovits holds that "developing communicative competence in a language requires conditions in which communicative needs exist" (1971, p. 24). Many situations in the ESL society provide precisely such communicative needs. Second, the use of English as medium of instruction for at least a significant part of the education process dramatically raises not only the learner's exposure to the language, but the potential success of the instruction as well. G. Richard Tucker (1968) has written on the value of the medium of instruction in language learning (see Conrad and Fishman quote at the beginning of this section).

Both ENL and EBL societies feature an inverse learner-user ratio. Here the language is used by all those who speak it natively, and those studying it formally in school constitute a subset of those users. Taking the United States as a case, the 23 percent of the population that is in school (excluding tertiary) (U.S. Government Census Bureau, 1978, p. 148) yields an inverse ratio of roughly one learner to 4 1/3 users. EBL societies could have even much higher inverse ratios where a smaller segment of the population is in school, where fewer years of schooling are the norm, where English was not taught in school, and so on.

Language Acquisition

Features 8 through 11 in the table deal with how, and for what reasons English is learned and used within the four societal types.

Dominant Type of Motivation

"Language is much more than an instrument; among other things, it is also an expression of personality and a sign of identity" (Haugen, 1971, p. 288). The work of Lambert and Tucker (1972, p. 347ff. and elsewhere) is well known. They distinguished two types of motivation, instrumental versus integrative, and demonstrated that achievement in FL learning correlated positively with integrative motivation (the desire to identify with the cultural norms and values of the group whose language one is learning) and correlated negatively with instrumental motivation (the desire to learn the language in order to accomplish certain personal goals). The Lambert dichotomy covers only two of the three functions of language articulated in the preceding Haugen quote. Smith (1972) cited a third type of motivation related to the human organism's need for self-expression.

In a 1978 paper J. B. Pride has gone beyond the previously held notion that the types of motivation operated independently, and to the exclusion, of each other in calling for the need to "recognize the interplay of several types of motivation." The importance of this view of motivation as a single complex attitudinal unit composed of instrumental, integrative, and expressive motives operating interdependently can hardly be overstressed. Whenever anyone uses English it is, in part at least, to serve some purpose, that is, instrumental. The fact that one is learning and using English, for whatever purpose, reflects at least some degree of willingness to identify with others who use the language, integrative. Finally, the purposes for which one learns and uses English, one's feelings of identification (even if they be negative) with others who use it, and the type of English one uses in a given speech event (Pride, 1978), all express something of one's personality.

Though all three components are present in most instances, different situations can condition the dominance of one or another of the three motives. In societies in which English is an FL, those who learn the language need it principally as a tool in their work, that is, for instrumental purposes. It is necessary for certain highly restricted and specialized professions only. In the ESL society English is a requisite tool for success in the professions in general, reaching well down into the upper echelons of blue-collar jobs such as work gang foreman, and one learns and uses English in order to be a part, that is, integrate himself, into the socioeconomically advantaged group.[6] In the ENL society there is no active choice for most persons of whether to learn English or not, but the way in which he makes use of language—his use of stylistic variants, and so on—plays an important role in the expression of his individual personality. He might well learn special peer group or occupational registers for integrative motives, but his overall dominant motivation in acquiring and using English will be expressive. The same motive is dominant in the EBL situation, owing to the native language status of English. The question of integrative motivation is clearly secondary, since one is already a member of the English-using group.

Reference Group for Integrative Component

Feature 9 needs little exposition. Since the purpose of English in the EFL society is for international rather than internal communication, both the reference group and the linguisitc model aimed at are clearly external to the society itself. The function of English in the ESL society, on the other hand, is to facilitate communication between groups internal to the society. In the ENL and EBL societies as well, the groups with which one has primary communication are internal, rather than external to the society.

Secondary External Reference Group

It is widely acknowledged that the speakers of the new Englishes are loath to recognize the distinctive character of their English and, rather, insist that they speak one or another of the major ENL varieties. Kachru (1976, pp. 230–232) found that the majority of Indian university students and teachers of English not only preferred British English, but a significant number felt they were speaking it. In the EFL society in which there is no internal communicative function for English, the external reference group is the only significant one; while in the ESL society the internal group is, in actual fact, primary, with the external group being secondary. This is attested by the fact that most Indians returning from study in the United States or the United Kingdom do not speak de-Indianized English, and that the few who do are deprecated. Thus the real norms that condition linguistic behaviour are Indian, but the ideal norms that condition professed attitudes are British.

In contrast to the ESL case, most ENL nations identify with their own variety of English and eschew that of other ENL nations. Americans do not model their linguistic behavior after British norms, and vice versa. There is one important exception, however. LePage (1968, p. 441) reports that "many educated West Indians are unwilling to admit that their dialect differs at all from English English (the model language)." The existence of the strong secondary reference group here is the legacy of colonial rule and the introduction of standard English to the general populace through mass education which it initiated. It is bound to pass as the sociolinguistic adjustment processes of adding standard English to the local English-based creoles which are the native varieties of most persons in these West Indian countries run their course resulting in the "post-creole continuum" described by DeCamp (1971b).

Native English speakers in EBL situations, on the other hand, seem most likely to identify secondarily with other Creole speakers in nearby ENL Caribbean nations.

Degree of Informal Learning

It is generally accepted that children have a good command of all systems of their native language by, or shortly after, the time they enter school. This mastery comes about very largely through informal learning with very little formal instruction on the part of parents and others.

What is acquired through this informal learning is a local or colloquial variety of English; whereas the schools offer instruction in, and through the medium of, the standard variety of English current in the particular society. It is generally assumed, therefore, that native speaker competence in the standard language is acquired through formal learning. A careful look at the situation, however, suggests that this variety, too, is learned informally.

The failure of the schools to adequately teach the three R's and the failure of English courses at all levels, from grade school through university freshman composition courses, are perhaps the commonest themes in education in ENL societies today. The adolescents who are the clients and end-products of the universal education are so linguistically divergent from all other norms of society that adolescent speech is recognized as a separate variety or register by educators and linguists alike. The special forms that characterize adolescent speech are generated, transmitted, and learned by means of mechanisms that are completely independent of the formal instructional component of the educational process, though recess times, playgrounds, locker rooms, and other informal settings around the school play an important part.

Thus the bulk of the language acquisition of the high school graduate takes place informally first in the home and, later, through peer group contacts. When such graduates need to write a formal letter, undergo a job interview, speak in a public meeting or carry out any of the other activities cited by Labov (1966) as requiring the formal style of the language, they are linguistically ill-prepared to do so. At most they will possess learned rather than acquired competence (see Krashen, 1978) in the standard variety. In many cases they would resort to the use of a specific model looked up in a reference book or observed in practice so that their language performance would not be based on the formal instruction sat through in school. Therefore, learning of even the standard variety in ENL countries is largely informal as well, hence the designation for ENL of "maximal" for feature 11. The same is probably true for the EBL societies, though there may be fewer support mechanisms in some cases for the informal learning of the standard variety, such as newspapers, public meetings, and the like.

The EFL societies provide the opposite extreme with nearly all learning of English accomplished through formal instruction. Lieberson (1972) points out the "precarious balance" between French and English in Montreal. English is an FL within the French community, the large body of ENL speakers within the city notwithstanding. Despite this, "English is mainly transmitted through the schools" (1972, p. 250). The majority of EFL societies (those not within a larger ENL society) have even fewer informal means for the learning of English.

The ESL situation lies between the two extremes just outlined. In these societies, children in English-using families or areas are typically exposed to a good bit of the language in the home or on the streets so that they have some basic competence in English before entering school. Once in school, English will play a major role in all peer group communication. The presence of indigenous languages as well in these domains means that the opportunities for informal learning will be quantitatively less than in ENL nations, but sufficient to provide the users with a viable competence in the home-grown informal variety of English which is one of the hallmarks of the ESL situation. A second hallmark seems to be, as with ENL societies, a more passive than active competence in the standard variety. A third characteristic, the wide differences between the colloquial and the standard varieties, contributes to the difficulty of acquiring competence in the formal variety. To the extent that it is successful, learning is more the product of indirect informal means, such as English-medium instruction, exposure to reading material, public functions, and radio broadcasts, than of studying English as a subject. The difference between the ESL case and the ENL one with respect to informal learning of English is one of degree, not kind.

Language Attitude

Though it is a complex composite feature, language attitude is generally treated by sociolinguists in terms of the relative presence or absence of prestige that a language holds in a given society. In linguistically complex societies, degrees of prestigiousness become important. Stewart (1968, p. 53) states that a classical language like Latin or Greek will have higher prestige than English, which he sets as a prime example of a standard language with high prestige. I suggest this is not a realistic ranking since it seems not to be reflected in people's actions. In societies in which both are present, far more people elect to study, use, and promote English than any of the classical languages. Platt (1977a) has taken a more empirically sound approach in stating that English has higher prestige than Mandarin in Singapore.

The significant components making up high prestige are well summarized by Kloss (1966, pp. 15–16) as "rich literary heritage, high degree of language modernization, considerable international standing, or the prestige of its [the language's] speakers." If all factors are present, they will be additive and highest prestige will result. The presence of only some of the factors, however, can be effectively neutralized by the absence of others. Of course, the relative degree of any one of these features can place one language above or below another in a multilingual setting, and rapid changes in one component can alter the relative ranking of languages dramatically. In 1968, studies of the language attitudes in the Philippines showed Filipino (Tagalog) low with respect to English (Tucker, 1968), but a mere five years later surveys showed Filipino preferred over English in most activities (Bautista and Luzares, 1972).

It might at first seem that English would possess high values of all of the four factors of prestige just cited, in whatever society. This is clearly not the case. High prestige of English is only assured in two of the four societal types: ENL where it is the sole or clearly dominant language, and ESL where its "overarching role" (Pride, 1978) elevates its prestige relative to the local languages. In fact, as was seen earlier, when a local language has reached a sufficiently high state of modernization to adequately replace English in certain key formal domains, English is forced out of the role of SL into that of FL. This change (now taking place in India, Malaysia, and the Philippines, foreseen by Fishman in 1971, p. 388) has its corollary in the reversal of the relative prestige of the two languages. This seems to indicate that international standing is the least important of Kloss's four factors. Rustow (1968, p. 97) assigns overriding importance to "whether one or several of them [languages] have a substantial literary tradition" but the cases just cited do not appear to substantiatiate this.

The conditions determining the relative prestige of English are so varied, particularly in the EFL and EBL societies, that it is not possible to establish specific degree of prestige for the language in each of the four societal types. Therefore a binary feature has been employed denoting simply whether high prestige of English is certain or uncertain, indicated by a + and a +/−, respectively, in plotting features 12 and 13. It may appear redundant to include two discrete dimensions when the designations for both are identical. A single feature, however, would mask the fact that English, or any language, may have one level of prestige to its speakers and quite another in the society at large. The two features are kept separate here as a reminder to test for both when applying the taxonomy to specific English-using societies.

Prestige to Users

It has been pointed out that English is "certain" to have high prestige to those who use it in both the ENL and ESL societies. In certain EFL nations, such as Japan and Western Europe, people take great pride in their ability to use English, while in others where a local language or an alternative European language is dominant, people tolerate the need to use English as a necessary evil. Abdullah (1979, personal communication) reports that this is a growing tendency in Malaysia, particularly among Malays. Thus high prestige of English is "uncertain" in EFL nations. A similar antipathy toward English can be found during the colonial era of some ESL nations as part of a larger complex of anticolonial attitudes. These would seem to be quite ephemeral, however, since the generations born after independence would see English as a fact of life within the local situation, rather than something associated with a group of colonial rulers that they have never known.

It may seem surprising that native English speakers in EBL societies do not always hold their mother tongue in high regard, until recalling that in many we are dealing with creolized varieties of English. In Ferguson (1959) and elsewhere, studies of diglossia have amply documented not only the lack of prestige, but the outright deprecation of the "low" variety of a standard language, be it dialect as with Hindi speakers in Fiji and many parts of India (Moag, forthcoming a) or Creole as in Haiti and other French-speaking areas of the Caribbean and Indian Ocean. Wherever a post-creole continuum exists in an EBL enclave, featuring a range of social variants with Creole at the bottom and standard English at the top end, speakers will view English with high prestige just as they do in the ENL Caribbean nations, notwithstanding the fact that educators in the West Indies decry the speech of many of their countrymen as "bad talk" (LePage, 1968, p. 438). On the other hand, where the creole operates in the absence of the standard, with a separate language (Spanish) functioning as the superposed variety, English speakers will consider their language to be without prestige. Voorhoeve (1971, p. 309) mentions the lack of prestige of Saramaccan and other English-based creoles to their own speakers in Surinam where Dutch is the "high" language.

Prestige in the Society at Large

The certainty of high prestige of English in ENL and ESL societies is a function of its use within a broad range of formal domains as well as of the sociocultural and sociopolitical standing of those who use it in them. In contrast, general prestige is particularly uncertain in EFL societies depending not only on the hierarchical standing or lack thereof, of those who use it, but on the degree of modernization of the dominant or official language in the society as well. In nations such as Japan and Indonesia, English is very highly regarded as may be seen, among other things, by the amount of loanwords found in the local national languages (Baird, 1978, and Alisjabana, 1974). In Latin American nations and former French colonies in Africa, on the other hand, English has low status vis-à-vis the dominant Spanish or French with the corollary of relatively few

English loanwords present in them. The Spanish-dominant EBL societies are the same in this regard, with the low status of the English users an additional contributing factor.

Bilingualism

Definitions of bilingualism differ greatly. The traditional view is represented by Bloomfield's (1933, p. 56) "native-like control of two languages." Some more recent scholars have been much more flexible regarding the degree of proficiency necessary. Kachru (1965, p. 393) speaks of a "cline of bilingualism," including pidginized varieties at one end. Haugen (1956, p. 10) states that one of the languages can vary from a smattering to literary mastery. Subsequently, several important scholars have adopted the position that bilingualism cannot exist without biculturalism. These include Haugen (1970) in revision of his earlier definition, Jakobovits (1971), and Gumperz (1970). This view would appear to rule out the person with limited and specialized ability in English who uses the languge for instrumental purposes. A popular distinction made in the 1960s is also culture-based with a "compound bilingual" whose two languages can serve equally to express the same culture, and the "coordinate bilingual" whose two languages express two different cultures.

A more balanced and all-encompassing definition of bilingualism is that of Mackey (1968, p. 556), who calls it "a behavioural pattern of mutually modifying linguistic practices varying in degree, function, alternation, and interference." In Mackey's framework, degree is a complete index of proficiency in both languages composed of the four skills and five levels of language (phonological-graphic through semantic). He also includes stylistic levels which in this taxonomy are handled by a separate feature (20). His function component equates to language use as treated in features 2–7. A noteworthy facet of his scheme is the subdivision into "external function" involving communication with or comprehension of other speakers or sources, and "internal functions," such as counting, reckoning, praying, cursing, dreaming, diary writing, and so on (1968, p. 565). Mackey's "alternation" involves codeswitching (not treated here), and his "interference" refers to what is dealt with here in feature 25.

Four dimensions of bilingualism are plotted in the chart and discussed in the following sections. Features 15 and 16 are closely related.

Individual versus Societal Bilingualism

Fishman has tried to rule out the idea of societal bilingualism by saying "bilingualism is essentially a characterization of individual linguistic versatility whereas diglossia is a characterization of the social allocation of functions to different languages" (1971, p. 295). Weinreich and many following, however, have preferred to speak of bilingual communities as well. Fishman (1971) himself refers frequently to societal bilingualism. Relative to the purposes of this paper is the statement by Kloss (1966, p. 15), "In calling a speech community bilingual we imply application not only to a few high-ranking bureaucrats and some scholars but also to a sizeable segment of the population." Thus, bilingualism will be "societal" in ESL societies and "individual" in EFL ones. Furthermore, the knowledge and use of FLs in ENL nations will be an individual, rather than a societal, phenomenon. Statistically significant non-English-speaking groups should be treated as EFL enclaves within the larger ENL society (c.f. French speakers in Montreal). In EBL societies, bilingualism is clearly societal. In two mixed communities, with a total population of 1471, surveyed by Reyburn (1975, p. 112), 595 of the 772 native English speakers (77 percent) also had competence in Spanish.

This feature correlates with the segment of the population using English, plotted as feature 2. Kloss (1966, p. 15) proposes four possible compositions of the bilingual segment of the population in the societal category—all males, all breadwinners, all literates, or all secondary school graduates. The fourth, of course, is a subset of the third. All of these seem to be either too broad or too narrow to represent accurately the membership of the English bilingual sector of the populace in the ESL societies with which I am familiar. Four, on the other hand, would describe the English-knowing, though not necessarily English-using, groups in the subgroup of EFL nations, including Mauritius and the small monolingual African and Pacific nations asterisked in Table 2.

Type of English Bilingualism

In considering degrees of proficiency in another language, it seems that the most basic split is between those who have some functional, if limited, competence in that language as opposed to those with no useful competence, rather than between those with differing degrees of useful competence. The person whose contact with an FL is limited to studying it as a school subject is in no sense bilingual, but anyone using it in his professional or private life, even in very restricted activities, is. After coining the term "functional bilingualism" to account for the degree found in EFL societies, I discovered that the same term had been used in describing the graduates of the Filipino-dominant education system in the Philippines (Bresnahan, 1979).

"The degree of proficiency in each language depends on its function, that is, the uses to which the bilingual puts the language" (Mackey, 1968, p. 557). Thus, the broader uses of English in the ESL case will condition a higher degree of English proficiency. The designation "coordinate" for this feature suggests two distinct cultures, which is only partly true. English is the language of modern westernized culture in many ESL societies, but this is not really the same culture extant in any of the ENL nations. Kachru (1976, p. 225) has pointed out the nature of the Third World Englishes as "culture-bound codes of communica-tion. . . [used] in these countries [the Third World] to teach and maintain the indigenous patterns of life and culture." For the urban resident in the ESL society who has become detached from much of his traditional culture, there is doubtless a single amalgamated local urban culture the more westernized elements of which tend to condition his English and the more native elements of which tend to condition his L1. The complementary distribution will vary according to the individual's education, social standing, and the like. If there is a "cline of bilingualism" (Kachru, 1969), there must be a corresponding "cline of biculturalism" in ESL societies, even if the complementary cultural strains form a unified culture at the higher level. The same "coordinate" designation is posited for EBL societies, and the bilingualism in ENL societies, where it exists, will be functional, but with reverse English-FL proficiency (see the next section).

Language of Higher Proficiency

Feature 16 is, in part at least, a function of feature 15. Obviously, where there is functional bilingualism, higher proficiency obtains in the L1. Fishman (1976, p. 63) states that such a context sensitive view of language dominance has gained sway over the earlier context free view. Ideally, coordinate bilingualism should reflect equal competence in both languages. In fact, this seems to be a hypothᴖsis seldom realized in practice. Most ESL nations have "transitional biling   education" (Fishman, 1978, p. 409), where the mother tongue is only used until pupils are able to operate in the English-medium classes characterizing the system as a whole. This, along with the English dominance in the media, government activities, and significant use in informal activities, all outlined earlier, tends to produce L2- (English-) dominant bilinguals in the ESL case, though this decreases as one goes down the social scale. In discussing Fiji, I have referred to this situation as "skewed bilingualism" (Moag, 1978a, p. 3). The EBL case is here cited as L1-dominant. Linguistically sophisticated tourists report that natives of St. Maarten are English-dominant with limited competence in Dutch. Coordinate bilingualism might well be skewed in favor of the L2 in some Spanish-dominant EBL situations though Reyburn's data for Honduras and Nicaragua (1975, p. 112) clearly indicates L1 (English) dominance.

English Skills Attrition

In the French community of Montreal, already defined as an EFL enclave, Lieberson (1972, p. 252) discovered in a longitudinal study covering a 40-year period, that, even after allowing for immigration and other demographic factors, "the existence of unlearning [of English] is still found among the population who were not immigrants to Canada in the intervening decades." Lieberson observes that French speakers in Montreal learn and use English only in the domains of school and work, as mentioned earlier. When persons cease to be active in these domains, their English proficiency declines to the point that after a few years they report themselves as monolingual to census enumerators. This is further supported by the fact that "the decline among men is more a middle-age phenomenon, while women tend to begin their decline in bilingualism at earlier ages" (Lieberson, 1972, p. 252). These beginning points correlate with the time of retirement and of assuming domestic duties a few years after the completion of schooling respectively. In light of this, feature 17 has been given the designation high for EFL societies.

Persons in ESL settings will suffer some attrition of English proficiency, since they, too, consecutively lose contact with the English-supporting domains of school and work, but this will be more moderate and take place at a slower rate owing to continuing English use in the domains of governmental activities and, more importantly, the media, social activities, and, often, shopping, and even home. Attrition will be low in ENL and EBL settings principally due to its L1 status there.

LINGUISTIC FEATURES

The six features treated under the rubric of linguistic features are more closely concerned with the internal structure and the variations within it, of the English as used in the four societies. None of them is purely linguistic, however, as they are all directly related to various social factors in the respective situations. Detailed studies of the differences in internal structure of English in the four types is most clearly needed, but it lies beyond the scope of the present paper.

Competence Versus Performance Models

It is a foregone conclusion that each ENL nation has its own variety of English which provides a native model for those living there. It seems clear that the same will be the case for EBL societies. Since the function of English in EFL societies is communication with outsiders, it has also been generally accepted that the appropriate model in their case is the native variety of the ENL society with which that country has the most contact. The "international English" proposed by Smith (1978) and Lester (1978) seems to have a nonnative competence model, but has had no significant impact as yet.

At the same time, there have been opposing opinions concerning the appropriate model for ESL societies. The more traditionalist view typified by Prator (1968), among others, holds that one or another of the ENL varieties is the only legitimate one for English in any nonnative context. The relativist or "pragmatic" view is well summarized in Kachru (1977) and recognizes the value of nativized, or indigenized (Moag and Moag, 1977, p. 3) models for societies in which English serves essentially the function of internal communication. The pragmatic view allows for the recognition of the already established second language varieties, such as Indian English, West African English, and so on, but neither view takes into account the fact that English learners and users from Germany, France, Latin America, Japan, and other EFL countries can also be easily identified by the highly predictable characteristics of their English performance and that despite this there are no indigenized emerging varieties in these countries.

To account for the disparity between idealized (target) and actual (learner) norms, I have split the concept of model into competence model and performance model, respectively. Thus, the EFL English user has a native, or external, competence model but a nonnative, or internal, performance model, the latter being the result of the user's own mother-tongue interference plus other interlanguage features, both reinforced by the similar performance of local teachers. The dominance of the native competence model is corroborated by the fact that the accepted ideal means for improving one's English in any EFL society is a stay in an ENL country.

In the ESL society, both competence and performance models are nonnative. A native competence model often persists as a part of the colonial heritage, but this has no reality for the clients of the education system, as it does in the EFL situation. The external reference group has only a very secondary role in the competence model. This difference in competence model provides a further theoretical base to Bickerton's observation that ESL societies "will produce varieties of language intermediate between pidgin and 'good foreigners' version,' e.g., the English of Fiji or the Philippines" (Bickerton, 1977, p. 55). Both models are, of course, native in the ENL and EBL situations.

Variation Within English

Language variation, like bilingualism and other topics taken up in this taxonomy, has a very substantial literature, and only a few major points may be reviewed here. Ferguson and Gumperz (1960) distinguish three types of variation—geographic, social, and stylistic—pointing out that a person is generally a native speaker of just one geographic or social dialect but that several styles may exist within the repertoire of the same speaker (1960, pp. 9–10). Halliday et al. (1964, p. 149) drew a primary distinction between two types of language variation: dialect, which they define as "variety according to the user," and register, which they define as "variety according to the use." Of the five features plotted under this heading in Table 1, the first is user-based, while the remainder are use-based.

Lectal Variation

ENL societies have both regional and social varieties which their speakers acquire natively. The Dialect Atlases of the United States and the work of Labov and others in urban social dialects are very well known. DeCamp (1971a, p. 28) points out the operation of both these dimensions in Jamaica with the social dimension being of particular interest. Rather than a single social variant, a person controls a range of variants along the Creole-standard English continuum. Conditions in EBL societies are less well reported. Edwards (1974) seems to refer only to social variation on San Andres.

In ESL contexts, user-based varieties divide along communal, that is, mother tongue or sometimes dominant language, lines. In India, for instance, there is Bengali English, Tamil English, Panjabi English, and so on (Kachru, 1977). The fact that these varieties tend to be regionally distributed in India and Africa is incidental, for the same phenomenon exists in other nations where communities have no regional base, such as Fiji and Malaysia where Indians, Chinese, and indigenese (Fijians or Malays) each exhibit distinctive varieties of English. A similar situation exists within EFL societies where there are two or more ethnic or linguistic groups. Particularly noteworthy examples may be found in the English of Arabs and Africans from former French colonies. Of a couple I knew from Algiers, the wife spoke with a heavy French accent and French-influenced syntax and discourse, while the husband's English showed no French influence but heavy influence from Arabic. I have coined the term "lingualect" (Moag, forthcoming c) to refer to these language-based varieties of English. Baird (1978) reports dramatically different varieties of Japanese English from educated versus uneducated speakers, but this may not be a true lectal variation, as he indicates that educated speakers control both. Therefore, this is not included in the designation under EFL.

Stylistic Variation and Language Distance Between Varieties

Styles are generally held to vary along the formal-informal dimension (Labov, 1966), with written and spoken language having separate, but overlapping, continua. Stylistic variation would appear to be minimal in the EFL context, with the principal difference being between spoken and written styles (Baird reports this for Japan). There will be no highly informal styles, since only formal activities are conducted in English. The range will probably be somewhat greater in EFL nations where tourism from ENL countries is big business.

Highly differentiated formal and informal styles have been reported for several ESL countries. The latter include Singlish (in Singapore), colloquial Fiji English, Nigerian Pidgin, and so forth. I have written elsewhere (Moag and Moag, 1977, and Moag, forthcoming b) that these varieties develop as the result of local people using English for informal activities for which their classroom English instruction provided no model. This accounts for the much higher degree of interference from local languages in them (see the next section). Krio in Sierra Leone and Pidgin in Nigeria are exceptions in that they entered those nations prior to, and independently of, standard English (Mafeni, 1971, p. 95), but they show the same high level of native language content. Though much further research is needed in the area, it is my observation in Fiji English that few intermediate styles exist in ESL societies between the formal standard variety and the informal colloquial one. Platt attests intermediate styles in Singapore English (1977b). Thus, the number of stylistic variants is few, but the language distance between them is considerable. If we take Baird's educated spoken Japanese English and the uneducated (pidginized) varieties as stylistic variants, we have a situation in which the number of styles is few, but the language distance between them maximal. However, this seems to be a unique case and not typical of EFL nations in general.

"Language distances within the code matrix are lowest in some highly urbanized communities such as we find in parts of modern Europe and in the United States. ... the distinction between standard and local dialects has almost diappeared. ... Some social speech distinctions persist. . . [and] there are a number of distinct formal and informal subcodes" (Gumperz, 1968, pp. 469–479). The picture that this suggests, several stylistic variants with minimal language distance between them, has an interesting minor exception. The number of intermediate styles on the post-creole continuum apparently is very large in Jamaica, and the distance between the two extremes is also very great according to the measures of dialect distance employed by Bailey (1971). Thus, distance between variants is conditioned by the degree of social stratification versus that of modernization and integration of the society (Gumperz, 1968, pp. 469–470), a factor that is independent of the role of English in the society. Since the ENL nations that are still highly stratified are statistically insignificant, only the dominant ENL pattern of minimal distance is shown in Table 1.

Since distance between varieties is keyed to factors of social and economic development, one can predict that the distance between the standard and colloquial varieties will progressively shrink with increased modernization and integration of these societies. This will be manifest in two ways. On the one hand, the standard exerts a significant influence on the informal variety, particularly at the lexical level, while on the other hand, the colloquial variety exerts a strong influence on the local standard, as reported by Wong (1978) for Malaysian English. The situation in EBL societies, once again, varies according to whether or not standard English plays a role. If so, it will present a picture mirroring that of Jamaica such as Edwards (1974) describes for San Andres. If not, the number and distance between variants would be much smaller.

Range of Registers

Register is a narrower category than stylistic variant. Whereas formal or informal style applies to a range of domains, register applies to specific domains or subdomains. It can be as general as, say, public speaking or as highly restricted a topic as language variation. Registers have generally been conceived of in lexical and, to a lesser extent, grammatical, terms, but I am in agreement with Halliday (1975, p. 26) who gives a more abstract definition in semantic terms: "A register can be defined as the configuration of semantic resources that the member of a culture typically associates with a situation type."

Since register is keyed to domain, the range of registers in English in a given society will vary directly with the range of activities conducted in the language in that society. The narrow range of activities in the EFL society conditions a minimal range of registers, the broad range of activities of domains in the ESL society and EBL societies conditions a moderate range of registers, and the full range of activities in ENL societies results in a maximal range of registers in the English used there.[7]

Number of Rapid Speech Forms

Rapid speech tends to be viewed as a subcategory of informal style. In studying English in San Andres, Edwards et al. (1978) found that each stylistic level in the vertical continuum had a horizontal rapid speech variety associated with it. They coined the technical term "patois" to refer to these horizontal variants. This is another way in which some EBL societies, at least, replicate the patterns of ENL societies where there is also a maximal number of rapid speech forms. The case is just the opposite in EFL societies in which there appear to be no rapid speech forms for the one or two oral speech styles. ESL societies, are, once again, intermediate between the two extremes. It has been my observation, for example, that in Fiji only a few stereotyped rapid speech forms are current, such as *gonna* and *wanna*.

Interlanguage Features

The interlanguage hypothesis (Selinker, 1972) has sparked large scale interest and considerable research. Its author now regards the five characteristics of interlanguage cited in the original article as incomplete (Selinker, personal communication). Here I will attempt to plot only the two characteristics that seem most directly applicable to the present purposes.

Transfer from Other Languages

Selinker's original characteristic is "transfer from L1," but I have modified that in order to account for the probable influence of Spanish and Meskito on the L1 English of certain EBL societies. Since Reyburn's survey indicates a goodly number of bi- and trilinguals, a moderate degree of other language influence is posited for these cases. Such influence is, needless to say, minimal for ENL societies.

The designation maximal appears in the EFL column because, though there are individual exceptions, the nonnative performance model has a heavy impact in these societies. The fact that English acquisition takes place mainly after the so-called critical age, that is, in adolescence or adulthood, is a factor of great importance. It is just not possible for most learners to reprogram their phonetic output rules. An added factor, to be sure, is the very high proportion of time-use obtaining for the L1 as opposed to that for English. In the ESL context, where English is acquired earlier and the time ratio for the two languages is skewed in favor of English, transfer from the L1 is only moderate.

Overgeneralization of Rules

The degree of overgeneralization of rules in EFL and ESL societies contrasts with that of L1 transfer, largely due to the lack of an informal variety in the former. Ferguson (1959) points out that the "low" stylistic variety in a diglossic situation will always be somewhat simpler grammatically. Overgeneralization is one of the chief ways in which simplification is accomplished. We find examples from Malaysian English (Wong, 1978) and Fiji English (Kelly, 1975) of the informal variety simplifying by adopting the unmarked form in all cases, thus eliminating the marked forms for third person present singular verbs, plurals of nouns, and the like. Therefore, the designation maximal is given for ESL societies, while only moderate appears for EFL ones. Minimal rather than nil appears in the ENL column since some conflation does occur in colloquial ENL varieties, such as the collapse of the third person plural object pronoun and the distinct plural demonstrative into the single form *them*.

CONCLUSION

The taxonomy tested in this paper has been shown to be valid in terms of the distinctive character of each category tested. The EBL category is identified for the first time here, hence has less supporting data for some of the feature designations cited. In terms of individual features, the specific designation for one particular type of society will be shared with one other type, sometimes two. Taking all of the features together, however, the cluster of designations for a given societal type is truly distinctive from the set for any other. ENL and EBL are the types with the highest number of shared features (12), and EFL and ESL are the two types with the least number of shared features (2). Other contrasts are clearly intermediate with between four and seven shared features.

The highest generality yielded by the matrix is the overall importance of language use patterns in determining other aspects of the situation and character of English in whatever society. Language-use patterns condition features of language acquisition, language attitude, bilingualism, performance model, language variation, and interlanguage. In devising the matrix, perhaps a useful tool has been created for the analysis of a variety of situations. Though designed to classify English-using societies, the matrix should be equally useful in ascertaining the role and character of other languages such as Indonesian, Spanish, French, Russian, Swahili, and Hindi which have differing functions in various nations, or within the boundaries of the same nation. The role of a single language in a given society can be plotted with a single-column matrix, while its situation in two or more societies requires only the addition of the requisite number of columns. The matrix could also be used for plotting the situation of several languages within the same society, or even of two or more languages within different societies, so long as the columns were given appropriate headings. Though a certain degree of completeness was attempted, there are doubtless other features whose inclusion would yield a clearer picture or added insights.

The taxonomy not only sheds light on those conditions that may be stable in English-using societies but also on sociolinguistic processes, such as the reduction of variation as a concomitant of modernization and integration, which accounts for the dynamic character of the situation of English in some societies. Inclusion of certain features has pointed up the lack of empirical data and the need for much more rigorous testing of the admittedly rough taxonomic tool presented here. It is intended to serve a useful function if some of the questions and theoretical issues raised here can point the way to more insightful and meaningful research on English sociolinguistics in the future.

NOTES

1. The ESL, ENL, and EBL lists are, actually, quite complete. The EFL list is very incomplete, since most of the nations of the world fall in this category. The United Nations, for example, has 150 members, all of which are EFL save 33: 14 ESL plus 19 ENL nations. All nations having EBL communities are, of course, EFL in terms of the total national society. The EFL list is complete, however, in terms of including nearly all of the transitional societies and modernizing monolingual former colonies of Anglophone powers which formerly have been regarded as ESL. This has meant that only a single representative from broad categories, such as Latin America and North Africa, could be included.

2. The Central American British protectorate of Belize may be a case of even closer competition between languages. The U.S. State Department publication, *Background Notes*, indicates that some 40 percent of the populace are native Spanish speakers with 20 percent more speaking it as a second language (which apparently does not happen with Afrikaans in South Africa). Figures for the number of native English speakers are not given, but based on simple subtraction of figures for all other groups, it would appear to be also around 40 percent. I have so far found no figures on the number of second language speakers of English, perhaps the most critical piece of data in the equation. Belize is certainly deserving of more detailed study.

3. H. J. Cedergren, a linguist at the University of Montreal, is a native English speaker from Panama. She reports that there are two distinct EBL groups there, one in the Canal Zone which tends to be monolingual, the other in Panama proper which is fully bilingual. Both are descended from West Indians who came as laborers in the late nineteenth and early twentieth centuries. Formerly, according to her experience, there were newspapers and radio stations serving these communities, but these have disappeared, apparently, as a part of a larger pattern of increasing pressures toward integration into the majority Spanish-speaking culture.

4. These relate principally to what Fishman (1977) identifies as the uses of English as an international language, that is, technology, big business, and higher education.

5. R. K. Barz (1979) of Australian National University in an unpublished paper on Hindi in Mauritius refers to the newspapers there as "carrying articles mainly in French, with some English content." Further, referring to the reading habits of Mauritians, he reports, "magazines and newspapers in French remain unchallenged as the primary source of information and comment."

6. The expressive motivation is also very strong in ESL situations since English is both thoroughly embedded in, and a carrier of, the local culture. This point is covered in more detail later in this paper.

7. Dr. R. R. Mehrotra of the English Department, Banares Hindu University, Varanasi, India, is doing detailed research on the registers of Indian English. He reports finding a significant number of registers across a broad range of domains which seems to support the designations in the ESL column in Table 1. Though in transition to EFL status, the limited segment of the populace using English in India still has it as a second rather than foreign language.

REFERENCES

Alisjabana, S. Takdir. Language policy, language engineering and literacy in Indonesia and Malaysia. In Joshua A. Fishman (ed.), *Advances in Language Planning*. The Hague: Mouton and Co., 1974, 391–416.

Bailey, Beryl L. Can dialect boundaries be defined? In Dell Hymes (ed.), *Pidginization and Creolization of Languages*. London: Cambridge University Press, 1971, 341–348.

Baird, Scott J. Performance varieties of Japanese English. Paper presented at the Conference on English in Non-native Contexts, June 30-July 2, 1978, University of Illinois.

Banjo, Ayo. Language policy in Nigeria. In David R. Smock and Kwamena Benstsi-Enchill (eds.), *The Search for National Integration in Africa*. New York: Collier and Macmillan, 1975, 206–219.

Barz, Richard K. The cultural significance of Hindi in Mauritius. Unpublished paper delivered at the International Conference on Indian Ocean Studies (ICIOS), Perth, Australia, August 15–22, 1979.

Bautista, Lourdes S., and Luzares, Casilda E. Judging personality from language usage: 1971 sample, *Philippine Journal of Linguistics*. June 1972, 3, 1, 59–65.

Benedict, Burton. *Indians in a Plural Society: A Report on Mauritius*. Colonial Research Studies No. 34. London: Her Majesty's Stationery Office. 1961.

Bickerton, Derek. The nature of a creole continuum, *Language*. 1973, 49, 3, 640–669.

Bickerton, Derek. Pidginisation and creolisation: language acquisition and language universals. In Albert Valdman (ed.), *Pidgin and Creole Lingusitics*. Bloomington: Indiana University Press, 1977, 49-69.

Bloomfield, Leonard. *Language*. New York: Holt, Rinehart and Winston, 1933.

Bresnahan, Mary I. English in the Philippines, *Journal of Communication*, Spring 1979, 29, 2, 64–71

Brosnahan, L. F. Some aspects of the linguistic situation in tropical Africa, *Lingua*. 1963, 12, 54–65.

Bughwan, D. Indian South Africans—Their language dilemma, *Humanitas*, 1972, 2, 1 (Pretoria), 61–65.

Chatterji, Suniti Kumar. Calcutta Hindustani: A study of a jargon dialect. In *Select Papers* (Anglia-Nibandha-Chayana). New Delhi: People's Publishing House, 1972, 204–256.

Conrad, Andrew W., and Fishman, Joshua A. English as a world language: The evidence. In J. Fishman, R. L. Cooper, and A. W. Conrad, *The Spread of English*, Rowley, Mass.: Newbury House, 1977. 3–76.

DeCamp, David. Introduction: The study of Pidgin and Croele languages. In Dell Hymes (ed.), *Pidginization and Creolization of Languages*. London: Cambridge University Press, 1971a, 13–42.

DeCamp, David. Toward a generative analysis of a post-Creole speech continuum. In Dell Hymes (ed.), *Pidginization and Creolization of Languages*. London: Cambridge University Press, 1971b, 349–370.

Edwards, Jay. African influences on the English of San Andres Island, Colombia. In David DeCamp and Ian F. Hancock (eds.), *Pidgins and Creoles: Current Trends and Prospects*. Washington, D.C.: Georgetown University Press, 1974, 1–26.

Edwards, Jay, Rosberg, Michael, and Hoy, Luis "Modesto" Pryme. Conversation in a West Indian taxi: An ethnolinguistic analysis. *Language in Society*. 1978, 4, 295–321.

Europa Yearbook. *Africa South of the Sahara 1979–80, Vol. II*. London: Europa Publications Ltd., 1979.

Ferguson, Charles A. Diglossia, *Word*. 1959, 15, 325–340. Also in Dell Hymes (ed.), *Language in Culture and Society*. New York: Harper and Row, 1964, 429–439.

Ferguson, Charles A. The language factor in national development. In Frank A. Rice (ed.), *Study of the Role of Second Language in Asia, Africa, and Latin America*. Washington, D.C.: Center for Applied Linguistics, 1962, 8–14.

Ferguson, Charles A., and John J. Gumperz (eds.), Linguistic diversity in South Asia. *International Journal of American Linguistics*. 1960, 26, 3, part III.

Fishman, Joshua A. *Language Loyalty in the United States: The Maintenance and Perpetuation of Non-English Mother Tongues by American Ethnic and Religious Groups*. The Hague: Mouton and Co., 1966,

Fishman, Joshua A. The sociology of language: An interdisciplinary social science approach to language in society. In Joshua A. Fishman (ed.), *Advances in the Sociology of Language*. The Hague: Mouton and Co., 1971, 217–404.

Fishman, Joshua A. The spread of English as a new perspective for the study of "language maintenance and language shift." In Braj B. Kachru (ed.), *Studies in Language Learning, Special Issue on Dimensions of Bilingualism: Theory and Case Studies*. Spring 1976, 1, 2. 59–104.

Fishman, Joshua A. Knowing, using, and liking English as an additional language, *TESOL Quarterly*. 1977, 11, 2. Also in Joshua A. Fishman, Cooper, R. L. and Conrad, A. W. *The Spread of English*. Rowley, Mass: Newbury House, 1977, pp. 302–310.

Fishman, Joshua A. Bilingual education: What and why? In Margaret A. Lourie and Nancy Faires Conklin (eds.), *A Pluralistic Nation: The Language Issue in the United States*. Rowley, Mass.: Newbury House, 1978, 407–446.

Fishman, Joshua A., Cooper, R. L. and Conrad. A. W. *The Spread of English*. Rowley, Mass.: Newbury House, 1977.

Garvin, Paul and Mathiot, Madeleine. The urbanization of the Guarani language: A problem in language and culture. In A. F. C. Wallace (ed.), *Men and Cultures; Selected Papers of the Fifth International Congress of Anthropological and Ethnological Sciences*. Philadelphia: University of Pennsylvania Press, 1956. Also in Joshua A. Fishman (ed.), *Readings in the Sociology of Language*. The Hague: Mouton and Co., 1968, 365–374.

Gumperz, John J. Types of linguistic communities. In Joshua A. Fishman (ed.), *Readings in the Sociology of Language.* The Hague: Mouton and Co., 1968, 460–472.

Gumperz, John J. Verbal strategies in multilingual communication. In R. D. Abrahams and R. C. Troike (eds.), *Language and Cultural Diversity in American Education.* Englewood Cliffs, N.J.: Prentice-Hall, 1970.

Gumperz, John J., and Naim, C. M. Formal and informal standards in the Hindi regional language area. In Charles A. Ferguson and John J. Gumperz (eds.), *Linguistic Diversity in South Asia: International Journal of American Linguistics.* July 1960, 26, 3, 92–118.

Hall, Robert A., Jr. The life cycle of pidgin languages. *Lingua.* 1962, 11, 151–156.

Hall, Robert A., Jr. Pidgins and creoles as standard languages. In J. B. Pride and J. Holmes (eds.), *Sociolinguistics.* Harmondsworth, England: Penguin Books, Ltd., 1972, 142–154.

Halliday, M. A. K. Language as a social semiotic: Towards a general sociolinguistic theory. In Adam Makkai and Valerie Makkai (eds.), *The First LACUS Forum 1974.* Columbia, South Carolina: Hornbeam Press, 1975. 17–46.

Halliday, M. A. K., MacIntosh, A., and Strevens, P. *The Linguistic Sciences and Language Teaching.* London: Longmans, 1964; Bloomington, Indiana: Indiana University Press, 1966.

Haugen, Einar. *Bilingualism in the Americas.* Publications of the American Dialect Society, No. 26, University of Alabama Press, 1956.

Haugen, Einar. On the meaning of bilingual competence. In R. Jakobson and S. Kawamoto, *Studies in General and Oriental Linguistics.* Tokyo: TEC Corporation for Language and Educational Research, 1970.

Haugen, Einar. Instrumentalism in language planning. In Joan Rubin and Björn H. Jernudd (eds.), *Can Language be Planned?* Honolulu: The University Press of Hawaii, 1971, 281–289.

Holm, John. The creole "copula" that highlighted the world. In J. L. Dillard (ed.), *Perspectives on American English.* The Hague: Mouton and Co., 1979.

Jakobovits, Leon A. The psychological bases of second language learning. *Language Sciences.* February 1971, 14, 22–28.

Kachru, Braj B. The Indianness in Indian English. *Word.* December 1965, 21, 3, 391–410.

Kachru, Braj B. Models of English for the third world: White man's linguistic burden or language pragmatics? *TESOL Quarterly.* June 1976, 10, 2, 221–239.

Kachru, Braj B. The new Englishes and old models. *English Teaching Forum (July 1977),* 1977, 29–35.

Kahin, G. M. *Nationalism and Revolution in Indonesia.* Ithaca, N.Y.: Cornell University Press, 1952.

Kelly, Sister Francis. The English spoken colloquially by a group of adolescents in Suva, *Fiji English Teachers' Journal.* 1975, 11, 19–43.

Kloss, Heinz. Types of multilingual communities: A discussion of ten variables. In Stanley Lieberson (ed.), *Explorations in Sociolinguistics.* Bloomington: Indiana University Press, 7–17.

Krashen, S. Adult second language acquisition and learning: A review of theory and applications. In R. Gingras (ed.), *Second Language Acquisition and Foreign Language Learning.* Washington, D.C.: Center for Applied Linguistics, 1978.

Labov, William. *The Social Stratification of English in New York City.* Washington, D.C.: Center for Applied Linguistics, 1966.

Lambert, Wallace E., and Tucker, G. Richard. A social psychology of bilingualism. In J. B. Pride and J. Holmes (eds.), *Sociolinguistics.* Harmondsworth: Penguin Books, 1972, 336–349.

LePage, Robert B. Problems to be faced in the use of English as the medium of education in four West Indian territories. In Joshua A. Fishman, Charles A. Ferguson, and J. Das Gupta (eds.), *Language Problems of Developing Nations.* New York: John Wiley & Sons, 1968, 431–441.

Lester, Mark. International English and language variation. Unpublished paper, East West Center, 1978.

Lieberson, Stanley. Bilingualism in Montreal: A demographic analysis. In Joshua A. Fishman (ed.), *Advances in the Sociology of Language Vol. II.* The Hague: Mouton and Co., 1972, 231–254.

Mackey, William F. The description of bilingualism. In Joshua A. Fishman (ed.), *Readings in the Sociology of Language*. The Hague: Mouton and Co., 1968, 554–584.

Mafeni, Bernard. Nigerian pidgin. In John Spencer (ed.), *The English Language in West Africa*. London: Longman, 1971, 95–112.

Mihalic, F. *The Jacaranda Dictionary and Grammar of Melanesian Pidgin*. Brisbane: Jacaranda Press, 1971.

Moag, Rodney F. Bilingualism-biculturalism: Where is it going in the Pacific? *Directions*. 1978a, 1, 3–7.

Moag, Rodney F. Standardization in pidgin Fijian: Implications for the theory of pidginization. In A. J. Schütz (ed.), *Fijian Language Studies: Borrowing and Pidginization*. Suva, Fiji: The Fiji Museum (Bulletin No. IV), 1978b, 68–90. Also in S. A. Wurm and Lois Carrington (eds.), *Second International Conference on Austronesian Linguistics: Proceedings, Fascicle 2, Eastern Austronesian*. Canberra: Pacific Linguistics, 1979, 1147–1184.

Moag, Rodney F. Linguistic adaptations of the Fiji Indians. To be published in Vijay C. Mishra (ed.), *Rama's Banishment: A Centenary Tribute to the Fiji Indians*. Auckland: Heinemann. Forthcoming a.

Moag, Rodney, F. The life cycle of non-native Englishes: A case study of Fiji and the South Pacific. To appear in Braj B. Kachru (ed.), *Other Tongue: English in Non-Native Contexts*. Forthcoming b.

Moag, Rodney F. A hierarchical typology of variation in English and how it varies according to the role of English in the society. To appear in *Proceedings of NWAVE 8*, special number of Montreal Working Papers in Linguistics. Forthcoming c.

Moag, Rodney F. and Moag, Louisa B. English in Fiji, some perspectives and the need for language planning. *Fiji English Teachers' Journal*. 1977, 13, 2–26. Also in J. C. Richards (ed.), *New Varieties of English: Issues and Approaches*. Singapore: SEAMEO Regional Language Centre (Occasional Papers No. 8), June 1979, 73–90.

Moag, Rodney F. and Moag, Louisa B. Plotting language use patterns, an added tool for teachers and materials writers. Workshop presented at the annual meeting of Teachers of English to Speakers of Other Languages, Mexico City, April 1978. Being revised for publication.

Noss, Richard B. *Language Policy and Higher Education in South-East Asia*. UNESCO—International Association of Universities Joint Research Program in Higher Education, 1965.

Paauw, Scott H. The role of the media in Indonesia, Singapore, and Malaysia, In Rodney F. Moag and Scott H. Paauw, (eds.), *Papers in Multilingualism*. University of Michigan Papers in Linguistics, Spring 1980.

Parliament of Fiji. *Report on the Census of the Population, 1976*. (Parliamentary Paper No. 13 of 1977.) Suva, Fiji: Parliament of Fiji, 1977.

Platt, John. ". . . Or, what you will," *Hemisphere: An Asian-Australian Monthly*, 1975, 15–18.

Platt, John. A model for polyglossia and multilingualism (with special reference to Singapore and Malaysia). In *Language in Society*. 1977a, 6, 361–378.

Platt, John. The sub-varieties of Singapore English. In W. Crewe (ed.), *The English Language in Singapore*. Singapore: Eastern Universities Press, 1977b.

Prator, Clifford H. The British heresy in TESL. In Joshua A. Fishman, Charles A. Ferguson, and J. Das Gupta (eds.), *Language Problems of Developing Nations*. New York: John Wiley & Sons, 1968, 459–476.

Pride, J. B. Communicative needs in the learning and use of English. Paper given at the East-West Center Conference on English as an International Auxiliary Language (April 1978), Honolulu, Hawaii, 1978. Published in revised form in J. C. Richards (ed.), *New Varieties of English: Issues and Approaches*. Singapore: SEAMEO Regional Language Centre (Occasional Papers No. 8), June 1979, 33–72.

Reyburn, William D. Assessing multilingualism: An abridgement of "problems and procedures in ethnolinguistic surveys." In Sirarpi Ohanessian, Charles A. Ferguson, and Edgar C. Polomé (eds.), *Language Surveys in Developing Nations: Papers and Reports on Sociolinguistic Surveys*. Washington, D.C.: Center for Applied Linguistics, 1975, 87–114.

Rosenbaum, Yehudit, Nadel, E., Cooper, R. L., and Fishman, J. English on Keren Kayemet Street. In Joshua A. Fishman, Robert L. Cooper, and Andrew W. Conrad (eds.), *The Spread of English*. Rowley, Mass.: Newbury House, 1977, 179–194.

Rustow, Dankwart A. Language, modernization, and nationhood—An attempt at typology. In Joshua A. Fishman, Charles A. Ferguson, and J. Das Gupta (eds.), *Language Problems of Developing Nations*. New York: John Wiley & Sons, 1968, 87–105

Sekhar, A. Chandra. *Census of India*. New Delhi: Republic of India, Office of the Registrar General, 1971.

Selinker, Larry. Interlanguage, *International Review of Applied Linguistics*. 1972, 10, 3, 209–231. Also in Jack Richards (ed.), *Error Analysis: Perspectives on Second Language Acquisition*. London: Longman Group, 31–54.

Sibayan, Bonifacio P. Language policy, language engineering and literacy in the Philippines. In Joshua A. Fishman (ed.), *Advances in Language Planning*. The Hague: Mouton and Co., 1974, 221– 254.

Simpson, Sam. *The Part-European Community in Fiji*. Suva, Fiji: South Pacific Social Sciences Association, 1974.

Smith, D. M. Some implications for the social status of Pidgin languages. In D. M. Smith and R. Shuy (eds.), *Sociolinguistics in Cross-Cultural Analysis*. Washington, D.C.: Georgetown University Press, 1972, 47–56.

Smith, Larry E. English as an international and intranational language: A report on the Honolulu conference. Paper presented at the Conference on English in Non-native Contexts, June 30–July 1, 1978, University of Illinois.

South Africa Statistics 1976. Pretoria: Republic of South Africa Department of Statistics, 1977.

Stewart, William A. A sociolinguistic typology for describing national multilingualism. In Joshua A. Fishman (ed.), *Readings in the Sociology of Language*. The Hague: Mouton and Co., 1968, 531–545.

Tucker, G. Richard. Judging personality from language usage: A Filipino example, *Philippine Sociological Review*. 1968, 16, 30–39.

United States Government Census Bureau. *Statistical Abstract of the United States*. Washington, D.C.: Government Printing Office, 1978.

Voorhoeve, Jan. Varieties of creole in Surinam: Church creole and pagan cult languages. In Dell Hymes (ed.), *Pidginization and Creolization of Languages*. Cambridge: Cambridge University Press, 1971, 305–315.

Wong, Irene F. H. English as an international auxiliary language in Malaysia. Paper presented at the Conference on English as an International Auxiliary Language, East-West Center, Honolulu, April 1978.

Wurm, Stephen A. Pidgins, creoles, lingue franche, and national development. In Albert Valdman (ed.), *Pidgin and Creole Linguistics*. Bloomington: Indiana University Press, 1977.

3 THE USES, USERS, AND FEATURES OF ENGLISH IN SINGAPORE

Mary Tay

INTRODUCTION

In this paper I want to describe the characteristic uses, users and features of English in Singapore to show what problems are encountered in using current linguistic terminology to describe language use and language variation in a multilingual country. I conclude with some suggestions about how to determine teaching goals and standards of correctness in countries where the well-established varieties of English are not spoken.

USES OF ENGLISH

Let me begin by considering the characteristic uses of English in Singapore against the background of the linguistic situation.

Singapore is a multiethnic and multilingual country. Its population of about 2¼ million is composed of 76 percent Chinese, 15 percent Malays, 7 percent Indians, and 2 percent others, including Eurasians, Europeans, and Arabs (Arumainathan, 1973). The linguistic situation is even more complicated than these ethnic categories suggest. It may be described as one involving "a variety of unrelated languages each with its own literary tradition" (Rustow, 1968, p. 102). These languages are: Hokkien, Teochew, Cantonese, Hainanese, Hakka, Foochow, and Mandarin (all with a common Chinese literary tradition but mutually incomprehensible when spoken), Malay (traditionally identified as the language of the Malays), Tamil (the language of the majority of Indians), and English.

In recent years, English has become an important language in the republic. Six main uses of English may be identified:

1. English as an official language.
2. English as a language of education.

3. English as a working language.
4. English as a lingua franca.
5. English as a language for the expression of national identity.
6. English as an international language.

English as an Official Language

When Singapore became independent in 1965, the government decided that there would be four official languages: Malay, Mandarin, Tamil, and English. In practice, this has meant that newspapers; radio and TV programmes; important public notices issued by the government; and the addresses of government bodies such as the Ministry of Education are in all four languages.

In countries where English is used as an official language, it should not be considered a "foreign" language because it has become indigenised. In the Singapore context, English is never referred to as a "foreign" language. Foreign languages are languages such as Japanese and French which are now taught in some schools in addition to English and one of the other three official languages. Besides, the distinction between "English as a first language" (EFL) and "English as a second language" (ESL) is blurred in the context of multilingualism and, in the case of Singapore, the bilingual policy in language education.

English as a Language in Education

Since independence, the national policy has been to give equal treatment to all the four official languages in its educational structure. Thus education is available in English-medium, Chinese-medium, Malay-medium, and Tamil-medium schools up to the secondary level. In addition, all four languages are available as second languages at both primary and secondary levels.

The place of English in education is best understood in the context of the bilingual policy. Bilingualism has a special meaning in the Singapore educational system. It does not mean the learning of any two languages, but of English and one of the other three official languages. English is taught right from the first year in primary school either as a first or second language.

In the context of education in Singapore, the term "English as a first language" does not necessarily mean that it is the first language of the student either in terms of the order of acquisition (the first language learned in childhood) or of proficiency (the best language), but that it is the English taught in English-medium schools. Similarly, the term "English as a second language" is used to refer only to the English taught in non-English-medium schools. As a result of this distinction, second language techniques and materials are considered essential in the case of English as a second language but not in the case of English as a first language.

This distinction between first and second language is valid so long as those who study English as a first language come from homes where English is spoken most of the time. But when the students of English as a first language come from homes where English is not the dominant language, perhaps second language teaching techniques should also be used in teaching English as a first language. It is well known that in a number of so-called English-medium schools in Singapore, some of the children are much more fluent in Mandarin than in English. Besides, as the most recent policy is to give almost equal emphasis to both first and second languages in primary school, the media distinction is likely to be less important and the present distinction between English as a first language and English as a second language less useful.

With the implementation of the bilingual policy, English has come to occupy a unique position in the educational system. In future years, English is likely to become even more important as a language in education for two main reasons. First, student enrollment in the English-medium schools has more than doubled in the past 30 years. In 1947, 31.6 percent of all the school-going children in Singapore were in English-medium schools; in June 1975, the percentage had increased to 69.4. (Ministry of Education Reports; Yearbook of Statistics, Singapore 1975/76). Second, the switch in the medium of instruction from Mandarin to English at Nanyang University in 1975 is an indication of the growing importance of English in tertiary education. It is still possible to major in Chinese Language and Literature or Malay Language and Literature and thus avoid the use of English to some extent, but they are certainly not the most popular courses.

In the Singapore educational context, therefore, there are real problems in the use of the terms English as a first language and English as a second language. Lee (1974) has suggested that the languages taught in school be referred to as "first school language" and "second school language." We would then talk of "English as a first school language" (EFSL) and "English as a second school language" (ESSL) when we talk of English in the context of education in Singapore. However, we would continue to use ESL in its more universal sense to mean that speakers of ESL are those for whom English is a second language in terms of proficiency.

In the context of education, however, it does not matter too much what term we use to describe English. What is infinitely more important is that there should be a clear understanding of language learning strategies and a set of clearly defined teaching goals, standards of acceptability, and teaching materials based on sound pedagogical principles. If these are absent, the teaching of English will still have its problems no matter how we choose to label English.

English as a Working Language

English is the dominant working language in Singapore. It is the language of government administration and legislation. Thus, on such documents as the Singapore identity card, driving licence, and vehicle registration book, only English is used. Legal contracts are also written only in English.

With the possible exception of some Chinese firms, English is the only language used at job interviews regardless of whether the job is in the civil service or in the private sector. Thus competence in English is an important criterion in recruitment and even in promotion.

English as a Language for Intra- and Interethnic Communication

As the majority of the educated Singaporeans can speak at least two languages, they have a choice of what languages to use in intraethnic and interethnic communication. English is just one of several languages available to the educated Singaporean in such communication.

Among the earliest Chinese immigrants to Singapore, Hokkien was widely used when one Chinese spoke to another Chinese. Some used Mandarin, but few used English or Malay in intraethnic communication among the Chinese. Among the Malays, the language of intraethnic communication was Malay; among the Indians, Tamil.

These patterns of intraethnic communication have changed noticeably in the last 20 years. Today, English and Mandarin are much more widely used in intraethnic communication among the Chinese. In fact, many of the young Chinese in Singapore cannot speak the so-called Chinese "dialects" with any degree of fluency. Among the Malays, Malay continues to be used in intraethnic communication, although English has also come to be used alongside Malay. Among the Indians, English is beginning to replace Tamil as the language used in intraethnic communication.

The patterns of interethnic communication also show interesting changes. Traditionally, when a Chinese spoke to an Indian or Malay, he used English or Bazaar Malay (a pidginised form of standard Malay). Today he is likely to use English more often. The same change in the pattern of interethnic communication is observable among the other ethnic groups.

Because of the increasing use of English and Mandarin in the schools, and the fact that a number of Indian and Malay parents are beginning to send their children to schools where English is taught as a first language and Mandarin as a second, we can expect that in the future English and Mandarin will be the most commonly used languages both in intra- and interethnic communication, at least among the more highly educated. Hokkien and Bazaar Malay may continue to be used in intraethnic and interethnic communication, but their use will be more widespread among the less well-educated.

With the increasing use of English and Mandarin by many different types of speakers in a wide range of situations, "local" English and "local" Mandarin present real challenges to the linguist who tries to describe their various subvarieties, and to the language teacher who has to be conscious of the subvarieties that he uses in various situations and to teach an "acceptable" subvariety in the classroom.

English as a Language for the Expression of National Identity

While ethnic identity is expressed by the use of one of the Chinese languages for the Chinese, Malay for the Malays, and Tamil for the Indians, national identity is usually expressed in some other language which is not associated with any of the three major ethnic groups in Singapore. This national identity by which a Singaporean identifies himself as Singaporean rather than as Chinese, Malay, or Tamil is best expressed through the use of English.

This use of English in the expression of national identity is well stated in the words of T. T. B. Koh, Singapore's representative to the United Nations:

> When one is abroad, in a bus or train or aeroplane and when one overhears someone speaking, one can immediately say this is someone from Malaysia or Singapore. And I should hope that when I'm speaking abroad my countrymen will have no problem recognising that I am a Singaporean. (Tongue, 1974)

The desire to be recognised as a Singaporean probably explains why the average educated Singaporean, including the language teacher, considers it important to aim at a standard indistinguishable from standard British English in the area of syntax but not in the area of phonology (pronunciation, rhythm, stress, and intonation) and vocabulary. It is the phonology and vocabulary, rather than the grammar, that identify a speaker as distinctly Singaporean. The use of English as a language for the expression of one's national identity also explains why the English of some Singaporeans is considered "near-native" rather than "native." Their speech is characterised by stress and intonation patterns that do not conform to those of the well-established varieties of English, such as British English and American English.

English as an International Language

As Singapore is at the crossroads of international communication, one very important use of English is as an international language. Smith has defined an international language as "one which is used by people of different nations to communicate with one another" (Smith, 1976, p. 38).

In discussing this use of English in Singapore, it is important to distinguish between English that is functionally international and that which is structurally international. In terms of function alone, one might say that *anyone* who uses English to communicate with someone from another country is using English as an international language. This would include the uneducated Singaporean taxi-driver who talks to the American, Australian, or Japanese tourist in some form of English. It would also include the educated Singaporean who speaks English at an international conference either at home or abroad.

Such a definition of English as an international language in purely functional terms overlooks some important considerations. There is the question of the variety of English that is used for international purposes, depending on the educational and linguistic background of the speaker. The type of English that is spoken by the highly educated Singaporean at an international conference is very different, structurally, from that spoken by the Singaporean taxi-driver. The former variety is quite close to standard British English; the latter is a pidginised form that is much closer to other pidgins than to standard English.

It is linguistically naive to talk of English as an international language as if it were characterised by certain structures that cut across educational and linguistic differences. Various linguists have drawn attention to the fact that native speakers of English use a "filtering process" in which they simplify their language when speaking to foreigners. The research (notably by Platt) that has been done in Singapore English shows that this filtering process is not confined to native speakers of the established varieties of English, such as British English. The speaker of Singapore English who has a wide lectal range adjusts his speech according to whether he is using English at the national or international level; one who has no such range obviously cannot.

An important consideration in any discussion of English as an international language is the question of intelligibility. Research on the mutual intelligibility of different varieties of English is still in its infancy. It may be noted, however, that even within a small country like Singapore, there are speakers who can speak a variety of English that is highly intelligible at the international level, and there are those who can speak a variety of English that is intelligible only at the national level.

Variables such as the educational and linguistic background of the speaker determine the variety of English that is spoken by a Singaporean in all the uses of English discussed in the first section of this paper. It is to these variables that I now turn.

USERS OF ENGLISH

I have demonstrated that in recent years the role of English in Singapore has taken on new dimensions at the official, educational, occupational, social, national, and international levels. All these dimensions should be carefully considered in describing the characteristic features of English in Singapore and in the formulation of teaching goals. However, a description of English in Singapore would be incomplete without a description of the users of English and the user variables that must be considered in discussing the Singapore English speech continuum. English has not only become a more widely used language in many spheres of life; it has also come to be used by many more speakers of diverse linguistic origins, differing proficiency and so on.

Let us now look at some of these user variables that influence the variety of English that is used.

Age

The age of the user of English is an important variable. The 1970 census shows that there is an inverse correlation between age and literacy in English: in the 15–19 age group we find about 50 percent literate in English, whereas in the 40–44 age group the rate is only 19 percent. The 1975 *Survey Research Singapore* survey also revealed that in the 15–20 age group 87.3 percent could understand English, whereas in the over-40 age group the percentage of those who could understand English was only 27.5.

Not only is the younger generation more literate in English than the older generation, but there is reason to believe that the age of the participant influences the variety of English that is spoken by him and to him. Among Singaporeans who are over 25 years of age (that is, those who finished secondary education before the implementation of the bilingual policy in 1966), there is a marked difference in the English used by those who studied in English-medium schools and that used by those who studied in non-English-medium schools. The former are generally more proficient in English. It is particularly in the area of code diversity that the English-educated group is considered more proficient than the non-English-educated group. Among Singaporeans who are under 25, however, this difference, though still observable, is less marked. This is probably because, with the implementation of the bilingual policy, there is equal or near-equal emphasis on two languages: English and another language. Thus proficiency does not vary too much between those who learned it as a first school language and those who learned it as a second school language. In fact, some students are more proficient in their second school language than in their first school language.

The influence of age on the variety of English that is spoken is also seen in the fact that those who can speak and write near-perfect British English are generally from the over-25 age group.

Age is also an important variable in that it often distinguishes a developmental variety of English from a non-developmental one. Thus it would be misleading to characterise Singapore English in terms of the features found in the speech of school children for theirs is a "developmental variety" (or an interlanguage) that has not yet stabilised. In the case of adults who have stopped learning the language, however, the variety of English that they use may be described in terms of "a non-developmental lectal continuum."

Sex

This variable influences the speaker's language in the area of vocabulary. Some vocabulary items used in Singapore English may be described as being characteristic of male speakers only. These are items acquired by boys during military training and are usually hybrids of English and Hokkien. For instance, the word *kooning* meaning "sleeping" is a hybrid of the Hokkien *koon* meaning "sleep" and the English *-ing* ending used to mark the present continuous tense. As girls in Singapore do not as yet have to enlist for military service (or "be called up for National Service," according to the Singapore idiom), these items are usually outside their vocabulary. Whether they will eventually pass into common use is left to be seen, but at present there is a considerable number of "army vocabulary" items which are understood and used only by male speakers who have recently completed National Service. In Singapore, all male citizens must do two years' compulsory military service when they reach the age of 18.

Proficiency

The effects of schooling in English-medium or non-English-medium schools on proficiency have been discussed in an earlier section. Here I would just like to discuss the effects of proficiency on language choice and choice of topic.

In a multilingual society like Singapore, proficiency often determines not only which language will be used for communication, but also the amount of switching from one language to another. For instance, a Singaporean who is bilingual in English and Mandarin will choose to speak Mandarin to someone if he knows that this person is proficient in Mandarin but not in English. If they are both bilingual, they will probably switch from one language to the other many times in the course of their conversation.

Proficiency also determines which variety of a language will be used. For instance, a speaker who has a command of the whole range of the Singapore speech continuum (from the acrolectal to the basilectal varieties) will choose to use only the basilectal variety when speaking to someone who can speak only this variety. On the other hand, a speaker who has a command of only the basilectal variety will, of course, have to use it all the time, irrespective of what he is talking about and to whom. This explains why a speaker with a command of the acrolectal variety uses it in speaking to a foreigner if he does not expect the foreigner to understand the basilectal variety. If he thinks the foreigner understands the basilectal variety and if the situation is an informal one, he will still switch from one lect to another. A speaker who does not have the same lectal range is, of course, unable to do this.

Proficiency determines what topics will be discussed in which language. For instance, most Singaporeans are able to discuss academic topics in either Mandarin or English but not in their first language (first in order of acquisition) which may be Hokkien, Malay, Tamil, or some other "ethnic" language. They will therefore choose Mandarin or English and avoid using their first language for this purpose. On the other hand, they may be proficient in speaking on other topics, such as family life or religion, only in their first language.

Attitudes

A person's attitude toward the language he uses and the way that other people use it is an important variable that affects not only his own motivation in learning and using the language, but also the particular variety of English that he speaks or chooses to speak.

The general language attitude of the Singapore population is seen in the desire to become bilingual (and this means the use of English and one other language). English is generally accepted as a useful language to know as it opens the door to employment, further studies and interethnic communiation. It is interesting that in a recent survey of language use among secondary four pupils in Singapore (Chia, 1977), those who considered English the most useful language did so, not because of a desire to identify it as their "own" language, but because of its "usefulness." On the other hand, those who considered Chinese the most useful language did so mainly because they felt that it was their own language.

Most Singaporeans recognise the fact that they speak English differently from the so-called native speakers of English. They are, of course, exposed to some of these native varieties, particularly British and American English, in the film world. They accept these differences but are quite content to speak English their "own" way as long as they can be understood by fellow Singaporeans *and* foreigners.

Role

Differences in the role of the participants affect both the choice of language used and the variety of language used. As an example of the former, take the case of a teacher of English in a classroom situation. He uses English in his teaching because he is playing the role of English teacher. He and/or his students may be equally conversant in another language, but that language would be the wrong one to use in his role as English teacher. Outside the classroom, however, he might use another language with his pupils, especially if these pupils have difficulty expressing themselves in English. There his role is that of a friend, and this switch in the language used might be an indicator of the change in role. There are, of course, those who carry their role as English teacher beyond the classroom and feel that they should talk to their pupils in English under all circumstances to encourage them in their use of English.

As an example of the influence of role on the variety of language used, take the case of the same English teacher. In the classroom, he will be very careful about the "variety" of English that he uses in teaching English. He will use the highest variety that he can speak. He remembers the role he is playing is that of English teacher. However, when he is not teaching English he may drop to the basilectal variety in an attempt to establish rapport with his pupils, for his role is now that of a friend. This switching may, of course, be unconscious or subconscious.

I have chosen the example of the English language teacher because I think it also illustrates the dilemma this person faces in the choice of the variety of English to be used in teaching. For language learning to be successful, particularly at the primary level, the teacher's role must be both that of teacher and friend. It is not surprising, then, that he should switch from one variety to another. The higher varieties of Singapore English are associated with formality and are not considered appropriate in informal situations.

Linguistic Background

The linguistic background of the user of English influences the variety of English that he uses in a number of important ways.

First, interference from the speaker's first language to his second language (for those who have a definitely clear-cut first and second language) explains why Malay, Indian, and Chinese speakers of English have different features in their pronunciation.

Second, as many Singaporeans learn two or more languages simultaneously, it is difficult to state in which direction interference occurs. English could be the speaker's L1, L2 or L3 in terms of proficiency and even L7 in terms of order of acquisition.

Third, as English is so widely used among many speakers who come from diverse linguistic backgrounds and who are bilingual, if not trilingual, the variety of English spoken is affected, not only by the speaker's own linguistic background, but also by the linguistic background of the other people in that community. For example, an English speaker in Singapore may not be able to speak Tamil but his or her English will probably show characteristic influences from Tamil if he or she learns English from someone who speaks English with Tamil features of pronunciation.

FEATURES OF ENGLISH

What I have suggested so far is that when we talk of English in Singapore, we need to consider what the language is used for, who uses it, and to whom. Let me now describe the characteristic pronunciation, grammatical and lexical features of English in Singapore.

I agree with Platt's characterisation of Singapore English as a speech continuum:

> Singapore English is a speech continuum, comparable to the post-creole continuum in Jamaica described by DeCamp. . . or in Guyana described by Bickerton. . . . There is a whole range from the 'lowest' variety, the *basilect*, through the medium range, the *mesolects,* to the 'highest' variety, the *acrolect*. (Platt, 1977, p. 84)

I agree with Platt also in that

> There is of course, a gradation along the scale but for convenience's sake, I shall divide the speech continuum into an acrolect, a mesolect, and a basilect. (Platt, 1977, p. 84)

Let me now amplify the defining features of each of the three varieties of Singapore English according to the data that I have gathered. I will highlight the pronunciation features that differ from those of received pronunciation (RP) and the grammatical features that differ from those of standard British English (SBE).

Pronunciation Features of Singapore English

Acrolect

This variety of Singapore English differs from received pronunciation in rhythm and intonation, stress patterns, vowels, and consonants.

Rhythm and Intonation.   English in its RP pronunciation is said to have a "stress-timed" rhythm. This means that stressed syllables recur at equal intervals, but unstressed syllables are unequally spaced in time (Pike, 1946, p. 35; Abercrombie, 1967, p. 97). This type of rhythm has also been called "morse-code rhythm" (James, 1940, p. 25). English in its Singaporean pronunciation (even in the acrolectal variety), however, has a "syllable-timed" rhythm. This means that all syllables recur at equal intervals of time, stressed or unstressed. This "machine-gun rhythm" (James, 1940, p. 25) is one of the most important features of Singapore English.

The intonation patterns of English in its RP pronunciation show a fairly wide pitch range and many different pitch patterns. It has been observed that English in its Singaporean pronunciation has a much narrower pitch range and not as many different pitch patterns (Tongue, 1974). This difference probably explains why the speaker of British English can use intonation to express himself in many ways that the speaker of Singapore English cannot. It is also intonation that sets apart Malay, Chinese, and Indian varieties of Singapore English.

Stress Patterns.   The stress patterns of Singapore English differ from those of English in its RP pronunciation in four main ways:

1. Equal stress in words that have primary and secondary stress:

R.P.	Si. P.
ce-le-<u>bra</u>-tion	*ce-le-bra-tion*
an-ni-<u>ver</u>-sa-ry	*an-ni-ver-sa-ry*

2. Absence of stress distinctions to mark different parts of speech:

R.P.	Si. P.
in*crease* (verb)	in*crease* (verb and noun)
*in*crease (noun)	
*ob*ject (noun)	
ob*ject* (verb)	ob*ject* (verb and noun)

3. Difference stress placements:

R.P.	Si. P.
*fa*culty	fa*cul*ty
*co*lleague	col*league*
advan*tage*ous	ad*van*tageous
*cha*racter	cha*rac*ter
eco*nom*ic	*eco*nomic
spe*cif*ic	*spe*cific

4. Use of contrastive stress at sentence level where normal stress is used. Thus in RP, the word *bag* in *shopping bag* is not normally stressed in a sentence like "I want a new shopping bag" unless the speaker wishes to contrast *bag* with *list* as in "I want a new *shopping bag*, not *shopping list*." The speaker of the Singapore English acrolect however, often stresses *bag* in sentences where no such contrast is intended.

The features rhythm, intonation, and stress patterns immediately set Singapore English apart from other varieties of English.

Vowels.   Differences in vowels in Singapore English include:

1. *Vowel length and quality.*   In RP certain vowels are distinguished from one another by a three-way contrast. For example, there is a three-way contrast between /i/ and /iː/ in words like *bit* and *beat*, /u/ and /uː/ in words like *pull* and *pool* and /ɔ/ and /ɔː/ in words like *cot* and *caught*. The contrast is one of tongue position: front vs. back; length: short vs. long; and tenseness: tense vs. lax. In Singapore English only the first two contrasts are made.

2. *Diphthongs.*   Certain diphthongs in RP such as /ou/, /ei/, /ɔə/ and /ɛə/ in words like *go, day, four,* and *there* are reduced to /o:/, /e:/, /ɔ:/, and /ɛ:/. In other words, they are pure long vowels without the glide in the diphthong.

3. *Schwa in unstressed syllables.*   In RP the schwa vowel /ə/ is found in the unstressed syllables before the primary stress in some words. For example, in the words *familiar, conclusion, upon, available,* and *official,* the stress is on the second syllable, and so the vowel in the first syllable is reduced to a schwa. In Singapore English the vowel in such syllables is usually not reduced to the schwa but has its full vowel qualities [æ], [ɔ], [ʌ], [a], and [o].

Consonants.   The acrolectal variety of Singapore English has a system of consonants that closely resembles that of RP. However, while the 24 consonant phonemes are kept apart, the same allophonic distributions are not found in Singapore English. The main differences in their allophonic distributions are as follows:

1. *Release of stops in final position.*   In RP the stops and affricates /p t k b d g tʃ dʒ/ are partially released when they occur at the end of a word. In the acrolectal variety of Singapore English, they are not released at all.

2. *Voicing.* In RP the opposition 'voice' versus 'voicelessness' occurs among all the stops, affricates, see (1), and fricatives /f v θ ð s z ʃ ʒ/ in all word positions. In the acrolectal variety of Singapore English, these stops, affricates, and fricatives are not voiced in word-final position. Thus *believe* is pronounced as *belief; teethe,* as *teeth; ones,* as *once;* and *rouge,* as *rooch.* Conversely, where voiceless alveolar and palato-alveolar fricatives are used in RP, their voiced counterparts are used in the acrolectal variety of Singapore English, especially in intervocalic position. Thus words like *uses* (noun), *December, price,* and *version* are all pronounced with the voiceless fricatives in RP but with the voiced fricatives in Singapore English.

Mesolect

The mesolect variety of Singapore English differs from RP in all the features mentioned under the acrolect as well as in the following features:

Aspiration of Voiceless Stops.   In RP the voiceless stops /p t k/ are aspirated when they are in initial position but unaspirated or weakly aspirated in unstressed syllables. In the mesolect variety of Singapore English, these voiceless stops are weakly aspirated or unaspirated in all word positions.

Simplification of Consonant Clusters.   Final consonant clusters are often reduced. In the following examples, RP has two consonants at the end of each word: *went, just, find, ask, told, seventh, complaint,* and *behind.* In the mesolect, only the first consonant in the cluster is pronounced. Medial consonant clusters are also reduced especially if a /d/ or /l/ is in the cluster. Thus in the following examples, RP has two or more consonants in the clusters: *hundreds, revolving, also.* In the mesolect, the /d/ or /l/ are omitted.

Variable Lack of Final Stops or Substitution by Glottal Stops.   In the mesolect, the final stops of RP are not only unreleased (as in the acrolect), but they are often omitted altogether or replaced by glottal stops. Thus words like *chop, cut, pork, crab, mad,* and *big* are pronounced with a final glottal stop instead of with /p/, /t/, /k/, /b/, /d/, and /g/.

Substitution of /t/ for /θ/ and /d/ for /ð/. Thus the *th* sounds in words like *three* and *this* are pronounced as *tree* and *dis* in the mesolectal variety.

Basilect

The basilectal variety of Singapore English differs from RP in having a higher proportion of all the features mentioned under the acrolect and mesolect as well as in some other features. These features are mainly the substitution of one consonant for another.

Substitution of voiceless alveolar fricative /s/ for voiceless palato-alveolar fricative /ʃ/ and vice versa. Thus *sugar* and *should* are sometimes pronounced with /s/ while *supermarket* and *soup* are sometimes pronounced with a /ʃ/.

Substitution of /l/ for /r/. Thus the /r/ in words like *forever, practice, fried, rice,* and *radio* are all pronounced with a /l/. This lack of contrast between some consonants means that at this level, there are not as many consonants as RP.

Two observations about the basilectal variety of Singapore English may be made:

1. Many of the pronunciation features of the basilect are those that the average teacher can comfortably handle as "errors" in a classroom situation. On the other hand, features of the acrolect and mesolect may be pointed out as errors, but the teacher may not always be able to produce the "correct" RP pronunciation.

2. Some of the features of the basilect also help to identify a speaker as typically Chinese, Malay, or Tamil. For example, the absence of the /f/ – /p/ distinction is typically Malay, the absence of the /v/ – /w/ distinction is typically Indian, and the absence of the /r/ – /l/ distinction is typically Chinese.

Grammatical Features of Singapore English

Acrolect

There are no significant or consistent differences between the grammatical features of the acrolect variety of Singapore English and those of standard British English.

Mesolect

This variety of Singapore English differs from standard British English in the following grammatical features:

1. *Word order in indirect questions*:
   May I ask where is the stamp counter?
   I'd like to know what are the procedures.

2. *Use of present continuous tense for simple present*:
   I'm having a business in High Street.
   I'm running an electrical shop.
3. *Indefinite article deletion*:
   May I apply for car license?
   You got to have proper system here.
4. *Lack of plural marking in nouns*:
   One of the lecturer told me to see you.
   Very few student can come on Friday.
5. *Lack of marking in verb forms*:
   He always go there every Sunday.
   She study so hard.
   My friend work in the bank.
   You have check my security.

Basilect

The basilect variety of Singapore English differs from standard British English in having a higher proportion of all the features mentioned under the mesolect as well as in some other features.

1. *Generalised "is it" question tag*:
   You're teaching us today, is it?
   The new committee has been formed, is it?
   The Director is busy now, is it?
2. *Word order in embedded structures*:
   I fill in exactly the man told me what to fill in.
3. *Do-deletion in direct questions*:
   Government pay you for what, man?
   You think what?
   Then how we manage to cope?
   Why she want to be like that?
   What you want?
   What license you want to take?
4. *Lack of marking in verb tenses*:
   We gone last night.
   We seen *Tarzan* last night.
   Everybody down there see me before.
5. *Verb pattern*:
   Would you mind take me go?
   He no bring come.
   You go there ask.
6. *Concord*:
   All this are wrong.
   All the clerk here are busy.

7. *Subject deletion with the use of "can" or "cannot"*:
Can or not?
Cannot.
Why cannot?
8. *Use of single verb or complement to replace subject + verb structures*:
Is he angry with me?
Angry.
Are you coming?
Coming.
Have you eaten?
Eaten. (or Eat already.)
9. *Object deletion*:
Can I renew?
They said they will send to you.
10. *Copula deletion*:
This part not filled in.
My handwriting not clear.
His teaching not so good.
11. *Use of modal auxiliaries*:
That will depends.
I will like to make a complaint.
12. *"Got" as "have" and "there are"*:
You got long hair.
Where got enough time?
Here got so many American teachers.
He got pots of money.
13. *Use of particles like la, man, ah, and ha*:
Hurry up la.
Government pay you for what, man?
You are doing all these fantastic things, man.
How is this like, man?
Wait ah.
What is it you want ha?

Lexical Features of Singapore English

Acrolect

The lexical features of this variety of Singapore English differ from those of standard British English mainly in the use of certain words that have acquired a different meaning in the Singapore context. A typical example is the use of the word *bungalow* in Singapore to refer to a two-storied building.

Mesolect

In this variety of Singapore English, the vocabulary differs from that of standard British English, not only in the way just mentioned, but also in the use of loans from Chinese, or Malay. Thus the use of such words as *jaga* (from Malay, meaning *watchman*), *padang* (from Malay, meaning *field*), and *towkay* (from Chinese, meaning *proprietor*) is a common feature of the mesolect.

Basilect

This variety of Singapore English is characterised by the use of words that are normally classified as slang or colloquialisms. Thus the use of slang like *frus* or *sabo* and colloquialisms like *shake legs* (from a literal translation of Malay *goyang kaki*, literally to shake legs and meaning completely at leisure) and eat snake (from a literal translation of a Hokkien phrase meaning to try and get away without doing work) immediately characterise the English spoken as a basilectal variety of Singapore English.

HOW SHOULD WE LABEL ENGLISH IN SINGAPORE?

Which of the terms ESL or EFL best describes the uses and varieties of English in Singapore?

Let us take the term EFL first. No attempt has ever been made to describe Singapore as an EFL country. This is as it should be. English has never been considered a foreign language because of its status: as an official language, an important language in education, a dominant working language, a lingua franca, and a language for the expression of national identity. English is not foreign but has indigenised. English is now widely used in many spheres of life by many speakers of diverse linguistic backgrounds, proficiency, and so on. When a Singaporean learns English, he is learning it both to communicate with other English-speaking people outside his country *and* to communicate with people within the country. The fact that EFL does not fit the Singapore context does not, however, invalidate the use of the term altogether. There are countries like Japan, the Republic of China, and Korea where English is basically a foreign language in terms of its status, its restricted societal functions, and the fact that it has not indigenised (that is, spoken widely and with native-speaker fluency by a large group of people within the country).

Singapore has often been described as an ESL country. This term is used to distinguish it from countries like the United States, the United Kingdom, and New Zealand where English is spoken by the majority of the people as a native language. The distinction between a native and a second language creates a number of difficulties in a multilingual country and needs clarification. The precise definition of native language varies and is not always clear. However, one can say that two main factors are usually borne in mind in the definition of the term. The first is priority of learning. Thus a language to be called native must have been the first-learned language. Priority of learning, however, is not always easy to determine in a country like Singapore which is characterised by polyglossia *and* multilingualism. A child may learn two or more languages simultaneously. Are we then to talk of "childhood acquisition of two or more native languages" (Diebold, 1961, p. 99)? There are difficulties here because one of these languages, such as Mandarin, may be forgotten in adult life through disuse. Both languages are therefore not equally native in adult life.

What is even more disturbing is the fact that absolute priority of learning may not even be needed for a speaker to achieve native fluency in the language. Many of the Singaporeans who are able to speak English with native fluency did not learn it as their first language. However, English has become their dominant language as a result of education in English and constant use in social interaction. Of course, there are also those who learned it as their first language in childhood and have continued to use it as their dominant language in adult life.

Priority of learning, therefore, is not always a significant consideration. The second assumption underlying the native–second language distinction is the assumed importance of an unbroken oral tradition. There are those who emphasize that a native or first language must have been learned in early childhood:

> One could say arbitrarily that any language learnt by the child before the age of instruction, from parents, from others, such as a nurse, looking after it, or from other children, is an L1. (Halliday, McIntosh, and Strevens, 1964, p. 78)

The point that is emphasized in this definition is the primacy of the oral tradition and the lack of interference from other languages. In a multilingual country, this assumption may be seriously questioned for two reasons:

1. Although a first language tends to influence a second-learned, it is equally true that a second-learned language can also influence the first.
2. Talk of a "pure" oral tradition is somewhat simplistic, because, although a child acquires his speech before he learns to read and write, his speech will contain features of the written language if he continues to use it in adult life.

The assumed importance of an unbroken oral tradition, therefore, is also questionable. Despite these difficulties in the definition of native language, however, one aspect of its use is particularly relevant to the Singapore context. Where native is equated with first language in the sense of dominant language or primary language—the language of its speaker's intimate daily life (Catford, 1959, p. 165)—it serves as a useful definition to distinguish between those for whom it is a dominant first language and those for whom it is essentially a second language.

Our definition of the native speaker will therefore be modified as follows:

1. A native speaker of English is not identified only by virtue of his birthright. He need not be from the United States, the United Kingdom, Australia, New Zealand, or one of the traditionally native English-speaking countries.
2. A native speaker of English who is not from one of the countries mentioned in (1) is one who learns English in childhood *and* continues to use it as his dominant language *and* has reached a certain level of fluency. All three conditions are important. If a person learns English late in life, he is unlikely to attain native fluency in it; if he learns it as a child, but does not use it as his

dominant language in adult life, his native fluency in the language is also questionable; if he is fluent in the language, he is more likely one who has learned it as a child (not necessarily before the age of formal education but soon after that) and has continued to use it as his dominant language.

According to our definition of native speaker, there are many more native speakers of English in Singapore than are normally identified in census reports. One problem with using census data in identifying a person's native language in a multiethnic country is that a person may identify Hokkien, Cantonese, or Tamil as his mother tongue or native language because that is his ethnic language, although he may not be any more fluent in it than, for example, in English or Mandarin.

In describing English in Singapore, we should consider not just the fact that English is used for communication with people of other nations or for communication with any fellow nationals but who uses it—the speaker's educational, socioeconomic, and linguistic background—and in what situation he uses it—formal, semiformal, or informal. When English is used as an international language, mutual intelligibility is the most important consideration. I have tried to show how the different varieties of Singapore English differ from British English. It would be interesting to see how these differences affect mutual intelligibility. We would need much more empirical data before we can say conclusively that the acrolect is intelligible, but the mesolect or the basilect are not. At present we can say that the acrolect is likely to be more intelligible to one who speaks British English because it is more similar to it than the mesolect and basilect.

WHAT VARIETIES OF ENGLISH SHOULD WE TEACH?

In the Singapore context, it is neither feasible nor desirable to teach a variety of English that is indistinguishable from standard British English. When we consider writing in English, we can and should set such a standard. In fact, many of the deviations in grammar that are listed in Tongue (1974) and Crewe (1977) are the teaching points of many English language courses in Singapore. However, for reasons that I have mentioned in the preceding sections (the desire to express one's national identity and the need to recognise the fact that English has indigenised), in matters of pronunciation, stress, rhythm, and intonation, the acrolect would serve as an adequate teaching model.

The attitude of the English language teacher is important in the Singapore context. He should not condemn features of the basilect as substandard or uneducated, but point out that they may be used not only among the uneducated but also by the educated if they wish to mark the dimensions of informality, rapport, solidarity, and intimacy (Richards and Tay, 1977). Besides, the English language teacher in Singapore should be aware of the great amount of lectal switching that goes on all the time. He will not therefore condemn expressions like "stop shaking legs and get back to work la" as substandard but consider its appropriateness in terms of (1) the formality of the situation (it would be appropriate in an informal but not a formal situation), (2) the participants involved in the communication (it would be appropriate for a Singaporean to talk to another Singaporean like that but not to a foreigner), and (3) the media (it would be appropriate in speech under certain conditions but never in serious writing except in novels that attempt to produce colloquial English).

The aim of learning English in Singapore should be to develop native fluency in the different lectal norms as they are distinct functional varieties. Each of these lects has its own rules of grammatical well-formedness, code diversity, speech act rules, and functional elaboration. This is borne out by the fact that a foreigner who tries to imitate the basilect does not succeed too well and his efforts are often described as not genuine. The mesolect and basilect will continue to be used in Singapore and nothing can stop this trend. It is also evident that children acquire the basilect fairly early in childhood, and they have to be taught the mesolect and acrolect if they have to use English for functions other than those served by the basilect.

Thus it is important to distinguish between formal instruction in English and its use by English-speaking members of the society. In formal instruction in school, teachers should certainly aim to teach the acrolect and expect their students to add the acrolectal features to their already acquired basilectal features. Upgrading the teachers' English would then be seen as basically one of lectal expansion (perhaps from the mesolect to the acrolect) but not of making it look more like British English.

CONCLUSION

The use of English in Singapore is unique in many ways. To understand its uniqueness, a teacher of English should understand the complexity of the linguistic situation, the bilingual policy in education, the many different uses of English in social interaction, and the varieties of English spoken. It is evident, therefore, that teaching goals and standards of correctness suitable for one country may not be suitable for another and it is at the national level that such decisions should be made.

Our thinking of such terms as ESL and EFL would be clarified if we sought to understand, not just how English is used in the world in general, but how well these terms characterise the uses, users, and features of English in the many different countries in the world that use this language loosely called "English." Then we might hope to make some progress in the teaching of the English language as a first, second, foreign, or international language.

REFERENCES

Abercrombie, D. *Elements of General Phonetics.* Edinburgh: Edinburgh University Press, 1967.
Arumainathan, P. *Report on the Census of Population, 1970.* Singapore, 1973.
Catford, J. C. The teaching of English as a foreign language. In R. Quirk and A. H. Smith (eds.), *The Teaching of English.* London: Secker and Warburg, 1959.

Chia, S. H. An investigation into language use among secondary four pupils in Singapore—Pilot project. In W. J. Crewe (ed.), *The English Language in Singapore*. Singapore: Eastern University Press, 1977, 157–188.

Crewe, W. J. (ed.). *The English Language in Singapore*. Singapore: Eastern University Press, 1977.

Diebold, A. R. Incipient bilingualism. *Language*. 1961, 37, 97–112.

Halliday, M. A. K., McIntosh, A., and Strevens, P. *The Linguistic Sciences and Language Teaching*. London: Longman, 1964.

Hymes, D. (ed.). *Pidginization and Creolization of Languages*. Cambridge: Cambridge University Press, 1971.

James, Arthur Lloyd. *Speech Signals in Telephony*. 1940.

Lee, S. L. *A Survey of the English Language Teaching Situation in the SEAMEO Countries*. Phase 1. Country Profiles. RELC, Singapore, 1974.

Pike, K. *The Intonation of American English*. Ann Arbor, Mich.: University of Michigan Press, 1946.

Platt, J. T. The sub-varieties of Singapore English: Their sociolectal and functional status. In W. J. Crewe (ed.), *The English Language in Singapore*. Singapore: Eastern Universities Press, 1977, 83–95.

Richards, J. C., and Tay, M. W. J. The la particle in Singapore English. In W. J. Crewe (ed.), *The English Language in Singapore*. Singapore: Eastern Universities Press, 1977, 141–156.

Rustow, D. A. Language, modernization and nationhood—An attempt at typology. In J. A. Fishman, C. A. Ferguson, and J. Das Gupta (eds.), *Language Problems of Developing Nations*. New York: Wiley & Sons, 1968, 87–106.

Smith, L. English as an international auxiliary language. *RELC Journal*. 1976, 7, 1, 38–42.

Tongue, R. *The English of Singapore and Malaysia*. Singapore: Eastern Universities Press, 1974.

Section **2**

*BILINGUAL
AND BICULTURAL
BACKGROUND*

4 NIGERIAN ENGLISH: AN INTRODUCTION

Munzali Jibril

HISTORICAL BACKGROUND

Nigeria, a West African country, has a population of over 80 million people and occupies a land area of 355,174 square miles. It is the most populous country in Africa and has the largest concentration of black people in the world. Before Britain colonised Nigeria in the nineteenth century, the country consisted of disparate kingdoms, empires, and city-states, some of whose domains extended far beyond Nigeria's present borders.

The earliest contact in recent times between Europeans and West Africans was in the second half of the fifteenth century when Portuguese ships stumbled on West Africa in their search for a sea route to India. The Portuguese established trade contacts with West Africans, and between 1481 and 1495 the King of Benin (in what is now Bendel State of Nigeria) sent an ambassador to Portugal, which responded by sending missionaries and trading agents (Crowther 1962, p. 57). But with the opening up of the New World, the legitimate and innocuous trade in commodities was replaced by the savage trade in human beings. British and other European slave traders established trading posts and other preliminary infrastructures of colonialism all along the coast of West Africa, so that by the nineteenth century when the slave trade was abolished, Britain had enough naval presence to bombard Lagos (1851) and thus prepare the ground for its annexation which came ten years later. By the close of the century, Britain had colonised the whole of the southern part of Nigeria, and, by the turn of the twentieth century, even the larger and more remote hinterland in Nigeria's present North had succumbed to British gun-power. In 1914 the protectorates of northern and southern Nigeria were amalgamated into a single political unit—Nigeria—which achieved independence in 1960.

Missionaries had been active in the coastal towns well before the formal involvement of the British in local politics. The first school in Nigeria was established by missionaries in Badagry in what is now Lagos State in 1842 and by 1910 the number of schools in Yorubaland had risen to 120. This early start of the Yorubas was to give them an unassailable position as the most influential group in the modern sector of Nigeria's economy. The Holy Ghost Fathers, who were to dominate missionary activity in the east, arrived there in 1884. But the north was even slower to embrace Western education. Not until 1909 was the first European-type school established in Kano by the colonial government, since, unlike in the south, missionaries were not allowed to operate in Muslim areas.

According to Ajayi (1965, Introduction) many of the missionaries operating in Nigeria in the 1840s were not native speakers of English. Some were German, some French, and the native speakers of English who were available came largely from Scotland and America. Most of the liberated slaves who were settled in Freetown, Sierra Leone, were Yoruba and returned to Nigeria to become missionaries and teachers. These and other non-English missionaries formed the bulk of the teachers of the language in the nineteenth century, and one could speculate about the nature of their influence on present-day Nigerian English.

Nigeria operates a federal system of government consisting of 19 states and a central government headed by an American-type executive president. Between 200 and 400 languages are spoken in Nigeria, though no reliable figure is available. Of these, three are regarded as the major languages: Igbo in the east, Hausa in the north, and Yoruba in the west. English is the official language and lingua franca among the educated, for the uneducated find it more realistic to learn the other Nigerian languages than to learn English when they settle in parts of the country other than their own. Perhaps not more than 30 percent of Nigerians know English, but it is nevertheless the language of the modern sector—of education after the first three years at school, of government, of commerce, and of the mass media. No fewer than ten daily newspapers are published in English, and there is a network of radio and television stations serving the whole country in English and local languages. The new Nigerian Constitution makes no explicit statement about the status of English, but it is mentioned (section 51) as the language in which the business of the National Assembly may be conducted, though the three main languages may also be used "when adequate arrangements have been made therefor." The *National Policy on Education* also states that each Nigerian child should be "encouraged to learn one of the three major languages other than his own mother-tongue." It is clear, therefore, that while the usefulness of English is recognised, the ground is being prepared for the eventual evolution of a national language.

NIGERIAN ENGLISH?

Most Nigerian speakers of English think that Pidgin English is what is meant by Nigerian English, since in their view they speak and write the Queen's English.[1] Even Nigerian linguists are not unanimous in their assessment of the citizenship status of English in Nigeria. Is it "Nigerian English"? Nigerian English is defined as a language belonging to Nigeria but "still in communion with its ancestral home . . . altered to suit its new African surroundings" [to borrow from Achebe (1965) as quoted by Young (1971)]. In this case, we would be at liberty to set our own standards, create our own idioms, and so on with confidence and without apology. Or is this English "the English language in Nigeria"? In this case, it is like an expatriate working on a short-term contract in Nigeria, housed in a secluded Government Reservation Area, and generally inclined not to seek any genuine social intercourse with the local people to the extent that when he begins to learn the local language or to wear local clothes he is regarded with grave suspicion.

Strong arguments can be advanced to support or refute either opinion. But what do we mean by "Nigerian"? Does a linguistic feature have to be common to all Nigerians to qualify for the label "Nigerian"? Certainly not. And to prove this, let us consider an analogous situation. One of the most prominent markers of British English is the non-realisation of post-vocalic *r*. But the British accents, such as those of Scotland, Northern Ireland, and Gloucestershire that retain post-vocalic *r,* are not by this reason any less British.

We may now proceed to ask: what happens if, as is very often the case, a linguistic feature that is identified as a marker of a particular speech community also happens to "belong" to a cognate, though separate speech community? In other words, does a linguistic feature have to belong to Nigeria and nowhere else to qualify as "Nigerian"? An example of such overlap is the southern Nigerian pronunciation of the RP vowel /ʌ/ as [ɔ] which is also current in Sierra Leone, Liberia, and the West Indies. In such a case, we should be prepared to accept that this feature is not only Nigerian but also Sierra Leonean, Liberian, and West Indian. After all, we use several, not one, features to establish dialect boundaries. If we can tell a Nigerian accent or text, we are usually able to do so because a number of co-occurent features which *collectively* mark the accent or text as originating from Nigeria are all present. Thus when we hear, say, a Freetown accent which has [ɔ] consistently instead of [ʌ], we are still able to conclude that it is not Nigerian because the voice quality, among other things, is so radically different from that of any Nigerian accent.

Having established the criteria for assessing linguistic Nigerianness, it is worth our while to consider the problem of acceptability. Would most Nigerians accept "next tomorrow," for instance, as good English? An expression such as "next tomorrow" (for the more cumbersome but standard "day after tomorrow") runs across the continuum from Pidgin English to the speech of the most educated and most highly placed Nigerians, but there are a few who happen to have been taught to avoid such expressions and who would therefore reject it as unacceptable. In any event, even those who are not sure that this expression is bad English would be inclined to reject it, because, by merely being asked to judge it, its status is rendered suspect; and linguistic insecurity, which is a potent factor even among first language speakers, prompts the respondent to be on the side of caution. Therefore, it would be more advisable to determine acceptability, not through opinion-sampling, but through the examination of actual usage. It would be sufficient to demonstrate that a certain social group uses a certain linguistic feature to establish that it is acceptable to them.

Having thus clarified some of the theoretical issues involved, we may now take a very quick overview of Nigerian English, beginning with pronunciation. We will take a few sensitive variables in each branch of spoken English in order to illustrate the nature of divergence from RP.

PHONOLOGY

The dental fricatives /θ/ and /ð/ serve as our consonantal variables. When these are not realised as in RP—and very few people know how to or care to so realise them—they are realised as [t] or [t̪] and [d] or [d̪], respectively by one group; and as [s] and [z], respectively, by another group. It is safe to define the groups in the following terms: those who realise these fricatives as in RP are Nigerians who have been taught to pronounce them in this way or who have learned to do so and who think it worth their while to strive to reproduce these sounds perfectly. The "dentality group" ([t], [d]) are those who do not belong to the first group and who come from any of the nine southern states or parts of Kwara, Benue, and Niger States, or who are from the other northern states but have been exposed to southern models of pronunciation or think it worth their while to cultivate such a model. The third group, the "friction group," consists of Nigerians who belong to neither of the first two groups and who come from the northern states. It would be useful to designate these three types of pronunciation as types 1, 2, and 3, respectively.

Three RP central vowels /3ː/, /ʌ/, and /ə/ will suffice to illustrate the vowel system of Nigerian English. Type 1 speakers would of course pronounce these as in RP or as very close approximations of RP. Type 2 speakers would pronounce /3ː/ in a word such as *fur* as [ɔ], that is, [fɔ], and in a word such as *birth* as [ɛ], that is [bɛt̪], and in a word such as *earn* as [aː] or [ɛ], that is, [aːn] or [ɛn]. They would pronounce RP /ʌ/ consistently as [ɔ] so that *come* is [kɔm], *country* is [kɔntɾi], and *brother* is [bɾɔda]. This group would also replace RP schwa with a range of fuller vowels according to the orthographic form the schwa takes. Thus *teacher* is [tiːtʃa] or [tɪtʃa], *versus* is [vɛsʊs], *administrator* is [admɪnɪstɾetɔ], and so on. Type 3 speakers, on the other hand, would pronounce RP /3ː/ as [aː], so that *fur* becomes homophonous with *far* as [faː], *birth* becomes [baːz], and *earn* becomes [aːn], as in one variety of type 2 pronunciation. RP /ʌ/ is realised fairly consistently by type 3 speakers as [a], so that *come* is [kam], *country* is [kantɾʊ], and *brother* is [bɾaza]. In type 3 pronunciation the schwa receives a fairly consistent treatment as [a], so that *teacher* becomes [tiːtʃa] as in one variety of type 2, *versus* becomes [vaːsas], and *administrator* becomes [ædmɪnɪstɾeta].

The area of word stress is particularly revealing in an examination of Nigerian English, whose peculiar rhythm can be traced substantially to its handling of word stress. Type 1 speakers generally follow RP patterns. Type 2 speakers employ a radically different system from that of RP, best exemplified by examining polysyllabic words and adjective+noun phrases. *Socialism* is, for instance,[sɔːʃɪaːlɪzm] [‿‿ ¯¯ ‿], and *cultural imperialism* is [kɔltʃɔɾal ɪmpiːɾɪaːlɪzm] [¯ ¯¯ ‿‿ ¯¯ ‿]. The vowel that bears the greatest prominence is in fact the one that is not stressed in RP, namely [ə] in *socialism* and *imperialism*. Type 3 pronunciation of these words would be [sɔːʃɪəlɪzm]and [kaltʃaɾal ɪmpiːɾɪəlɪzm] [¯ ¯ ‿‿ ¯ ¯ ‿ ‿], which are much nearer RP than type 2.

In the area of sentence stress we find the three groups almost merging. In Nigerian English a word such as *from,* which in RP has two forms, weak and strong, has only one unchanging form [fɾɔm] or [fɾam] , which is pronounced on a low tone like the RP weak form of the same word. Certain other words, such as *on, have,* and *was,* however, have strong and weak forms only in the sense that when they occur finally in the sentence (for example, "I have," "it's on") they are pronounced with a falling tone rather than with the normal tone which they have in other contexts. All this leads us to make the point that Nigerian English generally makes no use of word stress for emphasis or contrast. Very often, Nigerians think it fashionable to use the strong form of a word such as *was* in a sentence such as "I was in Lagos" when the context calls for no such emphasis.

As a result of the fact that this important area of English is seldom taught in Nigeria, Nigerians use the intonation patterns of some of the local languages when they wish to highlight some information through intonation. To illustrate this, let us imagine that an angry boss accusingly tells his secretary "You weren't in the office" and she wishes to insist that she was. The reply would be "I was in the office" with a rising tone on [fɪs] if the secretary is a type 2 speaker. This same intonation pattern is always used to contradict an earlier statement or to express indignation. The word that should have been stressed, *was,* is glossed over, for, in accordance with the semantic structure of Nigerian languages it is not as important as *office* in this context. A type 3 speaker, on the other hand, would utter the same sentence with a fall on [fɪs], again with *was* being merely glossed over.

Pronunciation spelling often provides students of language with extra evidence to confirm what they already know is happening. This is no less true of Nigerian English. A letter to a national newspaper, for instance, has "from the time the *formal* NPP splitted which gave birth to GNPP"[2] and a bank statement of an account sheet has "*Rurar* Branches." In both *formal* and *rurar* we have evidence to prove that word-final [l] is being deleted in at least one type of Nigerian English—that designated as type 2. In the case of *formal,* it has become homophonous with *former* which is the word the correspondent meant to use. In the case of *rurar,* the printer knows that there is a silent letter at the end of the word, and *r* is a more likely candidate than any other.

Another source of confusion involves the loss of distinction between [θ] and [t] in type 2 pronunciation, as the following extracts from an issue of a national daily reveals:

> The Public Service Commission, in good *fate* would consider the purse of the government before promoting people.
>
> . . . that Nigeria has become the world's prime dumping ground for every kind of *thrash.*[3]

In the first extract *faith* is confused with *fate* because both are [feit] or [fɛt] in the speech of the reporter or the typist. In the second extract *trash* is confused with *thrash* for the same reason.

In another issue of the same newspaper the following police notice appears:

> Both Gidmon and Angwan are *fund* of smoking, frequenting hotels, beer bars, and brothels.[4]

In this case *fond* is confused with *fund* because RP /ʌ/ is [ɔ] in the speech of the writer or the typist.

And finally, something from a type 3 speaker:

> He told the administrator . . . that the system would not only arrest petrol shortage in the state, but would also check *filfering* by unscrupulous tanker drivers.[5]

Here, /p/ and /f/ are confused because of their status as free variants in the language (Hausa) of this type 3 journalist or typist.

SYNTAX

We may now turn from phonology and move to syntax. Here we concentrate on the more common areas of divergence from standard or World English. In its written form, Nigerian English can be viewed as a continuum ranging from Pidgin to something that is unmarked and cosmopolitan. It is tempting to equate points on the continuum with educational attainment, for there are certain kinds of English that a university graduate would not write and certain others that a primary school graduate cannot write. But the generalisation collapses in the case of secondary school graduates, among whom we find those who write more like university graduates as well as those who write more like primary school graduates. Furthermore, certain areas of English syntax, notably prepositional usage, defy complete mastery even by those who are otherwise writers of World English, which justifies the setting up of Pidgin as the starting point of our continuum. There are also those whose formal education terminated at the primary school level, 20 or 30 years ago when "standards were high" and who, through years of exposure to the language, have been able to improve their written and spoken English to the extent of being better than many a young university graduate.

Uncountable nouns are susceptible to pluralisation in Nigerian English, especially in cases where the reason for their classification as uncountable is not obvious. Words such as *information, equipment, violence, advice,* and *accommodation* very often appear as plural. There is mother-tongue interference here, since when the relevant English rule has not been learned, the tendency is to fall back on the mother tongue.

The articles, definite and indefinite, are also susceptible to omission where they ought to be inserted, and insertion where they ought to be omitted, as well as being substituted for each other. Examples are:

1. "Make no attempt therefore, to *give history opportunity* to chronicle the fact that in seeking to eliminate a Nigerian or group of Nigerians from a political tournament, we fertilize the soil to eliminate Nigeria as a corporate entity from the map of Africa."[6]
2. "But he said that my fertility was being tampered with by *evil* spirit."[7]
3. "Nigerians also exerted *very high degree* of maturity."[8]
4. "Nigerians and many citizens of *the Third World oil producing countries* are being made to suffer."[9]

Another area of English grammar in which Nigerian English diverges from World English is that of tense. In Nigerian languages tense is not as important as aspect in the verbal system, and such distinctions of tense as are made are not as fine as those made in English. This fact, coupled with indifferent teaching, makes divergence from World English inevitable. A politician speaking on television, for instance, said:

It was during that time these people *make* some arrangement with law enforcement agencies. . .

which was perhaps a slip of the tongue but which nevertheless illustrates what we are discussing. In this politician's language, Hausa, the main verb of the sentence need not be marked for tense once the time of action has been specified earlier, thus "it was during that time." In another text, a would-be chief thanks and cautions his friends in a newspaper advertisement:

I therefore thank . . . friends all over the federation and overseas, who by cablegram, telegram, letters and personal call *congratulate* me and my family on the above title, and to inform them as well that the title has not been conferred on me by the authority. . . . I therefore implore all those who *send* me money and articles as present to withhold it till further notice.

We will ignore some other points equally worthy of comment in this interesting passage, and comment only on *congratulate* and *send.* In Yoruba, this advertiser's mother tongue, it is perfectly normal to use the unmarked form of the verb in this context, and the utterance would still be unambiguous without the tense being specified, as indeed it is in this English version. Similarly, *those who send* is clearly those who *intend* to send and the fact that they are asked to *withhold it* suffices to show that the action has not yet taken place, hence the redundancy of marking the verb for futurity.

There are also scattered but systematic tendencies to diverge from the word order of World English, construct sentences based on false concord, and add inflections to some words on the basis of analogy with words in the same grammatical class. The first of these can be illustrated by a quotation from an Igbo-speaking government functionary: "to solve this our common problem." This tendency to use demonstrative + possessive expressions is very common in Nigeria and is traceable to Shakespeare, the Bible, and other early modern English texts rather than to Nigerian languages. Two instances of false concord constructions can be seen in the preceding passage, "and to inform them as well" (that is, "I therefore thank . . . and to inform . . .") and "to withhold it" (that is, "money and articles"). The tendency to inflect words on analogy can be exemplified by this quotation from a politician in the heat of a political debate on television: "Our party is the only one that is *brandly* new." The occurrence of *splitted* has been noted earlier.

But the point of greatest divergence in Nigerian English from World English—assuming that the latter *is* consistent in its rules for handling this area of English grammar—is prepositional usage. The eccentricities of English in this area and the nature of the problem confronting the second language learner have been well captured by Fillmore (1968), Banjo (1969), and Adesanoye (1973).[10] Even the most cursory examination of the English functional and contextual equivalents of any preposition of any Nigerian language (strictly speaking, any multipurpose particle) will reveal the divergence of Nigerian languages from English in this area. Agasokoa (1978), for instance, finds that a single particle in Bassa-Nge, a language spoken in Kwara State, has at least five equivalents in English:

be lazhi	*in* the morning
be yesi	*at* night
be bici nyi	*on* foot
be egwa nyi	*by* hand
be Mana	*with* Mana

and similar patterns can be readily found in other Nigerian languages. This divergence and the impossibility of ideal teaching leave no choice for Nigerian English but to go its separate way in this as in other areas.

A circular letter signed by a senior government official reads:

This is to inform all . . . state students that the Secretary *for* . . . State Scholarship Board will be coming to . . . soon.

Most Nigerians are not quite sure whether a secretary is *for* (as in Pidgin), *of,* or *to* a body, institution and so forth.

A prepositional usage that is fast creeping into the speech and writing of the most educated Nigerians is *by,* in expressions of time where *at* would be used in World English. An obituary in a national newspaper reads:

With deep grief we announce the untimely death of . . . which said event took place at the Ahmadu Bello University Teaching Hospital, Kaduna *by* 12.30 a.m. on Saturday. . . .[11]

In the same issue of the same paper, a senior international civil servant of Nigerian nationality is quoted as saying:

The first intergovernmental meeting on this project has been held and arrangements are *in hand* for the convening of the second meeting. . . .

though it cannot be established whether he was misquoted. And, finally, this extract from a letter to a newspaper from a group of four MCAs (members of the (dissolved) Constituent Assembly):

Since the intentions of obtaining the signatures made public are contrary to that for which we appended our signatures, we do hereby publicly dissociate ourselves *with* the National Union Council.

SEMANTICS

Semantics is perhaps the most interesting area of language to examine when a language has been implanted in a virgin land, or, as in this case, imposed on top of the Tower of Babel. We will consider semantic innovation in Nigerian English in four categories: new words from Nigerian languages, calques, extensions of meaning of words already in the English lexicon, and new collocations for words already in the lexicon.

Perhaps the longest list is that of words from Nigerian languages for which there are no English equivalents, mostly food items, clothes, and names of traditional institutions or objects. When such words are used, they are usually enclosed in inverted commas, so that they are not yet part of the lexicon, strictly speaking. *Danfo* is one such word, from Yoruba, and used to refer to tiny uncomfortable buses whose drivers are notorious for recklessness. Another word is *buka,* of Hausa origin (*bukka,* hut) but injected into English through Yoruba. It refers to a small wooden or other roofed enclosure usually erected by the roadside where cheap food may be bought and eaten, in other words, a make-shift restaurant. A number of such *bukas* have sprung up on a university campus in Nigeria, and where they provide a much-needed alternative for students who wish to avoid the cafeteria and have a really decent but cheap meal—not, however, in a *buka* but in a *bukateria.*

In our second category of semantic innovation, calques, as indeed in all other areas of semantics, Yoruba will be seen to be the dominant source language for several reasons. Yoruba has been providing the bulk of teachers, missionaries, journalists, and other professionals since the nineteenth century, and this preeminence has continued with more vigour in present-day Nigeria. The position of Lagos, a Yoruba city, as the capital also enhances this role of the language.

Many of the expressions in this category are greetings, such as *you're enjoying,* which is a translation of the Yoruba *Eku igbadun* (literally meaning "I greet you as you enjoy yourself"). It is not altogether unlike the British "Enjoying yourself?" In Yoruba culture, as indeed in many an African culture, all happy events, such as buying a new car, getting a new job, passing an examination, are celebrated with a party, where the happy event is *washed* in drinks. It is common now to hear the expression, especially in the West and Lagos, "We'll wash it!" when somebody breaks the good news of a happy event to friends. Another expression of Yoruba origin is *next tomorrow* which was noted earlier. It is a translation of the Yoruba *otunla* (literally meaning "new tomorrow"). Expressions such as *to put sand in someone's gari* and *chewing-stick* are of indeterminate origin. The first means to threaten someone's livelihood or to interfere with someone's good fortune; *gari* is cassava flour used as staple food in southern Nigeria. *Chewing-stick* is not the Nigerian equivalent of chewing gum, but a short stick that is chewed to produce a rough brush-like edge which is then used to brush the teeth.

The third category is that in which English words have had their meanings extended in order to express uniquely Nigerian experiences. *To declare surplus* is to host a party—presumably because only those who have money to waste can host parties. A *drop* is not a fall in some figure or other, but the longest distance a passenger may travel in a taxi for the minimum fare. In Nigeria, taxis drive along specific routes picking up passengers, with each passenger paying the same fare no matter at what point along the road he wishes to *drop*. Any journey farther than the specific routes attracts a higher fare. New meanings are given to the English words *soup* and *stew*. *Soup* refers to the thinner and easier to cook dish which is not sipped, but taken with *eba* (a meal of gari mixed in boiling water) or some other similar meal. *Stew,* on the other hand, refers to the more elaborate curry which is used in the company of rice, yam, or beans. And, finally, there is the use of *well done* as a greeting for people at work, which serves well the function of similar expressions of good-will for people at work which abound in Nigerian languages. In this category also belong expressions, such as *sorry* as an expression of nonapologetic sympathy, which are so universal that they are bound to make their way into the mainstream of English.

The fourth category is that in which English words have been combined in a new relationship. Examples are *pounded yam,* a meal of boiled yam that has been pounded in a mortar with a pestle, and *motor-park,* which is a bus and taxi station from which travellers may board vehicles to other towns.

CONCLUSION

Nigerian English, which is part of the continuum of West African English, is yet to be adequately described. Most statements on it are merely pre-analytical hunches, even though a full description may confirm rather than contradict them. Many of the forms highlighted here are frowned upon by teachers of English and by the West African Examinations Council. But it is naive to expect a language such as English in Nigeria to respond to remote control when every observable factor dictates that it respond to the various pressures being exerted upon it by its Nigerian circumstances.

It may be argued that there are more Nigerians studying in Britain and America at the present time than at any other time, that more Nigerians now visit these and other English speaking countries than ever before, that more books and films than ever are now flowing into Nigeria from these sources, that more Nigerians now listen to news broadcasts originating from these sources, and that all this is going to counter the internal pressures on English and thus minimise its divergence from World English.

But we only have to look at the nature of these internal pressures on English to realise how difficult it is to neutralise them. First, there is pressure from the mother tongue, with its own set of rules which are often in conflict with those of English and upon which the Nigerian learner of English frequently falls back. There is also pressure from Pidgin English with its deceptive similarity to English. Then there is pressure from the complexity of English itself—its misleading spelling, hybrid vocabulary, and eccentric prepositions, all of which defy complete mastery. And this situation is not helped by the Nigerian teacher of English, who is more often than not a literature graduate to whom the English language is nothing but a beautiful grand mystery. Finally, there is pressure from society—the kind of English the Nigerian learner reads in newspapers and in locally written textbooks, and the kind of English he hears from everyone around him.

There is evidence—from an on-going study of Nigerian English that I am undertaking—that Nigerians do not place a high premium on acquiring close imitations of native accents of English, and that consequently they do not modify their accents significantly even after living in Britain or America for up to eight years; or if they do, they do not disown their original Nigerian accent but rather use it whenever they speak to their fellow Nigerians. Indeed the cultural climate in Nigeria at the present time discourages any tendency towards a perfect, native-like accent, though there is no corresponding aversion to impeccable written English.

As more and more people learn English in Nigeria so will the international intelligibility of Nigerian spoken English fall. This is nothing to worry about, since the role of English in Nigeria is largely in internal communication, and the few businessmen, officials, diplomats, and students who have to communicate with people abroad in more cosmopolitan English can be trusted to learn to make more or less the same necessary adjustments that a university professor from Chicago must learn to converse with a miner from Rotherham.[12]

NOTES

1. Labov, 1966, p. 480, for instance, found that:
   New Yorkers also showed a systematic tendency to report their own speech inaccurately. Most of the respondents seemed to perceive their own speech in terms of the norms at which they were aiming rather than the sound actually produced.

2. The *New Nigerian*, August 1979. NPP stands for Nigerian People's Party and GNPP stands for Great Nigeria People's Party, two of the five political parties in present-day Nigeria. Note the inflection of "split."

3. The *New Nigerian*, December 27, 1977, p. 23 and p. 1, respectively.

4. The *New Nigerian*, December 19, 1977, p. 9.

6. The same letter as in note 2.

7. "The Coming of the 'Holy Spirit.' " *Lagos Weekend*, September 28, 1979, p. 5.

8. *Punch*, January 3, 1979, p. 4.

9. The *New Nigerian*, June 2, 1978, p. 4.

10. Fillmore (1968, p. 15) writes:
    Prepositions in English or the absence of a preposition before a noun phrase, which may be treated as corresponding to a zero or unmarked case affix, are selected on the basis of several types of structural features, and in ways that are exactly analogous to those which determine particular case forms in a language like Latin: identity as (surface) subject or object, occurrence after particular verbs, occurrence in a construction with particular nouns, occurrence in particular constructions, and so on.

Banjo (1969, p. 145) writes:
    The difficulties of the Yoruba learner of English in the area (where we have an enormous split situation) are further aggravated by the idiosyncrasies of English usage shown in the semantic features of most of the prepositions. Thus, we have *at Ikeja* but *in Lagos* and *in Nigeria, at Christmas* but *on Christmas Day*, not to mention *in the air* and *on the air*.

Adesonoye (1973, p. 205) admonishes that:

> To improve the English language performance of most first-variety users of written Nigerian English more than passing attention must be given to prepositional forms: it is well known, in fact, that the question of prepositions, even to an L1 user, is not always an easy proposition, and the problem is compounded in the case of the unwary L2 user who may unwittingly substitute inappropriate forms from his first language.

11. The *New Nigerian,* December 12, 1977, p. 19.

12. In writing this paper I have relied rather heavily on Jibril (1976) which was written under Dr. Loreto Todd's skillful supervision. I am even more grateful to her for reading the draft of this paper and making valuable suggestions though I must dissociate her from any responsibility for the many imperfections that are still conspicuously present.

REFERENCES

Achebe, C. English and the African writer. *Transition.* 1965, 18. Also in Achebe, C. *Morning Yet on Creation Day.* N.Y.: Anchor Press, 1975.

Adesanoye, F. A study of varieties of written English in Nigeria. Unpublished Ph.D. thesis, University of Ibadan, 1973.

Agasokoa, P. *The Interference of Bassa-Nge on Spoken English.* Unpublished B.A. (Ed.) dissertation, Bayero University, 1978.

Ajayi, J. F. A. *Christian Missions in Nigeria, 1841–1891.* London: Longman, 1965.

Banjo, A. L. A contrastive study of aspects of the syntactic and lexical rules of English and Yoruba. Unpublished Ph.D. thesis, University of Ibadan, 1969.

Crowther, M. *The Story of Nigeria.* Faber, 1962.

Daily Times Publications. *The Constitution of the Federal Republic of Nigeria.* Lagos, 1979.

Federal Ministry of Information. *Federal Republic of Nigeria: National Policy on Education.* Lagos, 1977.

Fillmore, C. J. The case for case. In E. Bach and R. T. Harms (eds.), *Universals in Linguistic Theory.* New York: Holt, Rinehart and Winston, 1968.

Jibril, M. M. Towards an analysis of the English language in Nigeria. Unpublished M.A. dissertation, University of Leeds, 1976.

Jibril, M. M. Regional variation in Nigerian spoken English. In E. Ubahakwe (ed.), *Varieties and Functions of English in Nigeria.* Ibadan: African Universities Press, 1979.

Labov, W. *The Social Stratification of English in New York City.* Centre for Applied Linguistics, 1966.

Young, P. The language of West African literature in English. In J. Spencer (ed.), *The English Language in West Africa.* London: Longman, 1971.

5 SOCIOCULTURAL CONSTRAINTS AND THE EMERGENCE OF A STANDARD NIGERIAN ENGLISH[1]

Funso Akere

INTRODUCTION

The history of the development of the English language in West Africa dates back to the beginning of the establishment of trading contacts and, later, of colonial empires on the West African coast by the British. In less than two centuries, English developed from being ordinarily a contact or trade language between British and American merchants and slave dealers on the one hand, and African middlemen on the other hand, into several varieties characterized by marked linguistic, social, and cultural features.

Within this period, the English language has assumed the status of a native language (that is, a mother tongue) in Liberia;[2] it is regarded as an L2 and the official language, lingua franca, and the language of formal school education in Sierra Leone, Gambia, Ghana, and Nigeria. The English language has become creolized in Sierra Leone,[3] and its pidginization is evident in parts of Nigeria and Ghana.[4] Even in French-speaking parts of West Africa, the development of English as an effective foreign language is fast becoming an important aspect of the language planning policy of several countries.

Through the various stages of development, the English language in West Africa has acquired certain peculiarities which are a product of the different environments within which it is learned and used. Environmental influences deriving from linguistic, social, cultural, political, and economic factors have combined to produce the varieties of English that can easily be identified in West Africa. The emergence of West African dialects of English is a function of both linguistic and sociological processes of change in language use and function in a contact situation.

The English language was not only superimposed on the indigenous languages, it also became the medium through which the educated elite in English-speaking West Africa wrote and talked about aspects of their culture.

As a result of the adoption of the English language, certain aspects of the culture of the British people became gradually adopted by the educated elite in West Africa.

It must be pointed out that just as changes (linguistic and nonlinguistic) have occurred to produce American, Canadian, and Australian dialects of English in native-speaker environments outside Britain, so also have some other kinds of change occurred to produce Indian and African dialects of English in a second language situation. Nigerian English has come to be recognized as one such dialect of English.[5]

From a purely linguistic standpoint, it could be argued that the varieties of English that have emerged in most of former British West Africa necessarily bear the marks of the different indigenous languages with which English has come in contact, and over which it has become superimposed. Differences that may occur between British or American standard English and the dialects of English in West Africa can be traceable to interference in a contact situation. But the phenomenon of linguistic interference cannot be solely responsible for the considerable differentiation that now exists between British standard English and the varieties of English in West Africa. Such varieties are bound to exhibit the different sociocultural features of the linguistic/ethnic groups using English as a second language.

To the extent that social and cultural characteristics differ among the various cultural groups of the English-speaking world, heterogeneity in the pattern of English language usage is bound to occur in the various linguistic communities. The pattern of standardization or change that the language exhibits in a particular environment will be related to the degree of homogeneity, in both linguistic and cultural features, which exists among the community of users. As Luckman (1975) observes:

> The existence and the functioning of languages and the changes they undergo are closely linked to concrete social structures and the dynamic relations between individuals, groups, institutions and society.

Nigerian English, therefore, has to be seen as a product of its own general social context.

This paper examines the extent to which sociocultural features, in addition to purely linguistic problems, influence or constrain the emergence of a standard Nigerian English. Consideration is given to culture-specific features, such as kinship terms and their usage, greetings, forms of address and the system of deference, social expectations, ethos, value orientations, and patterns of conceptualization generally as they affect the usage of English in Nigeria.

VARIETIES DIFFERENTIATION IN NIGERIAN ENGLISH

Several sociolinguistically oriented studies in language variation in recent years have shown that the picture of a language as a uniform, invariable, and unchanging phenomenon has given way to one of considerable heterogeneity within the context of its use. The English language clearly exhibits this trait in its native-speaker and non-native-speaker environments.

The standardizing influences of a common orthography as used in the formal system of school education, in addition to the social importance that is attached to one particular dialect of English in British native speaker environments, have no doubt been responsible for the emergence of the variety of English known as standard English. The forces that combine to produce a standard variety of English in native-speaker communities are not necessarily the same in the evolution of the standard varieties of English in nonnative speaker speech communities.

It must be emphasized that language is an activity of people. And, as Bailey and Robinson (1973)[6] have pointed out, "because the forces of standardization have not yet completely leveled the individuality resulting from genetic make-up and rearing, removed the human impulse to gather in manageably small groups, or erased the cultural differences that distinguish group from group or nation from nation, language must be as various as the groups who use it and the activities they engage in." This theoretical standpoint underlines the fact that considerable variation is bound to exist in Nigerian English, and a great deal of attention is now being focused by language researchers in Nigeria on the parameters for identifying varieties in Nigerian English.[7]

Varieties differentiation can be viewed from many perspectives especially in the context of the users and uses of English in Nigeria. In terms of the various indigenous languages with which English co-exists in Nigeria and the different ethnic groups who use them, the English language as used in the different ethnic communities will exhibit influences or interference features from the ethnic languages of its users. These interference features can occur at phonological, lexical, syntactic, and even semantic levels. Thus it is possible to talk of Yoruba, Igbo, Hausa/Fulani varieties of English.

At another level of differentiation, the formal acquisition of English is bound up with the system of formal school education. Since the official medium of instruction and learning from primary school to university in Nigeria is English, proficiency in the language will no doubt be closely linked with the level of formal educational attainment, hence variety differentiation produces such terms as educated and noneducated varieties of English.[8] At yet another level of differentiation, a form of hybridization resulting from the early contacts that English had with some coastal languages in Nigeria produced what is now known as Pidgin English or Nigerian Pidgin.[9] It is in these respects that one can talk of the many dialects of English in Nigeria.

The question that then arises relates to whether or not there is a standard Nigerian English. This question has been variously examined by many language analysts in Nigeria. There are those who hold the view that a pattern of standardization in Nigerian English is only just evolving, and that it is unfair to quote the many grammatically deviant structures written or spoken by poorly educated Nigerians, young school leavers, and those still at school, as features of Nigerian English. These features are characteristic of people with very poor proficiency and a generally low level of communicative competence. Salami (1968) for instance has argued that most of the nonstandard usages found in Nigerian newspapers published in English, in the essays of Nigerian students, and in the speech of many English-speaking Nigerians, are in fact "mistakes and solecisms," and that it will be improper, therefore, to label these mistakes as Nigerian English.[10]

The contention in this argument and in many others like it is that if the point of reference for the analysis of Nigerian English is necessarily to be a British or American standard English, it is only proper to take the educated variety of Nigerian English for a comparative analysis, so that whatever features distinguish this variety from British or American standard English can be regarded as general features of Nigerian standard English. In a recent detailed study of certain characteristics of Nigerian English, Adetugbo (1977a) concludes that English language usage in Nigeria has its own characteristics that set it apart from any native English variety. The differentiating features occur at various levels of grammatical structure ranging from preposition usage, pronoun substitutions, and reference, to subjunctive forms, modal auxiliary usage, lexical choice, and so on.[11] They also occur at the level of phonological realizations and semantic representations.[12] Adetugbo asserts that these features are not mere deviations from the norms of the native speaker's standard English, but that they constitute features that characterize standard Nigerian English.

Such heterogeneity in Nigerian English is to be expected in view of the many factors that constrain its evolution and spread. As others have pointed out, the characteristic linguistic problems of interference attaching to the acquisition of English in a second language situation are quite prominent. Besides, since the principal source of acquisition is through the formal school system via non-native-speaker teachers, the acquisition of competence (both grammatical and communicative) is bound to be developmental and, to a large extent, generally imperfect. It is only in very rare cases that an ideal level of absolute proficiency or native-speaker competence can be reached to produce a standard Nigerian variety of English that has a measure of uniformity comparable to a native-speaker standard. What constitutes standard Nigerian English, therefore, can be regarded as an aggregate of heterogeneous grammatical structures common to Nigerian usage, several pronunciation peculiarities, and socioculturally constrained usage of certain lexical items, and the semantic interpretations and generalizations given to these items.

SOCIOCULTURAL DETERMINANTS OF LINGUISTIC FORMS AND THEIR USAGE

In this section I want to examine in some detail those aspects of Nigerian English usage about which not much has been written. English in Nigeria derives from the general social context within which it functions, thus it necessarily bears the marks of the sociocultural features of that setting. The sociocultural patterning of certain usage forms in Nigerian English constitutes an important aspect of the study of standardization in Nigerian English. The peculiarly Nigerian adaptations of a number of English linguistic forms relating to greetings and forms of address, kinship terminologies and terms of address, and the use of English personal pronouns in the expression of deference within the honorific systems in social relationships in the indigenous culture all show what is uniquely Nigerian in the variety of English that has evolved in Nigeria.

General Social and Situational Contexts of English Language Usage

English is used for multifarious functions in Nigeria. The multilingual and multiethnic composition of the Nigerian community requires a lingua franca for the purpose of interethnic communication and understanding. The introduction of the English language appropriately solves this problem, at least for an important section of the population. As a matter of fact, it could be argued that the multiethnic situation in Nigeria, and the accompanying emotional attachment to ethnic identity by various groups, required the adoption of a neutral language. Therefore, the decision to adopt English as the official language and the lingua franca would be said to be a guided one.

Sentiments such as the preceding, over the imposition of the English language on some West African countries, were not uncommon in the nineteenth century even among black intellectuals such as Edward Blyden:[13]

English is, undoubtedly, the most suitable of the European languages for bridging over the numerous gulfs between the tribes caused by the great diversity of languages or dialects among them. It is a composite language, not the product of any one people.

In Nigeria today, the English language not only bridges the communication gaps between different ethnic groups in the country, it is also used as the medium for enacting social or interpersonal relations among literates who belong to different linguistic/ethnic groups.

In many (elite) primary family setups where interethnic marriages have taken place, the language of interaction between husband and wife may be English; indeed this is generally so. Children born into such homes would first of all acquire the English language in order to be able to communicate with their parents. Although they may acquire either of their parents' languages later on, for the most part the general elements of the indigenous culture and the patterns of social relations are acquired and practiced through the medium of the English language.

Apart from these, other levels of interaction ranging from educational and economic to political require the use of the English language for effective transactions, at least among the educated elite. In institutions of learning, from secondary school to university, the multiethnic nature of their composition requires that students, as well as teachers, relate and interact through the medium of the English language, which therefore becomes the primary exponent of the various subcultures that converge in such institutions, and the main vehicle for enacting the various social relationships that emerge from such cultural diffusion. This is also the picture of the pattern of interactions in national political or economic organizations like government ministries and corporations. Here, as Luckman[14] has rightly observed, the socialization of individual consciousness and the social moulding of personality are largely determined by the language in use.

Sociocultural Constraints

Studies in the linguistic manifestations of culture patterning have generally concentrated on identifying correlations between categories in the indigenous language spoken by a people and categories of their culture. The Whorfian concept of language as "a guide to social reality" has been followed up in several other studies, and conclusions have been reached which confirm the close relation between a language and the culture of the society that uses it.

Little attention has been paid, however, to the sociolinguistic consequences of the use of a nonindigenous language within the domains of an indigenous culture. The English language, having been transplanted from its native cultural domain, is now being used to convey the cultural norms and concepts of the various ethnic groups in the Nigerian society. Basic differences in cultural categories, norms, and concepts undoubtedly exist between the British and the Nigerian societies. These differences will no doubt manifest themselves in certain features (both lexical and semantic) of the English language as used in the two societies. In the words of Edward Sapir,[15] "the worlds in which different societies live are distinct worlds, not merely the same world with different labels attached."

The facts of the situation are: the real world of the native English-speaking society is built unconsciously on the English language habits of the people; the real world of the Nigerian society is built unconsciously on the native language habits of each of its ethnic groups. The languages used in the two real worlds cannot be considered, as Sapir puts it, "as representing the same social reality." It is within the same real world of the Nigerian society that the English language is made to function. The sociocultural constraints on the emerging forms and functions of the English language in Nigeria are analyzed in the following sections. The observations that are made in respect of usage are relevant for the English-speaking classes of the Yoruba, Igbo, Hausa/Fulani, and Edo groups of Nigerians.

English Kinship Terminologies in Nigerian English

English terms for kinship relationships seem quite straightforward when used within the native English cultural context. The terms father, mother, son, and daughter are what they are within the nuclear family unit, and they are used only in reference to that domain. The term family itself is, in the Western sense, composed of a grandfather, grandmother, father, mother, and their children.

English kinship terms in Nigerian English however have acquired wider semantic features than this in order to be able to cope with the intricate pattern of kinship relationships and kinship categories of the various ethnic cultures. There is a commonality of features in the pattern of family organization among the various ethnic groups. The term family, among any of the major ethnic groups, may apply to several different categories. On the simplest level is the elementary family, which is the same thing as family in the Western sense of the word. There is also the polygynous family, made up of a father, his wives, and all their children. Within this context, there will be one father, several mothers, and a group of full and half siblings all of whom would be referred to as brothers or sisters. In addition, there is the extended family setup, traditionally made up of a father and his sons, or a group of brothers if the father is dead, their wives, sons, and unmarried daughters. Today the extended family network covers all members who can trace their consanguinity to a single paternal or maternal origin.

Thus, when a Nigerian English user makes reference to a brother or sister, it could be to a relation in any one of the three levels of family organization.

Apart from their use as terms in close family relationships, the terms father, mother, brother, and sister are often used in reference to distant relations, or even to people who are very close, but not related by blood. The inherent system of deference within the Yoruba culture may warrant that a person who is not one's paternal or maternal progenitor be referred to as father or mother if the person is as old as or older than one's real father or mother. Here age and the deference attaching to it seems to be the constraining factor.

Age also seems to constrain the use of terms like cousin, niece, or nephew. If a person with whom one enters any of these relationships is very much older, one is not likely to refer to him or her as cousin, niece, or nephew; the term uncle or aunt is likely to be used in such circumstances.

Outside one's immediate ethnic community, or when in a foreign country, a common township identity, or even some ethnic identity, is sufficiently close for terms like brother, sister, cousin, uncle, and so on to be used for each other. In places like Lagos, London, or New York, two people from the Igbo ethnic group or two Yoruba people or Edo people without any consanguinial or affinal relationships can refer to each other as brother or sister.

Cultural Constraints on the Forms of Greetings in Nigerian English

Many of the various forms of greetings in native-speaker English are generally used in Nigerian English also, but with considerable modifications (not necessarily in structure) to suit the diverse cultural considerations attached to greetings among the people. Among the Yoruba and many other cultural groups in the country, greetings are more than mere instances of phatic communion, or openings for establishing social interaction.

In the indigenous cultures, there are greetings for almost every sphere of activity. Greetings are used for expressing empathy or sympathy, as the case may be, in situations of joy or of sorrow, on the birth of a child, the death of a relation, and so on. That the full forms of English greetings, such as *Good morning, Good afternoon, Good evening,* and so on, have such a high frequency of occurrence in Nigerian English is not surprising. The formality of the full forms matches or equates with the pattern of deference that age or status imposes on social relationships in the Nigerian context. Younger people find it very appropriate to use the full forms in greeting older people or persons of higher socioeconomic status. The terms *Hi, Hello,* and *How are you* can be used by older or senior persons to younger or junior ones, but not vice-versa. Such verbal behavior coming from a younger person would be regarded as off-hand. Informal forms like *Morning, Afternoon, Hi,* or *Hello* are most frequently used among equals.

Special greetings or greetings for special occasions are a common feature of Nigerian English. The multiplicity of festivals such as the Christian festivals of Christmas, New Year, and Easter, and the Muslim festivals of Salah and Rahmadan call for special greetings which can be said in advance or in arrears depending on whether the person being greeted is met before or after the festival. Another form of greeting most commonly used is "Congratulations." Nigerians would congratulate a person on the minutest form of achievement: on the passing of even a minor examination, for making a pilgrimage to Mecca or Medina, and so on; and even for the achievements of a relation or a friend. If my friend X has just earned a promotion at work, another friend might see me and say "Congratulations." If in utter surprise I asked "What for?" the reply could be, "Becauase your friend X has just earned a promotion!" One is bound to thank him for this!

Because the native speaker's language does not possess linguistic markers for such functions, the Nigerian user of English simply substitutes the nearest equivalents in English for them. Thus, a form such as "You are welcome," or simple "Welcome," as a type of greeting for a person just returning from a journey, or for a visitor who has just arrived in the country, is never used in this sense in British or American English. The form *sorry* in English is intended as a genuine apology for a mistake or wrong-doing, for causing some inconvenience to somebody, or as an expression of regret for an action not intended but whose result adversely affects or inconveniences another person. In Nigerian English, the semantic field of *sorry* has become extended. It is used, in addition to the above, as an expression of sympathy or pity for a person involved in an accident, even for his tripping, knocking his toe against a stone, and so on. In a classroom situation for example, if a lecturer accidentally drops his lecture notes or a piece of chalk, his students would say "Sorry Sir." The forms *careful* or *watch it* are rarely used in Nigerian English, most probably because of their imperative forms which make them sound rather rude when addressed to an older or senior person. Since the indigenous languages have linguistic markers for these cultural nuances, equivalent forms in English are either found for them or other forms of English usage are modified to cope with them.

An important consideration in the selection of greeting forms, also the decision to greet or not to greet, who greets who first, and so on, is the kind of social relationship between the interlocutors; thus, variables such as cordial or noncordial, age and/or status differential, and intimate or nonintimate considerations, act as constraining factors. If the relationship between interlocutors is cordial, greetings are exchanged freely with the deference attached to age or status differences influencing the choice of forms. Older persons will however expect to be greeted first. Younger or junior persons would generally use the full forms with the addition of the lexical items *Sir* or *Ma/Madam* as substitutes for honorific reference as in "Good morning Sir" or "Good evening Ma!"

In university communities, academic titles like doctor (Ph.D.) or professor are attached to greetings by students, and by colleagues who are not quite intimate. Junior administrative and technical workers in the university would use the abbreviated forms of these titles in greeting. Forms such as "Good morning Doc," or "Good afternoon Prof" are often heard. Their users employ them with an assumed air of familiarity with their addressee.

Forms of Address in Nigerian English

It will not be an easy task to attempt to summarize within the scope of this paper the complex structure of dyadic relations in intraethnic and interethnic interactions conveyed in the system of address rules in Nigerian English. The intricate network consists of an underlying pattern of address forms expressed in the various indigenous languages in the country, and then the transference of these sociolinguistic rules of address from the native-culture-based languages to the English language, not necessarily in the form of direct translation equivalents but in the form of the substitution of English address labels for locally structured patterns of dyadic relations.

I will try to compare the forms of address used in Nigerian English with those of British or American English. Here we will be dealing with two widely divergent cultural groups, both of which have the use of the English language as a common factor. But the fact remains that, while one group uses the English language as an L2, the other uses it as its native language. The contention is that a shared language does not necessarily mean a shared set of sociolinguistic rules of address.

Titles and Proper Names.   Several studies of communicative interactions in most dyadic relations have shown that the selection of certain linguistic forms is governed by the relation between the speaker and his addressee. This is true of most cultural groups. But the convergent social variables that determine the linguistic forms to be used, especially in terms of address forms, vary from culture to culture. The studies of Brown and Ford (1961) on the forms of address in American English and other studies in British native-speaker contexts show that English forms of address consist mainly of a single binary contrast: FN or TLN, that is, the choice between the use of the first name (FN) and the use of a title with the last name (TLN).

American English forms of address show three logically possible dyadic patterns: the reciprocal exchange of FN, the reciprocal exchange of TLN, and the nonreciprocal pattern in which one person uses the FN and the other TLN. While mutual TLN goes with distance or formality, mutual FN goes with a greater degree of intimacy. In nonreciprocal address, the TLN is used to the person of higher status and the FN to the person of lower status. Thus, one form is said to express both distance and deference; the other form expresses both intimacy and condescension.

These patterns are equally applicable among the various groups of Nigerian users of English. The system of first-naming is used among friends and age-mates. Older people can employ nonreciprocal FN for younger people or people of lower status in information situations. However, the pattern for the use of TLN in Nigerian English shows only slight similarities with the American pattern just described. Some marked differences exist between usage in American English and Nigerian English usage. These will be pointed out presently. Differences exist, also, in the degree of importance attached to titles in the Nigerian social context.

The underlying principles that seem to modify TLN usage in Nigerian English derive from the people's social evaluation of achievement. Great effort is exerted in the amassing of wealth toward conspicuous consumption. Among the Igbo people, for example, this was expressed traditionally in the form of title-taking, that is, joining a titled society by paying a high initiation fee and giving a series of feasts to the members, and in the form of second funerals.[16] The pervasive use of titles and multiple titles as forms of address in Nigerian English is connected with such expectations.

Ervin-Tripp (1969) refers to the list of occupational titles or courtesy titles accorded people in certain statuses as an identity set. The following lists show Ervin-Tripp's identity set in American English usage compared with terms in the identity set in Nigerian English usage:

A. *American English Usage*

Cardinal	Your Excellency
U.S. President	Mr. President
Priest	Father (+ LN)
Nun	Sister (+ religious name)
Physician	Dr. (+ LN)
Ph.D., Ed.D., etc.	Doctor + LN
Professor	Professor + LN
Adult, etc.	Mister + LN
	Mrs. + LN
	Miss + LN

B. *Nigerian English Usage*

Head of State	Your Excellency
Military Governor	Your Excellency

Nigerian English Usage (continued)

A traditional Oba[17]	Your Highness
A traditional chief	Chief (+ LN)
Physician	Doctor (+ LN)
Ph.D., D.Sc., etc.	Doctor (+ LN)
Professor	Professor (+ LN)
Engineer	Engineer (+ LN)
Architect	Architect (+ LN)
Priest	Archbishop (+ LN)
	Bishop (+ LN)
	Archdeacon (+ LN)
	(Revered) Canon (+ LN)
	Father (+ LN)
	Revered (+ LN)
Nun	Sister (+ LN)
Muslim Pilgrimage title	Alhaji (+ LN)—(Male)
	Alhaja (+ LN)—(Female)
Adult	Mister (+ LN)
	Mrs. (+ LN)
	Miss (+ LN)
Muslim	Malam (+ LN combination)

Certain usage features distinguish Nigerian English from American usage as lists A and B show. The use of parentheses in both lists shows items that can be optionally deleted as forms of address. In the American examples, LN can be deleted with Priest and Nun titles only. In Nigerian English usage, however, three groups of titles would need to be identified. These are:

(i)	*(ii)*	*(iii)*
Deferential	*Revered*	*Common*
Chief......	Archbishop	Mister
Doctor	Bishop	Mrs.
Professor...	Canon	Miss
*Alhaji	Revered	Malam
*Alhaja. ...	Father	

As address forms in referential usage, items in the three groups would normally combine with LN if the referent is not present at the scene of utterance. But when the referent is present seniority in age or status will constrain the use of LN after a title in either of the deferential and revered groups. LN tends to be deleted and only titles preceded by the definite article *the* are used.

Thus, if a highly placed personality who is a chief, a professor, or a bishop is present at the scene of utterance, a younger or junior person would not normally address him or refer to him using his title plus his last name. So, instead of *Chief* + LN, *Professor* + LN, *Bishop* + LN, and so on, *the Chief, the Professor, the Bishop,* and so on would be used.

As forms in direct address the titles in group (iii) can be used while LN is optionally deleted. But with the forms in groups (i) and (ii) LN deletion can take place only if age and status are not marked for seniority.

Multiple titles or title combinations often used in Nigerian English include:

1. (*Chief Doctor* + LN) where the person is either a medical doctor or a Ph.D. holder who has also taken a chieftaincy title.
2. (*Alhaji Chief Doctor* + LN) = a person who is a medical doctor or Ph.D. holder who has taken a chieftaincy title and has also made a muslim pilgrimage to Mecca and Medina.
3. (*Doctor* (*Mrs.*) + LN) = a married woman who holds a doctorate degree or is a medical doctor.
4. (*Chief Doctor* (*Mrs.*) + LN) = a married woman who holds a doctorate degree or is a medical doctor and has taken a chieftaincy title.

Among the Yoruba and Igbo, titles are displayed with relish and held in such high regard that an addressee might feel offended if not addressed by his correct title or title combinations. There are some unusual cases where a wife is a medical doctor but her husband is a nontitled adult; when it comes to writing name-plates for identifying their residence, a combination like *Mr. and Dr.* (*Mrs.*) + LN is not uncommon. The husband's ambition would probably be to take a chieftaincy title so that *Chief* can replace the nonprestigious *Mister.*

Kinship Terms of Address.   A few kinship terms of address are frequently used in Nigerian English. Forms like *Dad, Mom, Uncle, Auntie, Brother,* and *Sister* have taken wider semantic references as address forms in Nigerian English.

Generally, the forms Daddy and Mommy are used in direct address not only by children to their parents but also to people who are as old as or older than their parents; they are also used as deferential forms within the family by husband and wife. During the early years of marriage when the children are still very young it is quite common for husband and wife to address each other by their first names. But when the children become older, a wife would start addressing her husband as *Daddy* and the husband would address the wife as *Mommy,* especially in the presence of the children. One form that is very common is for a husband to address his wife as *Madam.* A common feature of usage among women and young girls in government offices, in the marketplace and among street traders in urban centres is the use of the terms *Daddy* and *Mommy* as address terms for adult men and women. Such usage does not convey any relational association. Street hawkers and market traders wanting to sell their wares use the forms frequently for car owners who stop by to buy some commodities at the road side. Such usage carries deferential overtones in relation to age differences and status. Immediate bosses in their places of work get addressed as either *Daddy* or *Mommy* by subordinate young officers.

The use of the terms *Uncle* and *Auntie* also bears close similarity to the pattern sketched for *Daddy* and *Mommy.* Deferential considerations are the primary motivation for using the terms *Uncle* and *Auntie.* They do not necessarily involve blood relationship.

In literate homes, the children are encouraged to address male and female relations older than the children as *Uncle* and *Auntie,* respectively. This is also extended to visitors by children. This feature of usage was observed recently by the present writer among Nigerian families in Britain. Naturally enough, some form of solidarity exists among groups of African people living in Britain. There, Nigerians tend to belong, at least psychologically, to one big family. To children born in Britain every Nigerian adult male who visits their home is an *Uncle* and every adult female is an *Auntie.*

In a rather interesting way, Nigerian children in Britain have started to generalize the use of the terms *Uncle* or *Auntie.* It follows, therefore, that from these children's point of view, besides their parents, every other black man who is an adult must be an *Uncle* and every other black woman must be an *Auntie.*

CONCLUSION

The evolving pattern of standard Nigerian English usage exhibits several interesting features that deserve detailed sociolinguistic analysis, as I have attempted to show here. There is need for further research to establish the most significant aspects that are distinctively Nigerian in standard Nigerian English.

What has happened here in Nigeria, as this study reveals, and in other places where some cultural assimilation of the English language has taken place (say for example, in India) is that the resources of a second language are superimposed on an intricate system of social and kinship relationships, and on a completely different pattern of cultural outlook and social expectations. The differences in cultural outlook and social expectations between British culture, on the one hand, and indigenous Nigerian cultures, on the other hand, become quite obvious in the resulting pattern of address forms and greetings that characterize Nigerian English. The close similarities between some of these forms in Nigerian English and their translation equivalents in indigenous Nigerian languages show the extent to which the English forms of address and greetings have become modified or semantically extended to suit local communicative needs.

In a similar study of Indian English, for example, Kachru (1966) identified socially determined speech functions, such as modes of address or reference, greetings, blessings/prayers, abuses, and curses, as being related to the Indian context of culture. In Indian languages, there are fixed formal exponents for these contexts, but these are sometimes transferred to their L2 (that is, the English language) for those contextual units that are absent in the culture of the English language.

In the Nigerian situation, the kinship terminologies of the culture of the English language are adopted for expressing the kinship relationships in an indigenous culture with which English bears no analogous kinship nomenclature. The intracultural variations in the uses of these linguistic forms in Nigerian English may be assumed to be systematically related to the constituents of subculture patterns. These include aspects of the social structure, cultural definitions of the situation of action, respect and deference in social relationships, the cultural philosophy and the value system, and their patterned interrelations. Ethel Albert (1972) made similar observations in her study of speech behaviour in the African Community of Burundi. The sociolinguistic reality is that Nigerian English cannot but exhibit features of the cultural life and of the pattern of social behaviour of the people who use it.

NOTES

1. This paper was first presented in the Regional Standards of English section of the Sociolinguistics Program, Ninth World Congress of Sociology, Uppsala, Sweden, August 14–19, 1978. From *Anthropological Linguistics,* vol. 20, no. 9. "Reprinted December 1978, with the permission of F. Akere and *Anthropological Linguistics.*"

2. Liberia is the only black African country in which English is a native language. English is the first language of the country's black elite. It is also the only country in Africa which owes its English to American blacks returned from the Americas rather than directly to British rule in the continent. See Ali A. Mazrui (1973).

3. In Freetown, Sierra Leone, Krio is the first language of many inhabitants. It is also the lingua franca between the Creoles and the indigenous people in and around Freetown.

4. Pidgin English is used along the coastal towns of Nigeria and Ghana. In Nigeria Pidgin is the code of wider communication among the various ethnic groups in Bendel, Rivers, and Cross River States.

5. See Adetugbo (1977a).

6. See the "Introduction" in Bailey and Robinson (1973) pp. 1–8.

7. The theme of the 1978 Annual Conference of the Nigerian English Studies Association which was held at the University of Ibadan was "Varieties of English in Nigeria." This emphasizes the claim that attention is now being paid to varieties differentiation in Nigerian English.

8. I have avoided using the terms standard versus nonstandard in this particular context because of the social implications that these terms have in their American or British usage.

9. There is some controversy at the moment about the use of the terms Pidgin English and Nigerian Pidgin. Some scholars feel that Pidgin in Nigeria is not a variety of English and could not therefore be called Pidgin English. Others think that since Pidgin in Nigeria developed from the contact between English and some coastal Nigerian languages, a large proportion of its word stock derives from English lexical items, and until a statistical count of its vocabulary stock is taken, Pidgin in Nigeria will continue to be called Pidgin English. I think that a great deal more research into the structure and lexical characteristics of Pidgin in Nigeria needs to be carried out.

10. See Salami (1968) for his particularly uncompromising arguments on this issue.

11. Adetugbo (1977a) provides several examples of these forms in Nigerian English.

12. See Adetugbo (1977b).

13. Edward Blyden's words are quoted in Ali Mazrui, 1973, p. 62.

14. See Luckman (1975).

15. See Edward Sapir (1929) pp. 207–209.

16. The Yoruba of Nigeria also have an equally elaborate system of funerals.

17. A traditional ruler in Yoruba society is called "Oba" the Yoruba equivalent for "King." In Nigerian English, an Oba is referred to with the address form "His Highness . . ." followed by the title "Oba" plus his name, and then his official chieftaincy title. For example the Oba of Oyo in Oyo State would be referred to as: "His Highness Oba Lamidi Adeyemi, the Alafin of Oyo."

REFERENCES

Adetugbo, A. Nigerian English: Fact or fiction? *Lagos Notes and Records,* 1977a, 6, 128–141.

Adetugbo, A. Is there a Standard Nigerian English phonology? Mimeograph, 1977b.

Albert, Ethel. Culture patterning in speech behaviour in Burundi. In J. J. Gumperz and D. H. Hymes, *Directions in Sociolinguistics.* London: Holt, Rinehart and Winston, 1972.

Bailey, R. W. and Robinson, J. L. *Varieties of Present-Day English.* London: Macmillan, 1973.

Brown, R. W. and Ford, M. Address in American English. *Journal of Abnormal and Social Psychology,* 1961, 62, 375–385.

Ervin-Tripp, S. M. Sociolinguistics. In J. A. Fishman, *Advances in the Sociology of Language.* The Hague: Mouton, 1969.

Kachru, B. B. Indian English: A study in contextualisation. In C. E. Bazell, J. C. Catford, M. A. K. Halliday, and R. H. Robins, *In Memory of J. R. Firth.* London: Longmans, 1966.

Luckman, Thomas. *The Sociology of Language.* Indianapolis: The Bobbs-Merrill Co. Inc., 1975.

Mazrui, Ali A. The English language and the origins of African nationalism. In R. W. Bailey and J. L. Robinson, *Varieties of Present-Day English.* London: Macmillan, 1973.

Salami, A. Defining 'Standard' Nigerian English. *Journal of the Nigerian English Studies Association,* 1968, 2, 2, 96–105.

Sapir, Edward. The status of linguistics as a science. *Language,* 1929, 5, 207–214.

6 LEARNING TO SAY IT BETTER: A CHALLENGE FOR ZAMBIAN EDUCATION

Robert Serpell

Within the Zambian speech community we need to recognize two dimensions of linguistic variation: "the dialectal and the superposed" (Gumperz, 1968, p. 225). Furthermore, "the distribution of linguistic variants is a reflection of social facts" (Gumperz, 1968, p. 225). I propose in this paper[1] to examine some of these social facts in Zambia, and to explore their implications for an educational policy designed to help students become more articulate.

THE ZAMBIAN SPEECH COMMUNITY

The task of providing a systematic account of the Zambian speech community has only recently begun. Regional variations in the rural areas were a major focus of enquiry in the Zambia Language Survey. As Guthrie (1948) pointed out some time ago, the application of purely empirical, linguistic criteria to the classification of Bantu languages results in an impasse. After plotting geographical boundaries (*isoglosses*) on the map for lexical, grammatical and phonological features, "what actually happens is that each of the criteria gives good results in at least one area but not in another" (Guthrie, 1948, p. 26). Even the unit of analysis is difficult to define. "Thus in deciding what is to be regarded as a distinct language, and what a mere dialect, not only do we have no watertight linguistic test to apply, but we have to bring in other considerations which are entirely non-linguistic" (Guthrie, 1948, p. 29).

One such consideration with obvious practical significance is that of intelligibility. Might we not define as separate languages those codes that are so different that a person competent in one cannot understand when the other is spoken? Kashoki tried this experiment on secondary school students who claimed never to have been exposed before to the languages in which he tested their comprehension. Not surprisingly, these students, who were competent speakers of Bemba, Lozi, Nyanja, or Tonga, understood rather little of any of the other codes when passages were played to them on a tape recorder. This technique would be well-nigh impossible to use with closely neighbouring communities, since their speech codes are in practice intermingled. Moreover language contact is not usually a symmetrical process, and informants may be unaware of the nature of their exposure to the vocabulary and forms of another speech code. For instance, loanwords introduced into Bemba from Swahili, Portuguese, and Kabanga are often so well disguised that competent speakers are quite unaware of their exotic origins (Kashoki, 1975, p. 714).

The asymmetrical nature of language contact between Zambian speech codes is most clearly illustrated by urban speech patterns. In the two major urban centres a lingua franca is widely used for communication among people who do not share a language in which they are fully competent. On the Copperbelt the prevalent lingua franca is Bemba, while in Lusaka it is Nyanja, while in small centres like Livingstone and Kabwe the situation is less clearly defined (Mytton, 1974, p. 22). This means that a Lozi speaker who comes to stay in Lusaka is much more likely to learn Nyanja than a Nyanja speaker is likely to learn Lozi in the same city. This is not a mere consequence of the numerical preponderance in Lusaka of families originating from the Nyanja-speaking Eastern Province. The Nyanja code has acquired the status of general currency in the city, so that, regardless of their regional origins, two Africans meeting in a public place for the first time will generally opt for it as the medium of their first attempt at communication.

The use of a lingua franca raises two further important features of the Zambian speech community: the first is individual multilingualism, the second the influence of situational context in a speaker's choice of code. Clearly, since only a limited proportion of each city's population are first language speakers of the local lingua franca, the remainder must make up a substantial number of bilingual individuals. When we add to this the widespread use of English in Zambian towns, we arrive at the conclusion that many urban Zambians are familiar with at least three different codes. There is no reliable evidence of how fluent these individuals are in each of the codes they speak. But Mytton's extensive survey of the mass media audience in Zambia found (using a very conservative criterion of language differences) that adults living in the urban areas claimed on average to know about 2.8 languages, while those in the rural areas claimed an average of 1.9 (1974, p. 22).

Given that a person speaks more than one language, what determines which code he will choose on a given occasion? One answer which comes immediately to mind is that a multilingual person will always choose the code that he thinks his listener understands. But in a society of multilinguals, the speaker can assume that most of his listeners understand more than one code. Speaker and listener share a repertoire of several codes within which his selection will carry social meaning. One dimension of this meaning is laid down by the status of English as the superposed language of formal communication. Another is the expression of ethnic affiliation. Just as in Oakland, California, "the use of Black

English promotes cohesion among Blacks" (Kernan, 1971, p. 148), so two urban Zambians from the same minority ethnic group may express their solidarity by choosing to converse in the code of their ancestral, rural home.

The classification of codes by social status or ethnic group is, however, too static a conception to do justice to the variety of social meanings expressed by code selection in a multilingual community. "What one empirically observes . . . is not 'customs' so much as 'cases' of verbal behaviour, illustrating very often processes of over- and under-communicating statuses (processes of 'impression management')" (Pride, 1970, p. 300). Goffman, to whom this last expression is due, has pointed out that "it is not the attributes of social structure that are here considered, such as age and sex, but rather the value placed on these attributes as they are acknowledged in the situation current at hand" (1959). Thus Parkin reports from another multilingual African city, Nairobi, that:

> In a particular conversation English is seen to express, say, social exclusiveness, as against Swahili which may express social inclusiveness. In another conversation, this set of values may be reversed . . . people do not adhere rigidly to the stereotyped evaluations. They use the manifold behavioural connotations of different languages . . . (1974, 212–214).

To this social-psychological potential of code selection we should add that the availability of these several speech registers puts at the speaker's disposal a remarkable range of nuances. This is particularly evident in the presentation of topics that concern the interaction between different cultures. In both the social and the semantic field, the choice of code by multilingual speakers is often a highly creative exercise.

One further distinguishing feature of the Zambian speech community requires emphasis, namely the fluidity of its verbal repertoire. In describing the social significance of code selection, I have simplified the situation by implying that a whole message or conversation is transmitted in a single code. In practice, however, we find among Zambian multilinguals a great deal of switching to and fro between codes. Mkilifi (1972) has described similar "language mixing" among Swahili-English bilinguals and trilinguals in Tanzania.

It is often difficult to draw a firm line between the use of "borrowed" lexical items and code-switching in urban Zambian speech. Consider, for example, the following Lusaka statement:

> Napita ku *office* kwake. Manje napeza kuti *he's not available.* (I went to his office, but then I found that he was not available.)

The second intrusion from English tends in context to imply a note of irony, as if the words are being quoted from a secretary whose supercilious manner is accentuated by the imputed choice of the high-status English code. But the earlier intrusion passes almost unnoticed, since it is an accepted designation for this kind of place of work. Thus the first item is a case of borrowed vocabulary, the second a case of code-switching.

Certain linguistic indicators (critical characteristics) may be relevant to this distinction, such as the length of the intruding segment, or the extent of phonological transformation (for example, *office* rather than *ofisi*). But the main criteria lie in our understanding of the social context in which the words are used, which may well be highlighted by prosodic and paralinguistic indicators such as intonation and facial expression. Other instances of mixed language seem to fit either description equally well, for example:

Nikonda mowa too much. (I really dig beer.)

The fluidity, or lack of clear "compartmentalization," of the codes (Gumperz, 1968, p. 230) is apparent in urban Zambian speech throughout the three linguistic subsystems: lexical, grammatical, and phonological. Thus, in addition to the lexical intrusions cited, we find constructions based on English word order imposed on a string of Nyanja or Bemba words, and, of course, extensive phonological restructuring of English words when they are "borrowed." The predominant patterns of intrusion seem to be from English into the Bantu codes for lexis and grammar, and from Bantu into English for phonology. But there are some reversals of these orders at all levels, for example:

1. "This *ka*-problem will soon be solved." (*ka* = little)
2. "This is a really nice record, *than* all those others you have been playing." (This construction is probably based on an attempt to equate *than* with the Bemba *ukucila*.)
3. The name of the town, Kafue, is pronounced by many Lusaka residents with a diphthong [yu] immediately after the [f], following English phonology.

These very varied patterns of code mixture pose a complex problem of criteria when it comes to identifying "errors" in the spoken or written usage of Zambian students (see the section on dialects and errors).

I have stressed in this description the highly flexible and fluid nature of speech in the Zambian community. By contrast, the formal institutional structures of the society tend to emphasise distinctness among the various categories of language. In a valiant attempt to systematise the range of codes, Kashoki presents a table listing over 80 names of indigenous African "languages and/or dialects" spoken in Zambia. These are arranged in about 25 clusters with close "linguistic affinity," which in turn fall into 14 groups sharing some "vocabulary and grammatical characteristics." Only ten of these groups (according to data collected in the 1969 population census) have more than 1 percent of the population who speak one of their varieties as their "mother tongue" (the range for these ten is from 2 percent to 34 percent). One variety in each of seven of these groups has since independence been given recognition as an official language of the state. These official languages are used for written and oral government propaganda and for a limited part of the primary school curriculum on a regional basis. They are also used with various time allocations in radio broadcasting, which is centralised and beamed to all parts of the country.

In addition, English permeates all these official activities as a separate, nationwide code which in most respects carries a superior status. Thus central government officials deliver their public speeches in English, their statements being then translated into the regional official language by an interpreter; English is the medium for 38 percent of radio "air time," as compared with a maximum of 14 percent for any of the other languages (Mytton, 1974, p. 16); and English is officially the medium for all primary education except for three "Zambian languages" periods per week. Other indications of the high status accorded to English are the facts that virtually all television programmes are exclusively in English (two notable exceptions have been the programmes "Zam-Arts" and "The Police and You"), and that both the national daily newspapers are exclusively in English. Journalism in the other seven official languages is mainly confined to fortnightly newspapers published by Zambia Information Services, which (with the one exception of *Imbila*) are almost exclusively read by residents of rural areas (Mytton, 1974, p. 62). English was claimed as a mother tongue by about 1 percent of the residents of Zambia in the 1969 population census.

OPTIONS FOR LANGUAGE POLICY

The contrast between the social realities of the Zambian speech community and the institutional structure of language policy has several dimensions. It has often been observed that the high official status accorded to English is anomalous in a nation that has recently thrown off the yoke of British colonialism. The structure of language embodies a powerful expression of a culture's moral and intellectual standards. Surely then it is politically inconsistent to opt for teaching our children the language of a culture whose moral standards the nation has explicitly rejected. In reply it is argued that English is chosen for its impartiality in a multiethnic community, where assigning nationwide status to any one of the indigenous languages would be divisive.

Both these opposing positions seem to share the theoretical assumption that a superposed language will eventually replace the other codes, so that the Zambian community will become effectively monolingual. This seems to me, however, most unlikely to happen in practice, in view of the tendency for different codes to acquire specialised social connotations and in view of the creative potential inherent in this diversity. Ferguson (1959) argues from an analysis of four other states in which diglossia prevails (Switzerland, Egypt, Haiti, and Greece) that "there are only a few general kinds of development likely to take place" (p. 248). He outlines several major alternatives: (1) the functional separation along lines of diglossia may persist for a long time; (2) the lower status code which prevails in the nation's communication centre (or centres) may become the standard code for the whole community, either with or without a considerable admixture from the high-status code; (3) several low-status codes may become standard in different regions; (4) the only condition under which the high-status code is at all likely to become the nationwide standard is "if it is already serving as a standard language in some other community and the diglossia community, for reasons linguistic and non-linguistic, tends to merge with the other community" (Ferguson, 1959, p. 248).

Clearly it is the third of these alternatives, along with the prospect of concomitant political fragmentation, that the policymakers in Zambia have sought to prevent by the establishment of English as a unifying force. What about the second alternative? Bemba is the most widely used low-status code on the Copperbelt and Nyanja in Lusaka, while Lozi and Tonga are widely used in the line-of-rail towns to the south of Lusaka. The dominant code in rural towns away from the old line-of-rail is more easily inferred from the ethnic composition of their surrounding rural areas. According to Mytton's survey (1974, p. 22), Bemba and Nyanja are each understood by about half the adult population of Zambia. Unfortunately, however, his figures do not show how much these two halves overlap—in other words, we do not know what proportion of the population speaks neither of these two linguae francae. But even supposing that proportion to be small, the problem of reconciling these two major "competing" codes remains.

A survey that I conducted in two suburbs of Lusaka in 1969 (Serpell, 1970) compared the comprehension of Nyanja by children from various family backgrounds born and brought up in Lusaka. Our test was in the medium of Eastern Province Chi-Chewa, the dialect of Nyanja used for official purposes in Zambia. Children of Bemba-speaking families in Grade 6 were about three years behind their classmates from Nyanja-speaking families on this test. These children had in fact been through the pre-1966 lower primary school curriculum, and had thus not only been exposed to Nyanja on the buses and in the streets but also in the classroom as the medium of instruction for four years. Comparison of these children with others who had only recently arrived in Lusaka from Bemba-speaking regions showed that the Lusaka environment had indeed taught the resident Bemba-speaking children a great deal of Nyanja, but this still fell far short of the competence acquired by children speaking Nyanja in their homes.

One element in common between the Nyanja of Lusaka and the Bemba of the Copperbelt (sometimes known as Town-Nyanja and Ichi-Copperbelt) is their considerable admixture of English. Is it possible that a standard mixture of these three codes (a Bemba-English-Nyanja or a Town-Bemba-Nyanja?) could emerge as a nationwide medium of communication in Zambia? Mkilifi (1972) argues

It is very unlikely that a new spoken language in the form of Swahili-English pidgin or creole will emerge in Tanzania . . . bilinguals of Swahili and English constitute a very small percentage of the total population. . . . Also there are social constraints working against the development of such a code. Swahili is gaining tremendous prestige as the national language. There is now a conscious effort on the part of bilinguals to improve their proficiency in Swahili. . . . What is likely to happen is that the functions of Swahili and English will be more and more clearly demarcated until the two languages reach a stable functional relationship. (1972, pp. 211–212)

There are two main differences in Zambia. First, about a quarter of the total adult population and nearly half of those living in town (Mytton, 1974, p. 21–2) claim to speak English as a second language; the proportion in the younger generation is likely to be much higher. Second, the status of unmixed (or "pure") varieties of Bemba and Nyanja in relation to official national issues is far less prestigious than is the case for Swahili in Tanzania.

Neverthelesss it seems unlikely that a full-scale fusion of Nyanja, Bemba, and English will occur in the near future. Nyanja loanwords feature only very modestly in Kashoki's descriptions of Town Bemba (1972, 1975). And, although a fair amount of code-switching takes place between Nyanja and Bemba, my own impression in Lusaka is that most people retain a clear sense of the distinctness of these codes. Thus, while fusion is not an inconceivable long-term development, it does not seem to be a plausible target for a present language policy, any more than the objective of homogeneous imposition of English or any other of the widely spoken codes. As a matter of principle, language change cannot be engineered, I believe, unless the strategy adopted is closely geared to the social structure and dynamics of the speech community. The essential character of the Zambian speech community lies in the diversity and the fluidity of its repertoire. Thus any policy that conforms to this principle must as Kashoki (1973) has advocated, "recognise diversity as a national asset and consciously encourage its *positive* exploitation." The key to planning for national unity through linguistic diversity lies in fostering diversity within individuals rather than between different groups.

THE MULTICULTURAL INDIVIDUAL

In most discussions of culture contact, there is a tendency to refer back (partly for clarity of presentation) to a paradigm (or standard pattern) of total isolation. A contrast is drawn, for instance, between the Navajo of North America, the Mandarin of China, and the Luvale of Africa, three communities that have scarcely ever been in contact with each other. In this instance, race, language, culture, and education are interrelated within each community and contrast with each of the other groups. For certain purposes of exposition such comparisons are both valid and interesting. But there is a danger in our constant recourse to this paradigm that we may lose sight of the fact that such total isolation is the exception rather than the rule among cultures of the modern world. In that respect, it is really not a useful paradigm since it is quite atypical.

A second guiding assumption that colours most accounts of culture contact is that it is characterised by inequality. Thus coexisting cultures are often presented as superposed. The colonial experience in Zambia has left us with a whole array of binary oppositions which tend to get aligned into an oversimplified pattern of parallel contrasting values like Table 1. Any policy that attempts to reverse the polarity of one of these contrasts finds itself confronted with opposing associations along the total array. For instance, attempts to promote

TABLE 1   *Parallel Cultural Contrasts in the Colonial Ideology*

superior	foreign	cash	urban	modern	advanced
inferior	indigenous	subsistence	rural	traditional	primitive

indigenous cultural music or languages as symbols of the new society encounter resistance because of the association of traditional culture with the rural subsistence economy. To break out of this deadlock we need to dismiss all a priori connotations and consider each item on its intrinsic merits. I will suggest that in practice much of Zambia's social life shows a healthier eclecticism than most propagandists would have us believe.

Most people in Zambia have access to a dual cultural repertoire generated by the juxtaposition and intermingling of two formerly isolated sets of traditions, those of Africa and those of Europe. Rather than opting for one stream to the exclusion of the other, most individuals in my experience make use in varying degrees of two strategies: coordination and fusion. Both approaches are eclectic and in that sense represent a resistance to the blanket superimposition implied by Table 1. In *coordination* we find contextual specialisation, while *fusion* involves adaptation. In the case of language, these two processes have already been described. The sensitivity of code-switching to the social situation shows how the bilingual individual coordinates his two codes by treating each as specially suited to a given context. In the case of words borrowed on a more permanent basis from one code into another, there is extensive phonological adaptation, so that the loanword, once appropriated, may cease to be recognisable to monolinguals familiar only with the originating code (for example, *imishiishibeeti* from *bedsheets*; *fosholo* from *shovel*).

The same two processes can be seen at work in other cultural domains. In music, for instance, a great deal of fusion takes place. Kubic (1974) has vividly described the creative borrowing that goes into the compositions of a Malawian musical group, the Kachamba Brothers. The converging influences of European and African prototypes on this music are mediated by a long history of interaction. On the one hand, the American input to modern Western popular styles of music has been greatly affected by jazz, to which blacks brought an African tradition. On the other hand, the major immediate influences on the Kachambas come from *Kwela* and *Simanje-manje,* two Southern African styles that have emerged from a fusion of indigenous and Western music in the last 20 or 30 years.

It is characteristic of every cultural encounter and transculturation that those involved tend first to recognise in the 'hybrid' forms the cultural traits of their own group, as they are familiar with them. This can lead to the phenomenon of extremists on both sides claiming the cultural product entirely for their own culture, or attributing it to whichever culture they identify with. . . . What European listeners feel to be 'Western' often really coincides with traditional structural traits in the African realm and is experienced by African musicians as distinctly African. (Kubik, 1974, pp. 14–15).

The coordination of two or more distinct cultural styles is also witnessed in many Zambian musical groups. It is a matter of professional pride for them to include in their repertoire some rumba "numbers" of Central African origin as well as some soul music and some rock-and-roll from America. Depending on the occasion, and often on the immediate response they elicit from their audience, the bands bring out more and more of the style that seems most appropriate. Musical styles thus operate very much like the linguistic codes just discussed in their sensitivity to situational pressures and opportunities. Since much of Zambian music is accompanied both by words and by dancing, there is a rich field here for further analysis. What themes, for instance, in lyrics are most effectively set to music in each style, and what are the social connotations of dancing to the various styles? In the present context the implication of central importance is that multicultural versatility is widely recognised in the field of music as a highly desirable quality for the Zambian performer.

In the realm of personal decoration we can again see examples both of fusion and of coordination. Hairstyles in Zambia reflect traditions of plaiting which are indigenous to this region of Africa as well as adaptations of European styles (such as parting, waving, and buns) to suit the constraints and the opportunities created by the structure of negroid hair. One such adaptation, the so-called Afro style, together with a ready-made, removable version (the Afro wig), was imported wholesale from the West where it was developed by Afro-Americans. A curious debate has arisen over this style, which was supposedly conceived in the United States as an attempt to recapture the spirit of an African tradition, but in Zambia now appears to be acquiring the connotation of a foreign cultural product. Coordination is best exemplified by women's choice of dress. When attending funerals in town, and when visiting villages for any reason, many urban Zambian women exchange their knee-length skirts for a full-length *chitenge* wrap. The role-playing nature of this change of attire is highlighted by men who will sometimes don a *chitenge* over their Western trousers in order to join in a traditional dance at a wedding, and then remove it before resuming their seat.

Weddings in Zambian cities illustrate the complexity of coordination in matters of dress. Very often, when a well-to-do Zambian couple are wed, there will be three largely independent ceremonies: (1) a traditional African cere-mony conducted in one or more private homes, (2) a Christian service performed in a church, and (3) a reception held in a public hall. At the first of these ceremonies (whose actual timing relative to the others varies from one instance to another), the bride and most other female participants are dressed in rural style with a *chitenge*. In the church, the bride is clothed in white with a veil in the style of English church weddings, and the groom and guests wear almost exclusively clothes of the smartest, formal, English style. The gathering proceeds from the church to the reception without a change of clothes, but here the attendant women from the traditional ceremony (who were discreetly nonparticipant, or even absent, at the church service) return to the scene. In some cases, they assert their presence on the church steps, ululating their approval of the ceremony that has just taken place. Very often they do so as the newly wed couple take the floor for the first dance of the reception, while the band plays a waltz or a foxtrot. The resulting spectacle of the bridal couple waltzing erect in their Western clothes and Western embrace to the tune of Western music, while their mothers clad in African *chitenge* dance round and round them, bending double and clapping their hands against their mouths in a shrill ululation, nicely symbolises the harmonious celebration of one and the same event in two contrasting cultural styles.

My concern in citing these examples has been to show that language use in Zambia shares with many other facets of social life the pervasive characteristics of coordination and fusion among diverse cultural traditions. At this juncture I wish to rebut a value judgment made by Turnbull (1962) in his book *The Lonely African*. Observing that Africans often see no inconsistency between certain Christian and pagan practices (which, according to orthodox Christianity, are fundamentally contradictory), he interprets this as evidence of a basic super-ficiality in approach to both cultural traditions. The urban African is thus portrayed as a lonely aimless individual who has fallen between two stools and has no reliable frame of moral reference. I have argued on the contrary that the bicultural individual is keenly aware of social frames of reference and draws both eclectically and creatively on his dual cultural heritage.

The notion that, unless a person is thoroughly steeped in every aspect of a cultural tradition, his thinking is superficial and devoid of sincerity arises from the unfamiliarity of the bicultural experience. What needs to be realised is that very few individuals in any society have a thorough knowledge of every aspect of a culture, and this is especially true of the modern world. One man can interpret in depth the artistic tradition that gives meaning to a certain style of furniture, while another recognises the literary allusions in a public speech, and yet another notes with appreciation the technical improvements that make a new brand of automobile. The fact that few people combine all three of the strands of knowledge required for appreciating these different dimensions of culture illustrates the fact that a culture is enshrined in the behaviour of the whole society collectively. Even in closer-knit societies with a subsistence economy, it is common to find that certain groups have greater knowledge than others about specific dimensions of the culture. The technologies of house-building, of pottery, and of weaving are often restricted to a single sex, as are the rituals associated with adolescence and childbirth. Certain medical and religious practices are often confined to a highly specialised individual or family. Now it may be argued that the "partly acculturated" individual learns random bits and pieces of the new culture, which do not hang together as a coherent role and thus do not fit in with the society as a whole. But this account shifts the inadequacy from the individual to the group. It may well be correct to say that modern African cities have inadequate institutions based on incompletely absorbed features of Western culture. The bureaucracy is a fine example. But how much does this affect the individual's psychological health? Very little, I suspect. Just as with bilingualism, diglossia serves to bring into play the individual's greatest skill where it is needed, so more generally the bicultural individual learns to use his piecemeal knowledge of the two cultures in ways appropriate to the social situation.

We should also note that bicultural societies have their own special structure and dynamics about which the individual learns a great deal. The insights generated by cultural conflict and by untranslatability constitute a source of culture in themselves to which the bicultural individual has special access. Thus the growing community of bicultural people shares an undocumented culture which permits communication on a plane that monocultural people do not understand. Indeed much of the charge of superficiality comes from a prejudiced assumption that unless items of an old culture are used in traditional ways they are being abused and lack any real significance. Just as people talk of a "debased language," they see the mutual adaptation of African and European cultures as a form of degeneration, rather than as the growth of a new and potent culture of the modern African city.

The language policy for which I wish to make a case is directed towards the promotion of this new culture. This means opting neither for a romantic revival of traditional African culture from the past, nor for a blind superimposition of an imported Western culture, but rather for an eclectic African modernity in which the diverse strands are effectively organised towards ambitious but realistic goals. Such goals are normally defined in terms of social and economic characteristics; but my concern here is with their psychological dimensions. The key term at this level is versatility. An articulate Zambian citizen, I submit, needs to be able to put his thoughts and feelings into speech in many different ways. His aim must be to communicate not only intelligibly but effectively with various kinds of people about various topics and on various occasions. To achieve this aim the student requires a wide range of competence in several different codes and a sensitivity to context that will guide his choice of code.

DIALECTS AND ERRORS

The English spoken in Zambia by the African population differs in several notable ways from the English spoken in Britain. There are also well-known contrasts between British and American English, and between southern and northern English in England. It is conventional to refer to the latter contrasts as dialectal variations, whereas there are two schools of thought about the variants found in Zambia. One school treats these variants as evidence of a Zambian English dialect, while the other considers them as errors arising from inter- ference between the speakers' first (Bantu) languages and their control over the rules of standard English.

Even those who recognise the existence of nonstandard dialects do not always regard them as equally expressive or logical as the standard version of the language. Thus Bereiter and his associates (1966) conclude that "the language of culturally deprived children . . . is not merely an underdeveloped version of standard English, but is a basically non-logical mode of expressive behaviour" (p. 113). Labov (1969) has made a concerted attack on this position. He has shown, for instance, in expressions such as "they mine" (meaning "they are mine" in standard English), that "the deletion of the *is* or *are* in nonstandard Negro English is not the result of erratic or illogical behaviour: it follows the same rules as standard English contraction. . . . The appropriate use of the deletion rule, like the contraction rule, requires a deep and intimate knowledge of English grammar and phonology" (Labov, 1969, p. 203).

How much of what is currently held up as faulty English in Zambian classrooms can be reinterpreted as a valid nonstandard dialect? It seems to me that one crucial criterion lies in Labov's distinction between erratic or random variations and systematic, rule-governed usage. If we can show that a feature of English spoken in Zambia is systematically predictable with reference to a grammatical "rule," the mere fact that the rule in question does not feature in the grammar of standard English should not deter us from recognising it as a valid dialectal variant.

With all the emphasis I have placed in the first section on the diversity and fluidity of the Zambian speech repertoire, the reader may well question why I should now wish to give prominence to any rules. The reason is a basic, logical one. We do not wish to prejudge in this situation what is going to emerge as an accepted set of rules, but this does not mean that we can dispense with the idea of rules altogether. A useful distinction in this context is made by Searle (1965) between regulative and constitutive rules. The grammatical rules of a language constitute, or define, the very nature of communication in that medium, much as the rules of chess constitute what it is to play the game. When we ask what are the rules of Zambian English, we are not requesting some authority to announce some regulations to constrain the speech behaviour of the Zambian community. We are concerned rather to establish how communication takes place in this community, much as an observer must know the rules of chess if he is to understand how people play the game.

There is, however, a demand for regulative rules in relation to language in Zambia, and this comes from the classroom. Teachers wish to know what is the standard at which they should direct their students to aim. They recognise the existence of various forms of English, but they feel the need to identify an ideal as a yardstick against which to measure their students' tentative variations. When the constitutive rules of a language are well established they provide a useful criterion for this kind of regulative exercise. This is why schools are the largest market for books about grammar, in which the author seeks to make explicit the intuitive knowledge of native speakers. The dilemma we face in Zambia is that this classroom application of linguistics is pressing for definite answers before the constitutive rules of Zambian English have settled down.

In an earlier reference to the difference between dialects and errors, I laid special emphasis on phonemic distinctions:

Some consistency must be maintained even if only to ensure intelligibility of one Zambian's English to another Zambian. It would seem particularly important that phonemic distinctions be preserved. (Serpell, 1968, p. 93)

Johnson and Isoardi (1971) take the same position for English in Papua New Guinea:

The 'sounds' made by a Cockney, a New Yorker, a Queenslander or the Queen are likely to be very different, but all of these native speakers of English will tend to preserve a basic system of relationships among the sounds they make, and it is by interpreting this system of relationships, not by identifying particular sounds, that we are able to 'decode' into a message the acoustic signals which our ears receive. . . . A Papua New Guinea accent is as acceptable as any other provided that the accent our pupils have is genuinely an accent of English; i.e. that, regardless of the precise acoustic quality of the sounds they utter, they maintain the phonemic distinctions of English, and are not attempting to communicate an English language message through the phonemic system of their native language.

I am no longer quite so sure about the paramount importance of phonemic distinctions. The dialects spoken by black Americans must surely be "genuine" accents of English, since the speakers do not for the most part have any other means of communication. Yet according to Labov (1970) "Black English" completely obscures the phonemic distinctions within such minimal pairs as *three/tree, jar/jaw, six/sick, row/road,* and *boil/ball.* Theoretically the threat to communication posed by disregard of a phonemic distinction lies in the possibility it creates of a listener misidentifying one member of such minimal pairs for the other. In practice, however, most spoken utterances contain a large element of redundancy, that is, they provide several different cues by which the listener can decide which word is intended. Thus the homonyms in standard English *sore* and *saw* are seldom mistaken for one another since the contexts in which they are used tend to make it abundantly clear which of these two same-sounding words the speaker intends (thus, "my leg is very sore"; but "I saw him on the road").

Presumably the normal redundancy of speech permits most black Americans most of the time to "decode" the "Black English" introduced into the communication system by the addition of a whole range of extra homonyms. I say "presumably" on the supposition that, if this were not so, the dialect would tend to shift in order to improve communication. In Zambia we may have less faith in such an assumption, since the Bantu languages from which Zambian English phonology derives its extra homonyms have dynamics of their own which continue to place a premium on the observance of certain rules and categories that have no direct relevance to communication in English and sometimes conflict with the demands of the English code.

One particular point of interest for our present discussion is whether the dialect complicates the task faced by children learning to read. Melmed (1971) concludes from his research in California that "black students encounter the same problems that SE (Standard English) speakers encounter when they read or hear homonyms for the first time. The BE (Black English) dialect speaking child, however, is less aware of the homonyms he uses because the teacher is also ignorant of them" (Melmed, 1971, p. 66). Melmed emphasises the need for teachers who are native speakers of SE (or should we say WE, White English?) to "be schooled in linguistic as well as social and ethnographic characteristics of speech behaviour . . . the understanding of BE features, the appreciation of black culture and language tradition, and an awareness of the intricate interaction between the speaker and the speech situation must all enter into decisions made while black children learn to read" (Melmed, 1971, pp. 77–78).

Now, the dialect of English spoken by most Zambian primary school teachers is controlled by much the same pattern of interference from Bantu phonology as the speech of the children they are teaching. Thus the particular problem of communication which has bedevilled the education of minority group black children in the United States does not find a strict parallel in Zambia today. But according to Melmed's analysis the success of most black American children learning to read depends in large measure on an opportunity that is seldom afforded to Zambian children. Melmed found that Grade 3 black children in California schools experienced no more difficulty than white children in discriminating among the *written* forms of the homonyms which they pronounced interchangeably and which they failed to distinguish acoustically when they were spoken in SE. He concludes that "these third graders have had enough exposure to SE in their every-day activity to aid them in recognition of the printed SE word" (p. 74). This kind of exposure is, of course, extremely rare for most Zambian children, whose parents and teachers tend to speak the Zambian dialect of English. And indeed, I have found that Zambian school-children do misidentify, even in the written form, one member for the other in such minimal pairs as *glass/grass, ship/sheep,* and *wet/wait* significantly more often than English-speaking children with a comparable level of general mastery of English (Serpell, 1968, section IV). Both Melmed (1971) and Kernan (1971) have observed that most black Americans have a dual repertoire which enables them to switch from BE to SE. If Melmed's conclusion that black American children learn to read by "translating" from one dialect into the other is correct, we may need to consider the promotion of some analogous form of dialect stratification in Zambian English usage.

In the realm of semantics, dialectal variations are widely recognised by language teachers as differences in register. Thus in the formal register we might say "this work is totally unacceptable," while in the informal register the same message could be expressed as "this work is no bloody good." Teachers are less inclined to call one of these forms incorrect than they are in the case of phono-logical variants. Thus it may be that I am on safer ground when suggesting that certain turns of phrase in Zambian English call for acceptance in the Zambian curriculum. I have in mind such well-known expressions as shown in Table 2.

Spoken in context, I have never witnessed any of these expressions give rise to a failure of communication between a Zambian and a non-Zambian. They are sufficiently well established in general usage to qualify for recognition as standard conversational idiom. Nothing more than a tradition of orthodoxy stands as an impediment to accepting these forms in suitable contexts within the

TABLE 2   *Non-Problematic Zambianisms*

Zambian English	British English
far much better	far better
cope up with	cope with
just now	in a moment
Is it?	Did you?
hoping you	I hope you are well too.
I'm enjoying	I'm enjoying myself.

school curriculum. Teachers in Britain face similar problems when they have to decide whether to accept forms such as *ain't, isn't,* and *is not.* There is, however, a second category of "Zambianisms" which appears more controversial (see Table 3).

As we proceed in Table 3 along the continuum from (1) to (9) we encounter a progressively serious threat to communication between a Zambian and an Englishman in the difference between their dialects. I would say from informal observations that many of the expressions in the left-hand column of Table 3 are as commonly used in Lusaka as those in Table 2. But the average secondary school teacher in Zambia from a British background will have little hesitation in designating the forms of Table 3 as incorrect. If you write these forms down, the

TABLE 3   *Problematic Zambianisms*

Zambian English	British English
1. Please will you borrow me this book?	Please will you lend me this book?
2. He refused.	He denied it.
3. Oh, by the way?	Oh, really?
4. These people are strangers.	These people are visitors.
5. I am from town.	I have just come from town.
6. too much	very much
7. I hope the police are coming.	I think the police are coming.
8. He hasn't heard what you said.	He hasn't understood what you said.
9. Hasn't he gone yet? —Yes	Hasn't he gone yet? — No

argument goes, readers outside Zambia will tend to misunderstand what you mean. And here is the crux of the matter: should language teaching in Zambia be addressed to an international audience when English is being used or is English to be treated, like Lenje, as a code to be taught for use in the Zambian speech community? What of Nyanja? Should the Malawi standard form of Chi-Chewa be taught, or should Zambian variants be acknowledged and officially approved? Clearly the intelligibility of Bemba to many people in Zaire along the Luapula River, of Luvale in Angola, of Lozi in Zimbabwe, of Nyanja in Malawi, of English in Kenya, and so on is an important asset for the travelling Zambian who has mastered one of these codes. But should this cross-national intelligibility become a criterion for establishing standardised forms?

It may be argued that the case for English is somewhat different from that of the other languages I have mentioned. English is *par excellence,* a language of international communication and there is little point in teaching it to Zambians if they cannot use it outside the borders of their country. If this were so, then in my view English would have no place in the lower grades of the Zambian primary school curriculum. You do not start teaching a child to communicate with foreigners before he can even communicate with his family and neighbours. I have advocated (in Serpell, 1978) the retention of English in the lower primary curriculum because I believe it serves, and is likely to continue to serve, an important communicative function within the Zambian speech community. It is this function of English that I feel should guide the decisions, therefore, about which forms to accept within the language when teaching it in Zambian schools. The growth of standard Zambian English idioms is evidence of appropriation. The sense that the language belongs to this community is an important step towards demystification of its status and lays the ground for more creative, less derivative patterns of English usage than presently characterise much of what appears in print in Zambia.

As I indicated, the language situation in Zambia is in a state of flux such that it is impossible to lay down rules for classroom usage that will not appear arbitrary from one point of view or another. The best guideline for the teacher in this difficult situation seems to lie in two complementary principles: an awareness of the social nuances of variations in speech behaviour and an open-minded and pragmatic approach to the treatment of unorthodox forms. I should like in conclusion to illustrate these principles with two communicative events that I have recently witnessed in Zambia.

The first event took place in the context of an intelligence test addressed by a Bemba-speaking woman psychologist to a young girl in grade 4 of a village school near Mporokoso. The tester (T) asked the child (C) in Bemba to tell her the names of the days of the week:

T: Lumbula amashina ayaba mumulungu uno
C: Monday, Tuesday, Wednesday . . . Thursday . . . Friday . . .
T: Walaba? (Have you forgotten?)
C: (nods)

T: Cisuma. Bushiku nshi ububalilapo lintu tatulafika pali cibili? (All right. Which day comes before Tuesday?)
C: Cimo (Monday).
T: Bushiku nshi tubalilapo ninshi tatulafika pali chine? (Which day comes before Thursday?)
C: Citatu (Wednesday).
T: Bushiku nshi tubalilapo ninshi tatulafika pacibelushi? (Which day comes before Saturday?)
C: Cisano (Friday)
T: Bushiku nshi tubalilapo ninshi tatulafika pa Mulungu? (Which day comes before Sunday?)
C: Cibelushi (Saturday)

Note that because of the context in which she has learned the information, the child attempts to respond to a Bemba question in English. But the psychologist's intuition suggests to her that the child may in fact know more about the topic in question in Bemba than in English. So she proceeds with the questions in Bemba, disregarding the child's use of English names for the days. As a result, the child is eventually able to show that her competence extends over Saturday and Sunday, which merely lie beyond the scope of her English vocabulary. In this situation it seems that the child's formal education has led her into a self-defeating attitude. She feels that in addressing a teacher-figure she should use the English names for the days. But in so doing she limits her scope for demonstrating her actual competence. The psychologist's sensitivity to the social and intellectual aspects of the child's language use enables her to steer her into a more successful medium.

My second story comes from Lusaka and concerns a conversation overheard between two children aged 8 and 9 years. The girl who is younger is Bemba-speaking by upbringing on the Copperbelt but now lives in a predominantly English-speaking family with the boy who has grown up using English at home. They both attend school in Lusaka where, of course, they are taught in English. The topic of their conversation is a very sticky bar of chocolate which they are sharing on the back seat of a car. The girl (M) speaks first:

M: "Look, D., my chocolate is sweating!"
D: "Chocolate doesn't sweat: it melts."
M: "But *this* chocolate is *sweating*! Look!"

On this occasion the girl refuses to accept the designation of her utterance as incorrect. Confident of the meaning of the word *sweating* she insists on drawing her friend's attention to the phenomenon that has caught her imagination. I wonder with some misgivings how many teachers would spare M's usage the red pen if she were to write it down, and recognise in her innovation the creative use of a new expression to communicate most successfully the author's idea.

In conclusion, I must emphasise that in neither of these last two sections have I proposed a definitive answer to the problems of language policy in Zambia.

The logical requirement that a language must embody constitutive rules certainly means that some verbal utterances will qualify for the designation incorrect. But at the present time in Zambia the nature of these rules at the levels of phonology and semantics cannot be specified in a precise and uncontroversial manner. The issue of prime importance seems not to be whether what is said or written conforms with some pre-established standards, but rather whether it succeeds as a communicative act. And in Zambia we have seen that for any given situation the words that will ensure this are likely to be different from those that express the same idea best in another situation. This is why this paper is not entitled "learning to say it right," but "learning to say it better." The definition of what this means, and the discovery of how to help children acquire this kind of articulacy, is the great challenge facing those who must determine a language policy for Zambian education.

NOTE

1. This paper was presented at the Zambian Language Group Conference on Language and Education in Zambia, held at the University of Zambia, Lusaka on August 31, 1975. It was reprinted from *Language & Education in Zambia,* by S. S. Chimuka, M. E. Kashoki, H. P. Africa, and R. Serpell, with the permission of the Institute of African Studies, University of Zambia, Lusaka, Zambia.

REFERENCES

Bereiter, C. et al. An academically oriented pre-school for culturally deprived cildren. In F. M. Hechinger (ed.), *Pre-School Education Today.* Doubleday, 1966, 105–137.

Ferguson, C. A. Diglossia. *Word.* 1959, 15, 325–340. Reprinted in P. Giglioli (ed.), *Language and Social Context.* Harmondsworth: Penguin, 1972.

Goffman, E. *The Presentation of Self in Everyday Lift.* Garden City, N.Y.: Doubleday, Anchor Books, 1959.

Gumperz, J. J. The speech community. In *International Encyclopaedia of the Social Sciences,* Macmillan, 1968, 381–386. Reprinted in P. Giglioli (ed.), *Language and Social Context.* Harmondsworth: Penguin, 1972.

Guthrie, M. *The Classificaiton of the Bantu Languages.* London: Oxford University Press, 1948.

Johnson, R. K., and Isoardi, D. Introduction to discrimination exercises for use with Papua New Guinea pupils learning English as a L2. In *Phoneme Discrimination.* Papua: Teaching Methods and Materials Centre, University of Papua New Guinea, 1971.

Kashoki, M. E. Town Bemba: A sketch of its main characteristics. *African Social Research.* 1972, 13, 161–186.

Kashoki, M. E. Language: A blue print for national integration. *Bulletin of the Zambia Language Group.* 1973, 2, 1.

Kashoki, M. E. Migration and language change: The introduction of town and country. *African Social Research.* 1975, 19, 707–729.

Kernan, C. M. Language behaviour in a black urban community. *Monographs of the Language Behaviour Resarch Laboratory* (Berkeley: University of California). 1971, 2.

Kubik, G. The Kachamba brothers' band: A study of neo-traditional music in Malawi. *Zambian Papers* (University of Zambia: Institute of African Studies). 1974, 9.

Labov, W. The logic of nonstandard English. *Georgetown Monographs on Language and Linguistics.* 1969, 22. Reprinted in P. Giglioli (ed.), *Language and Social Context.* Harmondsworth: Penguin, 1972.

Labov, W. Language characteristics—Blacks. In T. D. Horn (ed.), *Reading for the Disadvantaged: Problems of Linguistically Different Learners.* New York: Harcourt, Brace & World, 1970.

Melmed, P. J. Black English phonology: The question of reading intereference. *Monographs of the Language Behaviour Research Laboratory* (Berkeley: University of California). 1971, 1.

Mkilifi, M. H. A. Triglossia and Swahili-English bilingualism in Tanzania. *Language in Society.* 1972, 1, 197–213.

Mytton, G. *Listening, Looking and Learning:* Report on a national mass media audience survey in Zambia (1970–73). Lusaka: University of Zambia, Institute for African Studies, 1974.

Parkin, D. J. Language switching in Nairobi. In W. H. Whiteley (ed.), *Language in Kenya.* London: Oxford University Press, 1974, ch. 8.

Pride, J. B. Sociolinguistics. In J. Lyons (ed.), *New Horizons in Linguistics.* Harmondsworth: Penguin, 1970, ch. 16.

Searle, J. What is a speech act? In M. Black (ed.), *Philosophy in America.* Allen & Unwin and Cornell University Press, 1965, 221–239. Reprinted in P. Giglioli (ed.), *Language and Social Context.* Harmondsworth: Penguin, 1972.

Serpell, R. Selective attention and interference between first and second languages. *Communication* (Lusaka: University of Zambia, Institute for Social Research). 1968, 4.

Serpell, R. Chi-Nyanja comprehension by Lusaka school-children: A field experiment in second language learning. *Human Development Research Unit Reports* (University of Zambia: cyclostyled). 1970, 16.

Serpell, R. Learning to say it better: A challenge for Zambian education (unabridged original paper). In S. S. Chimuka, M. E. Kashoki, H. P. Africa, R. Serpell, *Language and Education in Zambia.* University of Zambia, 1978.

Turnbull, C. M. *The Lonely African.* London: Chatto & Windus, 1962.

7 ENGLISH IN CAMEROON: EDUCATION IN A MULTILINGUAL SOCIETY

Loreto Todd

HISTORICAL OVERVIEW

The first recorded contact between Europeans and Cameroonians was in 1472 when a Portuguese navigator, Fernaõ do Po, reached the Cameroon coast (see Figure 1). The Portuguese visit coincided with a migration of shrimps and so the Portuguese called the river that flowed into the bay at Douala, Rio dos Camaroẽs (River of Shrimps), and this is the name that occurs in 1500 in Juan de la Cosa's map of the area. At first, it was applied only to the river and the bay; then to Douala and the coastline; and gradually, by extension, to the entire country.

Between the fifteenth and nineteenth centuries Portuguese, Spanish, Dutch, French, and English trading ships visited Cameroon, but no permanent European establishment was built on the mainland until 1844 when the English Baptist Missionary Society established a school and a church at Bimbia (near Douala). In 1858, the Baptists, under Alfred Saker, established a permanent settlement at Victoria. From here, the English of the missionaries, many of whom were Krios[1] and manumitted slaves, began to spread to other parts of the country.

Between 1850 and 1884 the British were more or less in control of coastal Cameroon and, on several occasions, the coastal chiefs appealed to the British government and to Queen Victoria asking to have their country officially annexed.[2] By 1884 the British had decided to make their long-standing association with Cameroon official, but, while Edward Hyde Hewett was on his way to sign the treaties with the Cameroon chiefs, the Germans forestalled him and, on July 12, 1884, *Kamerun* became part of the German Empire.

Although German now became the official language of the country, a pidginised English was used by Germans and Cameroonians, especially on the

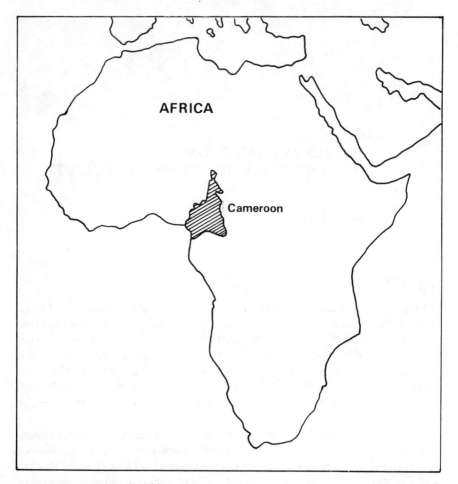

FIGURE 1   Position in Africa

large, coastal plantations which the Germans established and which drew their labour force from many different ethnic groups. Pidgin English was also well established in the noncoastal zones by the early years of the German rule. Rudin (1938, p. 358) claims that the Bamenda people used Pidgin in preference to German or any one vernacular language. And he adds:

> In the grasslands of North Western Cameroons there were so many dialects that the various tribes spoke and still do speak Pidgin English to make themselves understood by others in their periodic market days.

During World War One most of the Germans left Cameroon, and in 1919, as a result of the Treaty of Versailles signed on July 1, 1919, Cameroon was mandated by the League of Nations to France and Britain. Approximately four-fifths of the country went to France and was integrated into the system of direct government that applied to all of France's West African colonies and one-fifth went to Britain (see Figure 2) and was governed from Nigeria.

On January 1, 1960, the French sector became independent, and, as a result of a plebiscite held in the Anglophone[3] zone on February 22, 1961, the southern Cameroons and the République du Cameroun were reunited as the Federal Republic of Cameroon.[4] (The northern Cameroons voted to remain united to Nigeria.) English and French became the official languages of the new Federal Republic, with English as the language of administration and education in the Anglophone area and French fulfilling similar roles in the Francophone section. From 1961 onwards, the federal government committed itself to the establishment of full and widespread bilingualism. On May 20, 1972, a national

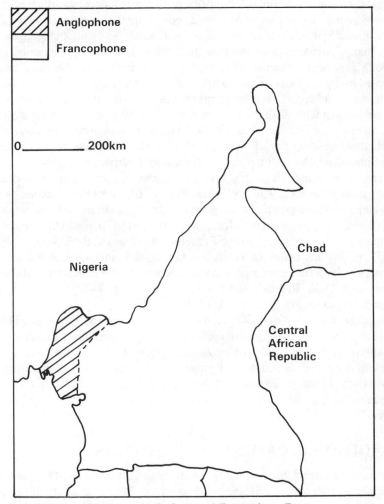

FIGURE 2   Cameroon: Anglophone and Francophone Zones

referendum was held on the proposed creation of a unitary, bilingual state. As a result of the referendum, the United Republic of Cameroon came into being on June 2, 1972, and the new unified state pledged itself to the promotion of national bilingualism.

THE MULTILINGUAL NATURE OF CAMEROON

Sub-Saharan Africa is one of the most multilingual areas of the world in terms of the ratio of population to languages, but it is not yet possible to be precise about how many distinct languages exist there. *Current Trends in Linguistics* (pp. 759–900) contains a checklist of over 5000 names that have been given to languages in the region, but it does not even attempt to answer such questions as: How often has one language been listed under more than one name? How often have mutually intelligible dialects been represented as distinct languages? Or how many languages have been omitted from the list? The impossibility of making precise statements about sub-Saharan multilingualism can be accounted for by two facts. First, no full-scale linguistic survey of the area has yet been made, and second, it is by no means easy even for linguists to know when we are dealing with distinct languages, related languages, or related dialects.

Cameroon, which is often called "Africa in miniature" because of its multiethnic makeup (see Figure 3) offers a clear example of sub-Saharan multilingualism. As with the rest of the region, however, it is still not certain exactly how many languages co-exist in the country. The semi-official publication, *Cameroon Today* (Debel 1977, p. 16) claims that there are "some two hundred ethnic groups" among the country's "seven million inhabitants." This figure is in agreement with Johnson's estimate (1970, p. 48) that "there are as many as 136 languages" in the Francophone zone and the Courades' claim (1977, p. 78) that there are 51 distinct languages in the Anglophone section. However, in a more comprehensive document, the *Linguistic Atlas of Cameroon,* Dieu, Renaud, and Sachmine (1976, pp. 1–32) assert that 300 distinct languages are spoken in Cameroon.

In addition to the 200 to 300 vernaculars, which may be classified as local, domestic, and oral, there are two official languages, French and English; one widely used but officially unrecognised lingua franca, Cameroon Pidgin English; a number of African languages of wider communication, including Basa, Bulu, Douala, Ewondo, Mungaka, and Hausa; and a nonindigenous language, Arabic, which is highly valued for its religious and cultural significance.

TRADITIONAL CAMEROON EDUCATION

Although the Portuguese first made contact with Cameroon in 1472, there was little obvious European influence on Cameroon culture[5] until the nineteenth century when permanent settlements began to be established by missionaries and traders on the coast. The Nigerian novelist, Chinua Achebe, has frequently

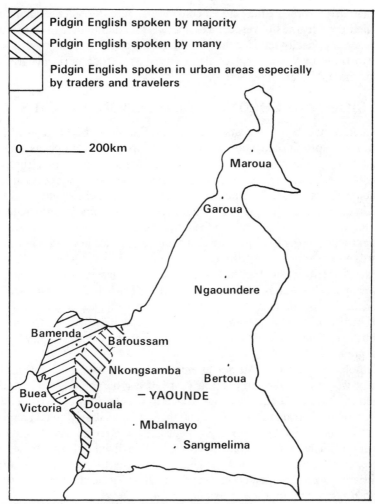

Pidgin English spoken by majority

Pidgin English spoken by many

Pidgin English spoken in urban areas especially by traders and travelers

0 ———— 200km

Maroua

Garoua

Ngaoundere

Bamenda
Bafoussam

Nkongsamba

Bertoua

Buea
Victoria   Douala

− YAOUNDE

· Mbalmayo

· Sangmelima

FIGURE 3   Areas Where Pidgin English is Spoken

insisted that "culture" did not arrive in Africa with the white man and the same is certainly true of education. Traditional Cameroon education was oral and exemplary. By means of myths and folktales,[6] children were taught the history, religion, and philosophy of their people; by means of proverbs and aphorisms, the value of cooperation was stressed and people were reminded that "when a hand rubs the foot, the foot also rubs the hand" and that "a man who walks alone will fall into error"; by means of worksongs, manual labour was transformed into an enjoyable communal activity, and many types of work, such as clearing the land or building a house, were rhythmically systematised; in songs and dances, legends were relived and traditions reinforced; by means of instruction and demonstration, girls were taught to grow and cook food, to look after the very old and the very young, and to make simple garments, while boys learned to hunt and fish, to prepare the land for cultivation, and to protect the family. Both girls and boys learned to respect age and wisdom and to delight in life. Such education was ideally suited to the traditional way of life, and, although it is now being modified by Western values, it has survived in Africa and in all parts of the world where Africans have settled.

MISSION AND COLONIAL EDUCATION POLICIES

Although contact between Cameroonians and Europeans began in the fifteenth century, no specific education policy was adopted by Europeans until the middle of the nineteenth century.[7] The English Baptists were the first Europeans to establish schools on the Cameroon mainland. The education provided by the missionaries was gospel-oriented and the teaching of literacy was meant as a prelude to teaching Africans to read the Bible and to promote Christianity. At first, the Baptists used English as the chief medium in their schools, but they were extremely eager to acquire at least some of the local languages as a means towards a more rapid evangelisation of Cameroon. By 1884 when the Germans annexed Cameroon, the Baptists had established 24 mission stations, each with a vernacular school, and in addition, they had five English-medium schools. The American Presbyterians who worked in the less multilingual east of the country used both English and Bulu in their missionising activities. They had been firmly established in the southeast for just over ten years by the time of the German annexation.

Catholic missionaries did not attempt to evangelise Cameroon until the country was under German control. In 1890 a group of German Catholics arrived in Douala. Their immediate concern was the spiritual welfare of the workers on the German plantations, and they found that they could communicate by means of German and Pidgin English, the preferred lingua franca of the plantations.[8] The early Catholic missionaries attempted to learn the vernaculars, especially Douala, Ewondo, and Basa, into which they translated a number of Christian texts. Eventually, however, they found it easier to concentrate on Pidgin English and, to a lesser extent, on German.

With the establishment of German authority, the English Baptists handed over their mission lands and institutions to the German-speaking Basel missionaries who selected two indigenous languages, Douala and Mungaka, as their main instruments of evangelisation. The American Presbyterians were allowed to remain in Kamerun when they agreed to substitute German for English in all their activities. And the Catholic missionaries, as we have seen, were German-speakers who, from their earliest days in Cameroon, used German and Pidgin English.

For a time, the German administration permitted the use of vernacular languages in education, but, as the Douala language began to spread, the German government decided to curb the growing influence of the Douala people. Accordingly, in 1907, Governor Seitz announced that standard German was to be the main medium of instruction in all schools in Kamerun. He

TABLE 1

Run by	Schools	Number of Pupils
Government	4	833
Government	1 (Muslim)	(figures not available)
Baptists	57	3,151
Basel	319	17,833
Americans	97	6,545
Catholics[9]	151	12,532
	629	40,894

was prepared to admit the use of a vernacular language within its own speech community, but, on the whole, vernacular education was discouraged. At this time only primary, trade, and seminary schools existed in the country, all post-primary education being provided in Germany. Table 1 indicates the nature and extent of education within Cameroon before the outbreak of the First World War. Thus, at the end of Germany's period of colonisation, only a small fraction of Cameroon's population was being educated. A few spoke German well, many had picked up enough German for simple, basic communication, but the majority of the population still spoke only the vernaculars or Pidgin English.

In the Francophone zone, as of 1921, French was to be the sole medium of instruction. Teachers were forbidden to use either the vernaculars or Pidgin English and were urged to discourage such usage among their pupils. Post-primary education was given in French[10] and, until 1960, when Francophone Cameroun became independent, the textbooks used in Cameroon schools were identical to those used in France. Statistics for the period are not readily available, but Table 2 gives an estimate of the number of Cameroonians receiving education in the Francophone zone in 1958. In addition, there were 1050 students receiving tertiary education abroad.

TABLE 2

Type of Institution	Percentage of School-Age Children Receiving Education
Primary Schools	69.2
Secondary Schools	1.5
Technical Schools	0.6
University	(not opened until 1962)

Thus, under French colonial rule, although Arabic-medium schools were permitted in the Muslim north, vernacular education ceased in the Francophone zone. French became the only written language of the area, and the vernaculars were restricted to oral communication outside the field of education. The French attitude toward the vernaculars in Cameroon was the result of a desire to encourage the use of standard metropolitan French throughout the colonies. They believed that a standard metropolitan French was the most suitable medium for Western education and French culture.

The British had a different language policy. Not only did they tolerate Pidgin English in the police force, in missions, and on plantations, but they were eager to promote and expand vernacular education. Throughout Nigeria and the Cameroons it was recommended that the vernacular language of the village, town, or region was to be the chief medium of instruction for the first four years of primary school education. English was then to be taught and used during the next four years. It would be inaccurate to claim that vernacular education was uncommon during the British colonial period, but it must be admitted that a variety of English was often used even in the first year of primary education. The choice of English in the classroom resulted from three factors: first, the high prestige accorded to English by the people, especially the teachers; second, the knowledge that many children did not stay at school more than three or four years; and third, the available teachers did not always speak the language of the area in which they were employed.

Throughout the period 1921–1960 vernacular education in the Anglophone zone declined. In 1935, for example, 89.3 percent of the children receiving primary education were being taught in vernacular schools. By 1959 this percentage had fallen to 1 percent, and in 1960 vernacular education was abandoned. It is perhaps worth stressing that the decline in vernacular education was due more to the influence of Cameroonians than to that of the British. The final disbanding of vernacular schools was due to a Buea Ministerial decree, dated September 27, 1958, and drawn up by Cameroonians. The crucial sentence in the decree reads:

English is to be the medium of instruction in Primary Schools and all the text books are to be in English.

During the early period of the British rule, secondary education was available to Cameroonians in Nigeria and three secondary schools were opened in Anglophone Cameroon between 1938 and 1955. These were a Catholic school for boys at Sasse in 1938, a Protestant school for boys at Bali in 1948,[11] and a Catholic school for girls at Okoyong in 1955. Training colleges were also inaugurated. Between 1925 and 1959, eleven colleges were opened, and by 1959, these provided some teacher training for 664 Cameroonians. In 1952, a technical school was opened with 38 students; this number had increased to 173 by 1959.

In Anglophone Cameroon post-primary institutions were run by missionaries and staffed largely by expatriates. English was the sole medium of instruction in them, and many Cameroonians insist that the quality of the English acquired at this period was better than at any time since.

POST-COLONIAL EDUCATION POLICIES

Francophone Cameroun became independent in 1960 and, just over a year later, the southern Cameroons voted to be reunited with the Francophone zone. The new government was anxious to extend education and to establish a language policy that would be acceptable to both sections of the federated state and of value to the country as a whole. It therefore adopted French and English as the official languages of the state. This was not because it undervalued local languages or local culture. The selection was based on practical expedience. No single vernacular could be selected as a language of national unity, and it was neither possible nor desirable to standardise and use all the Cameroonian mother tongues. A bilingual approach was also adopted towards education. From nursery schools upwards all education was to be in either French or English, with bilingualism in these two official languages being encouraged and being specifically catered for in a number of secondary schools and in the university.

The policy adopted was meant to extend education, making it available to all Cameroonians. When the country became independent "only 420,000 children were attending primary school" (Debel, 1977, p. 66). Now, less than 20 years later, approximately 90 percent of all children receive some education, and the percentage is as high as 99 percent in the Douala area.[12]

THE TEACHING OF ENGLISH
IN THE FRANCOPHONE ZONE

When the French took over the government of part of Cameroon, they attempted to impose standard French as the medium of instruction throughout the education system and as the sole official language for administrative purposes. Comparatively few Cameroonians in the Francophone zone received any post-primary education (even in 1958 the figure was as low as 1.5 percent of the children of school age) but those who did, attained a relatively high standard of French and some of them had also a reading knowledge of English.

As soon as East and West Cameroon were reunited, however, the teaching of English became an essential part of the curriculum in all secondary schools. In years 1 and 2, students received between 3½ and 5 hours of English each week. This was reduced to a maximum of 3 hours for students preparing for the BEPC (Brevet d'Études du Premier Cycle), but was subsequently increased to 5 or more hours a week for those students studying for the baccalauréat.

Two main criticisms were levelled against this system. First, the way English was taught differed in no fundamental respect from the way it was taught in France. The main emphases were on the written skills—reading, writing, and translation—and little attention was paid to the more immediately useful skills of talking and listening with understanding. The second criticism was that the bilingual process began too late. Cameroonians like Fonlon (1963) urged that bilingual training should begin early, possibly in the first year of primary school. Such views were discussed, praised, and condemned, but the policy advocated by Fonlon was not officially sanctioned until 1972.

Immediately after the creation of a unitary state in May 1972, however, there was a government pledge to encourage the teaching of English in primary school and a commission on the introduction of English into Francophone primary schools was held in June 1973. Despite a sincere desire to attain the early bilingualism advocated by the ministry of education, it was realised that the introduction of a second official language in primary school posed serious problems. The members of the commission felt that it was essential for the children to attain full proficiency in French before being confronted with English. There were fears that a too-early exposure to English (which would be a third or even fourth language for many of the children) might impose an intolerable learning burden and might result in failure to keep different language systems distinct. On the other hand, the commission did not want to delay the teaching of English too long and thus fail to take advantage of young children's linguistic capabilities.

It was eventually decided that Francophone children should begin to learn English from their first year in primary school. For a three-year period, 2½ hours a week for the 30 weeks of the school year would be devoted to English. It was estimated that after such exposure to English, the children would have mastered the basic grammar and a working knowledge of Cameroon's second official language.[13]

Despite government wishes and commission recommendations, however, it is by no means easy to introduce English into all Francophone primary schools. Qualified teachers are not always available, and many headmasters feel that the language burden being placed on children is too great. Nevertheless, it is still official policy to pursue and extend bilingualism, and the University of Cameroon is taking a keen interest in the debate. In November 1975, a seminar on bilingualism held there reaffirmed the necessity for including English in the primary school curriculum. The seminar concluded that bilingualism (in the two official languages) was essential to the well-balanced Cameroonian citizen, and it stressed the belief that three years of English in primary school would enable most Francophones to use English in their daily lives—enable them, that is, to converse with Anglophones, to listen to the radio, to read newspapers, and to write simple letters. The importance of introducing bilingualism in primary schools becomes clearer when it is remembered that fewer than 25 percent of children receiving primary education will go on to secondary schools.

It is still too early to claim either success or failure of the plans to encourage bilingualism in Francophone Cameroon by introducing English in primary school. It is true that there is a strong desire among young people to learn English. Many who did not have the opportunity at school attend evening classes or try to learn English by radio. It is also true that employment opportunities are greater for bilinguals than for monolinguals and that bilingual civil servants can earn more than their monolingual colleagues. Nevertheless, it is still possible for Francophones to get on very well without English. Theoretically, all documents are issued in both languages, but the practice rarely lives up to the theory. Many decrees, for example, carry the footnote: "To be published in English and French throughout the Republic, the French text only to be legally binding"; and all British and American films are dubbed in French. Thus French remains the chief language of government and of entertainment, and the onus of bilingualism falls mainly on the Anglophones who make up only one-fifth of the population.

THE TEACHING OF ENGLISH
IN THE ANGLOPHONE ZONE

Since 1960, all teaching in Anglophone schools is theoretically[14] through the medium of English,[15] and the available statistics certainly prove that there has been a dramatic increase in the number of children receiving education in the Anglophone sector. School attendance increased from approximately 64,000 (that is, 27 percent of the children of school age) in 1959 to 210,000 (that is, about 70 percent) in 1971. The academic year 1970–1971 seems to have seen a peak in the percentage of children attending school; the best available estimate for 1978–1979 is that approximately 65 percent of school-age children are being educated. Perhaps as significant as the overall increase in school attendance is the improved position of girls. In 1960, only 25 percent of the school population was made up of girls but this had increased to 42 percent in 1970 and to an estimated 45 percent in 1978–1979. Table 3 provides a graphic illustration of the increase in education in the 12 years between independence

TABLE 3

Year	Primary Schools		Secondary Schools		Teacher's TC		Technical Educ.	
	Schools	Pupils	Schools	Pupils	Coll.	Pupils	Coll.	Pupils
1960	470	73,400	?	?	?	?	1	173
1962	590	95,159	6	903	8	925	?	?
1964	686	116,852	12	1658	12	1374	?	?
1966	748	163,720	15	3388	12	1875	6	1428
1968	764	183,402	15	4531	12	2037	9	1788
1970	761	210,243	19	5521	12	2281	14	3199
1972	691	188,974	21	6766	12	1423	17	3619

and integration into a unified state.[16] Thus, in 1972, 200,782 children out of an estimated school-age population of approximately 286,000 were being educated.[17]

In Anglophone Cameroon, in the majority of educational institutions from primary school to A-level college, education is meant to be through the medium of standard British English, although it is the intention of the government to introduce bilingual education into primary schools, paralleling the bilingual programme described for the Francophone zone in the preceding section.

THE VARIETIES OF ENGLISH IN CAMEROON

No one familiar with the multifaceted variation that occurs in monolingual communities—variation in terms of such parameters as region and class, age and education, loyalties and aspiration—will be surprised to learn that there is an almost infinite set of English varieties in Cameroon.

First, no Cameroonian acquires standard English as a first or only language. Therefore all varieties of Cameroon English are influenced by the mother tongues of their speakers. This is most apparent in the pronunciation of English. Vowel contrasts in all varieties of Cameroon English are fewer than in RP largely because there are fewer vocalic contrasts in Cameroon languages. Many Cameroon vernaculars[18] have a seven-vowel system such as shown in Figure 4 with varying numbers of diphthongs and/or triphthongs. Cameroon Pidgin also has this type of vowel system and thus the influence from both the mother tongues and Pidgin reinforce the tendency to simplify the vocalic contrasts found in British English. Thus, few Cameroonians consistently distinguish between /i/ and /ɪ/[19] as in *leave* and *live,* between /ɔ/ and /ɒ/ as in *caught* and *cot,* or between /ɑ/ and /æ/ as in *bark* and *back.* Central vowels and centring diphthongs are also avoided with the result that *church* becomes either /tʃɔs/

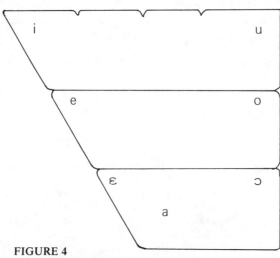

FIGURE 4

or /tʃes/ depending on the extent of one's education, and words like *beer* and *chair* are realised as /bia/ and /tʃia~tʃe/. Consonants too are modified. In the past, many Cameroonians had trouble with such consonantal clusters as *str*, *spl*, and *scr* and with distinguishing between the continuants /l/ and /ɹ/, but young speakers no longer seem to experience these difficulties. It is still true, however, that the articulatory setting tends to favour a dental rather than an alveolar realisation of /t, d, ɹ, l, s, z/ and that /θ/ and /ð/ are extremely rare.

It is not only at the level of phonology that the influence from the mother tongues appears. It can also be seen in vocabulary, in the use of local items for food, clothing, and government, for example:

ashu	—	a type of paste (similar to peanut butter in texture)
mbɔnga	—	a type of flat fish
abada	—	local suit for a man
danʃiki	—	local shirt
fɔn	—	chief
ntʃinda	—	messenger of the chief

in calques, such as:

man han	—	right
wuman han	—	left
tai fes	—	frown

in syntax, such as the following structures:

Take it go.   Bring it come.

and also in the use of such formulaic utterances as:

Go well.   Come well.
Stay well.

Second, there is a strong and growing influence from French on certain types of Cameroon English.[20] This is most obvious in the speech of Anglophones who live in a Francophone area and from which community I collected the following sentences:

After that we made a nice sorti and we amused ourselves fine
Come, arrosez. You must drink some wine or some /ɔdine/ (i.e., bière ordinaire)
I'm just coming from the Conseil d'Administration where I have been following up my dossier.

And *third,* the influence of Pidgin on Cameroon English could hardly be exaggerated. A *Sociolinguistic Survey of Cameroon* (carried out by the University of Yaoundé and not yet published) suggests that between 70 percent and 95 percent of urban Anglophones speak Pidgin and that up to 60 percent of urban Francophones have a working knowledge of the language. As with the mother tongues, the influence from Pidgin is all-pervasive. Its most obvious influence can be seen in the nonstandard use of such words as:

bush	— undergrowth, wild, uncultivated
foot	— foot, leg, trouser-leg
hear	— understand
skin	— body
sweet	— tasty (The soup is very sweet.)
whiteman	— European, Indian

Depending on the education of the speaker, it can have varying degrees of influence on the syntax of the speaker. For example, even the most highly educated Anglophones tend to use *not so?* as a universal tag:

He got married, not so?

and the *not so?* is clearly influenced by Pidgin's *no bi so?*

i bin mari, no bi so?

I have written as if mother-tongue-influenced English, French-influenced English, and Pidgin-influenced English were discrete varieties. To suggest that such divisions exist is, however, a gross oversimplification, because each of these varieties influences the other and each is itself a conglomerate of overlapping variants. In addition, most speakers are capable of modifying their performance to suit the circumstances (a wedding or a funeral, a party or a quarrel) and to suit the linguistic competence of their addressees. Cameroonians have had to learn to manipulate languages—vernaculars, and trade and official languages. They have discovered that the need to communicate often involves moulding and modifying their languages. And it is because of the need to communicate that all varieties of Cameroon English are, or can easily become, mutually intelligible. As Uriel Weinreich puts it (1964, p. viii):

> Two speakers who, when first brought together, had found their respective dialects mutually unintelligible, may in a few hours or a few days discover the clues to unimpeded intercourse. If cooperation is a pressing necessity every one will soon learn enough of the other man's language to establish communication.

THE ROLE OF PIDGIN ENGLISH IN EDUCATION

It is undoubtedly true that Pidgin English is the most widely used language in Cameroon.[21] It is also true that it is occasionally and increasingly being used by teachers in urban communities in the Anglophone zone as the only means of communicating effectively with their pupils. In view of these facts it seems reasonable to examine its possible role in education.

Despite the widespread use of Pidgin English in Cameroon, only Kisob (1963) has seriously suggested that it should be made an official language, or at least taught and emphasised as a lingua franca. Most frequently it is ignored or criticised because of its influence on standard English (Ngijol, 1964) or positively excluded from the classroom. And yet, in many ways Pidgin English is a Cameroon language.[22] It is structurally close to the vernaculars which are also reflected in its calques, idioms, and metaphors. It is the only language in Cameroon that is not associated with a particular tribe, region, or religion, or indeed, with a specific colonial government. It is often acquired by children in the Anglophone zone and in urban communities throughout Cameroon as one of their first languages. It has long been used as a vehicle for Cameroon culture and has been found perfectly adequate to the expression of Christian doctrine (spoken and written), parliamentary proceedings, and financial negotiations. In addition, it is a shared lingua franca with Cameroon's West African neighbours.[23] In view of all these positive factors, Pidgin warrants special attention as a possible language of education. And there is at least one negative reason which can be offered in support of its adoption. It has a marked influence on the English of Cameroon, in terms of phonology, lexis, and syntax. To have an education system that ignores such an influence is to give children less than they have a right to, by failing to make them aware of the different patterning of English and Pidgin.

There would be few linguistic or financial problems connected with the adoption of Cameroon Pidgin as a language of education, but there is one valid reason against its use in education and that is the attitude of the people. Most Cameroonians use and delight in Pidgin. They find it essential in travelling and trading, and it is, perhaps more than any other language, the vehicle for jokes, witticisms, and proverbial wisdom. But few Cameroonians would accept its formalised use in schools or colleges. If pressed on the subject, they admit that it is in no way deficient, but they feel that to use Pidgin or any other nonstandardised language could be educationally limiting. To most Cameroonians it seems foolish to tamper with an educational system that has already proved its worth, or to risk the quality of their children's education for the sake of a liberal experiment.

THE FUTURE OF ENGLISH IN CAMEROON

If any language other than English were in competition with French in Cameroon, it is likely that it would gradually disappear. And even English has suffered in that the onus of bilingualism has fallen on Anglophones, and their English, already under pressure from the vernaculars and Pidgin English, has been weakened. Nevertheless, English is important to Cameroon. It is the official language of Nigeria, Cameroon's most influential neighbour, and is rapidly becoming the world's most useful lingua franca. In addition, the Cameroon government seems determined to encourage and promote bilingualism. It would apear, therefore, that English will continue to be used and encouraged in Cameroon, but it seems to me that it will probably become like French in Nigeria—a valued but foreign language.

EXAMPLES OF CAMEROON ENGLISH

Samples of Standard English

1. A poem by a Francophone

In the beginning
The world was melancholy
For there was no music

And the Word created the word
And offered it
In love
To man

And man
Took the word
And set it to music

Since then
Since
Man expresses
The seasons of his soul
Through music

Ernest Alima

2. Part of a study of Noni, a Cameroon vernacular

Cameroonian languages, for the most part, have no written grammars; the thought patterns of the people have never been explored. This is the main obstacle to the sudy of native languages. For years the need has been felt by both Cameroonians and non-Cameroonians for grammars of native languages, and this has given rise to the language studies now mushrooming all over the country. *Noni Language Simplified* is an attempt by a non-linguist to contribute to these studies.

Engelbert Kofon

Standard English with Cameroonianisms

1. Speech
   This your Elizabeth Taylor, she's fine, a beautiful somebody but her legs are too small (i.e., thin) for her skin (i.e., body).
2. Letter
   I have not yet succeeded to see you but I will come to your office by nine o'clock and hope to meet you.

Extract from a Letter in English and Pidgin

I hope you're back from your short visit. I couldn't write at once because I was expecting to receive the post card you promised sending and of course because you were out of station.

How for your family? I think say all dem dey fine. Any time we you de write for them make you salute them fine for me. How for your short walker (i.e., visit)? You been see all your people well? How for you sef? You trong fine?

Sample of Cameroon Pidgin English

a wan tɛl yu hau wi bin gɛt dat ples fɔ Fontem. so di chif wei i bin
I want to tell you how we got that place in Fontem. So the chief who was the

fɔs bi, dɛm kɔl i sei Sumingi, i bin bi na hɔntaman. So wɛn i kɔmɔt
first (chief), they called him Sumingi, he was a hunter. So when he came

dat sai fɔ nia Mamfe i go insai bush fɔ go hɔnt. i kam bak wan dei,
to a place near Mamfe he went into the forest to hunt. He returned one day,

i bring plenti pipu kam si sei di ples fain. Dɛn dɛm
bringing lots of people to show them that the place was lovely. Then they

put dɛm smɔl haus fɔ dei. Dɛm kam bak tɔk fɔ dɛm kɔntri pipu
built little houses there. They returned home to tell their countrymen

sei dɛm dɔng gɛt sɔm ples i fain.
that they had found a place which was really nice.

NOTES

1. Between 1845 and 1887 there were 75 Protestant missionaries in southern Cameroon. Of these, 27 were British, 18 were Krios from Sierra Leone, 4 were Krio-speakers from Fernando Po, 6 were directly connected with Jamaica and the West Indies; the remaining 20 were Cameroonians. According to missionary archives (summarised in Gwei, 1966) English was used for preaching and teaching in the Victoria region, but quoted samples of the speech of the early non-British Christians certainly seem to be pidginised. Lewis (n.d.) who arrived in Cameroon as a missionary in 1884 gives such examples as: *Dat'll teach you not to lemme toot* (i.e., tote) *you tomorrow, ma beauty boy* (p. 54) and *Massa, what for you talk dem words about de Holy Spirit dis morning?* (p. 55).

2. Typical of such requests is the following letter written to Queen Victoria by King Akwa of Douala on August 7, 1879:

Dearest Madam,

We your servants have join together and thoughts it better to write you a nice loving letter which will tell you all about our wishes. We wish to have your laws in our towns. We wish to have every fashioned altered, also we will do according to your consul's word. Plenty wars here in our country. Plenty murder and idol worshippers. Perhaps these lines of our writing will look to you as an idle tale.

We have spoken to the English consul plenty times about an English government here. We never have answer from you, so we wish to write you ourselves.

When we heard about Calabar river, how they have all English laws in their towns, and how they have put away all their superstitions, on, we shall be very glad to be like Calabar now.

(Foreign Office Papers, 403/18, Letter 1)

3. Although I use the terms Anglophone and Francophone to designate the zones previously governed by Britain and France, the terms are, in fact, misleading. I do not wish to suggest that all or most of the population can speak English or French. Such a suggestion would be grossly inaccurate. It is impossible to give precise figures regarding the proportion of the population fluent in one or both of these languages but, even though French and English are the official languages of the country and used for government, law, education, medicine, and international affairs, they are spoken well by only a minority of Cameroonians.

4. The name of the country has been spelled differently by the various European governments that have ruled there. The Germans called it *Kamerun,* the French *Cameroun,* and the English *The Cameroons.* The official policy is that the country be referred to as Cameroun in French documents and Cameroon in English ones.

5. The culture of the Middle East seems to have exerted an influence on the northern parts of Cameroon from perhaps as early as the ninth century. Certainly, the Kanem Bornu Empire had spread as far south as the Cameroon grasslands by the eleventh century. However, since our main concern in this chapter is with English in Education it would be neither useful nor relevant to consider the influence of Islam on Cameroon.

6. Perhaps it will be of value to paraphrase a story which occurs all over Cameroon and which teaches children that cooperation is important but that common-sense may be vital to survival.

Once, there was a famine throughout the country and none of the animals could find anything to eat. The strong leopard searched all day and found nothing. The wise goat looked everywhere but always came home hungry. And the cunning tortoise sat quietly and thought of ways of satisfying his needs. At last he had an idea. He called Leopard and Goat and said: "When we hunt alone, we are unsuccessful. Let us hunt together and soon we shall have meat."

They all agreed. Next morning at dawn they started off together. Leopard went to the right, Goat to the left and Tortoise stayed behind. Suddenly, Tortoise saw a deer. He tucked in his head and legs and rolled like a stone towards it. The deer turned to the left and Goat charged. In terror the deer fled to the left and did not even see Leopard's open mouth.

Now they had meat, more meat than they had seen for a long time. Leopard turned to Goat saying: "Goat, you are everywhere renowned for your wisdom, you divide the meat." Goat looked at the deer and divided it into three equal amounts. Leopard looked at his share and was furious. He lifted his paw and struck Goat. Goat too now lay dead. Leopard turned to Tortoise saying: "Tortoise, why don't you divide the meat." Tortoise looked at the meat and looked at the leopard. He took one tiny piece of the deer's tail and pushed all the rest over to Leopard.

As they sat quietly eating, Leopard asked Tortoise: "My friend when did you learn to divide meat so well?" Tortoise pointed to Goat and said: "When I looked at his dead body."

7. It is probable that some Cameroonians had earlier been taken to Europe so that they might learn the European language and so be of greater help as interpreters on trading missions between Europe and Cameroon.

8. The plantations recruited workers from many parts of Cameroon and from Togo and Dahomey, and from the beginning Pidgin English was their lingua franca. In Yaoundé in 1975 I recorded the story of an old Ewondo who spoke only Ewondo and Pidgin. He had learned his Pidgin as a child on a banana plantation at Bota, near Victoria, prior to 1910 when his family returned to Yaoundé.

9. All the figures are based on Keller's *The History of the Presbyterian Church in West Cameroon* (1969). According to Monsignor Franz Hennemann in *Werden und Wirken eines Afrika-missionars,* however, there were 300 Catholic schools teaching 29,259 children by the time the last Catholic missionaries left in May 1916.

10. The first secondary school apart from seminaries in Francophone Cameroun was opened in Douala in 1940.

11. Sasse boys learned Latin while Bali boys learned French. Thus, at the time of reunification, ex-Bali students had an advantage in terms of federal employment.

12. The Muslim north has the lowest percentage of school-age children in full-time education, i.e., approximately 34 percent. Some Muslim schools in the north have also been permitted to use Arabic and French as the mediums of instruction.

13. It is worth stressing that the commission refused to sanction the use of Pidgin English in education and insisted on the teaching of standard British English and not a bastardised variety.

14. According to several Anglophone teachers that I have interviewed, it is no longer possible to use standard English as a medium of instruction in the first year of primary school. In the words of Mrs. Mary Mbunwe (a primary schoolteacher for 20 years): "For the first six months I have to use Pidgin. If I didn't, the children would not understand *one word.* Only after I have trained them in Pidgin can I begin to use proper English." (October 1979)

15. A different situation prevails in the Bilingual School established in Man O' War Bay (near Victoria) in 1963 and transferred to Buea in 1970. This school (like its counterparts in Douala and Yaoundé) takes an equal number of Anglophone and Francophone students and, for the first two

years of their secondary school education these students are taught through the medium of their first foreign language. In addition, they are taught the second foreign language for ten hours a week. By the third year, students are expected to be sufficiently bilingual to attend classes in either English or French.

16. The academic year 1972–1973 marked the first year of a centralised educational system and the start of a new phase of education marked by Francophone management from Yaoundé. It is not yet possible to quantify or evaluate the consequences of the new system, but many teachers have assured me that the standard of English is deteriorating.

17. The projected number of children of school age for 1980 is 400,000.

18. This statement is equally true of languages in both the Anglophone and the Francophone zones. The vowel chart illustrated, for example, could be used in a description of Lamso (a language from the northwest) and Bulu (a language from the southeast).

19. Failure to distinguish between such phonemes can also have an effect on spelling. A common Cameroonian mistake is *cleanic* for *clinic*.

20. Francophones who have a good command of French prefer to speak French and they do not intersperse their French with English. The Francophones who have studied English seriously tend to speak it very well and although they speak with a markedly French accent their English tends to be close to standard English in idiom and syntax.

21. Pidgin English is used on plantations, on work-sites, in church, in the market, in playgrounds, and in pubs, by preachers and by politicians. It is also the lingua franca of prisons, the armed forces, the police force, and the most commonly heard language in the law courts. See Figure 3.

22. It is only fair to state that Pidgin is no more homogeneous than any other oral language. It too shows considerable variation in terms of the region, age, education, and purpose of the speaker.

23. There has been much debate regarding the mutual intelligibility of West African pidgins and creoles. Undoubtedly, regional differences occur but there is enough common ground for these varieties to be made inter-intelligible. In October 1979 I played a tape-recording of a Cameroon folktale to a Nigerian (Igbo), a Togolese woman (educated in Ghana), and a Sierra Leonean woman. They all understood it and were immediately able to suggest in which ways Cameroon Pidgin differed from the variety they had learned.

REFERENCES

Courade, C., and G. Courade. Education in Anglophone Cameroon. Youandé: National Geographic Centre, 1977.

Debel, Anne. *Cameroon Today,* éditions j.a. Tours, 1977.

Dieu, M., Renaud, P., and Sachmine, M. L'atlas linguistique du Cameroun. *Bulletin de l'Alcam* (ONAREST, Yaoundé), 1976.

Fonlon, B. A case for early bilingualism. *Abbia* (Youandé), 1963, 4.

Gwei, S. N. *History of the British Baptist Mission in Cameroon.* Unpublished B.D. thesis, Ruschlikon-Zurich, 1966.

Johnson, W. R. *The Cameroon Federation,* Princeton: Princeton University Press, 1970.

Keller, W. (ed.). *The History of the Presbyterian Church In West Cameroon.* Prebook, Victoria, Cameroon, 1969.

Kisob, J. A. A live language: "Pidgin English," *Abbia 1,* Yaoundé, 1963.

Lewis, Thomas. *These Seventy Years: An Autobiography by Thomas Lewis, Missionary in Cameroon and Congo 1883–1923.* London: The Carey Press, n.d.

Ngijol, P. Nécessité d'une langue nationale,' *Abbia 7,* Yaoundé, 1964.

Rudin, Harry. *Germans in the Cameroons.* New Haven: Yale University Press, 1938.

Weinreich, Uriel. *Languages in Contact.* The Hague: Mouton and Co., 1964.

Section **3**

SECOND
OR FOREIGN LANGUAGE?

8   *INDIAN ENGLISH*

Sisir Kumar Das

As English has increasingly come into worldwide use, there is an acute need for more information on the language of a particular region and the ways in which it is used. As India is growing in importance not merely within the English-speaking world, but in the world as a whole, it becomes increasingly important to understand as precisely as possible the ways in which Indian English is different from the Englishes used elsewhere. Moreover, there is the interest to linguistics of studying a form of language transported a great distance from the areas to which it had previously belonged.

It is obvious that no one is personally acquainted with more than a few of the twelve million users of English in India, and in addition to this, English in India has nearly two centuries of usage to record. Therefore, the term Indian English is and has to be used rather loosely. One may legitimately ask if it has a set of coherent and homogeneous linguistic systems and if it is describable as the speech of an identifiable social group. Besides, one can have several categories of Indian English—English used by the student community of India in different regions, several varieties of English used by teachers of different institutions, English used for administrative purposes in India, and the innumerable varieties of English used by creative writers, journalists, scholars, businessmen, and other professionals. One can have also different varieties of English used in the north, south, east, and west of India. Every variety has its own spatiocultural features.

As far as I know, there has been no comprehensive study of any of these varieties. Papers have been published and seminars have been organized[1] on Indian English, but the explicitness, systematicness, and objectivity one expects from linguistic description have not been achieved. Therefore, conclusions arrived at are tentative rather than definite; and many of these conclusions are derived from purely subjective and severely restricted surveys. I include my paper also within this category. The only redeeming feature is the widening interest in sociolinguistic studies relating to various aspects of English used in India. In this paper, the scope of which is naturally limited, I do not want to give the impression that what is omitted is unimportant; and I can discuss no more than a very limited aspect of the use of English in India.

There are a large number of different Indian Englishes; indeed, much of the confusion regarding the discussion of Indian English stems from the false assumption that there is only one Indian English used by all users of English in India. Obviously this is an oversimplification. It is possible to divide Indian English into three broad categories: higher, intermediate, and lower. At one end of this cline we have a debased variety of Indian English, while at the other end we have forms almost entirely free from unusual features and immediately intelligible over the whole of the English-speaking world. All the three varieties deserve serious academic attention, but till today a complete description of any of these varieties has not been made possible. The first category is represented by writers like M. K. Gandhi, Jawahar Lal Nehru, C. R. Das, R. K. Narayan, Nirod Chaudhuri, and Raja Rao, who handle the English language skillfully and are acceptable throughout the English-speaking world. The last category includes speakers of English who are semi-literate or illiterate persons engaged in various kinds of professions. But the largest number of people using English belong to the intermediate category, most of whom have received a university education and have been taught English at the university level. Therefore, this variety of English may be called educated Indian English. I shall restrict myself to this variety of English because it is spoken and written by millions of Indians and on this variety depends the future of English in India.

To characterize the educated variety of Indian English the first problem is to isolate it from other kinds of English by selecting those elements that are distinctively Indian. But this is more difficult than is commonly supposed; it is difficult to separate educated Indian English from general English or standard English, because the influence of standard English on Indian English is very strong, especially on those users who have most contact with and at the same time are most influenced by the norms of standard English. On educated Indians the influence of British English has been continuous; newspapers, radio, and dictionaries continue to exercise a very strong influence on Indian English. And finally, there is the general language of learning and science, a written idiom shared with other English-speaking countries with the minimum of local variation.

It would be interesting to see how the English language, known for its resilience and mobility, is put to new uses in response to environmental needs. Certain features of register, stylistic nuances, unusual collocations and unusual syntax speak of the ingenuity with which the language is made to play new roles in India, and this brings into focus some of the salient features of educated Indian English today. Those of us who have received a university education and use

English for various purposes are only a small fraction of the entire community; this means that our English does not have to rub shoulders with the English of the farmhand and cobbler as in Australia. For none of us, except for the very small Anglo-Indian community, is English the mother tongue and this implies that English never becomes for us what it is for an American or an immigrant from a non-English-speaking country. For us English is an additional language, very useful and perhaps indispensable. Yet it is a language that does not have the intimacy or spontaneity of the mother tongue. We acquire this not as the German, Turkish, or Japanese immigrant to Great Britain or the United States acquires it under strong pressure from life itself; we acquire the language from schools and colleges.

Countries where English is used as the first language have an undeniable advantage: they are linguistically and culturally closer to each other, and most of the features of language change are shared by all the users in those areas. In an area where English is used as a second language, the pressures for language change are external and not internal as in the first language areas. And often these external pressures are imposed rather than shared. The second language tends to diverge in more directions than does the English of England or the United States. The first language countries, therefore, have the advantage of common agreement and their dialects to a great extent tend to be mutually supportive.

The very fact that English is taught in India as a subject has been a factor in promoting a somewhat exotic brand of English. It is somewhat more literary than is the English of a native speaker, or of those who acquire it in the process of living rather than in the process of being educated. The educated variety of Indian English leans heavily towards the poetic. Many Indians prefer poetic prose; this is perhaps because of such a tradition in our own literature. Figures of speech abound in the ordinary descriptive passages in Indian languages. The influence of the Sanskrit language and particularly the science of rhetoric in India determines even today the language behaviour in our country.

Besides, the teaching of English in schools and colleges has always been closely linked with the teaching of English literature. The needs of the language as a language have invariably been subordinated to the needs of the literature of which it is the medium. Teachers and students have as a rule been more concerned with the content of their texts than with the language. Few have truly imbibed or acquired the idiom of the language. The vast majority of the users of English have been dipped Achilles fashion into this strange stream. Whatever little attention has been paid to the study of language has been mostly in the sphere of mechanical drill in grammar and a misguided induction of the learner into the secrets of idioms such as *to make both ends meet, to have too many irons in the fire, on the eve of, apple of discord,* etc. Such locutions have been given disproportionate importance in the study of the English language in India. It may be said in extenuation of the teacher's part that this unhealthy practice has been forced upon him by the requirements of the examination paper; there is invariably a question on such idioms. Consequently one comes across such utterances as *I am in very good health and hope you are in the same boat; he is able to keep the wolf from the door;* and *life is not a bed of roses but a hard nut to crack.* They have not been taught to distinguish between living English and cliché-ridden phrases. Here is another specimen:

> My friends, let us explore all avenues before we abandon our last ray of hope. The hand of doom is upon us. We are in the very jaws of death, and must beware of the snake in the grass.[2]

"They have been at a great feast of language and stolen the scraps" was Moth's shrewd comment on the pedantry of Armado and Holofernes. Many of us have doubtless been to such a feast, but our academic appetite finds it fairly indigestible. An ill-assorted phrasal memory is the storehouse on which we draw. A phrase like *wedded to the path of violence* or *threshed out of all possible avenues* is very common in educated Indian English. Numerous infelicities or illogicalities of this sort occur in the English of fairly educated Indians. There are phrases and turns of expression that have arisen from a failure to picture clearly or understand exactly the things spoken of. For instance the expression *a thin end of the wedge* which is quite common in Indian English betrays ignorance of the fact that a wedge has only one thin end. Similarly the peculiar Indianism *outlook of life* exhibits a failure to realize that the word *outlook* suggests looking out and so may be followed by *of* only when referring to the person looking out. Other instances of the same kind are *to dabble with, get down* (for *get off*), *as best as you can, to pick up a quarrel, to be thick and thin* (meaning *intimate*), and *all round the year.*

The English used by an Indian shows traces of the educational process to which he has been subjected. His exposure to literary English has cut him off from the mainstream of living English. He is unable to use English for business or for purposes of everyday life. Consequently one finds in Indian English stately and elegant forms sanctified by literary tradition. Thus he tends to use *ancient* rather than *old, demise* rather than *death, bosom* rather than *chest, comely* rather than *pretty, resplendent* rather than *dazzling.* He can be *blithe* but seldom *happy, mournful* rather than *sad.* As a result he is apt to be formal and is likely to amuse native speakers of English. Not only does he talk like books, he tends to do so like old books. The following passage from the leading column of *The Times*[3] provides an appropriate commentary on the situation:

> They do not go, they proceed. They do not have, they are (or more often are not) in possession of. They do not ask, they make application for. Their minds, in so far as they may be deemed to have minds, are stocked not with the glories of knowledge but with irrelevant and unmemorable statistics, such as their father's nationality at birth and the date on which they were last inoculated against yellow fever. Once they kept things or gave them up; now they must retain or surrender them. Want (it is true) they do not know, nor need; but deficiencies or requirements are just as inconvenient. They cannot eat, they can only consume; they perform ablutions; instead of homes they have places of residence in which, instead of living, they are domiciled.

The Indian user of English *pursues after* a thing or *behaves friendly* towards a person having been *reared up* in a decent home. Such linguistic habits may strike one as odd.

At times the educated Indian is inclined to be unnecessarily pompous. He invariably acknowledges not *letters* but *communications,* and replies *to the same*; and he is so humble that he will constantly *beg to state.* Neither the teacher nor the clerk nor the civil servant drinks at the well of English undefiled. His reading is more or less confined to the output of the indigenous press. As he reads much more of the Indian variety of English than standard English, he has little chance of being weaned from his singularities of idiom. His vocabulary appears strangely incongruous in the contexts in which he employs them. When his efforts are *crowned with success,* he is likely to be *overjoyed*; indeed his *joy knows no bounds.* On the other hand, when his efforts fail, he is *nowhere* and wishes he could *breathe his last.* Men and women around him are mostly *gentlemen* and *ladies* and he either *hates* or *loves* them. Nevertheless he is partial to the *females* whom he constantly flatters as *the fair sex.*

The Indian user of English is not aware that the English language has its own special character. How important this is in English is clearly brought out by Sir Denison Ross:[4]

> It has long appeared to me that in the case of all living languages a large and important element essential to their complete mastery has been almost wholly neglected. This element is by no means easy to define, but, briefly, it may be said to comprise the national store of quotation and allusion which every educated individual acquires in his own language, both by conscious study and by unconscious assimilation from his childhood onwards and from which he draws in order to lend colour or to give emphasis to the spoken or written word. This stock-in-trade or repertory may be said to form the physiognomy of the language, as grammar and vocabulary form its anatomy.

> Just as many families have household words and expressions of their own invention which are meaningless to outsiders, so has each nation a fund of allusion which is often unintelligible to foreigners.

> In English this linguistic background is exceptionally rich, and without some acquaintance with it no foreign student can be sure of understanding all that he hears.

In an alien atmosphere and for the most part under the inexpert guidance of teachers themselves outside the tradition of the language, the Indian learner generally speaking acquires through the study of literature very little knowledge of the language as a living tongue. We are lamentably cut off from the cultural background of the language. How many of us can grow up, as the native learner does, in the company of English nursery rhymes, fairy tales, the Bible, the Book of Common Prayer, English history, English festivals, and English countryside? There is a wide gap between the two cultures and our ability to master finer points of the English language must necessarily be limited, and we cannot but use it with a difference. But many would probably not welcome such a mastery, possessed perhaps by an exaggerated sense of national pride, or seeing it as a form of academic chauvinism.

The centripetal pressures of local habits and attitudes also partly account for some of the peculiarities of Indian English. For instance, the word *outbooks* among Bengali users of English is very common. An Englishman may be puzzled by a neologism which is simply a literal translation of two Bengali words, referring to books outside the prescribed course. Dr. Johnson says "words change their manners when they change their country."[5] Many English words have similarly changed their character and acquired a peculiar Indian flavour. *Boy* in Indian English means a bearer in a restaurant; *source* implies influence; *compound* describes an enclosed area with buildings; *gentleman* is nearly always used to denote *man* or *person* perhaps because the corresponding Indian word is more polite than the English word *man* or *person*. *Teacheress* frequently occurs in Indian English and this is perhaps because most Indian languages have two different forms to denote sex whereas English uses one word. Compounds like *cousin-sister, free-ship, lathicharge,* and *service holder,* and collocations like *business minded, life companion, standing photograph, giving examination, foreign educated,* and *angry on a person* are more or less literal renderings of the native idioms. *Picketers* and *picketing* are being used by nearly all leading newspapers of India and the verb *gheraoed* had also been very widely accepted.[6] Some of these may be intelligible to native English speakers but are not usual in British English. Idioms from local languages when translated literally will produce barriers of understanding and one may legitimately ask whether such coinages or translations should be encouraged or not.

If an Indian translates the local idiom for hunger as *rats are exercising in my belly,* would he be understood? Are *caste-dinner, family protector,* and *flower bed* easily comprehensible to native speakers of English? The exigencies of national life have brought before us many expressions of this sort, but they convey images and attitudes outside the range of the Englishman's normal experience. For many of these expressions suitable English words and compounds exist, and they would not have interfered with the communication of thought processes that are characteristically Indian. Why should it be *bedding roll* in Indian English, when *bedding* would have done as well? How much of it is due to intellectual blindness and how much due to a genuine need arising from culture-specific situations? If a language system is wrenched off its rails and transgressions become too violent or remote, they may pose a serious problem of acceptability.

It may be argued that before classifying these expressions as acceptable or unacceptable it is necessary to keep in mind the culturally determined context of situation in which they occurred. The "test battery" suggested by Quirk and Svartvik[7] may be applied to determine their acceptability, but they seem to have ignored the contextual elements among factors determining acceptability. It has been said that what is acceptable in British English may not be acceptable in American English, and there are it seems no such things as universals of acceptability[8] since the situational components differ from place to place, person to person. Expressions like the following:

He likes his bed tea everyday,
One cannot get a good job without source,
I shall be obliged if you do the needful,
May I know your good name, please?

are quite common in the writing of educated users of Indian English. They are intelligible to native speakers but I doubt whether they would be prepared to accept them as authentic specimens of standard English.

It has been said that each socially or regionally differentiated form of the language has its own standard of purity and correctness.[9] Expressions like *I give you my word, cut jokes, presently* (at present), *my both hands, his all attempt, my objection against that, as he is fat so he is lazy* (equally fat and lazy), and *whole India* are so common that many educated Indians do not know that they are un-English. When this is pointed out to them they would justify themselves by repeating what Raja Rao had said: "We cannot write like the English; we should not. We can write only as Indian."[10]

Is it possible to say today that Indian English is a system and follows its own set of rules? Its basic patterns are certainly those of standard English, but what precisely are the phonological, lexical, and syntactic features that distinguish Indian English from standard English? All generalizations regarding any of these features are arbitrary and based on inadequate data. Patterns of sentences in Indian English, it is often said, are framed without regard to the normal restrictions of standard English. Typical examples will be *I asked Mr. Banerjee where does he live? He told me that he is coming, I have read this book last month, You are coming to the meeting, isn't it?* If educated users of Indian English write such sentences they are probably the result of intellectual blindness rather than adherence to particular laws of Indian English. Failure to handle some of the basic patterns of standard English cannot be said to have been firmly established in Indian English. If approximately 20 percent of the educated users of English produce such sentences will it be proper to look upon this as a regular feature of Indian English and can it be elevated to a norm?

Bad teaching at school probably has something to do with it. A shop in South Calcutta offers "Tray Tikuji." It is not something exotic, and inquiries will produce tray cloths and tea-cosy. This is merely the outcome of learning English by ear. In another shop, cardboard boxes proclaim that their contents are "Frogs." Inside there are neither amphibians, nor tram rails nor any ornamental fastenings; all that they contain are *frocks* which is itself an outdated word. More than one shop claims to be "closed on Sundays and half-closed on Mondays." Since the salesman looks sleepy on any day of the week it does not really matter. At a recent exhibition in Calcutta there was a Tiffany's stall. What could you buy there? Diamonds as at Tiffany's in New York? No, the Calcutta Tiffany's sold South Indian tiffins. Indians seem to have been doing their best to wreck the English language since it was introduced here 200 years ago. I am not advocating a fixed standard, rigid and inviolable and patronised by a small community. I am aware that the English language will not remain static in a second language situation; it will change imperceptibly but inevitably as the coastline of England changes every day. But the problem is whether it should be allowed to develop as something totally independent of the traditions of standard English.

It is well known that language is a social tool or a social organism. It is the product of the society that employs it and as it is employed it is engaged in a continual process of re-creation. But it is possible that in the process of re-creation a language is likely to differ materially from existing norms and may pose a very real problem—the problem of intelligibility. During the last 200 years the English language used in the United States or Australia has not diverged sufficiently from that of the United Kingdom to seriously hinder mutual intelligibility. We in India, therefore, would expect that those who use English would not deviate so far from some sort of general standard as to render it less useful than at present for purposes of communication with either native speakers or speakers of English in other countries. If some form of standardisation is not imposed at the school/college level, English in India in the not very distant future will be found disintegrating into quite incomprehensible dialects.

Many Indians choose to write in English in the hope of gaining readership among the large number of people outside India. If in doing this there is no breach of the fundamental principle of maintaining mutual intelligibility with other forms of educated English, the Indian writers need not be apologetic about the emergence of a truly characteristic national style. There are of course many writers in India who use English for an audience restricted to their own culture. In that case, they have the freedom to apply local standards of style and expression, and may ignore critics from an audience they never intended to reach. But if they venture beyond their own culture and try to reach a wider section of readers, they must meet the criticism of those who are concerned with the preservation of some kind of norm for purposes of international intelligibility. Variety and change are healthy, for they are evidence of vitality; but when English is modified by local standards to the point where it has purely regional utility, its important function as an international tool is lost. Few would say that waves of linguistic change should recede so that the purity of the language can be maintained. Ideally, English in India should be allowed a free growth restrained only by consideration of its utility—which must be greater than local efficacy.

NOTES

1. In 1972 a Seminar on Indian English was organized by The Central Institute of English, Hyderabad, and in 1979 at Delhi another seminar was held to discuss features of Indian English. See also *Critical Essays on Indian Writing in English,* M. K. Naik, S. K. Desai, & G. S. Amur, eds., Macmillan, 1977; *Indian Writing in English,* R. Mohan, ed., Longman, Delhi, 1973.

2. L. D. Lerner, *English Literature: An Interpretation for Students Abroad,* Quoted by V. R. Gokak, *English in India,* Asia Publishing House, Bombay, 1965, p. 130.

3. Sir Ernest Gowers, *The Complete Plain Words,* London, 1955, p. 76.

4. From the Introduction to *This English Language,* Longman Green & Co., London, 1939.

5. Samuel Johnson, preface to *The Dictionary of the English Language.*

6. Examples are taken from the *Hindusthan Times* (Delhi), *The Hindu* (Madras), and *The Statesman* (Calcutta)—leading newspapers of India.

7. Quirk, R., Svartvik, Jan. *Investigating Linguistic Acceptability,* Mouton and Co., The Hague, p. 100. Quirk and Svartvik indicate certain nodes fairly confidently in a general framework:

I: Lexical	II: Grammatical
(a) congruous	(a) established
(b) obscure	(b) divided
(c) incoherent	(c) ill-established
	(d) dubious
	(e) unacceptable

8. A. A. Hill, *Introduction to Linguistic Structures,* N.Y., 1958.

9. John Lyons, *Introduction to Theoretical Linguistics,* Cambridge University Press, 1968, p. 42.

10. From the Preface to *Kanthapura.*

9 INDIAN ENGLISH: A SOCIOLINGUISTIC PROFILE

Raja Ram Mehrotra

"Queen's English is absurd for our purposes, correct English is insufferably Nesfieldian and dull; what is needed is imaginative break-through English, the kind no one speaks in India, but conditions being ideal, would" (Lal, 1964). While it seems difficult to disagree with the first part of this statement, the second emphasizing the need for "ideal" conditions for the growth of a desirable kind of English may appear to many as wistful Utopian thinking.[1] An ideal is something that is never fully achieved. Our craving for the ideal, which is an extralinguistic problem, should not be allowed to get in the way of appreciating the real. That Indian English (IE) has already come to stay as a reality is evident from a recent survey of opinions conducted by Pride. Out of 50 scholars of English in India no fewer than 46 accepted IE as a reality, only four were not quite certain about their judgment (Pride, 1978, p. 30). The American scholar Thomas Pyles accords the same legitimacy to IE as to any other variety of English in the world. He observes: "There are, of course, in addition to American English, Australian English, Canadian English, South African English, Indian English, among others—all as legitimately English as that form of the language which happens to be spoken in the mother country" (Pyles, 1971, p. 238). Professor Quirk of the *Survey of English Usage* fame remarks about expressions of Indian English and Ghanaian English as "the distinctive parts of a worthy and serious whole, a self-respecting, established variety of English—different of course from British or American varieties but sharing much with them and little with Pidgin" (Quirk, 1972, p. 51). "The Indian," he adds, "usually speaks a form of English that is 'full' in a very obvious sense" (p. 490).

Thus we cannot agree with those who question the very existence of IE and proclaim "the claim that there exists a viable variety of English called Indian English is false" (Daswani, 1974, p. 37). The explorer who fails to discover any

150

trace of Indianness in IE despite the most sincere efforts reminds me of one who in search of the real heart of an onion goes on stripping it of so many layers that by the time the real onion is reached there is little of it left. The emergence of IE as a viable, vigorous variety was predicted by an eminent professor of English as early as 1940: "A little courage, some determination, a wholesome respect for our own idiom and we shall before long have a virile, vigorous Indian English" (Jha, 1940). Only three decades after this prediction, the assistant director general of the British Council declared IE to be "the most widespread dialect on earth" spoken not only in India, but over all of Southeast Asia, East Africa, the Caribbean, and Fiji (King, 1971, p. 2).

ATTITUDES TOWARD IE

The prevailing attitude towards IE during the past 100 years has unfortunately been one of disapprobation. Look at the various pejorative labels used from time to time to denigrate IE as "Baboo English" or "funny English" (*The Times*, 1882), "dog English" (Kindersley, 1938), "bandit English" (Lutze, 1968), "Desi English" (Ismail, 1974), "arre bhai English" (Lal, 1964), "a joke of stage and screen" (Earle, 1976), "a bear dancing, a dog walking on its hind legs" (Anjaneyulu, n.d.) and finally "a blind alley, lined with Curio shops, leading nowhere" (Bose, 1963). Impressions and opinions rather than well-documented descriptive statements and scientific analyses have loomed large over discussions on the subject. "Indian English can only be bad English" says Chalapathi Rao (Rao, 1965). And for Whitworth (Whitworth, 1932) it can only be incorrect English. His book *Indian English* is subtitled "An examination of the errors of the idiom made by Indians in writing English."

As early as 1882 a reporter of *The Times* (London) remarked that a "thoughtful Englishman" would think of Indian writing in English in the same fashion as "Cicero would probably think of much of the Ciceronian Latin that is written at our schools and universities" (*The Times*, 1882, p. 8). Such an attitude is in fact noticeable in respect of all nonnative varieties of English as is evident from the general statement made in the British Council's Annual Report of 1960–1961: "In becoming a world language English, some say, like any other common currency runs the risk of becoming worn, debased and subject to counterfeit. Its stamp is no longer authentic, it loses its clarity; it may become unrecognizable" (Sheshadri, 1965, p. 17). Ironically enough, what appears to be worn, debased, and counterfeit currency to some has taken on a new stamp, fresh authenticity and far greater circulation in the world at large than the so-called standard *pucca* and unadulterated form. It is indeed an interesting instance of the application of Gresham's law in linguistics with the modification that no amount of legislation can drive the so-called debased currency out of circulation. What is needed therefore is a change in attitude.

The narrow parochial outlook thriving on a built-in colour bar should be abandoned in favour of one that is broad, catholic, cosmopolitan. Mark Twain has rightly reacted to such snobbish pretensions in these words: "The King's

English is not the King's. It is a joint stock company" (Moss, 1973, p. xiii). Similar is the import of a timely warning given in an editorial note in *The Times Literary Supplement*: "English itself is a shared language in which we have no special proprietorial rights; all that matters ultimately is who can use it best. . .it is not reserved like a private telephone line exclusively for messages from England or even from America, but is a means of communication for all. We must learn to look outwards or die" (*Times Literary Supplement,* 1962, p. 591).

A popular myth about IE is to consider it both formally and culturally "deviant" (Mathai, 1951), a favourite word of the language policeman who is out to catch culprits, real or fictitious. Whatever in this and other nonnative varieties appears to be different from British English at the phonological, grammatical, and lexical levels is dubbed "deviant." I strongly believe that the term deviant cannot and must not be applied to IE, which is a respectable language variety existing in its own right. Variant rather than deviant appears to be the right word in the present context. As Subrahmanian referring to IE remarked, "It is not inferior or superior to the British or American variety, but different" (Subrahmanian, 1977, p. 23).

To say that certain features of IE are deviant presupposes that there is some other norm—a uniform, correct, accepted, already well-described standard form of the language—to which it must conform, and that even the slightest departure from the norm will make it deviant, substandard, and undesirable. Such a norm, it is believed, is embalmed in dictionaries, laid out for inspection in textbooks, cut and dried and rubber-stamped by terminology commissions. Ironically enough, standard English, inspired by such a norm, is virtually a foreign language even in England. The concept of a standard form patronized by a small minority, however powerful, is not acceptable to the modern mind. "The modern mind insists on having the process of standardization take the form of a democratic rather than an aristocratic process" (Sapir, 1931; quoted in Firth, 1964, p. 31).

The other implication of using the term deviant in the present context is that IE can be described only by constant reference to the "standard" and "uncontaminated" form of English. Kandiah explains it thus: "What this means is that IE will always be measured ultimately in terms of a standard which is outside of it and which it will in all likelihood never attain, so that it will always, by that standard, be found wanting" (Kandiah, n.d., p. 6). However, comparisons of this sort are not without pitfalls. While accepting the desirability of comparison between "English English" and IE Pride argues as follows:

Comparison does not demand the adoption of a descriptive (or indeed theoretical) framework suitable for just one of the varieties being compared. If this is done, then it seems to me that many features of the other variety are going to be inadequately treated, even lost from sight. And this may particularly be the case if one is concerned not only with syntactic (etc.) patterns but also, simultaneously, with speech functions and so forth. The 'Indianness' of Indian English is surely very much a function of the Indianness of being Indian. Comparison, I would say, to be valid on both sides of the coin has inevitably to be imperfect. Ultimately, it's up to the individual to decide for himself what are (for him) the most interesting comparisons to be made. Seeing one variety as 'deviant from' the other is simply prejudging an essentially relative matter. (Pride, personal communication)

"English English" and IE are each an efficient and fairly stable variety existing in its own right, each has its own frame of reference, each symbolizes a distinct sociocultural reality, each performs functions that are not identical, and each therefore must be described and compared in its own terms even at the cost of imperfect comparison. And variation such as this is inevitable as has also been pointed out by Firth: "It is impossible to transfer a language 6000 miles overseas and expect it to remain as it was or to develop it on the lines of the mother country" (Firth, 1964, p. 197).

Thus, despite the models set by the BBC and the Voice of America, IE could not but develop on lines of its own, independent of the mother tradition. The process of Indianization of the English language got a fresh boost after the departure of the native speakers from the Indian scene in 1947. English enjoys a special privilege in India. No other language in this country has been asked to do so many things in so many situations and at places so remote from one another both geographically and culturally. It is a truism that English tends to admit of greater variety and to move in more diverse situations in a nonnative multilingual setting than in its native surroundings. The number of second language speakers of English has constantly been on the increase and this has also contributed to its rich variation. There is considerable weight in the following remark of King: "The more widespread English becomes, the greater the potential variation" (King, 1971, p. 2).

VARIETIES OF IE

Several types of variation can be noticed in IE. First, there is the regional variation which is more conspicuous in speech than in writing. At the phonological level several kinds of Indian English are perceived, each showing unmistakably its allegiance to a regional language whose phonetic features influence it. Thus one can speak, among others, of Tamil English, Bengali English, Punjabi English, Hindi English or "Hinglish," and so on. This has well been demonstrated by a reader in a letter to the editor of *The Illustrated Weekly of India*:

Tamil English
    Eye yate yeleven yeggs. (I ate eleven eggs.)
    Meester Bharma uaj bhomitting in the bharandah, Sir! (Mr. Verma was vomitting in the verandah, Sir!)

Hindi English
    It ij terribull. Prejence is poor in i-school. (It is terrible. Prejence is poor in school.)

Punjabi English
    Go sutterait in the suttereet and ju bill find the house ju bant! (Go straight in this street and you will find the house you want.)

(Sharma, 1974, p. 6)

Among the Urdu speaking aristocratic and upper middle class Muslims of the Uttar Pradesh, wide opening or rounding of the lips while speaking is considered to be a sign of lack of decency and sophistication, and hence they find it difficult to learn and pronounce properly some of the English vowel sounds (Ansari, 1978, p. 81). Thus variation in speech is not only regional but also sociocultural. If you want to experience the rich variety of IE at the phonological level, ask a native from each of Bombay, Madras, Calcutta, Patna, and Amritsar to read the same text and you will not miss the rich mosaic that IE is. There are however people in every region who have done away with the regional accent and speak a relatively more neutral form of English.

Regional variation in the written mode is less perceptible except in cases where an attempt is made to translate into English ideas and idioms from a regional language. This tendency is common both in creative writing and in the use of English in day-to-day interaction. The following sentences (the first three from creative writing) are illustrative of the variety of English used in the Hindi/Urdu region:

Rats were running around his belly.
Don't eat my head.
Whosoever has the staff, has the buffalo.
Have you given key to the watch?
Wake me up when Banaras comes.

Similar illustrations can be provided from the English used in other regions. Note for instance the Punjabi speaker's expressions such as *King of Pearls, Dont do the siapa* (funeral mourning) *here* and the hybrid nicknames in Kannada English as given by Raja Rao in *Kanthapura,* such as *Waterfall Venkamma, Nose scratching Nanjamma, Fronthouse Akamma, Temple Rangappa,* and *Gold-bangle Somanna.* We may also note in this context the tendency to employ statement forms as questions in Bengali English by putting an interrogation sign at the end, as in the sentence "Kanu, he was safe?" taken from Bhabani Bhattacharya's novel *So Many Hungers.* This is because the syntactic distinction between a statement and a question is often conveyed in Bengali through tone and punctuation and not by word order (compare with Verma, in this volume).

Yet another kind of variation is noticeable in the division of IE into three broad categories: higher, intermediate, and lower. At one end of this cline we have the so-called degenerate form, pidgin, while at the other we have forms entirely free from unusual features and scoring nearly 100 percent intelligibility over the whole of the English-speaking world. There are some who are reluctant to consider the lower and the higher ends of the cline as truly representative of IE. "For any consideration of Indian English," says Daswani, "it is essential to ignore these extreme points in the continuum" (Daswani, mimeo, p. 3). And indeed, most deliberations in this area have been restricted to the description and analysis of the intermediate variety. It is the considered opinion of the present author however that all three types of IE are worthy of serious academic discussion, and any attempt to describe IE without paying due attention to any of these is bound to be partial, deficient, and biased. What Kandiah says about Lankan English is equally true of IE: "In trying to characterize Lankan English itself as a linguistic organism, then, the investigator would be obliged to treat any and every bit of English that issues from the mouth or pen of a Lankan as a valid datum for his purpose" (Kandiah, n.d., p. 34).

THE HIGHER VARIETY

Let us first consider the higher end of the cline, represented by men like Jawahar Lal Nehru, Nirad Chaudhry, C. D. Deshmukh, and Sham Lal, a former editor of *The Times of India,* who all possess what Bloomfield calls a "native-like control" of the English language (Bloomfield, 1935, p. 56). Quirk pays compliment to Nehru's command of English in these words: "And at the top of the scale we get a man like Mr Nehru, speaking an English perfectly comprehensible and acceptable throughout the English speaking world" (Quirk, 1972, p. 49). Deshmukh's essay "Hundred years of the University of Calcutta" written in 1957, as Pride testifies, "would very nearly pass as 'English English'" (Pride, mimeo, p. 29). A similar claim can be made about Nirad Chaudhry, Sham Lal, and several others. Writers like R. K. Narayan and Raja Rao have already crossed the national frontiers without difficulty or opposition. Iyengar is not exaggerating when he says: "At its best Indian writing in English compares not unfavourably with the best writing in Australia, Canada, or even in the United States and England" (Iyengar, 1961, p. 140). Among earlier masters of English in India we may mention C. R. Das, C. Y. Chintamani, Shiva Swami Aiyar, and Brijendra Nath Seal. The tradition of the Indian writers of good English at the higher end of the cline is more than a century old. One of the issues of *The Times* (London) published in 1882 (referred to already) has this to say in an editorial note: "A considerable portion of the English Press of India is written by natives; and many of these so-called 'Anglo-Native' papers are written with great ability and in excellent idiomatic English" (*Times,* 1882, p. 8). Thus there has always been in India a galaxy of writers and speakers whose English is neutral, near-native and autonomous.

INDIAN PIDGIN ENGLISH

We now pass on to the other extreme represented by Indian Pidgin English (IPE) spoken by certain uneducated and prestigeless professional groups. Although some, with Quirk, have emphatically asserted that "there is no denying that Pidgin exists in India" (Quirk, 1972, p. 49), little attempt has been made so far to collect samples of IPE from a variety of domains and registers so as to enable us to identify its distinct features and functions. Naturally therefore, books, monographs, and bibliographies on pidgins have failed to make even passing reference to IPE. But, as Huxley once remarked, facts do not cease to exist simply because they are ignored.

Perhaps the main reason behind this apathy has been the stigma attached to pidgins as a whole, as is evident from labels such as "bastard lingo" and "mongrel jargon" (Hall, 1955, p. 14) and "the poor relations in the world's language families" (Todd, 1974, p. 91). IPE was ridiculed as "dog English" (Kindersley, 1938, p. 25) some 40 years ago and the situation has not improved much since. A veteran among Indian English writers, Mulk Raj Anand defines pidgin English as "anyhow English" or "the higgledy-piggledy spoken English" and adds "the fittest place for it to remain is in the gutter" (Verghese, 1975, p. 11). It was contempt and hostility of this kind that provoked some to use the expression "Hands off Pidgin" resulting in gradual recognition for this form.

One of the earliest scholarly references to IPE appeared in *The Times* (London) even before the close of the nineteenth century. The pidgin referred to was spoken by servants and butlers in Madras. In the following example, an *ayah* (maid-servant) complains to her master about the stealing of butter by the butler who also tries to purchase her silence by offering her a little share of the loot:

Butler's yeveryday taking one ollock for own self and giving servants all half-half ollock. When I am telling that shame for him he is telling master's strictly arder all servants for the little milk give it—what can I say mam, I poor ayah woman. (*The Times,* 1882, p. 8)

The distinguishing features of this piece are its extremely limited vocabulary, its scanty grammar, and the pull of the regional language on pronunciation, syntax, and vocabulary. Pidgin of this kind was widely used in pre-independence days by the menial staff, particularly those living in metropolitan towns.

At present, pidgin English in India is spoken widely, mainly by semi-literate or illiterate professionals while talking to overseas tourists not conversant with the local language. In Varanasi, for instance, it is spoken by unlicensed and self-appointed tourist guides, small shopkeepers, hotel-bearers, street vendors, narcotics dealers, porters, beggars, boatmen, rickshaw pullers, taxi-drivers, and commercial agents locally known as *dalals.* Some of the locales where IPE can be heard are the tourist hotels, markets in and around Vishwanath Lane, clandestine shops dealing in narcotics, *ghats* (the river bank), and temples. I have studied pidgin English of some of these groups as part of my sociolinguistic survey of IE in and around Varanasi. Here is a specimen of a tape-recorded text of the pidgin spoken by a boatman giving details to a group of foreign tourists about the holy city Varanasi, particularly its burning *ghat* through which the boat carrying them is currently passing:

This Banaras very old city. Nobody know how old. Varanasi our very oldest city in India. Varuna plus Assi both jointed called Varanasi.

The most important temple the golden temple. The golden temple they bring the Ganges water. The first golden temple Biswanath. Second golden temple Nepali temple, near the river Ganga, the ghat name Lalita. Here three hundred sixty ghats. Main ghat Dasaswamedh ghat.

Our Hindu religion so many different kinds of god. Shiva was destroy god and Vishnu was power and Brahma was creator. But that is only for totally bluff. This is not so many god. God is one.

Burning place. Deadbody burning place. Here two burning place. One burning place small. One burning place big size. Small burning place not all time fire. Big size burning place twentyfour hours fire. Everyday twenty four hours burn the body. Here everyday one hundred, two hundred people cremated.

First people die. White colour the man, red colour the woman. People bring the body in burning place near the river. He wash the body in the Ganges. After body will keep and people go in government office. He write the name which person to death. Then government know how many persons to death. Often people come and bring wood. After going the manager pay him the money. Some person rich man pay much money. Some person poor man pay less money. After come there make five rounds and then start fire. After three hours body will finish and less piece of body throw in Ganges water. But four kinds of bodies no cremated. Small pox, small children, animals and sadhus. I now (no) burn the children. I now (no) burn the small pox. I now (no) burn the lepers. I now (no) burn the holy man. When he die, people bring one heavy stone, throw in both the Ganges river. Children no burn. They put the Ganga.

The passage when subjected to a rather crude analysis would seem to have the following features which may be said to be representative of IPE.

A. *Deletion*

1. The absence of copula:
   This Banaras very old city.
   The most important temple the golden temple.
   The first golden temple Biswanath.
   Second golden temple Nepali temple.
   Here 360 ghats.
   Main ghat Dasaswamedh Ghat.
   Here two burning place.
   One burning place small.
   One burning place big size.
   Varanasi our very oldest city in India.
   Varuna plus Assi both joined called Varanasi.

2. Lack of concordial agreement between subject and verb:
   He wash the body in the Ganga.
   Nobody know how old.
   He write the name which person to death.
   When he die, people bring one heavy stone.
   Some person rich man pay much money.
   Some person poor man pay less money.

3. Absence of verb in a sentence:
   Small burning place not all time fire.
   Big size burning place 24 hours fire.
   White colour the man, red colour the woman.
   The government know how many persons to death.

4. Absence of preposition:
   The golden temple they bring the Ganges water.

Second golden temple Nepali temple near the river Ganga, the ghat name
    Lalita.
One burning place big size.
After going the manager pay him money.
5. Omission of article:
Small burning place not all time fire.
People go in government office.
After three hours body will finish.
Second golden temple Nepali temple.
Big size burning place twenty four hours fire.
6. Omission of subject:
After going the manager pay him the money.
After come there make five rounds and then start fire.
7. Absence of the finites of *be*:
Here everyday one hundred, two hundred people cremated.
Four kinds of body no cremated.

   B. *Shifts in Meaning.*   Because of the scanty vocabulary in the possession
of IPE speakers, words sometimes signify a wider and more than usual range of
phenomena:
1. *Less piece of body* signifiying bones and ashes:
After three hours body will finish and less piece of body throw in Ganges
    water.
2. *Small pox* standing for people who died of small pox:
I no burn the small-pox.
3. *I* for *we* or *they* (see preceding example).
4. *Near* used in the sense of *on the bank of*:
near the river Ganga.
5. *Start* used in the sense of *light*:
they start the fire.
6. *Make* used in the sense of *take*:
Make five rounds of fire.
7. *No* for *not* and *don't*:
four kinds of body no cremated
I no burn the children.
8. *In* for *to*:
People bring the body in burning place
people go in government office.

   C. *Stylistic Features*

1. Simplification devices:
    a. Verb used attributively to avoid complex syntactic constructions:
    Shiva was destroy god
    instead of
    god of destruction
    god who destroys

  b. Adjective manipulated as verb, as in *jointed* used instead of *joined*:
      Varuna plus Assi both jointed called Varanasi
  c. Noun used as participle as in *name* instead of *named*:
      the ghat name Lalita
  d. Avoidance of constructions beginning with preparatory *there*:
      Our Hindu religion so many different kinds of god
      Big size burning place 24 hours fire
  e. Avoidance of complex and compound sentences:
      Some person rich man pay much money
      Some person poor man pay less money
  f. Avoidance of complex phrase structure:
      One hundred, two hundred people cremated.
      dead body burning place.
  g. Avoidance of passive voice construction:
      After three hours, body will finish.
      Less piece of body throw in Ganges water.
      Everyday twenty four hour burn the body.
      They put the Ganga.
  h. Incomplete sentences:
      No body know how old.
2. Reversal of word order:
   Everyday 24 hours burn the body.
   Small burning place not all time fire.
   Big size burning place 24 hours fire.
3. Redundant and superfluous use of the conjunction *and*:
   After body will keep and people will go in government office.
4. Use of demonstrative adjective with proper noun:
   this Banaras.
5. Use of the modifier *very* with superlative degree:
   Varanasi our very oldest city in India.
6. Adverb position; some end-position adverbs, including those of place and
      direction, are made to occupy the front position even when no contrast or
      emphasis is involved:
   After three hours body will finish.

It is evident from the foregoing analysis that IPE is an ad hoc means of communication arising out of the marginal contact and aiming at limited transaction. It is characterized like other varieties of pidgin, by features such as limited vocabulary, simplified structures, reduction in the number of grammatical devices, and shifts and manipulations in meaning which are often reinforced and clarified with the help of gestures. A remarkable characteristic of this speech is its fluency which may partly be due to the frequent repetition of the same utterances almost every day. IPE may have very low rating on the cline of Englishness, yet it well fulfils the restricted communicative needs that give rise to it. It is a curious phenomenon that the two extremes of the cline, the high variety and IPE, have to do mainly, if not exclusively, with communication and intelligibility at the international level, a function that is not normally shared by the intermediate variety. In this way, we see the same communicative purpose at the top and the bottom of the cline. It needs to be stressed here that a careful and systematic recording of IPE varieties and their subsequent sophisticated analysis from a sociolinguistic stance will not only add a new dimension to the study of and research into IE, but will also help in discovering and ascertaining the universals in pidgins spoken in different parts of the world.

THE INTERMEDIATE VARIETY

A majority of educated Indians use the intermediate variety whose distinct features are more prominently perceptible in the IE lexicon. Besides a large number of Indian words that figure in Indian English writing (Yule and Burnell, 1903; Rao, 1954; and Kachru, 1973 and 1975) some common English words are given new meanings not to be found in the varieties of English outside the Indian subcontinent. One of the meanings of the word *boy* in IE is a male servant or a bearer in a hotel as in the sentence, "Boy! Get me some toast." This meaning is nonexistent in British English. The term *four-twenty* meaning a *cheat* or *swindler* in IE is absolutely unknown outside the country. The word *source* is often used in IE in the sense of influence, particularly of a resourceful person. *Source* in this sense is not used in British English. In the sentence "What are the subjects that you offered at B.A.?" *offer* is used in the sense of *take* which is not to be found in English dictionaries and British usage. Similarly, *colony, family, tempo, compound, division, moderator,* and *weightage* are some other words that have special meanings in IE usage.

One may also note in this connection a tendency for neologism which is yet another step towards Indianization of English. New words are coined when the existing ones are found to be inadequate to convey the desired meaning in an Indian context. The word *teacheress,* for example, is very common in the register of matrimonial advertisement in Indian newspapers. The reasons behind this coinage are:

1. Indian languages have two different forms of a word on the basis of sex, for example, *adhyapak* (male teacher) and *adhyapika* (female teacher).

2. Using *teacheress* instead of *woman teacher* or *lady teacher* is economical and implies some saving for the advertiser (Mehrotra, 1975, p. 44). The sociocultural exigency is also responsible for several new collocations and compounds not to be found in British English, as in *bed-tea, latrin-pot, black-money, cousin-brother, half-pants, back paper, mass-cut, face-cut,* and *change-room* (dressing room).

Sometimes a new word is coined because it happens to be shorter and simpler than the existing one conveying the same meaning. Thus we have *free-ship* in preference to *free studentship, debtful* instead of *indebted,* and *spacy* in place of *spacious.*

Quite a few lexical items in IE are the result of hybrid formation, thus *lathi-charge, bhabhi-hood, coolidom, motor-gari,* and *double roti.* Often such formations are in the nature of fixed collocations and are bound by what Kachru calls "structural constraints" (Kachru, 1975, p. 63).

Even more interesting is the way in which Hindi words are made to behave with English inflexional endings added to them. Look at the following illustrations drawn from the private letters of some university students in India:

I *lagaoed* a lot of pull.
I *phiraoed* a couple of girls in the bazar.
Have you been able to *patao* that girl?
You must *maro* at least 80% marks if you want a good job.
Mr. Gupta was *gheraoed* for two hours last evening.

Some other examples of this type are *salammed, kukru kruing,* and *dhotied blackman.* An example of the kind given by Goffin is: "The engine does not *chal* properly" (Goffin, 1934, p. 21).

A related feature of IE is language-mix which frequently occurs in its various genres and registers. Look at the following sentences taken from *Stardust,* a popular film magazine in India:

Premnath is really *ajeeb,* he gave a fake *thappad* even without touching her.
Everyone is dismissing off my career saying "Oh, she *chamchofies* the big men."
One actor commented, "*Saala,* he has broken our *bhandas.*"
Another wife who understands the importance of *maskofying* hubby's heroines is Babita.
He spoke about how he had met many *vishwasghaats* in his personal life.
She created quite a few *nakhras* over this delay but Miss Pandit sat *chup.*
Now she can be of no more *matlab* to him.
She was looking absolutely *bekar, ekdum ayah* like.

Indian fiction in English is not lagging behind in accommodating words from the Indian languages in the framework of English sentences. Here are a few examples from the novels of Mulk Raj Anand.

"dont do the *siapa* here" (*Seven Summers,* p. 22).
"You have to keep the *ijjat* of the *paltan*" (*The Village,* p. 208).
"Dont *buk*" (*Untouchable,* p. 39).
"Sali, she-ass, deceitful bitch" (*Private Life of an Indian Prince,* p. 37).
"What is this buk-buk?" (*Private Life of an Indian Prince,* p 212).

It is evident that Indian words of nearly all form-classes are freely and often unconsciously used in IE, and these are adapted with necessary changes made to them according to the morpho-syntactic rules of the English language. This apparently signifies that the English-Hindi bilinguals are "on the road to merger of the two languages" (Ervin-Tripp, 1968, p. 204).[2] There appears to be a strong tendency to use in an English sentence such words and phrases from Indian languages whose equivalents are available in English. This may be partly due to the fact that the Hindi words come more naturally and appear more forceful in a given context than their English equivalents. *Sister-in-law* is no match for *sali*, and *idle talk* is a poor substitute for *buk-buk* in the illustrations given above.

The registers in which the language-mixing tendency appears more prominent are college slang, film reporting, matrimonial advertisements, astrological forecasts, religious discourse, private letters, market reviews, casual conversation, cookery, reporting a musical concert, Indian English fiction, and question-box in Indian periodicals. There are, on the other hand, registers and domains where Indian words of this kind are very sparingly used: airport announcements, news broadcasts, lectures and articles on science and technology, formal addresses, applications, testimonials, editorials, book reviews, obituaries, and official letters. It will appear from the foregoing that the language-mix phenomenon is more common in situations that are more informal, more personal, more relaxed, and sometimes more culture-sensitive. It has been rightly observed, "Formal style and language mixture are normally mutually exclusive" (Verma, 1976, p. 160). Again, it may be noted that in IE language mix is a feature of both spoken and written language. Here the Indian situation is different from that in West Africa where mixed language exists almost exclusively in the spoken form (Ure, mimeo, p. 7). It appears that language mix is a necessary offshoot of bilingual situations, particuarly when, as in the case of English-Hindi, the two languages have been in interaction within the same sociocultural complex for more than a century.

STYLISTIC FEATURES

One of the potent factors that marks IE as different from British English and lends it its distinct character is a set of stylistic features associated with it. One such feature is the tendency to write long involved sentences with complicated structures. Some years ago, Firth had this to say on the nature of the IE sentence:

> They have not learnt the habitual 'economy' of the native in social situations, and their sentences are often much too long, too complete, sometimes too grammatical. (Firth, 1964, p. 176).

The situation has not changed much since the time of Firth. Look at the opening sentences of Rajan's novel *The Dark Dancer*:

> There was nothing in the cracked arid earth to suggest that he belonged to it, or in the river, shrunk away from the banks that seemed almost to wrench its way through the landscape, startling the brown anger into green. The rail tracks ran forward like an act of will, straining across the flat baked plain, to the first muddle of houses; and then the road forked from it driving relentlessly through the mantle of dust to an end that might have been reached from any beginning. (Rajan, 1958, p. 1)

The two sentences are not only long (consisting of 40 and 47 words, respectively), but they also give one the impression of being overdrawn, dragged, and strained with high-sounding abstractions which distract the reader's attention from the real object. Some time back, an Indian scholar made a comparative study of the editorials published in *The Hindu* (Madras) and *The Guardian* (London) and brought to our attention the interesting fact that "the average number of words in a sentence in *The Hindu* is 30 and in *The Guardian* it is 23" (Sheshadri, 1965, p. 21). It is obvious that the Indians generally are not in favour of short, simple sentences. Often the sentences are so complicated that the main purpose gets expressed only at the end.

As regards choice of vocabulary, IE writers generally show a preference for the archaic and the erudite. Nirad Chaudhry once confessed: "As a rule, I remove all words which have not been good English for at least two hundred years. As I have found from experience, this pays" (Spitzbardt, 1976, p. 37). In fact, a certain amount of conservatism about the IE vocabulary is attributable to the study, emulation, and often cramming of the classics of the earlier centuries in educational institutions in India. Although in recent years, efforts have been made to include twentieth-century prose writers in our English syllabuses, students are yet to imbibe the living English words, phrases, and structures in their speech and writing. Probably a big hurdle in the way is their teachers' own English which has been nurtured mainly by the study of the eighteenth- and nineteenth-century classics in English literature, and hence they find it difficult to get rid of the obsolete or semi-obsolete expressions. Thus even today "the Indian graduate prefers a word like 'demise' to 'death' and will refer more comfortably to his 'unfortunate pecuniary circumstances' than to the fact of being 'poor' or not 'well off'" (Goffin, 1934, p. 28). According to the "In Memoriam" column of the Indian newspapers, people seldom die or pass away. They either *breathe their last* or *leave for their heavenly abodes.* In the invitations sent to us, our friends and relatives solicit our *gracious presence on the auspicious occasion* of the wedding of their sons or daughters. Krishnan, a character in *The Dark Dancer,* does not put his luggage in a taxi, but *consigns his belongings* to it. Sometimes a letter writer in India *in reply to one's favour of the 10th ultimo* has the honour to be *your most obedient servant.* Thus Indians writing in English generally show a liking for learned words and sonorous phrases even in situations where more familiar expressions would be more appropriate. Witness Firth: "English literature up to and including Addison is not a suitable security on which to issue current tokens of speech in the twentieth century" (Firth, 1964, p. 176).

Sometimes this tendency leads to humorous formations. One feels tempted to cite here the case of a clerk who asked for ten days' leave because "the hand that rocked the cradle has kicked the bucket." Mathai has narrated the story of a lecturer in English who, on seeing the sea for the first time, asked: "Is that the ship on the bosom of the sea" (Mathai, 1951, p. 98). Our people's inability to keep the literary and figurative English separate from contemporary functional English has given us such expressions as:

How is life spinning at your end?
We went through the pages of human mouths from village to village.

Land is a well full of honeyed ambrosia. In order to get at it we need buckets—the buckets of our intellectual capacity.

This appears to be the inevitable consequence of the advice often given to students by their teachers in the classroom to underline the unfamiliar words and learned expressions, learn them by heart and use them in their own speech and writing. This tendency towards verbosity, preciosity, and use of learned literary words aiming at some sort of rhetorical effect is all the more prominent in the domain of literary criticism as will be evident from the following excerpt from a book written by a university professor of English for the use of undergraduate students:

> Carlyle was a portent of tremendous explosive force which shattered a host of Victorian illusions and tore asunder the veil of complacency to reveal the rotten, cowering, shrunken soul shivering behind the pompous facade of the proud society. A man of rugged strength brought up under the severe discipline of adversity, Carlyle was a singular figure, rugged, gnarled and eccentric, with the burning wrath of the old Testament-prophet, clothed in the uncouth Teutonic jargon, alternating with the simplicity, beauty and picturesqueness of the Biblical passages of limpid grace and purity. He was an iconoclast of grammar and syntax, a poet as bold as Donne and Hopkins in whose hands the hard crust of language became a lump of kneaded clay to receive the full impress of all the angularities of his complex nature. (Rai, 1967, p. 348)

One can easily imagine the nature of the output when the young students are exposed to this kind of English. Kantak's reaction in this context offers a correct analysis of the language used by professors of English in India:

> When a Professor of English attempts creative prose we often notice a certain 'literariness' in his language rather than a literary quality—a kind of straining for literary effect, a tendency to cliche or stale poeticism, a preference for the abstract in the turn of phrase or vocabulary such as one might suppose would result from a constant preoccupation with the business of literary interpretation. (Kantak, 1968, p. 146).

Another important stylistic feature related to the foregoing is in the preference for exaggerated and hyperbolic forms. The following are illustrative:

I am bubbling with zeal and enthusiasm to serve as a research assistant.
I am hugely grateful to you.
With heaps of love and tons of kisses.
I wish to express my over-flowing devotion to him.
Our country is facing at the moment multitudinous hydra-headed problems.

One may also note in this context the tendency to use adverbs of degree, such as *more, most, very, extremely* with adjectives that are indicative of absolute or perfect forms. Look at these expressions which are very common in IE speech and writing: *most* essential, *very* vital, *extremely* excellent, *very* unique, *very* best, *very* perfect, *most* ideal, *most* permanent, and so on. The same tendency appears to be responsible for frequent cases of tautology in which several near synonyms are used where only one would have been sufficient: proceed further, closed sine-die for indefinite period, one year's continuous service without break, verbal talk, etc.

Lack of training in and exposure to the functional varieties of English, together with excessive preoccupation with bookish English, lead many to registral confusion. The following sentences taken from personal letters written by university students illustrate this point:

I am enclosing some prasadam herewith.
All subjects went bumper in examination.
Listen! due to certain happenings I was mentally troubled.
My dear Bachha, Hallo.
Over to Mummy.
See you, all the best.

CONTEXT OF CULTURE

Language has often been described as the carrier of cultural genes. Dialects of English have often been associated with one cultural trait or the other which receive special treatment in them. King has provided a break-up of this phenomenon in these words: "It should be remembered that dialects are associated with other than linguistic factors, e.g., cockney with impertinence or self-pity, Received Pronunciation with condescension or ineffectiveness, Texan with arrogance or crudity, Chichi with subservience or unreliability" (King, 1971, p. 4). Continuing in the same vein it may be asserted that IE is particularly associated with humility. Humility is universally acknowledged as an essential characteristic of the Indian culture since it is also reflected in Indian languages, particularly in their elaborate systems of honorifics and respect terminology. Naturally, therefore, IE usages reveal unmistakably traces of inordinate humility and subservience. An illustration of this can be seen in the way a researcher in India offers thanks to his supervisor in the introductory remarks of his Ph.D. thesis. Here is a typical example taken from an approved Ph.D. thesis:

I consider it to be my primordial obligation to humbly offer my deepest sense of gratitude to my most revered Guruji and untiring and illustrious guide Professor . . . for the magnitude of his benevolence and eternal guidance.

The excessive modesty of Indian users of English is also reflected in the phrase *Thanking you* written at the end of official letters even when there is absolutely no need for offering thanks. It is customary that thanks are usually given by way of gratefully acknowledging a benefit, favour, or the like. But in IE we freely offer thanks even in situations where a favour or benefit is absolutely out of the question:

I hope I satisfy your requirements. Thanking you.
I promise to take up the task with complete sincerity and dedication. Thanking you.
I offer myself as a candidate for the post of Research Assistant. Thanking you.

Similar meekness is seen in the wide range of collocates of the word *kind* in official correspondence in India, thus *kind* letter, *kind* consideration, *kind* presence, *kind* encouragement, *kind* information, *kind* attention, *kind* interest, and so on. Even the dean of a faculty in a university has been found using the work *kindly* while giving instructions to the undergraduate students:

Undergraduate students will *kindly* mention their class roll number on their application forms.

In business correspondence in India, too, one comes across a statement written in the same spirit: "Your esteemed order has been duly noted." Another instance that highlights this trait is the use of the word *august* in the opening remark by a speaker addressing a meeting: "I feel greatly honoured in speaking to this *august* audience." The use of *august* in such a context is appreciated in India, but in contemporary British usage it would have a jocular or ironic meaning. Likewise a notice at the entrance to the Vishwanath Temple in Banaras Hindu University says "Please allow the shoe-keeper to look after your shoes," instead of the usual "Take off your shoes here." An application from a student for financial assistance ends thus: "I pray with my two folded hands to your kind honour to have a kind consideration on my pitiable condition."

The word *request* in IE is generally used in the sense of pray and seldom in the sense of ask, the usual meaning of the term in the Queen's English. If while addressing a vice-chancellor a university employee writes "I ask you to grant me leave" or "Could I ask you to grant me leave?" instead of the usual form "I request you to grant me leave," he will be considered rude and may even invite disciplinary action. Then there is an additional factor, the consideration of status which determines the syntactic structure in which the word is going to figure. A subordinate addressing his boss in an office in India writes, "I request you to look into the case," while the boss writing to a subordinate will normally use the passive, "you are requested to look into the case." If the latter form is used by a subordinate, it may mean a downright insult.

An important perspective in the present context can be had by examining the extent to which an Indian English utterance is "Indian." In other words, there are kinds and degrees of Indianness in IE involving the specific linguistic, contextual, and interpersonal dimensions. IE in one context may be more "Indian" than in other contexts. Again, there may be varying degrees of Indianness in the speech or writing of the same individual which Kelkar (personal communication) calls "heightening or lowering of the Indianness." Thus when I speak to an Englishman I consciously try to achieve as much approximation to the native variety of English as I am capable of, although I will not do so while speaking to a fellow Indian. However, it is not always the person being addressed (in this connection an Englishman) who brings about a change in style. Sometimes the topic being discussed will also lead to a similar style switching. A teacher of English in India will be more careful about the accuracy of the English speech sounds, stress, and intonation in his speech while giving lessons on spoken English than when he is lecturing on *Far from the Madding Crowd* or *A Very Indian Poem in Indian English*. A similar variation in the degree of Indianness in the same individual may be noticed in the written medium as well. For instance, Mulk Raj Anand's English is much more Indian in his novels than in his book of sexology *Kamkala* or in his evaluations of works of art. One can appropriately therefore speak of degrees and kinds of Indianness in IE.

INTELLIGIBILITY

IE often poses a problem of intercomprehensibility. It is generally believed that dialects are mutually intelligible and hence IE should be intelligible to the speakers of all other varieties of English. This is not always the case. There is a great deal in IE, particularly at the phonological and lexical levels, that is incomprehensible in varying degrees to the speakers of English outside the Indian subcontinent. At times, English spoken in one part of the Indian territory is not correctly understood in another part. The presence of mutual intelligibility therefore is not an absolute fact and should admit a range of wide variations. As Robins points out, "Mutual intelligibility, however, is not an all-or-none matter and admits of degrees from almost complete and unhindered comprehension to nearly total incomprehension without special training" (Robins, 1966, p. 59). Postulating a cline of intelligibility seems inevitable in a situation like this.

It is common knowledge that educated native speakers of English, whether from England, the United States, Canada, or Australia, have no difficulty in understanding each other. Elaborating on this, Prator says, "They (the mother tongue types of English) have sprung from a common linguistic stock and have evolved at a relatively slow rate over the decades since they achieved their separate identities. Such changes as have occurred in them have been largely the result of little understood processes of internal evolution and have kept pace with other elements of social change; even after many years of semi-independent development these types of English are still characterized by a high degree of intercomprehensibility, especially as spoken by the well-educated" (Prator, 1968, p. 163). Mutual intelligibility among the native varieties is due to the fact that they use the same grammatical structures, share a more or less similar lexicon, have recognizable ranges of phonemic contrasts, and use similar patterns of stress and rhythm.

The position is, however, different with speakers of nonnative, second language varieties of English. For the purposes of intelligibility, the situation in countries where English is used as a second language has been represented as a pyramid. The uppermost section of this pyramid is said to be suggestive of internationally comprehensible English, the middle indicating a local standard intelligible all over the country, and the lowest being representative of pidgin which lacks intercomprehensibility (King, 1971, p. 3). This analogy cannot be applied to India for two reasons. First, the situation in this country from this standpoint divides itself into four sections (instead of three): the international, national, regional, and pidgin or local. Second, the design of a pyramid does not fit the Indian situation where the highest and the lowest points representing the international variety and pidgin are used by numerically small sections of the population.

Let us illustrate here the four levels of intelligibility in the case of IE. Certain items are intelligible only locally. One such item is *Lanketing* which means visiting Lanka, a shopping centre near Banaras University. Indian Pidgin English is also at times unintelligible as when the illiterate boatman talking to a foreign tourist pronounces *no* as *now* in the sentence "I 'now' burn the children" implying "I (we) don't burn the (dead) children."

Then, certain lexical items are intelligible only at the regional or state level. In most parts of South India the word *vessel* means *utensils*. *Vessel* is nowhere used in this sense in any part of North India. The husband of wife's sister is called *co-brother* in Karnataka and Tamilnadu, but *co-brother-in-law* in Andhra. These terms are also unknown in North India. The term *outbooks* meaning books outside the prescribed course is very common in West Bengal, but unknown in the rest of the country. Similarly, the fictional writings of Khushwant Singh and Mulk Raj Anand often create difficulty in understanding among non-Punjabi speakers on account of the pull of the regional language in them.

The regional variations in English speech discussed earlier also hamper intelligibility. A Bengali speaker once annoyed his Punjabi neighbour by his inquiry, "Do you have T.B.?" What the speaker actually meant was "Do you have T.V.?" At a Gujarati wedding recently an announcement was heard from the microphone, "The snakes are in the hole." It created panic among the guests. "Which hole?" was the unspoken hysterical question. There was a scramble for the exit until someone explained that the message was "The snacks are in the hall." It is evident from the foregoing that sometimes English used in one linguistic region in India is not understood in the other regions or by other mother-tongue groups in the same country.

We now pass to the international intelligibility of IE. Except for a small minority of Indians educated abroad, most speakers of English in India are not easily and correctly understood overseas. There have been numerous complaints to this effect. Stocqueler as early as 1848 refers to the puzzling incomprehensibility of English conversation in India which "wears strange suits" (Stocqueler, 1848, p. iii). King calls it a dangerous situation when native speakers of English find it possible "to hear, and not understand speakers of English from the Indian sub-continent" (King, 1971, p. 2). Quirk also speaks of "that admittedly foreign sounding English of the Indians" who are studying in his country (Quirk, 1972, p. 48). It is feared that English in the Indian subcontinent and in most African countries may, in the not very distant future, be found disintegrating into quite incomprehensible dialects. "If action is not taken," King warns, "English is going to diverge into a series of Germanic languages as Latin did into the Romance languages" (King, 1971, p. 2). I wonder if it is possible, or even desirable, to take any action at any level to compel or persuade these nonnative varieties to conform to the standard native model. The inevitable fact seems to be that the more widely English spreads in a country, the more internationally incomprehensible it becomes.

What is it in IE that stands in the way of its intelligibility abroad? One of the major hurdles is the fact that its phonological features make it distinct from the standard British variety. The vowel and consonant systems of IE are not identical with those in RP (Bansal, 1976). Among other phonological features of IE causing difficulty in international intelligibility, mention may be made of difficulty with some consonant clusters resulting in deletion of one of the consonants, substitution of some RP diphthongs by monophthongs, confusion between long and short vowels, a strong tendency for retroflexion, incorrect accentuation, neglect of weak forms, and the absence of characteristic English rhythm and intonation (Bansal, 1976 and Masica, 1966).

At the lexical level, intelligibility is hampered by interpolation of words from Indian languages, hybrid-formations, and neologisms which have been discussed earlier in this study. Of particular relevance in this context is the extension of semantic features of English lexical items. Notice, for instance, the following sentences, all drawn from the domain of education, which in a recent survey I conducted have been found to be perfectly intelligible on a pan-India basis but at the same time absolutely unintelligible to educated native speakers of English in Britain. (The special meaning in IE usage is given in parentheses.)

After abusing me he left saying he would *see* me outside the college. (He would beat me when he finds me outside the college.)

I came here by a *tempo*. (*tempo*: a three wheeler power-driven vehicle larger than an auto-rickshaw).

I bought a dozen *copies* for my daughter. (*copies*: exercise books).

This year there was no *mass-cut* in the college. (*mass-cut*: boycott en masse).

It is important to note that the cases of total incomprehensibility such as these are in no way attributable to cultural differences. Similar illustrations can be had from other domains in IE and this in effect belies the popular belief that cultural gap is the only factor causing incomprehensibility of IE.

Another interesting fact that emerged out of this survey is that numerous items in IE were found to be intelligible to some native speakers, while unintelligible to others within the same country, viz. England. For instance, when asked to explain what they understood by the IE expression "Her face-cut is very impressive," some native speakers of English gave the correct response scoring 100 percent intelligibility, that is, "Her profile is impressive" or "The shape of her face is very attractive," while others failed to understand the sentence correctly and came out with a variety of interpretations, some of them rather amusing: "She has good bones," "Her hair cut is very impressive," "Her facial scar is very striking," "She cut her face badly, poor girl," "Sounds as though she has been in a fight with the knives out," "Does the girl shave?" The question of international intelligibility of IE, and in fact of the other nonnative varieties of English, is no simple matter and calls for a good deal of caution in its handling.

Before winding up our discussion on this subject it may be asserted that only a small fraction of the Indian population, consisting mostly of academicians, scientists, diplomats, top industrialists, and business executives, is bothered about intelligibility at the international level. What primarily concerns the majority of the speakers of English in India is the comprehensibility of their speech and writing on a pan-India basis which in effect stresses the need for evolving—what R. H. Robins said recently in a personal interview with me— "one standard for the whole subcontinent." There is no denying the fact that it is much more important to understand one's own countrymen than to understand outsiders.

ACCEPTABILITY

A related issue is that of acceptability. Intelligibility and acceptability do not always go together. An utterance may be perfectly intelligible but not at all acceptable. For instance, the following IE expressions have in the course of my survey been found to be 100 percent intelligible to native speakers of English in Britain but at the same time totally unacceptable to them. They would never use these sentences themselves.

I would like to have bed tea every day.
The warden reached in time and cooled the matter.
You cannot get a good job without some source.
Please inform the staff concerned to do the needful.
He speaks chaste Urdu.
He passed the examination in the second division.
May I know your good name, please?

Often the native speakers themselves are not unanimous in their judgment on acceptability of an IE item. I asked 40 native speakers of English in a questionnaire if the following sentence, commonly heard in all parts of India, would be acceptable to them: "What subjects have you offered for your B.A. degree?" It was acceptable to 16, unacceptable to 24. Similar reactions were received with respect to the majority of IE samples. Look at the range of comments they made on another common IE sentence: "I hope this finds you in the pink of health" (some of these overtly contradict one another): "unacceptable," "not best English," "out of date," "pedantic," "stilted," "vulgar," "antiquated," "slightly archaic," "a non-U expression," "very upper class," "acceptable," and "a cast-iron idiom."

This leads us to the inevitable conclusion that we have to develop our own norms of acceptability instead of seeking every now and then the opinion of native speakers who, as we have just seen, are not unanimous in their pronouncements. We do not want our whole vocation to be an endless imitation of the Queen's English. The English used in India cannot but take its shape from the contextual spectrum of its speakers—their lifestyles, their thought, ways, and the very ethos they breathe. The norms of acceptability change from place to place and time to time. In this connection we cannot but admire the approach of an Edinburgh teacher who when asked to comment on an IE item in the course of my survey remarked, "I would not say it myself, but I would accept someone else saying it." Here is an attitude in the right direction. Then there are expressions that are neither fully acceptable nor fully unacceptable but can be shown at various points between the two extremes on the cline of acceptability in accordance with their role "towards the maintenance of appropriate patterns of life" (Firth, 1957, p. 225). As Greenbaum tersely remarked, "Whether a form is acceptable is not a question that can be answered simply. We have also to ask such questions as who finds it acceptable and in what contexts" (Greenbaum, 1975, p. 171).

NOTES

1. I owe a special debt of gratitude to John Pride without whose help and counsel it would have been a much less satisfactory paper. I should also like to record my indebtedness to Randolph Quirk, R. H. Robins, T. F. Mitchell, Rodney Moag, Ashok Kelkar, and Shiva M. Pandeya for helpful comments. For the shortcomings that remain the responsibility is entirely mine. I also wish to express my gratitude to the University Grants Commission, New Delhi and the British Council, London, for financial help in conducting the sociolinguistic survey of Indian English.

2. It would however be wrong to think that English has only been at the receiving end. It has impregnated the structure of Hindi and other regional languages with items of English vocabulary in no insignificant way. Here, by way of illustration, is an excerpt from the running commentary in Hindi of a cricket test match broadcast from All India Radio:

Abhi batsman *ne* ball *ko* silly mid on *par* push *kiya, wahan* fielder ready *tha, aur* ball *ko* Thompson *ne* field *kiya.*

Such type of language mix was also resorted to by the British officials while talking to the Indian subordinate staff in pre-independence days. Here are some interesting examples taken from a recent article (Menon, 1978).

Raju, *lejao* this *roti* and toast *karo* both sides.
Mali, this *ek* jungle plant *hai. Is liye* you need your *bahut pani* only *do dafa* every *hafta.*
Get *tumhara* bleeding *wardi saf karaoed.*

This kind of language flourished a great deal at the time of the last war when a large number of British soldiers and officers were sent to India with a view to expand the Indian army and subsequently interaction between the two groups grew considerably.

REFERENCES

Anjaneyulu, D. The problem of focussing the Indian image. In *Indian Writing in English: A Symposium.* Calcutta: The Writers Workshop, n.d.
Ansari, Iqbal A. *Uses of English.* New Delhi: New Statesman Publishing Co., 1978.
Bansal, R. K. *The Intelligibility of Indian English,* Monograph No. 4. Hyderabad: Central Institute of English and Foreign Languages, 1976.
Bloomfield, L. *Language.* Delhi: Motilal Banarasi Dass, 1935, 1963.

Bose, Buddhadeo. Indian poetry in English. In S. Spender and D. Hall (eds.), *The Concise Encyclopaedia of English and American Poets and Poetry*. London: Hutchinson Publishing Group Ltd., 1963.

Daswani, C. J. Pidginization in multilingual society: The case of English. Mimeographed.

Daswani, C. J. Indian English. *The Journal of the School of Languages* (Delhi). Winter 1974.

Earle, David. Indian English (Letter to the Editor). *The Indian Express.* November 17, 1976.

Ervin-Tripp, Susan M. An analysis of the interaction of language, topic and listener. In J. A. Fishman (ed.), *Readings in the Sociology of Language*. The Hague: Mouton and Co., 1968.

Firth, J. R. General linguistics and descriptive grammar. In *Papers in Linguistics 1934–1951.* London: Oxford University Press. First appeared in Transactions of the Philological Society, 1957.

Firth, J. R. *The Tongues of Men and Speech*. London: Oxford University Press, 1964.

Goffin, R. C. Some notes on Indian English. *S.P.E. Tract,* No. XLI. Oxford, 1934.

Greenbaum, Sidney. Language variation and acceptability. *TESOL Quarterly.* June 1975, 9, 2.

Hall, Robert A. *Hands off Pidgin English!* Sydney: Pacific Publications, 1955.

Ismail, Razia. Desi English. *Sunday Standard* (Delhi). October 20, 1974.

Iyengar, K. R. Srinivasa. The literature of India. In A. L. McLeod (ed.), *The Commonwealth Pen.* New York: Cornell University Press, 1961.

Jha, A. N. Presidential address at a conference of English professors, playwrights, critics, Lucknow, reported in *The Ceylon Daily News,* September 2, 1940.

Kachru, B. B. Toward a lexicon of Indian English. In B. B. Kachru, Robert B. Lees, et al. (eds.), *Issues in Linguistics*. Papers in honor of Henry and Renée Kahane. Urbana: University of Illinois Press, 1973.

Kachru, B. B. Lexical innovations in South Asian English. *International Journal of the Sociology of Language,* 4. The Hague: Mouton and Co., 1975.

Kandiah, Thiru. Disinherited Englishes: The case of Lankan English. Paper presented at the conference on English in non-native contexts held in June–July 1978 at the University of Illinois at Urbana-Champaign. To appear in *H. A. Passe Felicitation Volume.* Sri Lanka, n.d.

Kantak, V. Y. The language of Indian fiction in English. In *Critical Essays on Indian Writing in English*. Dharwar: Karnatak University, 1968.

Kindersley, A. E. Notes on the Indian idiom of English: Style, syntax and vocabulary. In *Transactions of the Philological Society.* 1938.

King, A. H. Intercomprehensibility—The Humpty-Dumpty problem of English as a world language. *The Incorporated Linguist.* January 1971, 11, 1.

Lal, P. Indian writing in English. In *Harvard Educational Review,* 1964, 34.

Lutze, Lothar. Linguistic prospects of the emergence of an internal contact language for India. In *Some Problems of Independent India*. South Asian Studies 4. New Delhi, 1968.

Masica, C. P. The sound system of general Indian English. Mimeographed. Hyderabad: CIEFL, 1966.

Mathai, S. The position of English in India. In E. Partridge and J. V. Clark (eds.), *British and American English since 1900.* London, 1951.

Mehrotra, R. R. Matrimonial advertisement: A study in correlation between linguistic and situational features. In *Studies in Linguistics* (Occasional Papers). Simla: Indian Institute of Advanced Study, 1975.

Menon, A. M. Hindi made in England. *The Indian Express,* April 3, 1978.

Moss, Norman. *What's the Difference?* London: Hutchinson Publishing Group, Ltd., 1973.

Prator, Clifford H. The British heresy in TESL. In J. A. Fishman, C. A. Ferguson, and J. Das Gupta (eds.), *Language Problems of Developing Nations.* New York: John Wiley & Sons, 1968.

Pride, John. Communicative needs in the use and learning of English. In *Indian Journal of Applied Linguistics.* 1978, 4.

Pyles, Thomas. *The Origin and Development of the English Language.* New York: Harcourt Brace Jovanovich, 1971.

Quirk, R. *The English Language and Images of Matter.* London: Oxford University Press, 1972.

Rai, V. *Landmarks in the History of English Literature,* Vol. III. Varanasi: Bhartiya Vidya Prakashan, 1967.

Rajan, B. R. *The Dark Dancer.* London: Heinemann, 1958.

Rao, Chalapathi. *Fragments of a Revolution.* Oxford: Pergamon, 1965.

Rao, G. Subba. *Indian Words in English.* Oxford: At the Clarendon Press, 1954.

Robins, R. H. *General Linguistics: An Introductory Survey.* London: Longmans, 1966.

Sapir, Edward. Language. In *Encyclopaedia of Social Sciences,* 9. New York: Macmillan Co., 1931. Quoted in Firth, J. R. (1964, p. 31).

Sharma, R. P. Desi English (letter to the editor). *The Illustrated Weekly of India,* Marh 31, 1974.

Sheshadri, C. K. British English and Indian English: A linguistic comparison. *Journal of the M. S. University of Baroda* (Humanities No.) XIV, April 1965.

Spitzbardt, Harry. *English in India.* VEB Max Niemeyar Verlag Halle (Seale), 1976.

Stocqueler, J. H. *The Oriental Interpreter and Treasury of the East India Knowledge: A Companion to "The Handbook of British India,"* 1848. Quoted in Kachru (1973, p. 356).

Subrahmanian, K. Penchant for the florid. *English Teaching Forum.* July 1977, 15, 3.

The Times (London). Baboo English. April 11, 1882.

The Times Literary Supplement. In common (editorial). August 10, 1962.

Todd, Loreto. *Pidgins and Creoles.* London: Routledge and Kegan Paul, 1974.

Ure, Jean. Code-switching and mixed speech in the register system of developing languages. Mimeographed, n.d.

Verghese, C. Paul. Indish or English. In *Essays on Indian Writing in English.* New Delhi: N.V. Publications, 1975.

Verma, S. K. Code-switching: Hindi-English. *Lingua.* 1976, 38.

Whitworth, G. C. *Indian English: An Examination of the Errors of Idiom Made by Indians in Writing English.* Lahore: The University Book Agency, 1932.

Yule, H. and Burnell, A. C. *Hobson-Jobson: A Glossary of Colloquial Anglo-Indian Words and Phrases, and of Kindred Terms, Etymological, Historical, Geographical and Discoursive* (1903). New edition by William Crooke. London: Routledge and Kegan Paul (1968).

10 SWADESHI[1] ENGLISH: FORM AND FUNCTION

Shivendra Kishore Verma

In my earlier papers (Verma, 1972a, 1972b, 1974) I have said that the Indian variety of English cannot be grouped with American English, Canadian English, Australian English, British English, and other mother-tongue varieties of English. It is a nonnative, second language variety and has a complex network of features contributed by the mother tongues of its speakers, by their cultures, and also by intralanguage analogical processes. It exists as a set of coherent, homogeneous linguistic systems and is describable as the speech of an identifiable social group. It is used by a community of people and institutions in India for interpersonal and interinstitutional communication in a wide range of contexts. These users are:

1. University and college students, and school students (trained at English-medium schools),
2. Teachers teaching at schools, colleges, and universities,
3. Officers and clerks working at all-India establishments, prestigious state establishments, railway, postal, shipping, airlines, and travel offices,
4. Mid-level and high-level workers working at prestigious hotels, restaurants, and business establishments,
5. Scholars participating in all-India seminars, workshops, and conferences,
6. All-India newspapers, magazines and journals,[2]
7. All-India bodies (governmental and nongovernmental) communicating with state-level bodies,
8. All-India bodies conducting competitive examinations for recruitment to all-India services,
9. Doctors, lawyers and other professionals conducting their business,
10. Members of prestigious clubs and other recreation centres, and
11. Creative writers writing their novels, stories, plays, poems, and essays in English.

Most of the members of this community are English-using bilinguals or multilinguals. They are highly skilled language switchers[3] and make alternate and effective use of their mother tongue(s) and English to cooperate with others and coordinate their activities. They use it both as an all-India link language and also as an intragroup contact language. English in India has to meet the demands that the local users make on it and serve functions that are specific to Indian culture (Verma, 1969, p. 366). The nature of Indian English is closely related to the demands that we make on it, the functions it has to serve. It interacts with a variety of Indian languages and yet it is not a regional or state language, it is an all-India language (India as a whole may be treated as its region). It is quite natural for it to have a marked Indian colour. Every dialect is a spatioculturally determined variety of a language: it is marked by socioregional features. Language change is a continuous process of adjustment between those of us who use the language and the situations in which we use it. What makes a variety a nonnative, second language variety is not individual linguistic variations or idiosyncrasies of writers but mother-tongue variations reflected in the use of that dialect. Whenever two or more languages come into contact, lexical items, phonological features, and also syntactic patterns manage to filter across from one to another. Gumperz (1964, pp. 1116–1117), highlighting the Indianness of Indian English, says that:

> An Indian may speak English with near-native control; he may read it, write it and lecture in it with great success. But when he uses English in India his speech will share many of the features of the other Indian codes with which English alternates in the daily round of activities. Indian English will thus deviate considerably from the norms current among native speakers of English in the American Midwest. This kind of deviation represents not a failure to control English, but a natural consequence of the social conditions in the immediate environment in which Indian English is spoken.

There is nothing abnormal about this situation. We must note that English does not necessarily mean British English or American English. There are a number of standard Englishes, for there are several English-speaking countries in each of which there is a standard English peculiar to that country. People are becoming more and more aware of different varieties of "white and black" English. "Obviously," says a British Council Report "fresh dialects of English will arise abroad—as they have done in English-speaking countries. Standards of acceptable speech will vary—as they do in Britain itself" (Quirk, 1962, p. 15). "The most important development of all," according to Halliday et al. (1964, p. 294), "is seen in the emergence of varieties of English that are identified with and specific to particular countries from among the former British colonies. In West Africa, in the West Indies, and in Pakistan and India . . . it is no longer accepted by the majority that the English of England, with R.P. as its accent, is the only possible model of English to be set before the young." In fact, in a number of countries in Southeast Asia and also in Africa L_2 varieties of English have begun to replace native varieties of English. "Such standards are determined by a particular society, in terms of that society's structure, and in terms of the purpose for which English is used in it" (Quirk, 1962, p. 16).

So long as English continues to have the status of a second language (and not a foreign language) in India, it will create its own local standard. If a language is used as a foreign language by a limited set of people in a very restricted set of situations, its users can follow a foreign model; but if it is used by a vast majority of educated people for a variety of purposes, it is bound to create a local model of its own. The users of English in India are exposed to Indian English, for it is Indian English that they hear all around them and read in local magazines and newspapers (English English is restricted to textbooks, foreign films, and radio broadcasts). Exposure plays a crucial role in language acquisition. We learn that variety of a language to which we are exposed. In the present context we can go to the extent of saying that there are no Indian users of English in India who use any of the features peculiar to Indian English.

These users of English are educated, urban, elite bilinguals (by educated in this context we mean those people who have had English-based education and have obtained at least their first degree). They are (as has already been mentioned) code-switchers—switching from their mother tongue to English and from English to their mother tongue according to the topic of discourse, setting (local/all-India), and addresser-addressee relationships. Their choice (between English and their mother tongues) is also conditioned by their concepts of appropriateness, effectiveness, and "getting the work done." Their assessment of the sociocultural setting prompts them to use a registro-stylistic variety of L_A in a situation marked X and on a topic M and then shift to a registro-stylistic variety of L_B in a situation marked Y and on a topic N.

$$L_A/Code_A \qquad + \qquad L_B/Code_B$$
registro-stylistic features   registro-stylistic features

It is quite common today for speakers of Hindi and other Indian languages to switch to English when talking about scientific principles or describing the working of some complex machinery. They use different varieties of their mother tongue in various situations in life, but when they have to use a technical register, they usually switch to English. This kind of register-oriented bilingualism may be labeled "registral bilingualism" (Verma, 1969b, p. 302).

We must, however, make a note of a very important sociolinguistic movement in India today. The various regional languages of India are all being consciously expanded in vocabulary and standardized in spelling and grammar, so that they can increasingly function as the exclusive languages of government and of higher culture and technology (Fishman, 1972, pp. 45-46). However, one of the most interesting features of this sociolinguistic situation is that the same person switches automatically from one code to another in the same discourse or even within the same utterance, or uses a mixture of two or more codes. In each instance, the speakers want to identify themselves with a different speech network to which they belong and from which they seek acceptance.

These languages (English and the Indian languages—I will refer to English-Hindi contact situations) have co-existed for so many years now that there are constant pressures to merge the two systems of the bilingual. To be more accurate, the pressure has led to the Indianization (for example Hindi-ization and Tamilization) of English and the Anglicization of the Indian languages. This intense interaction between the linguistic systems has resulted in a new variety of Hindi/Tamil/Telugu/Marathi and so on and also a new variety of English. There are purists who consider the mixed variety corrupt and maintain that it should not be used in polite societies. There are others (young learners and creative writers) who regard these varieties as natural and living products of languages in contact. One striking linguistic aspect of this situation is the fact that we find few of the strictures against structural borrowing and giving the nonnative language a local colour and flavour commonly reported in some linguistic literature.

The Indianness of Indian English is to be seen in two varieties of English in India—the creative writer's use of English (his own English and his characters' use of English) and the general use of English by a variety of people in a variety of situations. References in this connection have been made to such idiosyncratic creations as *flowerbed*, *rape-sister, sister-sleepers,* and a host of similar expressions that have been used in Indo-Anglian novels. They have been coined by individual creative writers to convey those thought processes that look maltreated in an alien language. They are register-bound—restricted to the register of short stories and novels. As translation equivalents of corresponding expressions in Indian languages, they are highly idiosyncratic and arbitrary. One might go to the extent of saying that in some cases they are bad translations. One of the most significant facts about these *flowerbed* types of creation is that they are not used even by their authors in their ordinary, everyday language. They are not deviations but arbitrary creations. They have been created in the process of finding translation equivalents of concepts and ideas deeply rooted in Indian culture, and of faiths and beliefs represented by what the characters might have said in their mother tongues.

M. R. Anand (1969, p. 280), explaining his own position, says: "I generally translate or interpret my feelings or thought from Punjabi or Hindustani into the English language, thus translating the metaphor or imagery of my mother-tongue into what is called Indo-Anglo-Indian writing, but what I prefer to call 'pigeon Indian' (not Pidgin-Indian)." The peculiar feature of this variety is that it is not typical of the language of the community; it is fully idiosyncratic; its rules are peculiar to the language used by individual novelists and story-tellers in their creative writings. If innovations are to become more than personal idiosyncrasies, others must imitate them and incorporate them into their everyday language patterns. Some of the sentences used by M. R. Anand and Kushwant Singh are not readily interpretable in the non-Hindi/Punjabi/Urdu area. These writers know the conventions of the standard dialect but deliberately choose not to follow them. Their creations are motivated by their desire to make

English an effective tool of Indian culture. "All idiosyncratic dialects have this characteristic in common that some of the rules required to account for them are peculiar to an individual. This has, of course, the result that some of their sentences are not readily interpretable, since the ability to interpret a sentence depends in part upon the knowledge of the conventions underlying that sentence" (Corder, 1971).

Second language varieties of English are reserved for use among specific individuals in a restricted range of situations. It is generally said that this variety cannot be used as a tool of English culture. The real issue here is not that Indian English cannot be used as a tool of culture, but that it cannot and is surely not designed to be a component of British, American, or Canadian culture. It is used as a vehicle of Indian culture to express culturally determined networks of activities that are typically Indian; for example, the social stratification in India, the caste systems, and a complex network of personal and societal faiths and beliefs. Halliday et al. (1964, p. 174) think that there is even a risk here of conveying an implication that the native languages are somehow inferior: "Those who favour the adoption of 'Indian English' as a model, from whatever motive, should realize that in doing so they may be helping to prop up the fiction that English is the language of Indian culture and thus be pepetuating the diminished status of the Indian languages." Creative writers in India using English as their medium feel that their variety of English comes naturally to them. Their choice of English is partly their personal choice and is partly motivated by their desire to reach an international audience. They use English as an alternative way of expressing their culture.

The problem for the Indo-Anglian writers is how to express, in English, moods and expressions that are typically Indian. They have used a variety of devices to solve this problem. To do this effectively they have had to borrow words and expressions from Indian languages or to produce translation equivalents of these expressions. Kamla Das has expressed this forcefully in the following lines:

> The language I speak
> becomes mine
> Its distortions, its queernesses
> all mine, mine alone.
> It is half English, half Indian
> funny perhaps, but it is honest
> It is human as I am human
> Don't you see?

(Summer in Calcutta)

In his foreword to *Kanthapura*, Raja Rao says:

The telling has not been easy. One has to convey in a language that is not one's own the spirit that is one's own. One has to convey the various shades and omissions of a certain thought-movement that looks maltreated in an alien language. I use the word 'alien', yet English is not really an alien language to us. It is the language of our intellectual make-up—like Sanskrit or Persian was before—but not of our emotional make-up. We are all instinctively bilingual, many of us writing in our own language and in English. We cannot write like the English. We should not. We cannot write only as Indians. We have grown to look at the large world as part of us. Our method of expression, therefore, has to be a dialect which will some day prove to be as distinctive and colourful as the Irish or the American. Time alone will justify it.

Raja Rao has highlighted a number of aspects of English in India. First, the users of English are all English-based bilinguals. Second, they cannot write like Englishmen and they should not, for their variety of English draws its sustenance from an atmosphere in which it interacts with Indian languages and Indian culture. Third, it is a dialect in its own right and is one of the languages of India's intellectual make-up. Talking about R. K. Narayan's English, Walsh (1964, pp. 128–129) says that "it is clear of the palpable suggestiveness, the foggy taste, the complex tang running through every phrase of our own English. What it has instead is a strange degree of translucence. Unaffected by the opacity of a British inheritance or by the powerful, positive quality of a language which as we use it can never be completely subordinated to our private purposes, Narayan's language is beautifully adapted to communicate a different, an Indian sensibility."

Mulk Raj Anand uses a number of devices to make his English express feelings and sentiments deeply rooted in Indian interpersonal relations. "His endeavour to naturalize the language depends on three devices. Most notable is the literal translation of Hindi or Punjabi idiom into English: thus, 'my counterfeit luck' (mera khota naseeb), 'is this any talk?' (yeh bhi koi bat hai), 'nothing black in the pulse' (dal me kala), 'made my sleep illegal' (neend haram kar dia). Secondly, he interpolates Hindi words in an English sentence indiscriminately. . . . ('Shut up *Saley,* Stop you *tain tain*'). The third device is changing the spelling of English words to suggest uneducated speech: 'yus' for yes, 'notus' for notice" (Mukherjee, 1977, pp. 240–241). These are some of the distinctive features of English in India as it is used by creative writers to communicate an Indian sensibility, but this represents only one variety of English in India. The other variety or varieties refer to the use of English as a general service language, an interstate link language and a language of science, technology, and research.

When people try to use a language to which they are not native, the opportunities for their first language to influence their second are almost limitless. New words are certainly needed to identify things and processes for which there is no name in British or American culture. *Co-brother,* for example, has no value in English but it has a precise, culturally determined value in Indian English. This is true of a host of other lexical items. "There is a psychological truth behind this kind of synthetic speech. It is this: even when Indians know English grammar and have been used to speaking the alien tongue for a long time, they tend to feel and think in their own mother-tongues. And often, the native speech enters into the shell of the sentence in the foreign language through certain indigenous words" (Anand, 1970, p. 8). "The English used in India, even by foreigners who are but temporary residents of the country is filled with

Indian expressions. Immersed in a new country, surrounded by foreign languages and familiar objects, it is easy for an English speaker to accept new terms for the new objects. The washerman quickly becomes the *dhobi,* the tailor the *durzi* and a European man soon becomes reconciled to answering to the title *sahib"* (Burling, 1970, pp. 171–172).

In English the word *colony* is used to mean country or territory that has been developed by people from another country and is still, fully or partly, controlled by a group or people from another country; alternatively, people with the same trade, profession, or occupation living together. In Indian English this word is used to mean a residential area or block of flats, for example, Rajendra Colony, Railway Colony, and so on. The word *compound* is used in India, China, Burma, Sri Lanka, and so forth to mean an enclosed area with buildings. Most probably, it is derived from the Malay word, *kampong* meaning *enclosure.* *Almirah* is used in Indian English for a cupboard and also for a chest of drawers. The word *prepone* does not exist in British English; in Indian English it means to decide to do something earlier than expected. Similarly, the expression *pin-drop silence* is not usual in British English; it is used in Indian English to mean absolute silence. This shows that certain common English words have a slightly different meaning in India from the meaning they have in Britain or in America. This again is a natural feature, for words derive their special or extended meaning from the sociocultural contexts in which they are used.

Indian English is a self-contained system and follows its own set of rules. This system is closely related to the core grammar of English English. The Englishness of this socioregional dialect lies in the fact that its basic linguistic systems are the same as those of English English. Its Indianness lies in the fact that, within the overall general framework of the systems of English English, it displays certain distinguishing phonological, lexico-semantic, and also syntactic features. In terms of linguistic efficiency, these patterns are as good as any other. They are not corrupt, but rather different forms of the same language. Acceptability is a matter of social convention. Grammaticality, on the other hand, is rule-governed. When we say that a particular sentence is well formed, we mean that it is well formed in the particular dialect being described. There is no logical or natural reason why the auxiliary verb should be in front of the subject in a question form. "It is generally conceded that somebody speaking or writing in his mother tongue is allowed to take liberties with the language, since after all 'it is his own language.' But somebody who had acquired the same language as a second language would be felt by many to be wrong to do the same; it would be an improper liberty for him to take, 'since it is not his own language'" (Graves, 1966). Graves said also of Vladimir Nobokov that "his one error lies in abrogating a native-born's right . . . to do what he likes with the language" (Graves, 1966, p. 49). We do not accept this position, for we feel that creative writers have a right to explore the sociolinguistic resources of the language(s) they use. Any human language can be expanded to express any human thought; it may mean stretching the language beyond what at any particular time is considered native-like usage.

Dialects and individual variations share a large number of underlying similarities. By studying the deeper underlying principles of syntax we are in a better position to appreciate how minor the differences among the variants of the same language are. There is a vast body of sentence-formation principles common to English English and Indian English. Both the dialects consider the following patterns ungrammatical:

I done have work my.
Mohan reached at Patna today.

Now consider the following sentence types:

A. *Complex Sentence Formation.*   When a sentence is (or a number of sentences are) subordinated to function as constituents of a matrix sentence, we get a complex sentence. English English imposes certain tense and pronominal restrictions on the choices in the embedded sentences; Indian English tends to relax these restrictions.

IE: When I saw him two days ago, he told me that he is coming.
EE: When I saw him two days ago, he told me that he was coming.
IE: I asked Hari where does he work.
EE: I asked Hari where he worked.
IE: Tell me clearly are you coming.
EE: Tell me clearly if you are coming.

In English English the subject-auxiliary inversion rule applies only to the free type of interrogatives. In embedded interrogative sentences, the interrogative transformation is not applied: in Indian English the distinction between embedded and nonembedded interrogatives is not maintained. Embedding in IE is accomplished not by the use of *whether* or *if,* but by means of a flip-flop in the embedded sentence instead. This is also seen in Black English vernacular (Trudgill, 1974, p. 73), for example, "I asked Mary where did she go." and "I want to know did he come last night."

IE: If they will be here by this evening, we may go out.
EE: If they are here by this evening, we may go out.

English English has a complex system of rules to generate question-tags; Indian English has reduced this complex network of rules to one simple rule, that is, suffixation of *isn't it* or *no.*

IE: You went there yesterday, isn't it? (no?)
        You are coming this evening, isn't it? (no?)
        He will come tomorrow, isn't it? (no?)
EE: You went there yesterday, didn't you?
        You are coming this evening, aren't you?
        He will come tomorrow, won't he?

B. *Interrogative Transformation.*   The interrogative transformation in English English shifts the first constituent of the auxiliary to the pre-subject NP position. If the auxiliary is not patent, it creates the dummy *do* and gives it all the features of the first constituent of the auxiliary. The WH question transformation replaces the item to be questioned by an appropriate WH word and shifts it to the front. Indian English has a much simpler system of transformations. It does not use the subject-auxiliary inversion rule, but rather intonation, or intonation plus the structure of a statement.

IE: What you are leaving?
EE: Are you leaving?
IE: Who(m) you would like to see?
EE: Who would you like to see?
IE: Where you are going?
EE: Where are you going?
IE: What he wants?
EE: What does he want?

	English English	*Indian English*
Yes/No Questions	Flip-flop obligatory	Flip-flop optional
Embedded Yes/No Questions	No flip-flop	Flip-flop favoured

C. *The Perfective Forms.*   In English English the present perfect establishes a link between the past and the present. It is not used in the environment of the simple past. In Indian English this distinction is neutralized.

IE: I have worked there in 1960.
EE: I worked there in 1960.
IE: I have read this book yesterday.
EE: I read this book yesterday.

This use of the present perfect with an adverb of time (definite past) is so very common in English in India that it is seen even in such important and formal documents as the following:

1. Biographical Notes: p. 767 (*Current Trends in Linguistics V*):
   He (i.e., A. K. Ramanujan) *has taught* English in Indian Colleges and Universities from 1950 till 1957 and is now Professor of Linguistics and Dravidian Studies at the University of Chicago.
2. From the will of late V. K. Krishna Menon (published in *The Hindustan Times Weekly,* Sunday, No. 10, 1974):
   I, Vengalil Krishna Menon, son of late Sri Kamath Krishna Kurup, residing at 19, Teenmurti Marg, New Delhi, do hereby execute this will and testament which is in addition to and apart from *the will I have executed in April 1974,* in respect only of my taravad and tavazhi property, movable and immovable.

Indian English tends to favour the use of the present continuous both for the present perfect continuous and the present continuous and does not maintain any distinction between *since* and *for.*

IE: I am writing this essay since two hours.
EE: I have been writing this essay for two hours.
IE: We are living here since six years.
EE: We have been living here for six years.

D. *Complementation.*   Complementation is a syntactic mechanism by which a sentence is subordinated to function as a complement of one of the constituents of another sentence. It is the nouns or verbs of the recipient sentences that impose constraints on complement types. A want-type of verb in English English, for example, does not take a that-sentence. Indian English does not impose any such constraints.

IE: Mohan wants that you should go there.
EE: Mohan wants you to go there.

It is clear, then, that Indian English uses a set of syntactic rules to generate the sentence types that were listed. These nonstylistic deviant (deviant when compared with the patterns of English English) syntactic patterns are typical not only of Indian English but of many nonnative, second, and foreign language varieties of English. In French English and also in German and Czech English one often comes across such sentences as "I have gone to the cinema yesterday." In Sri Lankan, Burmese, Indonesian, and Japanese English, WH questions, as in Indian English, are marked by noninversion:

When you will move into your new house?
How you managed to get to this place?

In Hungarian English (Katona, 1960), we find such sentences as:

How long you are in Budapest?
I learn English for two years.
I asked him that where he went.

In French (Wilkins, 1972, p. 194) it is not possible for the equivalent of *want* to be followed by a pronoun like *him,* which is both the object of *want* and the subject of the following infinitive. An infinitive can follow *vouloir* only if the main verb and the infinitive have the same subject. The construction that has to be used involves the French equivalent of *that,* so that in English we may find the French speaker saying:

His wife wants that he pays her grandmother a visit.

It might seem tempting to dismiss these patterns as nothing more than an accumulation of errors or foreignisms caused by the failure of the speakers to master standard English, but the plain fact is that such patterns have become so well established in Indian English that they get passed on from one generation to the next. They have assumed such stability and continuity that they can be seen more like dialectal innovations than ephemeral foreignisms. The sentences in the preceding list are all part of the grammar of a great many educated speakers of English. This variety does not prevent effective communication; it is capable of clarity, complexity, power, and tenderness. What is correct and what is not correct is ultimately only a matter of conventions within a society. This is not an argument in favour of "anything goes." It depends on who says it and when. Firth (1964, p. 176) makes a reference to Babuism in Indian English, by which he means badly overdrawn English. Babuism, however, is not by any means confined to India. It is again a characteristic feature of nonnative varieties and is a by-product of purely literary, text-based language teaching. By Indian English we do not mean a mixture of English and Indian languages. It is different from what has been called Spanglish (Edna Acosta-Belen, 1975, p. 151). Spanglish is generally described as a particular mixture of Spanish and English. It is true that Indian English has drawn words from most of the Indian languages and has created translation equivalents of concepts deeply rooted in Indian culture. It is also true that it has simplified a number of grammatical patterns of English English. And yet Indian English is not a mixture, it is an auxiliary language and has a rule-governed system.

Native varieties of a language do not permit any marked nonstylistic syntactic deviance. This reinforces the point made earlier on that Indian English is a nonnative variety of English. Yet it is a highly structured system. When we say that it is a system, we mean that it differs from other dialects in rule-governed ways. Indian English, for example, does not use WH + Aux + Subject + NP patterns in WH questions but the meaning is preserved by the formal device of WH + Subject NP + Aux + Mv + · · · · One might say that these two patterns represent two dialectally variant surface manifestations of the same deep structure. These differences show up in the transformational component of grammar. Underlying both dialects there is a network of semantically significant syntactic relations. We are interested both in the vast body of syntactic principles that are common to all varieties of English and in those surface features that are peculiar to particular dialects. Indian English is adapted to the needs, interests, and cultural pressures of the speech community that uses it, while at the same time making use of the main features of the structures and systems that constitute the common language. It does have, like all dialectal variations, its own idiosyncratic rules that make it distinct from English English both linguistically and culturally.

Creative artists have begun to feel that the time has come for us to consider seriously the question of a Bharat brand of English; every variety of English has gone through a process of "toasting" (i.e., acquiring marked local colour). One noticeable result of this toasting is that much of the formalism surrounding the use of English has been abandoned. The refinements of usage in countries where English has the status of an auxiliary official language are worthy of study.

So far English has had a comparatively confined existence in our country, chiefly in the halls of learning, justice, or administration. Now the time is ripe for it to come to the dusty street, market place, and under the banyan tree. English must adopt the complexion of our life and assimilate its idiom. I am not suggesting here a mongrelisation of the language. I am not recommending that we should go back to the days when we heard, particularly in the railway, 'Wer U goin', man?' Bharat English will respect the rule of law and maintain the dignity of grammar, but still have a Swadeshi stamp about it unmistakably, like the Madras handlook check chirt or the Thirupathi doll. (Narayan, 1974, p. 57)

Examining the phenomenon of Indian verse in English Parthasarathy says that "it is Indian in sensibility and context, and English in language. It is rooted in and stems from the Indian environment, and reflects its mores, often ironically" (Parthasarathy, 1976, p. 3). Writers in English are conscious of their Indianness because they exemplify the uneasy tensions that arise in using a language they are not born into. Ramanujan says that "English and my disciplines (linguistics, anthropology) give me my 'outer' forms—linguistic, metrical, logical and other such ways of shaping experience; and my first thirty years in India, my frequent visits and field trips, my personal and professional preoccupations with Kannada, Tamil, the classics and folklore give me my substance, my 'inner' forms, images and symbols. They are continuous with each other, and I no longer can tell what comes from where" (Parthasarathy, 1976, pp. 95–96).

English in India represents a cline[4] extending from noneducated varieties of English at one end (which are not at all intelligible) to an internationally accepted standard form of English at the other. In between these two ends we have a great range of language variations. The two ends do not represent Indian English. What we have called educated Indian English is between the two ends and is marked by the presence of a number of syntactic patterns which, when compared with the surface patterns of English English, may be called deviant. But a deep analysis of the syntactic systems of Indian English reveals that they are not oddities but rather rule-governed dialectal variations. Linguistically speaking it cannot be considered a corrupt language; it is just different. To interpret its difference as its limitation is to miss the point. It is true that we cannot set up regular rules or systems to explain the violations of agreement rules and misuse or omission of articles and prepositions. Their use is so erratic and nonpredictable that they cannot be treated as features of educated Indian English. Muriel Wasi proclaims this kind of English as a fractured version of English. "The careless use of prepositions, the careless use of idioms, many of them distinctly Indian, proclaims it as a fractured version of English that is now common in India. It may have flavour; frequently it does. But no language has ever become acceptable for the educated of the world on the mere ground that it has a flavour of its own" (Wasi, 1970, p. 21).

The question whether Indian English *ought* to be what it is, is an extralinguistic question. Our main thesis here is that all nonnative second language varieties are varieties in their own right and are characterized by phonological, syntactic, and lexico-semantic properties peculiar to these varieties. What is really remarkable in our context is that Indo-Anglian writers and also general urban educated users of English feel loyal to this language and take pride in shaping it into an Indian language with a typical Indian flavour. Its future will depend on its ability to co-exist peacefully with the Indian languages in an atmosphere of "give and take" and the role that it can be made to play as an efficient tool for intragroup and intergroup contacts in a multilingual nation.

NOTES

1. The word *Swadeshi* represents a national movement in the direction of using home-made, home-grown articles, and of reshaping borrowed/imported items/ideas to function effectively in our sociocultural contexts.

2. Although English is spoken by a very tiny percentage of India's population, it is the language in which the largest number of Indians read newspapers (total circulation figures of English-language dailies in India: 1,945,000; of Hindi dailies: 1,175,000—these figures are 1969 figures based on Jussawalla, 1974, p. 25). In fact, every state produces a few newspapers and magazines in English.

3. Some of them are bidialectals—using Indian English in ordinary discourse and English English in formal (written) discourse.

4. "One point, however, does need to be made about 'Indian English,' which hardly yet applies to the West African and West Indian varieties of the language: that the single label 'Indian English' is used to cover a very great number of different varieties of English. The label has been used to refer, at one extreme, to various semi-pidgins that are at first encounter quite unintelligible to speakers of American or British English and almost certainly also to each other, and at the other extreme, to standard English of the most acceptable and consistent kind, accompanied by an RP accent with only a single variation, namely the use of retroflex consonants (made with the tip of the tongue curled back) for /t/, /d/, /n/, /l/. It is quite clear that not all the kinds of variant English denoted by 'Indian English' are acceptable alternative models" (Halliday, 1964, pp. 295–296). We have already made the point clear that by educated Indian English we mean those varieties of English that are used by English-based educated bilinguals. These varieties lie between the two ends of the cline of bilingualism.

REFERENCES

Acosta-Belen, Edna. Spanglish: A case of languages in contact. Marina K. Burt and H. C. Dulay (eds.), In *New Directions in Second Language Learning, Teaching and Bilingual Education.* TESOL, Washington, D.C., 1975.

Anand, M. R. A plea for English for higher education. *Language and Society in India:* Transactions of Indian Institute of Advanced Study, Simla, 1969, 8.

Anand, M. R. Pigeon-Indian: Some notes on Indian-English writing. Seminar on Australian and Indian Literature, Azad Bhawan, New Delhi: January 12–16, 1970.

Burling, R. *Man's Many Voices.* New York: Holt, Rinehart & Winston, Inc., 1970.

Corder, S. P. Idiosyncratic dialects and error analysis. *IRAL*, 1971, IX/2.

Firth, J. R. *The Tongues of Man and Speech*, London: Oxford University Press, 1964.

Fishman, J. The sociology of language. In P. P. Giglioli (ed.), *Language and Social Context.* Harmondsworth: Penguin, 1972.

Graves, R. Language Levels. *Encounter.* May 1966.

Gumperz, J. J. Hindi-Punjabi code-switching in Delhi. *Proceedings of the Ninth International Congress of Linguists.* London: Mouton and Co., 1964.

Halliday, M. A. K., McIntosh, A., and Strevens, P. *The Linguistic Sciences and Language Teaching.* London: Longmans, 1964.

Jussawalla, A. *New Writing in India.* Harmondsworth: Penguin, 1974.

Katona, A. Grammatical difficulties of Hungarian students. *ELT.* 1960, XIV, 2.

Mukherjee, M. Beyond the village: An aspect of Mulk Raj Anand. In M. K. Naik, S. K. Desai, and G. S. Amur (eds.), *Critical Essays on Indian Writing in English.* Delhi: Macmillan Co. of India, Ltd., 1977

Narayan, R. K. *Reluctant Guru*. Delhi: Hind Pocket Books, 1974.

Parthasarathy, R. (ed.) *Ten Twentieth Century Indian Poets,* Delhi: Oxford University Press, 1976.

Quirk, R. *The Use of English*. London: Longmans, 1962.

Trudgill, P. *Sociolinguistics*, Harmondsworth: Penguin, 1974.

Verma, S. K. Problems of teaching Hindi as a second language in India. *Language and Society in India*, Transactions of Indian Institute of Advanced Studies, Simla, Vol. 8, 1969a.

Verma, S. K. Towards a linguistic analysis of registral features. *Acta Linguistica*, Budapest, 1969b, 3–4.

Verma, S. K. Syntactic irregularities in Indian English. Paper presented at the Seminar on Indian English organized by the Central Institute of English & Foreign Languages, Hyderabad, 1972a.

Verma, S. K. A linguist's view of English in India. *Indian and Foreign Review* 10, 1972b.

Verma, S. K. The Systemicness of Indian English. *ITL*. Belgium, 1974.

Walsh, W. *A Human Idiom*. London: Chatto& Windus, 1964.

Wasi, Muriel. Indian English. *The Education Quarterly*. New Delhi, 1970.

Wilkins, D. A. *Linguistics in Language Teaching*. London: Edward Arnold, 1972.

11 ENGLISH IN SRI LANKA: A CASE STUDY OF A BILINGUAL COMMUNITY

Chitra Fernando

INTRODUCTION

This study[1] describes the language situation of Sri Lanka (previously called Ceylon) and examines the factors governing the language choice of Sinhalese bilinguals while attempting to correlate such factors with domains and role relations. It also examines the way in which such correlations reflect social differences in Sri Lankan society. The use of two languages by the same speakers almost inevitably effects the forms of the languages so used. The use of English by Sinhalese speakers has led to the functional elaboration of both English and Sinhala. Bilinguals show varying degrees of proficiency in the languages they use. Such disparities in performance have led to differing patterns of bilingualism manifested in different phonological and grammatical features. Materials are drawn from the English of newspapers, fiction, drama, poetry, and personal knowledge.

English was brought to Sri Lanka by the British who succeeded the Dutch in 1796 as colonial masters of the island. In 1802 a proper civil administration was set up when, as a result of the Treaty of Amiens, Ceylon was officially declared a British Crown Colony. A process then began whereby English displaced both Dutch and the vernaculars, Sinhala and Tamir,[2] as the state language. It became the major language of administration, of law, of secular education, and of commerce.

It is difficult to assess to what degree Portuguese and, after it, Dutch were spoken by the indigenous population. Judging by brief scattered references in nineteenth and early twentieth century historical work (Tennent, 1850, and Pieris, 1914), knowledge of Portuguese and Dutch appears to have been confined to a section of the population. The interest of the Portuguese (1505–1658) and the Dutch (1658–1796) in Ceylon was narrowly commercial, their government largely military. There was no real interest in what Sir James Emerson Tennent termed "civil colonisation." To secure their military hold on Sri Lanka, the Portuguese for a period had encouraged intermarriage with the Sinhalese, an experiment which was tried with disappointing results "by a few of the highest and by large numbers of the lowest among the people" (Pieris, 1914, p. 117). This suggests that at least a section of the native population would have been bilingual. Tennent noted that "at the present time [that is, 1850] Portuguese is in almost universal use in all towns in the maritime provinces, and that Dutch is not only almost extinct but the descendants of the Dutch have betaken themselves to speak the language of Portugal" (1850, p. 68). Even in present-day Sri Lanka a creolised form of Portuguese is spoken among sections of the population living in towns and villages mostly on the east coast (Goonetilleke and Hettiaratchi, 1976). The majority of the descendants of the Portuguese and virtually all the Dutch colonials, however, eventually adopted English as a mother tongue. By the end of the nineteenth century, Dutch was hardly spoken in Sri Lanka and Portuguese had ceased to be used in middle-class social intercourse, though these European languages left their mark on Sinhala as well as on Sri Lanka English, both of which have many loanwords from these sources.

English, in time, also came to be adopted as a virtual mother tongue by a section of the multiracial non-European population of Sri Lanka comprising the Sinhalese, the Tamils, the Moors, and the Malays,[3] and as such became in varying degrees the language of their domestic and social intercourse and of their entertainment. The more Anglicised upper-class members of the Sinhalese middle-class group which was numerically the largest, as well as Anglicised upper-middle-class Tamils, began speaking English in infancy and used it for almost all purposes. Sinhala was used for talking to members of the older generation (for example, grandparents), to infants, to Buddhist monks, to servants, and to *hoi polloi* who, of course, quite properly spoke the vernacular. The less Anglicised members of the middle-class group, mid and lower middle, usually learned English at a much later stage and might have found it necessary to use Sinhala in their conversation with parents or members of the same generation such as siblings, particularly sisters who were monolingual or whose command of English was limited to comprehension. But whatever the degree of Anglicisation, both English and Sinhala were used in domestic and social intercourse among the members of the middle class.

The major incentives towards the acquisition of English by the Sri Lankans are quite clear. In pre-British Sri Lanka (and this would still be the case in certain parts of the country), an individual's occupation went together with his caste, both of which determined his place in the social hierarchy (Leach, 1960). For a man to change his occupation in a society that was still very feudal in its economic organisation was relatively difficult. Cultivation being socially the most acceptable occupation, the cultivator caste (*goigama*), itself subdivided, was at the top of the social hierarchy and was also the largest caste group. The other castes, fishermen (*karave*), cinnamon-peelers (*salagama*), washermen (*radauw*), carpenters (*waduwo*), tom-tom beaters (*berawayo*), and so on, were considered to be collectively inferior to the cultivators and were themselves, on the basis of convention, hierarchically ordered in relation to one another. With the opening up of coffee and, later on, tea, rubber, and coconut plantations the economy changed. The establishment of a modern bureaucracy together with the expansion of secular education provided forms of employment other than the traditional ones. English was the language of commerce, of administration, and of secondary and tertiary education. The study of English offered all Sri Lankans very substantial material advantages. To the noncultivator castes it offered, in addition, the possibility of moving away from a caste system based on hereditary occupation towards a class system based on education, government, or commercial employment and money.

The Sri Lankan middle class, which came into existence under the British, was a mixture of all races in Sri Lanka with the exception of the Veddahs (a jungle aboriginal tribe) and almost all castes. It was distinct from the rest of the population by virtue of its adoption of the English language in domestic and social intercourse, its British style of education and its Anglicised way of life. This way of life in many instances also included the Christian religion.

Christianity in the form of Roman Catholicism had been introduced to Sri Lanka in the sixteenth century by the Portuguese and had secured a certain number of indigenous converts, especially among the fisherman caste. Religious activity among the great majority of these Roman Catholics was carried out then as now in the vernaculars, as the Portuguese parish priests were strongly encouraged to learn Sinhala and Tamil (Pieris, 1914, p. 478) unlike the Dutch who relied mostly on interpreters (Tennent, 1850, p. 68). But with the rise of an Anglicised bilingual group in the nineteenth century, the Roman Catholic clergy began to use English as well as the vernaculars in the fulfillment of their duties. The members of other Christian denominations (the Presbyterians, Anglicans, Methodists, Baptists, and so on) were and are still drawn almost entirely from the Anglicised middle class, unlike the Roman Catholics who belong to all social levels. The language of religion for the former is largely, though not exclusively, English. The middle class also includes Buddhists, Hindus, and Muslims. The clergy in all these three oriental religions would normally know no English (the rare exceptions being the missionary Buddhist monk or Hindu priest). All Buddhist sermons are preached in Sinhala, but the language of the sacred texts is Pali, a *prakrit* of Sanskrit spoken by the Buddha. Tamil is normally used in the religious discourses of the Hindus and the Muslims, but certain of the sacred Hindu texts would still be accessible only through Sanskrit, while the *Koran* continues to be read in Arabic.

Though the original motives for the acquisition of English by the Sri Lankan middle class were primarily social and economic, once English became the language of the individual in domestic and social intercourse, it acquired certain emotional associations and even elicited a certain language loyalty. Some of these Anglicised bilinguals went to the extent of flaunting a claimed lack of proficiency in the vernacular mother tongue. Such a claim, since it was accompanied by a near-native control of English, associated the speaker with the sought-after English culture while simultaneously dissociating him from the despised local counterpart. English and the vernaculars were thus used in complementary spheres, English being always reserved for administrative, professional, intellectual, and the socially more prestigious areas.

Even for the ultra-Anglicised upper-class Sinhalese bilinguals the vernacular was the first learned language and the language of greater proficiency in the first five years or so. Those who were less Anglicised often picked up English only at primary school, sometimes as late as high school if they had been to a vernacular primary, and consequently spoke the vernacular for a much longer period than their more Anglicised peers. This was largely because the females of less Anglicised families had often only a minimal knowledge of English and hence functioned only as "receiver bilinguals" (Haas, 1953), that is, persons who understand two languages but speak only one. The situation for Tamil bilinguals was substantially the same as that described for the Sinhalese.

Code specialization in terms of English and the vernaculars would have been for Sri Lankan as well as for other colonial Asian bilinguals the most significant linguistic experience in childhood or early adolescence. Thereafter, and this generally coincided with the beginning of education at the primary or high school level, there was an increasingly distinct separation in the domains in which Sinhalese bilinguals used English and Sinhala and the roles in which they used one or the other. Tanner [(1967) 1972, p. 128] refers to a similar phenomenon regarding the use of Javanese and Dutch in Indonesia.

Tables 1 and 2 summarise the general pattern of domain and role relations with regard to the use of English and Sinhala by middle-class bilinguals in pre-Independent Sri Lanka, that is, before 1948.

DOMAIN SHIFTS IN THE USE OF SINHALA

From the 1920s onwards, particularly with the grant of universal adult franchise in 1931, the rumblings of nationalism grew louder and louder and finally culminated in independence in 1948. Independence led to sweeping political, social, and linguistic changes. The most important linguistic change was in the position of the vernaculars. In 1956 English officially ceased to be the language of administration and was replaced by Sinhala and a restricted use of Tamil. Later on, inevitably, it ceased to be the major language of education as well. The linguistic situation in post-Independent Sri Lanka is naturally very different and infinitely more complex than it was before 1948. Language choice is no longer the relatively clear-cut affair it was in 1948 and before. Twenty-eight years and a new generation later, we find that there has been a re-ordering in the domains and role relations in which English and Sinhala are used. English *seems* to have given way to Sinhala completely in all the public domains listed in Table 1, and its position in the personal areas appears weaker too. In actual fact neither in public nor personal areas is the situation a simple "takeover" by Sinhala (and Tamil) from English.

TABLE 1   *The Domains and Role Relations in which Middle-Class Sinhala Bilinguals Used English**

DOMAIN	ROLE
Family	Parent-Parent
	Older child-Parent
	Parent-Older child
	Older sibling-Older sibling
Friendship	Friend-Friend
Religion	R.C. or Protestant Priest-R.C. or Protestant Priest
	Priest-R.C. or Protestant Parishioner
	Parishioner-Priest
	Parishioner-Parishioner
Education	Teacher-Teacher
	Teacher-Pupil
	Pupil-Teacher
	Pupil-Pupil
Employment:	
Administrative	Peer-Peer
	Superior-Subordinate
	Subordinate-Superior
Professional	Professional-Professional
	Professional-Client
	Client-Professional
	Client-Client

*Both Tables 1 and 2 are based on my own personal experience and observations of the domains and roles in which Sinhala middle-class bilinguals used English. The correlations in these tables are, therefore, relatively impressionistic and represent only general patterns of linguistic behaviour. Both Tables 1 and 2 would generally hold for middle-class Tamil bilinguals as well, the only difference being that the vernacular used would be Tamil.

Let us look at the public domains of education and employment first. In pre-Independent Sri Lanka Sinhala (and Tamil) had been used as media of instruction only in the primary vernacular schools. Secondary and tertiary education as well as primary education in the nonvernacular schools had been solely in English. The distinction between vernacular and nonvernacular schools was abolished in 1948. What is more the vernaculars as media of instruction had begun to be introduced in all nonvernacular primary schools two years before, a program that has been steadily extended to more advanced years

TABLE 2   *The Domains and Role Relations in which Middle-Class Sinhala Bilinguals Used Sinhala*

DOMAIN	ROLE
Family	Spouse-(Monolingual or receiver bilingual) Spouse
	Parent-Infant or monolingual child
	Child-(Monolingual or receiver bilingual) Parent
	Older sibling-Infant or (Monolingual or receiver bilingual) Sibling
Friendship	Friend-(Monolingual or receiver bilingual) Friend
Religion	R.C. or Protestant Priest-(Monolingual or receiver bilingual) Parishioner
	Layman-Buddhist monk
Education	Teacher (of Sinhala or Pali)-Pupil
	Pupil-Teacher (of Sinhala or Pali)
Employment: Domestic	Master-(Monolingual) Servant
Administrative	Superior-(Monolingual or receiver bilingual) Subordinate

so that today at the tertiary level only certain sections of law and medicine are still taught in English. Though English has been superseded as the medium of oral instruction and written examination, "it will never be superseded as the language of books and articles. The economics of publication leaves room only for a few text books to be published in the local languages on all advanced subjects" (de Souza, 1969). Not only teachers but also students still require a working knowledge of English, at least in the area of reading comprehension, if they are at the secondary or tertiary levels of education. This need has resulted in the emergence of a new group of bilinguals who are not necessarily middle class and among whom are "receiver" as well as "sender bilinguals" (Haas, 1953).

As far as employment goes, a knowledge of English is still essential for most professionals, ranging from lawyers, doctors, engineers, and accountants to pharmacists, technicians, surveyors, nurses, and so on. In the commercial sector all business relating to the import-export trade requires a knowledge of English. Though Sinhala is the official language of administration, a fair amount of departmental as well as intradepartmental work is "unostentatiously done in English" and preference unostentatiously given to employees who know some English (de Souza, 1969). English still remains one of the languages of the law and both lawyers and litigants still use it.

In the domain of religion the new national spirit, on the one hand, has encouraged the Protestant clergy to extend their knowledge of Sinhala; on the other, the democratisation of secular education has increased educational opportunities all round so that it is not impossible to talk to a Buddhist monk in English, though this would still be the exception.

The most striking feature marking the use of English and Sinhala in present-day Sri Lanka is the invasion by Sinhala of almost all the areas held by English alone (see Table 3). But despite the change in the vernaculars from being

TABLE 3   *Language Choice Among Sinhala Bilinguals in Present-Day Sri Lanka**

DOMAIN	ROLE	LANGUAGE
Family	Parent-Parent Older child-Parent Parent-Older child Older sibling-Older sibling	(Sinhala and English) or Sinhala if receiver bilingual
Friendship	Friend-Friend	(Sinhala and English) or Sinhala if receiver bilingual
Religion	R.C. or Protestant Priest- R.C. or Protestant Priest Priest-R.C. or Protestant Parishioner Parishioner-Priest Parishioner-Parishioner Buddhist monk-Layman Layman-Buddhist monk	(Sinhala and English) or Sinhala if receiver bilingual Sinhala
Education	Teacher-Teacher Teacher-Pupil Pupil-Teacher Pupil-Pupil	(Sinhala and English) or Sinhala if receiver bilingual
Employment: Administrative	Peer-Peer Superior-Subordinate	(Sinhala and English) or Sinhala if receiver bilingual
Professional	Subordinate-Superior Professional-Professional Professional-Client Client-Professional Client-Client	(Sinhala and English) or Sinhala if receiver bilingual

*This table represents predominant general trends and like those given previously is relatively impressionistic in its observations. Like the former two, it would represent the situation among Tamil bilinguals with regard to their use of English and Tamil.

nothing to being everything, at least officially, English still has a grudgingly recognised but decided social, cultural, and economic value. Those with social, cultural and professional aspirations still wish to learn it. For many middle-class bilinguals it has very high prestige and for them would still be the dominant language in the domains of family, of friendship, and, if Christian, of religion. In the public domains it would have a nearly equal place with Sinhala and Tamil in education and in employment. *In practical linguistic terms what this means is that in spite of English no longer being the official state language, as a result of expanded secondary school education more people today learn English than ever was the case in colonial times.*

The expansion in English language teaching has led to the emergence of three main patterns of bilingualism in present-day Sri Lanka, three main groups of bilinguals who can be distinguished most readily in terms of the character of their English, the degree of Sinhala influence on it and the domains in which they use it. Kachru (1966) uses an arbitrary scale termed the "Cline of Bilingualism" divided into three measuring units, zero, central, and ambilingual, in order to rank bilinguals in terms of their proficiency in English. Though Kachru's terminology differs, the basic idea is virtually the same as that presented by Weinreich (1953, pp. 63–67): the degree of bilingualism is gauged in terms of the degree of structural interference from the mother tongue at the phonic, grammatical, and lexical levels. I would regard Kachru's zero bilinguals as receiver bilinguals and his central and ambilingual classes as sender bilinguals of varying degrees of proficiency in their use of English and the vernacular. Bilingualism, then, as treated in this paper includes not only "the practice of alternately using two languages" (Weinreich, 1953, p. 1), but also the wider phenomenon of "the knowledge of two languages" only one of which the bilingual actually uses [Haugen (1970) 1972, p. 307].

THREE PATTERNS OF BILINGUALISM

Group One

This group of bilinguals typically shows a highly Anglicised lifestyle and speaks a virtually uniform variety of English whatever its racial origin, that is, Sinhala, Tamil, or Malay. Such bilinguals are typically members of the legal, medical, and educational professions; civil servants; commercial executives; and so on, at the top and middle of the social scale. At the lower end they are clerks, nurses, stenographers, and so on, who would shade off into Group Two depending on their pronunciation and the degree to which they use English in domestic or social intercourse.

The English of this group has several distinctive characteristics, particularly at the phonological level. My description is by no means exhaustive. It only identifies some of the major phonological features of Sri Lanka English which serve to separate it from other forms of English as well as to establish various subvarieties within Sri Lanka English itself.

Phonological Features

1. Substitution of pure vowels for English (Received Pronunciation) diphthongs in words such as *boat, road, material,* and *criterion.* Instead of boʊt, roʊd, matɪərɪəl, krɑɪtɪərɪən, one has boːt, roːd, mətɪrɪəl, krɑɪtɪrɪən.

2. Failure to distinguish between labio-dental voiced fricative /v/ and labio-velar semi-vowel /w/ in initial position. Sinhala bilinguals of this group do not distinguish between the initial sounds of *vine* and *wine.* Some would also not distinguish /v/ and /w/ in medial and final position.

3. Substitution of the half-open front unrounded vowel /ɛ/ for the close-to-half-close unrounded front vowel /ɪ/ in the final syllable of words such as *marriage* and *carriage.* Initial syllables, however, show the Standard English /ɪ/, for example, *ridge* and *bridge.*

4. Substitution of schwa /ə/ for /ɪ/ in the past tense and past participle forms of verbs such as *mated, fitted* and *dated.* This substitution would also occur in the plurals of *roses, busses, badges,* and so on and the simple present third person singular forms, such as *catches, hisses* and *flashes.*

Such differences combine with differences of assimilation, elision, stress, pitch, and speed to mark the Sinhala bilingual as unmistakably different in English from a native speaker.

Grammatical Features

Grammatical features reflecting the influence of Sinhala do not occur with the same predictable regularity as the phonological features just discussed. They appear to be distributed differently over the group as a whole. If a systematic study were undertaken, such differences would probably prove to be correlated with social and educational variables. The usages, now being reproduced in dialogue in fiction, drama, and poetry, give an idiomatic flavor more than a problem of comprehension.

Lexical Features

The Sinhalese who adopted English found it lacking in means for effectively expressing many norms of their culture, its institutions, relationships, and elements. Hence the introduction into their English of social formulae such as the greeting *So how?* (Sinhala itin kohomədə?) and farewells such as *I'll go and come* (Sinhala (mɑ ŋ)gihillɑ ennɑ ŋ), which exist alongside British *How do you do?, Cheerio,* and *Good bye.* There are numerous loans, new uses of existing forms and new constructions based on Sinhala in Sinhalese English.

After the British conquest, English became the language of government, law, education, and employment, as noted earlier. Since English possessed administrative, legal, technical, and scientific registers already, no substantial functional elaboration was needed in these areas in Sri Lanka, especially as the governmental, legal, and educational institutions of Sri Lanka were closely modelled on their British counterparts. Haugen [(1966) 1972, p. 107] rightly observes, however, that elaboration also "involves the extension of linguistic function into the realms of imaginative and emotional experience. Here the enrichment comes more clearly from the artistic community." In the context of Sri Lanka, it was essential that English undergo elaboration if it was to be used for the expression in imaginative writing of distinctively indigenous experience.

The particular problem of elaboration in this area was taken up by the older bilinguals (that is, pre-1948) of this group. Having adopted English as their first language together with an Anglicised lifestyle, they were so acculturated in British ways that these bilinguals were virtually cultural aliens in their own land. And yet they were not British. Ludowyck (1972, p. 26) quotes from an unnamed Sri Lankan who conveys very vividly this "cultural schizophrenia" of the Sri Lankan educated indigene:

> White literature drives him (the native) further from himself. It disorientates him from his surroundings: the heat, the vegetation, the rhythm of the world around him. Already in childhood he writes school essays on "the season of mists and mellow fruitfulness. . . ." In the writing of the greatest playwright of the world, he discovers that he is Caliban and Othello and Aaron; in the testaments of the most civilised religion that he is for ever cursed to slavery.

The Sri Lankan writer in English came and still comes from this group of partly dispossessed individuals, "marginal men" caught between two worlds, still seeking an identity both personal and linguistic.

As far as language goes, the problem of the Sri Lankan writer belonging to this Anglicised group is one of *innovation*. The Sri Lankan speakers of English have transferred, often unconsciously, vernacular forms of speech, certain phonological features, syntactic features, words, and idioms into their spoken English. They have also invented new words to denote local objects and customs. But they are still very diffident about extending such usages to their writing (Fernando, 1973). They realise such usages are not standard and so are dogged by the fear of being guilty of that greatest of linguistic sins—a *Sri Lankanism*. Such attitudes would appear to support the point of view put forward by Weisberger (1933) who claims that bilingualism is capable of crippling for generations the creative abilities of the group where it prevails. This, of course, need not be inherently so. Much would depend on the social and cultural prestige of the dominant language and the acculturation in the bilingual group. In the case of the Sri Lankan bilingual of Group One, the sociocultural prestige of English is undisputed and his acculturation very substantial. As a result even when it comes to imaginative creative writing, he still feels safe to a very great extent only in the standard English passed on to him by his colonial rulers. He does not have the confidence to experiment with English artistically as native speakers would. He would think his own Sri Lanka English, with its distinctive grammatical features and lexis, good enough for informal colloquial chatter but certainly not for serious artistic purposes. In terms of such high purposes, Sri Lanka English would be seen as a debased form of standard English rather than a variety of English in its own right with its own norms. As a result the creative writing of the Sri Lankan in English is correct, relatively neutral, and undistinguished.

Sri Lanka English has so far been most widely used for farce and burlesque, held up for ridicule as much as the characters who spoke it. This sort of usage raises special problems for the nonfarcical writer who is brought to feel that Sri Lanka English is inconsistent with the tender, the lyrical, the pathetic, the tragic, and naturally the subline. More recently, there have been strong pleas made for the more widespread use of Sri Lanka English in the creative writing of those who choose to write in English (Kandiah, 1971, p. 92). The change in attitude is reflected in the work of some writers writing in English who make use of Sri Lanka English to convey some peculiarly local experience. But though these efforts at using Sri Lanka English for serious writing are encouraging and certainly more natural in a Sri Lankan context than attempts to reproduce standard English forms or British spoken idiom, there is a great deal of validity in the view held by some Sri Lankan literary critics that the greatest imaginative truth can only be achieved through the use of the vernaculars, Sinhala and Tamil, rather than through a dialect of a foreign language like English. In fact, the most significant creative writing in present-day Sri Lanka is in the vernaculars, not in English.

Group Two

Group Two bilinguals, generally of peasant, lower middle or working class origin, would regard English very much as a foreign language unlike the bilinguals of Group One, especially the older ones to whom it has become an adopted mother tongue. Differences of racial origin would show up quite clearly in this group. The English pronunciation of a Tamil bilingual of Group Two would be very different from that of a Sinhala bilingual of the same group.[4] The English pronunciation of the members of this group would set them apart not only from native speakers but also from the Sinhala and Tamil bilinguals of Group One.

Phonological Features

The pronunciation of this second group of bilinguals typically shows one or more of three major phonemic features that separate such bilinguals from those of Group One. These three features are of great social significance, since they stamp speakers as having learned English late and, therefore, not generally using English in the personal domains of family, friendship, and religion.

1. Substitution of the long half-open back rounded vowel /ɔ/ for the long pure vowel /o:/ of the Group One bilingual: *bo:t, ro:d* become bɔt, rɔd.

2. Substitution of the short pure vowel /o/ for the short open back rounded vowel /ɒ/ of the Group One bilingual in nɒt, pɒt, and so on.

These two substitutions have the result that Group Two bilinguals will reverse the forms *hall* and *hole,* from the standpoint of the Group One bilinguals:

> hall   hɔl – ho:l
> hole   ho:l – hɔl

Such features, being substandard in terms of the norms of Group One, have attracted a good deal of derision, so much so that Group Two bilinguals till quite recently were referred to contemptuously as "the not-pot cases" by the more snobbish members of Group One. But though they still continue to exist and increase, the term is hardly ever used today in view of the growing power of the lower middle and working classes as social forces. The widespread failure to distinguish /v/ and /w/, although evident to a native speaker of English, does not attract the same attention because it appears in the speech of Group One bilinguals as well.

   3. Substitution of the voiceless bilabial stop /p/ for the voiceless bilabial fricative /f/ of Sri Lanka English and vice versa in English words which use these sounds. Sinhala has no /f/ phoneme and speakers of Sri Lanka English (Group One) use a bilabial fricative as the closest substitute to standard English labio-dental fricative. The same type of reversal noted in (2) between *hall* and *hole* then takes place between words like *pan* and *fan* in the speech of these Group Two bilinguals.

   Phonology is important because it is the salient criterion that distinguishes bilinguals of Group One from bilinguals of Group Two. Members of Group Two are not significantly different from Group One in grammar and lexis. Generally they have acquired their English simply at a much later stage (in the upper forms at high school or at university). They acquire it for professional purposes, largely, and use it primarily in the public domains of education, employment, special social occasions (diplomatic functions or conference dinners), speaking with members of Group One, and so on, but do not usually use it in domestic or intimate social intercourse. It is features of pronunciation that distinguish their speech as such from that of Group One.

ALTERNATION AND RECIPROCAL INTERFERENCE OF ENGLISH AND SINHALA IN GROUPS ONE AND TWO

Both Groups One and Two consist of sender bilinguals though there are differences in the social and linguistic backgrounds of the members of each group. Group One may be seen in terms of two subgroups, the major variable being age. For older bilinguals (that is, those born before 1948) English would still be the dominant language in family, friendship, and religion (if Christian). Such bilinguals, "central" in terms of Kachru's cline, would have received all or a substantial part of their education in English. Consequently, they would not only speak English constantly in a variety of professional, social, and domestic situations, but their grasp of the language would receive additional reinforcement and refinement from the written word. The extent of their "communicative competence" [Hymes (1971) 1972] in English is, therefore, very high. These bilinguals, as already noted, when they have chosen to write creatively have predictably chosen to do so in English.

   The position of younger bilinguals in Group One (that is, those born after 1948) is somewhat different. For these bilinguals, and this is a very important factor, both speaking in English and code specialization in terms of domains and role relationships would come much later than it would have for their parents and older siblings. In the case of the last named age groups, such specialization, if upper class, generally began around five years or so whereas with the former it takes place roughly between nine and twelve years since now education is in the vernacular. This brings the younger members of Group One much closer to the members of Group Two in their use of English. In discussing code switching and the reciprocal interference of English and Sinhala at levels other than the phonological, contrasting the older bilinguals of Group One with the younger bilinguals of Group One and Two is a more accurate representation of the situation than maintaining the original division which was chiefly on the basis of pronunciation.

Code switching among these older bilinguals generally approximates to Weinreich's ideal bilingual who "switches from one language to the other according to appropriate changes in the speech situation (interlocutors, topics, etc.) but not in an unchanged speech situation, and certainly not within a single sentence" (Weinreich, 1953, p. 73). They would use Sinhala, generally to mon-olinguals or receiver bilinguals, only in limited domains (see Table 2). The effect of English on their Sinhala would appear mainly in the form of widely accepted and, therefore, mutually intelligible loanwords, for example, *bus, car,* and *shirt,* with the attached Sinhala suffix ek or ekə, if used in the singular:kɑ:r ekə *(the car)* or kɑ:r ekɑk(*a car*); but zero for the plural kɑ:r *(cars)*. Loan translations as well as other borrowings would also appear in the Sinhala of these older bilinguals (see the section on the influence of English on Sinhala that follows). The effect of Sinhala on their English has already been noted.

Even though code specialization in terms of personal domains and role relationships within them still takes place, for younger bilinguals the comple-mentary spheres of English and Sinhala are not kept as clearly apart as it generally was for the older generation. Younger bilinguals in both groups do not make what Haugen calls "a clean switch of codes" (1972, p. 314) in terms of interlocutors and topics, but resort instead among themselves to "ragged switching" (Hasselmo, 1961) where the bilingual will switch codes even within the confines of a single sentence showing no demonstrable correlation between code, on the one hand, and interlocutors, on the other. The immediate linguistic cause of such switching, "anticipational" or "consequential," could be the presence of some triggering element (Clyne, 1967, pp. 20, 84 ff). Ragged switching *together* with extensive transference of lexical items from English to Sinhala is so widespread that this particular form of bilingualism has been humorously called "Singlish." Singlish, of course, would be considerably toned down so as to appear more clearly either Sinhala or English if the interlocutor(s) were unfamiliar as well as being superior in age and position.

There are two other major reasons for this phenomenon of Singlish apart from the triggering factor already mentioned. Sinhala no longer has the social stigma it once had as the communicative medium of humble illiterate peasants. With the vastly increased use of Sinhala for education, topics that in the past one would normally have expected to hear discussed only in English are now discussed in Sinhala as well. Younger bilinguals regardless of whether they belong to Group One or Two are educated in the vernacular and are drawn towards vernacular writings, though often this attraction is diverted to English as a result of there being relatively few books in Sinhala. Such bilinguals generally acquire an increased proficiency in English as their intellectual horizons broaden and they turn to English books. They would then move towards the ambilingual end of Kachru's cline in terms of fluency in the two languages. Their creative writing, however, is in Sinhala.

The other major reason for the use of Singlish is the absence of what Weinreich (1953, p. 81) has termed "interlocutory constraint." When these younger bilinguals speak among themselves, forms can be freely transferred from one language to another without the interlocutors paying the penalty of mutual unintelligibility. This was not the case with their linguistically less proficient parents and older siblings the majority of whom had, perforce, to avoid ragged switching and who because they generally spoke Sinhala to monolinguals avoided extensive lexical transfers from English as well.

Lexical transfers, it has been noted, are an important feature of Singlish. Such lexical transfers would include not only loanwords, loan translations, and so on that have been absorbed into Sinhala, but also regular transfers peculiar to Singlish even where there are common equivalents in Sinhala. Some of these transfers are *to marry* (kɑ:sɑ:də bədinəvɑ) *to pass* (of exam) (səmɑrtə venəvɑ) *to kiss* (imbinəvɑ) *wife* (pɑvulɑ, no:nə), *husband* (minihɑ, mɑhɑttəjɑ), and *university* (višvəvidjɑ:ləjə). Speakers also resort to transfers which vary widely from individual to individual. In the instances of the transfers already cited, the speaker might find it convenient and more natural to use an English term to a fellow bilingual rather than an equivalent Sinhala term for reasons additional to lack of interlocutory constraint. The Sinhala terms may be strongly associated with monolingual usage as those alread quoted are, and if used by the bilingual give the speech an uncharacteristic flavour. There is also the fact that the lexis is daily expanding with new words being spontaneously or officially coined as part of the functional elaboration of Sinhala. Using the new Sinhala words, often derived from Sanskrit roots, could give the speaker's language an artificial literary flavour which is anything but colloquial. The introduction of English words, and such transfers vary with the individual, is an effort to maintain the informal colloquial dimension of the conversation. Lexical transference and ragged switching, which together constitute Singlish, generally signal considerable closeness and informality and is, thus, a more intimate code than "unadulterated" Sinhala. As such it occurs mainly between peers in the domains of family and friendship.[5]

The English of the younger bilinguals of Groups One and Two would show much stronger interference from Sinhala than that of the older bilinguals of Group One. The difference in this respect between the two different age groups would show itself in the stronger influence of Sinhala grammatical structures.

The extensive transference of certain Sinhala verb patterns, such as the reduplicative pattern of *I went jumping jumping,* and Sinhala word order as in *Bertie Uncle* and *Lucille Auntie,* and so on is apparent in the English of these bilinguals. The reciprocal interference of English and Sinhala is much stronger in the language use of younger bilinguals, but the difference between their English and that of the older group would still be a matter of degree rather than of kind.

The influence of English on Sinhala is much more dramatic and striking than the influence of Sinhala on English. The tendency to introduce English words into Sinhala is much more marked than the reverse. The bilingual who chooses to talk English rather than Singlish or Sinhala will only introduce those Sinhala words (names of local fauna, flora, and so on) that have become an accepted part of the Sri Lanka English lexis. But anyone who talks in Sinhala, even a monolingual, will inevitably use a relatively high proportion of English words or words of English origin. While ragged switching is acceptable among younger bilinguals, lexical transfers, with the exception of the items cited, are unidirectional from English to Sinhala or Singlish which is as a linguistic system more Sinhala than English based; that is, Singlish would show a higher proportion of Sinhala phrases and sentences than English ones. In other words Singlish is a subvariety of Sinhala, not a subvariety of English. The point made by Hasselmo (1972, p. 264) that whereas in speaking American-Swedish considerably more variation is permitted in the direction of English than would be the case in the reverse applies very closely to the Sri Lankan situation as well when the bilingual chooses to speak Sinhala or Singlish.

Group Three

Group Three consists of bilinguals whose fluency in English is small but who are typically of the same social background as those of Group Two, that is, either peasant, lower middle or working class, or of such origins. Their use of English is limited to the English period in the classroom. They are essentially receiver bilinguals who learn English only because it is compulsory to do so in all Sri Lanka schools. (Their counterparts would be found among the Tamils as well.) If the entire school-going population were given the opportunity to learn English, it would seem everyone had equal educational opportunities and, therefore, equal employment prospects in their chosen fields. English language teaching programs are not administered, however, with equal efficiency in all schools. Nor do all English language learners come from homes where English is the language of the family. Poor teaching, weak motivation, and little or no exposure to the language outside the classroom result in Group Three bilinguals having very little receptive or productive skill in English. Their position on the bilingual cline is towards its zero end. The type of employment open to these receiver bilinguals would be that of minor employee in the public service, bus conductor, postman, taxi-driver, and so on. But a small percentage enter university where they undergo intensive reading comprehension courses in

English in order to read the books in the library, nine-tenths of which are still in English. In time, some of these receivers master English sufficiently at the productive levels to function as sender bilinguals. They may, then, qualify for inclusion in either Group One or Two, the salient criterion being the phonological features they manifest in their pronunciation. The majority of bilinguals in present-day Sri Lanka would be of the receiver type.

Phonological Features

The pronunciation of Group Three bilinguals generally shows the three main phonological features already referred to as characterizing Group Two, together with others, such as the introduction of vowels into consonantal clusters that begin with /s/: iste:šən, iskru, iskul, and so on. This feature may appear in the speech of the Group Two bilinguals as well, but less frequently.

Grammatical Features

The bilinguals of Group Three would not normally speak or write English in any of the public or private domains mentioned or in any role other than that of the foreign language learner. What is most striking about their grammar in English is the extent of its deviation from standard English as a result of the influence of the mother tongue. [I have analysed such deviations with material gathered from the free compositions of secondary school pupils in the Colombo, Kalutara, and Kandy districts of Sri Lanka in an unpublished Master of Arts dissertation (Fernando, 1964).] All groups of Sri Lankan bilinguals show areas of departure from standard British English, but whereas the departure of Groups One and Two are slight, those of Group Three are radical and numerous. Whereas the English of the first two groups can be said to have a Sinhala flavour, the English of the third group has a marked Sinhala stamp.

Lexical Features

This third group of bilinguals has had little or no discernible influence on English generally in the country. For them, English is very much a second language formally taught them in school, as noted. Probably their own occasional use of the language may show interesting examples of mother-tongue influence on lexicon, but these have not been studied and are not found in the English normally spoken and written. As has been discussed, even a Sinhala flavour has been felt an embarrassment in public writing in English, and features of pronunciation distinctive of Group Two have been stigmatized. On the other hand, even though the members of this group are only receiver bilinguals from the standpoint of English, the practice of transferring lexical items, such as *to marry*, *to pass* (*of exam*), and *to kiss*, into Sinhala, already noted for younger sender bilinguals, is evident here, too. No code switching occurs among the bilinguals of this group but lexical transference even though on a more restricted scale than is the case in Groups One and Two would indicate the bilingual status of these speakers vis-à-vis monolinguals. It is also further evidence of the influence of English on the Sinhala of all sections of the literate population, a phenomenon examined more extensively in the following section.

THE INFLUENCE OF ENGLISH ON SINHALA

Sinhala has had an uninterrupted spoken tradition for over 2000 years but its literary tradition has been adversely affected by three factors (de Silva, 1972, pp. 41, 56):

1. Foreign invasions and conquests beginning with the Portuguese in the sixteenth century, followed by the Dutch and the British in the seventeenth and eighteenth centuries, respectively;
2. The substantial diminishing of prose writings largely as a result of Sinhala not being used for governmental or intellectual purposes;
3. The little prose writing that was done in Sinhala was by the monks and was not secular in its nature.

The use of Sinhala in secular writing in the modern period was, accordingly, almost nonexistent till well into the nineteenth century. The use of Sinhala for serious expository prose as well as for creative writing increased enormously in the early twentieth century. After Sinhala was declared the official language in 1956, English provided Sinhala with a model for developing registers connected with administration, commerce, and so on. The language and style of official regulations, letters, and reports are all closely modelled on their English counterparts. Modern Sinhala journalism has been very influenced by the style of British journalism, particularly with regard to reporting and editorials. This was not all. The spread of English language teaching as a result of secondary school expansion beyond the confines of an Anglicised elitist middle class together with the "renaissance" of Sinhala and the rise of a new Sinhalese intelligentsia in the late 1950s and in the 1960s has resulted in *English and its literature having more impact on Sinhala in the last 25 years or so than it ever did in the 150 of British rule.* Such influence is seen in the further development in Sinhala of relatively new literary genres like the novel and short story, and new developments in existing genres such as the emergence of a *vers libre* style in poetry. There is also the growth of a substantial body of literary criticism influenced by Western critical theory (Obeysekere, 1974). But significantly, Sinhala is still not the language of original research. Ferguson (1962) and Kloss (1952) use this particular function of language as a criterion in measuring language development. As far as Sinhala goes, even research work on Sinhala itself is carried out abroad and written up in English!

In sum, what is most striking about present-day Sinhala is, first, the enormous and impressive functional elaboration it has undergone, and second, the very substantial influence of English on Sinhala. These two phenomena are, of course, related, for the chief means by which Sinhala has undergone functional elaboration is by modelling itself on English.

The influence of English on Sinhala appears most strikingly at the lexical level. Literally hundreds of words have been borrowed into Sinhala. Many of these have been only slightly "reinterpreted" phonologically. Such words, generally short and without "difficult" sound clusters (that is, difficult from the standpoint of the Sinhala speaker) are used with the Sinhala suffixes ekə or ekɑk. *Car, shirt, bicycle, cigaret, sheet, bus, fridge* are kɑːr ekə, šeːt ekə, baisikəl ekə, šiːt ekə, bɑs ekə, (f)(p)ridʒ ekə. Other words with "difficult" sound clusters (often consonantal) in initial, medial, or final position adapted much more to the sound system of Sinhala are *class, station, pencil, telephone, saucepan, lamp, tank;* these appear as kəlæsijə, isteːšəmə, pænsələjə, tælipoːn ekə, sɑːspɑːnəjə, lɑːmpuvə, tæŋkijə.

A host of objects have been named with new compounds, using Sinhala morphemes and Sinhala analyses of meaning, so that their foreign origin is not apparent, for example, words for *crescent* (moon, curve), *hors d'oeuvre* (front food), *film* (picture strip), *kerosene* (earth oil), *train* (smoke vehicle) and *radio service* (sky lightning service). Some of these new items have older, more colloquial equivalents of foreign origin as in the case of *train* (koːččijə) and *film* (bɑiskoːp). The new equivalents are literary, evidence of the functional elaboration of Sinhala and would not normally be used colloquially. *Earth oil* and *front food* are usual in ordinary conversation and have been coined to aid communication with monolinguals particularly domestics. This is also the reason for several words which are direct loan translations from English, for example, those for *dining room, bath room, table cloth,* and so on. Other words, such as *aeroplane, town hall, fisheries corporation,* and *mother tongue*, have been introduced in Sinhala as direct loan translations and are part of its functional elaboration.

Such lexical borrowings from English, whether they are direct loans, new compounds derived from English, or direct translations, would be found in the Sinhala of all three bilingual groups as well as in the Sinhala of monolinguals. Singlish with its numerous lexical transfers is the most dramatic manifestation of the influence of English on the Sinhala of bilinguals, but it is peculiar, as already stated, to the younger bilinguals of Groups One and Two.

CONCLUSION

The choice of English rather than Sinhala by Sinhalese bilinguals in various domains, particularly the personal ones, still constitutes the most striking indicator of differences in education and social background and is thus the single most powerful class indicator even in present-day Sri Lanka. The degree to which an individual's English reflects mother-tongue interference is yet another powerful indicator of social class. The resistance to the use of Sri Lankan English in writing is linked to the still fairly widespread feeling that any functional elaboration of the standard, however necessary, in some way tarnishes its aesthetic qualities and its effectiveness as a literary tool.

The Sinhalese bilingual by virtue of choosing another language (that is, English) and speaking it in a particular way (Pattern One or Two) in specific domains, particularly the personal ones, demonstrates his membership past and present of a given social group, in this instance an elitist or nonelitist group. But the choice of English rather than Sinhala in particular domains reflects at the same time the individual's sense of his own identity, his separateness from the community as a whole. It is "a ritual act" which symbolizes not only a person's status in society but also his emotional and intellectual separateness in the wider context of the purely indigenous culture—its norms, its institutions, and its relationships. Language choice in present-day Sri Lanka reflects both these factors very powerfully, serving as it does not only to define a socially more favoured group from one that is less so but also distinguishing the "marginal man" from those who are more completely integrated with their own culture.

NOTES

1. I am deeply indebted to Dell Hymes for his detailed comments on earlier versions of this paper. I should also like to thank Dr. Alan Davies of the University of Edinburgh and Euan Reid of West Midlands College, Walsall, for their help with the same. Any shortcomings are my own. Reprinted from *Language in Society,* Vol. 6, 1977, with the permission of C. Fernando and Cambridge University Press.

2. Not being a Tamil speaker myself, except for brief references, I have chosen to confine this paper to Sinhala, the vernacular of the major racial group, and to English. Sinhala is an Indo-European language, originally a *prakrit* of Sanskrit. Tamil is a Dravidian language of South India.

3. The population of Sri Lanka by race according to the 1963 census figures (to the nearest thousand) is as follows: Sinhalese, Low Country and Kandyan (7,502,000); Tamils, Sri Lankan and Indian (2,287,000); Moors, Sri Lankan and Indian (681,000); Malays (33,000); Eurasians (45,000); Europeans and others (19,000). (Census and Statistics, 1970, p. 30).

4. Having no knowledge of Tamil, I am unable to identify the sources or effects of interference from Tamil on the English of Tamil bilinguals.

5. Compare code switching as a distinctive style among Chicanos in the United States under similar circumstances.

REFERENCES

Census and Statistics (Department of). *Statistical Abstract of Ceylon, 1969.* Colombo: Government Printer, 1970.

Clyne, Michael G. *Transference and Triggering.* The Hague: Martinus Nijhoff, 1967.

Ferguson, Charles A. The language factor in national development. *Anthropological Linguistics.* 1962, 4, 23–27. Reprinted in Anwar S. Dil (ed.), *Language Structure and Language Use: Essays by Charles A. Ferguson.* Stanford: Stanford University Press, 1971, 51–59.

Fernando C. E. *A Contrastive Study of English and Sinhala Grammar.* Unpublished M.A. dissertation, Sydney University, 1964.

Fernando, C. E. Between two worlds: An examination of attitudes and language in Ceylonese creative writing. *New Ceylon Writing.* 1973, 3, 31–46.

Goonetilleke, M. H., and Hettiaratchi, D. E. Portuguese speaking communities of Sri Lanka. *Sri Lanka Research Bulletin.* January 1976, 2, 9.

Haas, M. R. Results of the conference of anthropologists and linguistics. In *Supplement to the International Journal of American Linguists,* 1953, 19.

Hasselmo, N. *American Swedish: A Study in Bilingualism.* Unpublished Ph.D. dissertation, Harvard University, 1961.

Hasselmo, N. Code switching as ordered selection. In E. S. Firchow et al. (eds.), *Studies for Einar Haugen.* The Hague: Mouton and Co., 1972, 261–279.

Haugen, E. The stigmata of bilingualism. In Anwar S. Dil (ed.), *The Ecology of Language: Essays by Einar Haugen.* California: Stanford University Press, 1972, 307–323.

Haugen E. Dialect, language, nation. *American Anthropologist.* 1966, 68, 922–935. Reprinted in J. B. Pride and J. Holmes (eds.), *Sociolinguistics.* London: Penguin, 1972, 97–111.

Hymes, D. On communicative competence. Philadelphia: University of Pennsylvania Press, 1971. Reprinted in J. B. Pride and J. Holmes (eds.), *Sociolinguistics.* London: Penguin, 1972, 269–293.

Kachru, B. The Indianness in Indian English. *Word.* 1966, 21, 3, 391–411.

Kandiah, T. Review of *The Call of the Kirala,* by James Goonewardena. *New Ceylon Writing.* 1971, 2, 90–94.

Kloss, H. *Die Entwicklung Neuer Germanischer Kultursprachen.* Munich: Pohl, 1952.

Leach, E. R. *Aspects of Caste in South India, Ceylon and North-West Pakistan.* Cambridge: Cambridge University Press, 1960.

Ludowyck, E. F. C. Writing in English in Ceylon. *ADAM International Review.* 1972, Nos. 367–369.

Obeysekere, R. *Sinhala Writing and the New Critics.* Colombo: M. D. Gunasena, 1974.

Pieris, P. E. *Ceylon: The Portuguese Era,* Vols. 1 and 2. Colombo: The Colombo Apothecaries Co., Ltd., 1914.

Tanner, N. Speech and society among the Indonesian elite: A case study of a multilingual community. *Anthropological Linguistics.* 1967, 9, 3, 15–39. Reprinted in J. B. Pride and J. Holmes (eds.), *Sociolinguistics.* London: Penguin, 1972, 129–141.

Tennent, J. E. *Christianity in Ceylon.* London: John Murray, 1850.

de Silva, M. W. S. *Basha Visheyeke Lipi.* Colombo: Lake House Investments Ltd., 1972.

de Souza, A. T. A. The teaching of English, 4. *The Ceylon Observer.* April 21, 1969.

Weinreich, U. *Languages in Contact.* The Hague: Mouton and Co., 1953.

Weisberger, L. *Zweissprachigkeit.* Schaffen und Schauen. Quoted by Uriel Weinreich *Languages in Contact.* The Hague: Mouton and Co., 1953.

Section 4

REGIONAL STANDARDS

12 *ENGLISH IN THE PHILIPPINES*

Andrew Gonzalez

INTRODUCTION

In an earlier work on written Philippine English of the mass media (Gonzalez and Alberca, 1978), I spoke of the tendency of written Philippine English to be monostylistic, the most popular being a "composition style" learned in the English classroom by the educated Filipino.

A subsequent research project using a larger corpus and different from the one used in the 1978 study provides a better differentiation of styles and interesting examples of style shifting and shows a more comprehensive picture of the stylistic varieties of Philippine English and directions along which the English language in the Philippines is evolving.

With the help of a research assistant,[1] whole issues of Philippine newspapers and weekly magazines in English were analysed: foreign-authored articles and syndicated columns were eliminated, then the articles were classified into columns, feature articles, and editorials. In the course of the analysis, three styles (differentiated according to the dimension of solidarity) emerged: formal, informal, and familiar.[2]

By means of examples, the three styles distinguished will be characterised. The code-switching variety (English and Pilipino) is described and some qualitative extrapolations made on the possibility of a pidgin arising in the Philippines. Interesting cases of stylistic shift will be cited, typologised and frequency counts indicated. An attempt will be made to explain the probable causes behind these shifts, largely a result of the manner of acquisition of English among Filipinos. A more general conclusion on relative underdifferentiation of styles in written Philippine English will be drawn as a result of the data.

THREE STYLES OF WRITTEN PHILIPPINE ENGLISH OF THE MASS MEDIA

Consider the following examples (Exhibits 1 and 2).

Exhibit 1   Formal

What is now happening in the BIR [Bureau of Internal Revenue] has been happening there ever since. What is likewise happening in the other Government offices, agencies and some State-owned corporations, especially the revenue producing ones, has also been happening there ever since.

The delayed reaction of the President to all of these is quite understandable. Eliminating the undesirables from these public offices, and there must be quite a number of them, is solving only one half of the problem. Getting qualified replacements who will remain honest for at least some time is the other half of the problem.

The men handpicked by the President to head or staff these offices are honorable and respectable citizens in the community who have earned the privilege and the trust of the appointing authority because of their qualifications, theoretical expertise and sheer respect for the law and the institutions which those long before us have so painstakingly built. (Vicente Pascual, Jr., "Business Spectrum," *The Economic Monitor,* October 8–14, 1979, pp. 15–16.)

Exhibit 2   Informal

September is a super month for doing something about your waistline. After all, today's fashion is showing this portion of the female anatomy more and more. Here's one waist-whittler to try: Sit on floor, spread legs as far apart as you can, like a frontal ballet split. Then eagle-spread arms, keeping them parallel to the floor, elbows straight. Now twist to the left; follow your left hand with your eyes; then to the right. Twist only as far back as your muscles will allow. And only do as many times as your wind, physical fitness, and general health will allow. Note: When doing the exercise, avoid lifting your bottom. Keep hips square. No lifting of legs and bending of the knees allowed either. Try to point toes.

September is a super month for trying to unlearn self-defeating habits and attitudes. Easier said than done, but you can always try. A friend to talk to (one who really listens) helps a lot. To work on: smoking, over-drinking and over-eating; useless guilt feelings; anxiety; a drive to over-achieve. (Cover story of *Manila Women's Wear,* Vol. 5, No. 19, 1979, p. 7.)

The obvious graphic indicators or conventions for the nonformal styles are the use of contractions, the use of three dots, loanwords in italics (sometimes not), nicknames (see Gonzalez and Alberca, 1978, p. 58).

With the preceding examples, we are now in a position to call attention to more than graphic conventions.

Perhaps the most salient feature distinguishing formal from informal style is lexical choice. Note the use of lexical items such as *super* (meaning *very good*), *wind* (for *breath*), *bottom* (for the rear part of the human anatomy), and such collocations as *a lot* (for *much/many*), and *eagle-spread* used as a verb (a local adaptation or Filipinism for *spread-eagle*), and *portion of the female anatomy* (mock-serious).[3]

Syntactically, the most obvious difference is the use of ellipsis (or sentences with deleted parts) in informal style and the frequency of short sentences (simple). On the other hand, the formal style is characterised by long sentences (complex) with modifications and adverbial phrases, using processes of relativisation, complementation, and nominalization. The first two sentences of the formal example are cleft sentences, for example.[4]

The formal style is a good example of what I have elsewhere called the composition style in the Philippines: formal, elegant, in the tradition of essay writing popular before the war, a rhetorical style still being used as a model in our classrooms in the Philippines. It is the writing style the educated Filipino is most used to and therefore most comfortable in, since it is the kind of writing (composition) that he learned from models in school. It is also basically the kind of writing he reads in literary essays and to a certain extent in many of the printed materials in textbooks and scholarly studies (using the thesis or dissertation style) he is most used to. The register differs according to subject area, but the sentence structures most frequently used are characterised by extensive use of adverbial phrases and clauses usually of a qualifying type, complex sentences, serial enumerations with embeddings, use of the subjunctive mood in verbs, polysyllabic Latinate lexical choices rather than monosyllabic Anglo-Saxon words except for function words, and parallelism in words, phrases, and clauses. Exhibit 1 exemplifies this.

From a linguistic point of view, the most interesting style is the familiar one exemplified by the third sample (Exhibit 3).

Exhibit 3   Familiar

Maniwala ka kaya, pare, kung sabihin ko sa iyo that a mere whisper can cause death. It may even create chaos.

Tipong heavy and intro ko, pero it happened one night dito sa destitute place namin. Ganito iyon, listen carefully. Around ten thirty in the evening nang dumating sa bahay ni utol ang kanyang kubrador ng Jai-Alai na si Dencio. Huwag mo nang itanong sa akin kung legal ang pa-bookist nila. Magkakaroon pa tayo ng sub-plot, e. And then, may ibinulong kay utol. Na-diyan ako dahil medyo madrama ang affair nila. Pabulong-bulong pa. So, nireblocked ko ang aking sarili ng around 45 degrees angle patagilid sa kanila to avoid suspicion (actually that's the best angle for my clinical ears).

Thanks a lot at hindi pa rin kinakalawang ang mala-radar kong nunal sa tenga. I was able to hear everything. Detailed, Precise, and VIVID.

Sssssh . . . atin-atin lang ito. Narinig daw ni Dencio sa kanyang ninong na nagtratrabaho sa Sky Room ng Jai-Alai na "magkakalutuan" ng laro ngayong gabi. Patok na patok ang mga numerong 8-2-10. Inutusan pa raw nito ang kanyang ninang na mangutang ng five siks para makabili ng maraming tiket. Ito na raw ang pagkakataon nilang yumaman. ("Isang Maikling-Maikling Pamagat Para sa Isang Maikling-Maikling Kuwento," *Coed,* October 1979, pp. 36–37.)

TRANSLATION

Can you believe it, friend, if I were to tell you that a mere whisper can cause death. It may even create chaos.

It looks like my introduction is heavy [too serious], but it happened one night here at our destitute place. It was like this, listen carefully. [It was] around ten thirty in the evening when Dencio, his Jai-Alai bookie, arrived at the house of Brother [my brother]. Don't now ask me if their bookie-ing [betting] was legal. Because we might end up having a sub-plot. And then, [Dencio] whispered something to Brother. I went in their direction because their affair [happening] (seemed) to be full of drama. They were whispering to each other. So, I re-blocked myself[made a turn] at around a 45-degree angle sideways to avoid suspicion (actually that's the best angle for my clinical ears).

Thanks a lot [that] the radar-like mole in my ear was not yet corroded. I was able to hear everything. Detailed, Precise, and VIVID.

Ssssssh . . . this is only among ourselves. According to Dencio he had heard from his godfather who was working at the Sky Room of the Jai-Alai that the play that evening would be fixed. The number combination 8-2-10 was sure of winning. His godfather sent him to borrow money at 5/6 rates [for every ₱5 lent the amount to be repaid the next day would be ₱6] in order to buy many tickets. This was, according to Dencio, the opportunity for them to get rich. ("A very Short Title for a Very Short Story," *Coed,* October 1979, pp. 36–37.)

Here there is a deliberate attempt at familiarity, at bridging the distance between speaker and hearer (writer and reader) and of even sharing certain confidences with the reader, signaled by the Pilipino familiar-vocative, *pare* (*compadre*), literally *co-father,* the title one calls the godfather of one's son, hence, a name for ritual kinship; most loosely, *comrade.* The writer remarks, "*Ssssssh . . . atin-atin lang ito*" (Ssssssh . . . this is strictly among ourselves).

Note that the Pilipino portion predominates, with English portions inter-spersed. This style has been called Taglish (if the Tagalog portions predomi-nate, which they do in this sample) or Engalog (if the English portions predominate). It has also been called Halo-Halo or Mix-Mix (a Pilipino term).

A distinction has to be made, however, between a deliberate attempt on the part of the speaker who has competence in both codes to use the two codes alternately at clearly marked portions of the discourse (sentence level, clause level, and phrase level) and a speaker who resorts to the first language because he does not have enough mastery of the second language and in the process mixes the two languages to the point of ending up with a pidgin. The written versions of this code-switching variety clearly attest to mastery of both codes, not lack of competence in the second.

Undoubtedly, there are discourses in the Philippines (second language acquisition among children and adults, imperfect knowledge of English among the unschooled, especially outside of the major urban areas) that are closer to pidgin, but the point must be made that in printed discourse, evidence of competence in the two languages is quite clear. We do not have a pidgin but prose equivalents of what we refer to in medieval literature as macaronic verse, interspersing of utterances in English and in Pilipino for a certain function, in this case, to bridge distance (familiar style).

Rather than refer to this as Mix-Mix, a term that has a pejorative connotation, I would rather refer to it as the code-switching variety, which has no value-judgment connoted, a rather sophisticated variety as it presupposes competence in both codes. (A structural description of this code-switching variety has been provided by Bautista, 1974; for data on evidence of the pidgin-like type resulting from lack of competence in English, but not of Pilipino, see Olonan's, 1978, Paniqui, Tarlac data).

The article being discussed is interesting since it code switches between a familiar style of Pilipino and a moderately formal style of English—to achieve familiarity.

The use of the addressee *pare,* the code switching itself, the use of loanwords from English (*tipong heavy*), the use of an abbreviated name to refer to one's brother (*utol* from *kaputol*—brother), the use of slang (*patok na patok*—very sure, in case of betting, especially cockfighting) clearly puts the Pilipino variety in the familiar category.

The moderately formal style of English used is shown mostly in the choice of vocabulary (a Latinate textbook vocabulary):

a mere whisper can cause death (literary)
It may even create chaos

dito sa *destitute* place namin

listen carefully
legal
sub-plot
ma*drama*
ni*reblocked* (literary) . . . ng around *45 degrees*
to avoid suspicion
actually that's the best angle for my clinical ears
mala-*radar*
Detailed, Precise, and VIVID

What we have here is something approaching the formal style (in terms of lexical choice and collocations) and in terms of literary associations especially from English literature classes.

The function and the intention, however, are clearly familiar so that we have an occurrence in written Philippine English of the *familiar style* realised by a combination of *familiar Pilipino* and relatively *formal English.*

The example given of the code-switching variety represents one extreme, however, since it attempts humor. It is felicitous in its blending and achieves the kind of familiarity that one native speaker speaking to another is used to. Perhaps more common and more representative is another example (Exhibit 4).

Exhibit 4   Informal-Familiar (?)

The entire country was shaken to its roots kamakailan nang biglaang ilunsad ng pamahalaan ang isang kilusan sa pagsugpo ng organized gambling sa Philippine Basketball Association.

Ang biglaang pagdakip sa anim na katao ay result nang may ilang panahon ding lihim na pagsubaybay na isinagawa ng isang task force against organized gambling na personal na itinatag ng Pangulong Marcos.

Several quarters where [sic] unanimous in saying that for the last time, the authorities should spare no one and punish the guilty to clean the league once and for all. ("Kislap Sports" (authorless column), *Kislap Magazine,* October 4, 1979, pp. 36–37.)

TRANSLATION

The entire country was shaken to its roots a short time ago when suddenly the government launched a movement for the checking of organized gambling in the Philippine Basketball Association.

The sudden apprehension of six persons is [the] result of [a] prolonged secret follow-up which was done by a task force against organized personal gambling, which was established by President Marcos.

Note that in this article, code switching takes place at the clause and sentence levels (paragraph level if the paragraph consists of only one sentence).

What differentiates this sample from the preceding one is that even the Pilipino sample is written in the formal style manifested by the choice of vocabulary and the concatenation of relative clauses (characteristic of formal discourse in Pilipino).

The entire passage does not convey the same impression of familiarity as the earlier sample, but it is clearly meant to signal more proximate social position than the formal style. The fact that the writer code switches clearly signals that he wants to be closer to the reader than if he were using English alone.

It is not entirely clear whether this should be classified as informal or familiar. The use of two formal styles makes it typologically different. Perhaps we can consider it as an alternate type of informality (but not familiarity) parallel with the informal style written entirely in English.

In terms of strategies, one can advance the hypothesis that the Filipino speaker of English who is less adept in the informal style of English can achieve the same informality by maintaining two formal styles of his code and by code switching between them.

For the familiar style, he has the option of maintaining the entire discourse in familiar Pilipino or, as a second option, of code switching between his familiar Pilipino and near-formal English to achieve familiarity.

Running through this thread of formal style in Philippine written English—through informal style (formal Pilipino and formal English) and familiar style (familiar Pilipino and near-formal English)—is formal English, the style best mastered by the Filipino. It is the rare Filipino who has mastered informal English as such. This is what I mean by stylistic underdifferentiation of written Philippine English of the mass media.

A NOTE ON THE CODE-SWITCHING VARIETY OF PHILIPPINE ENGLISH

The code-switching style exemplified by Exhibits 3 and 4 has been linguistically analysed by Bautista (1974). Its uses, based on empirical data, have been described by Pascasio (1979); these empirical data confirm self-reports based on questionnaires (Barrios et al., 1974).

The data so far has been for the spoken medium of this code-switching style. The corpus in this study is based on printed samples.

From a linguistic point of view, such a code-switching style presupposes competence in both English and Pilipino. The code switching takes place systematically at word level (in which case it would be a case of simple loans or borrowings), phrase level, clause level, sentence level, and, based on this sample, paragraph level. The two systems do not mix but rather alternate. It is important to stress that this alternation presupposes mastery of at least one style of each code.

The variety is used by well-educated Filipinos who have mastered both English (in its formal style) and Pilipino (in its formal and informal styles, even familiar) and is used in the mass media (spoken and written) for a very distinct purpose: to establish rapport with an interlocutor or audience (*Atin-atin lamang ito*—This is strictly among ourselves) and to establish an atmosphere of informality, perhaps unconsciously excluding a native speaker of English who is familiar with only one code and likewise perhaps unconsciously establishing one's credentials as a nationalist, albeit Westernized. Historically, it seems to have arisen from the student subculture (especially at the tertiary level) in the Manila schools and universities, propagated via the newspapers (since graduates of these schools eventually work in these media) and the other mass media, and has been imitated by clerics engaged in the youth ministry (an attempt to speak the same language as the youth do; moreover, these same clerics have come from this subculture). It is now widely used in talk-shows in the mass media and even in class, when the teacher wishes to establish his credentials as being "with it" and in order to "break the ice" in his class.

This code-switching variety is not to be confused with another variety which unfortunately has not been thoroughly studied because of its occurrence only in speech and the difficulty of capturing an adequate corpus. Based on the literature on pidginisation and creolisation as well as the literature on interlanguage (Andersen, 1979), probably the best way to describe this variety is to call it a form of interlanguage (of a Philippine-language speaker, for the most part Tagalog, in the process of learning the formal variety of standard English). It is found first of all among children in school usually in the lower grades in the process of learning English in school; undoubtedly, if enough subjects can be studied, it will be found in the interlanguage of children in bilingual homes (where Pilipino and English are used) who are in the process of learning both Pilipino and English, and in the attempts of the unschooled to communicate in English with a strictly English-speaking interlocutor (for example, a tourist).

What characterises this type of interlanguage and distinguishes it from what I have referred to as the code-switching variety is the presupposed competence of the performer. In the code-switching variety, the performer has competence in both codes. In the form of interlanguage I am referring to, the performer does not have sufficient competence in both codes; he is attempting to communicate in English but because of insufficient linguistic resources has to resort to Pilipino and in the process mixes both systems at unpredictable points in the discourse.

The linguistic features of this mixing need to be studied. One can hypothesise that there will be subtle differences between this form of interlanguage and the code-switching variety exemplified earlier.

Unfortunately, in the literature, even among reputable linguists in the Philippines, this distinction has not been made and both varieties are interchangeably referred to as Halo-Halo or Mix-Mix (Pilipino) or Engalog (if the bulk of the discourse is more English than Tagalog) or Taglish (if the bulk of the discourse is more Tagalog than English). Since the mass media are the most accessible to study, it is the code-switching variety of the mass media that has been studied (Marfil and Pasigna, 1970, and Bautista, 1974) and the form of interlanguage ignored (see scattered examples in Gonzalez, 1979).

I have likewise studiously avoided the term *Sprachmischung* (language mixing) since it is too general to keep the two varieties distinct.

Historically, during the Spanish period, the Philippines developed a local Philippine-Spanish pidgin which later became creolised as Chabacano and is now spoken as a first language in parts of Zamboanga (and formerly in Ermita, Manila, and Ternate, Cavite, and seemingly in Davao City, although no trace of this remains, see Riego de Dios, 1976). The Philippine-Spanish creole arose from a pidgin, from the communicative needs of natives (Tagalogs or Bisayans) and their Spanish military masters. There was mutual accommodation (through simplification) and eventually a re-analysis and relexification of the language (in the process of creolisation) showing many features of other creoles, for example in terms of catalysis of bound morphemes into free morphemes (especially in the Philippine verb system) and the loss of surface form distinctions in the Spanish nouns. The syntax is primarily Philippine rather than Spanish.

The social conditions were such that some process of simplification and eventually relexification was necessary to make communication possible.

The accommodation undoubtedly was mostly on the part of the Castilian who had to adjust himself to the imperfect interlingual speech of the native and reduce his own communication to the core grammar using roots without the accretions of subtle grammatical distinctions of Castilian morphology and syntax and of collocational rules.

The question must be posed whether the same type of sociolinguistic situation obtains at present for a Philippine-English pidgin to arise. Sibayan (1979) predicts that such a pidgin is in the making. I would disagree on the grounds that the sociolinguistic circumstances that gave rise to Chabacano do not obtain at present for the evolution of a Philippine-English Pidgin, an English version of Chabacano. English now has a life of its own in the Philippines, albeit confined to the elites and the educated. It is among these elites and educated that communication in a veriety called Philippine English is carried on, with no psychological or social distance dividing these from the rest of the population as there would be in the case of foreigners. In fact, based on the studies of Castillo (1972), there is an integrative motivation for learning English, to identify oneself not with Americans but with the Philippine elites who speak English, in addition to the usual instrumental orientation providing motivation for learning English as a language of wider communication.

The models for English then are not Americans but Philippine elites (undoubtedly the mass media leaders will contribute a distinct subset of models since they have the best opportunity for propagating and disseminating their variety). As long as these elites continue to speak English, contact with the target language will continue and as long as English continues to be a medium of instruction in schools (at least for certain subjects under the Bilingual Education Policy), the interlingual variety will continue to approximate the target language, that is to say a Philippine English standard. This standard will be restricted as to stylistic differentiation and will develop distinct local features of its own, but it will be English rather than a pidgin. Pidgins arise when interlingual varieties are frozen at a certain state, because of lack of exposure to the standard and the model, because of distance from the speakers of the target language if two interlocutors do not share each other's first language. For the latter function (a common language among Filipinos), the lingua franca developing is Pilipino. Education continues to be prized in this country and the rate of retention of the people in the system is improving. There is continuing exposure to the standard. Literacy is high. These are not the sociolinguistic circumstances for the emergence of a pidgin. A local variety yes, but a pidgin no.

Undoubtedly, if the social conditions and circumstances suddenly change, a totally different set of implications and possible results must be hypothesised. For the time, however, the emergence of such a pidgin does not seem to me likely.

STYLISTIC INSECURITY

This uncertain mastery of or competence in stylistic differentiation manifests itself in interesting sudden shifts of style which show what I would like to call "stylistic insecurity," akin to "linguistic insecurity."

The most common manifestation of this stylistic insecurity is an initial attempt at informal or even familiar style (usually in a feature article or column) which suddenly shifts into formal style (see Exhibit 5).

Exhibit 5   "Croc teeth" export?

The battlecry in exports is "non-traditional products." Just as soon as it was sounded by Trade Minister Luis Villafuerte, a broad front of the export sector appears to have taken on the shibboleth. But, of course, the test does not lie in the shouting but the doing that counts in terms of dollars and cents ringing at the national cash register at the Central Bank.

. . .

In terms of broadening the export base or matrix of exportable products, the addition of completely new items fashioned by the creative minds and hands of Filipino technicians and craftsmen or the development of heretofore untraded commodities would be the better approach. For it is when the Philippines can draw up a list of exportable products even just a fourth as thick as tariff code schedules of products classified by the Brussels Trade Nomenclature (BTN) or the U.S. Standard International Trade Classification (SITC) of exports would we have truly succeeded in non-traditional product exports. ("Viewpoints," Leonardo F. Ignacio, *The Economic Monitor,* October 8–14, 1979, p. 7.)

Note that the title is meant to be informal and colorful; the first paragraph makes an attempt at informality, only to switch three paragraphs later to the traditional composition style, including inversion in the second sentence of the second paragraph.

Most columnists in Philippine dailies and weeklies, while dealing with personalia and town gossip, do so in the formal composition style, perhaps a recognition of their lack of mastery of any other style. They seem unable to write in any other manner. For example, "Celebrity World," a gossip column about local film personalities, is written in this formal composition style (Exhibit 6).

Exhibit 6

There are three things that will always remind me of my visit to Los Angeles this year: "Apocalypse Now," Universal Studios, and the heat. Oh, the heat! It went up to over-100 degrees, an abnormal situation which was compounded by smog. And it was already past summer.

The heat wave notwithstanding, friends and relatives now settled in this enticing county went out of their way to make my stay profitable. ("Celebrity World," Crispina Martinez-Belen, *Bulletin Today,* September 23, 1979, p. 35.)

Similarly, "Limelight," a society column about parties and personalities in Manila, is written in the formal composition style (Exhibit 7).

Exhibit 7

Irene Marcos who has always shied away from parties and birthday celebrations even last year when she turned 18, or even when she became the sweetheart of the Upsilon Fraternity was delighted when her three "Ninangs" [godmother] Meldy Cojuangco, Zita Feliciano, and Lourdes Montinola organized a disco-jam session to surprise Irene last week for her birthday. Very casually attired, she arrived with her former classmates, gangmates, friends, and relatives all greeting her with warm embraces and singing. It will be recalled that Irene was only four years old when the First Family moved to Malacañang, and come to think of it, she has already grown-up in the Palace and turned to be a nice young lady with lots of charm and wit. To a very nice girl, our best wishes. ("Limelight," Moreno in Manila, *Bulletin Today,* pp. 22–23.)

Except for the use of nicknames, terms such as *disco-jam session* (a Filipinism) and *gangmates* (another Filipinism), and a colloquial "come to think of it" which bridges the distance between writer and reader, the vocabulary is decidedly formal, including the syntactic construction for formal discourse, "It will be recalled."

On the other hand, there are instances when the writer purposely seeks to be formal (for example, a literary essay) and unwittingly shifts into informality (Exhibit 8).

Exhibit 8

Of course there are other factors that limit the well-meaning writer's choice of material for his article. One of them is the time required by research. For example, Manunuri [Critic] Hammy Sotto would devote months of painstaking research to a very informative piece about a neglected but important old Filipino movie; Bienvenido Lumbera, the elder Manunuri, cannot sit down and write a lengthy, taped interview with director Ishmael Bernal partly because doing this would mean hours and hours of transcriptions and organization, which other more pressing, personal and professional, concerns demand of him. After all, one doesn't just bang away at his typewriter and presto! turn in an instant interview article just to beat the deadline. It's not only unfair to the person interviewed to be written about so quickly, casually and perfunctorily, it's also a reflection of the attitude of the writer and his ability or inability to capture the essence of his subject. ("To praise or not to praise, that is the question," Mario A. Hernando, *Expressweek,* October 11, 1979, pp. 10–11.)

One indicator of informality is the use of the nickname Hammy in the first half of the paragraph; the rest is formal, however. In the sentence beginning with "After all," the style shifts to informal and continues until the end of the paragraph. The last sentence makes use of contractions (a graphic indicator of informality), but the last sentence manifests the usual lexicon of the formal style: *casually, perfunctorily, reflection, attitude, capture the essence of his subject.*

In the hands of less able writers, even more stylistically insecure, one ends up with an infelicitous mixture of styles, shifting from formal to informal (Exhibit 9).

Exhibit 9

"Parang perya ang palabas," laments another. ["The show is like a fair," laments another].

"So long as there are limits to plugs, I suppose, they are a necessary evil. We cannot escape it [them] and TV is one habit we cannot kick," remarks Lily Balinghasay, administrative assistant of Ford Foundation.

"The current advertisement overdose is inescapable. In our economic system, the existence of capital is essential. We have to generate funds. Efforts should be focused more on the upliftment of media," notes an Industrial Psychology professor at Diliman.

Orly Mercado, 1978 TOYM broadcast awardee, adds his own perspective to the problem. "Any analysis of media practice should consider that the broadcast media is [are] essentially a commercial industry. Rousing public opinion against the ubiquitous presence of TV ads is only a palliative, since one reason for the existence of media is profit. Still, a lot can be done."

Putting it all succinctly: "While media is [are] a very effective educational medium it has become a very loud mouth piece for product pushing," sighs one viewer who goes to the comfort room during the regular commercials and runs to the ref during the "casual plugs." ("Why there are too many TV commercials," Teresita Reyes, *Parade,* August 3, 1979, p. 16.)

Perhaps some kind of justification can be made for the sudden shifts of style in the article in Exhibit 9, insofar as different people are being quoted, each with his own style. The shifts in style are rather sudden, however, the first quotation being in Pilipino, the next in informal style, the third in textbookese, the fourth in formal style, and the fifth a mixture of formal and informal. Then the actual writer herself who for the most part in the rest of the article has maintained a formal style suddenly talks about the *comfort room* (a taboo reference in most journalistic writing of the West) and the informal *ref* for *refrigerator.* Even *casual plug* for a short advertisement represents a shift.[5]

THE FILIPINO'S UNDERDIFFERENTIATED PHILIPPINE ENGLISH STYLE

One would have to look at the social matrix of Philippine society and the patterns of language use in various domains of Philippine life to explain why the Filipino bilingual uses a somewhat restricted style of English (confined to the formal style). One would likewise have to look at the language acquisition patterns of Filipinos and the environments in which he learns English to account for this restriction.

Filipinos are for the most part bilingual, even trilingual (see Gonzalez, 1976, on the complementarity of roles of various languages in the Filipino's repertoire). As a child, he learns a local vernacular (if he grows up in a non-Tagalog speaking area); he learns Tagalog (the school variety, namely Pilipino) in his neighborhood (if he lives in a Tagalog speaking area or the Metro

Manila area) and from the mass media (radio, TV, and movies), and a formal variety (the standard) in school under the bilingual education policy. Side by side with Pilipino he learns English in school.

The variety or lect of English that he learns in school is the formal variety, which is used in class (when the teacher is not code switching between a language that the student understands and the one he is learning in the early stages of schooling), in textbooks, and science and mathematics classes. Outside of the classroom, even in the schoolyard and the corridors, he switches to the local language, either the vernacular or Pilipino, depending on the area. The only contact that the Filipino has with a different variety of English would be in literature classes (where different styles and even regional dialects of English may be used, depending on the source of the literary pieces and their tradition), on TV, and in the movies, if other "accents" of English are used. If the student does much outside reading of popular literature and fiction, the exposure to other varieties of English becomes more frequent and the chances of at least a passive awareness of these differences (in some cases even an active mastery of different styles) becomes possible. For the average student, however, especially with the emphasis now in school on English for academic purposes and on English for science and technology, the style must necessarily be the formal style, with various registers depending on the field of specialisation.

Beyond schooling, the uses of English continue to be important but are limited to certain domains. Most everyday business and commercial transactions in the Philippines (in the market, in grocery stores, and in most department stores) are done in the local language (if not Pilipino). Even in offices, the local language prevails. Only in reading technical materials, in journals, in newsletters, etc. does one begin to use English again, and this, once more, in its formal style. We need empirical data (see Pascasio, 1978) to pinpoint which transactions and which conversational exchanges in the domain of business are done only in English. One has the impression that in multinational companies and local companies with extensive foreign contacts, at least at the board level and at the top management level, English dominates, with the code-switching variety sometimes resorted to for establishing rapport with another Filipino; hence, the informal style is used on such occasions.

Outside of the business domain, except in travel outside the country, in international gatherings, and in formal ceremonies within the country, the only other domain where English is used is the domain of entertainment, insofar as certain radio and TV programs and movies continue to be in English, although a significant portion of entertainment (especially on radio and TV) is now in Pilipino.

Even in church, in the domain of worship, outside of Metro Manila, the language of worship is the local language, the sermon being given in it; in Metro Manila certain services are conducted in Pilipino, but the majority are still given in English, with the code-switching variety often used (once more to establish rapport).

The Filipino's English then tends to be monostylistic both because of the patterns of second language acquisition in Philippine life (the school setting) and because of the restricted domains of English in Philippine life (business, academia [the classroom], entertainment, and international contacts). The Filipino's repertoire is a rich one; his Philippine English is restricted simply because he has other codes and varieties of such codes at his beck and call for other functions. When he wishes to be intimate, he uses the local vernacular; when he wishes to be familiar, he uses the local vernacular, Pilipino, or a code-switching variety of English (with the English portion predominantly in the formal style). Only when he wishes to be formal does he use English and, if he is versatile enough in Pilipino, the standard literary variety of Pilipino (which he is quickly acquiring as a result of the present policy on bilingual education).

The number of Filipinos who acquire sufficient mastery of the informal, perhaps even intimate, varieties of English is rather limited. If one wishes to estimate this number, one has only to read the works of our journalists, who have undergone a self-selection process, to realise their stylistic limitations. The journalists who have mastered more than one style are quite few. Judging from the samples and the corpus analysed, the majority are restricted in their English styles, with those who can maintain the informal style consistently and competently being in the minority.

A cursory reading of Philippine literature in English would manifest the same types of restriction. Philippine fiction is for the most part written in a creative variety of formal Philippine English with many loanwords and references to Filipino culture and life, in an attempt to express the sensibility of the Filipino in a rather restricted style. If the Filipino attempts to be familiar and intimate, he will insert either whole excerpts in Pilipino or purposely exploit the potential of the code-switching variety, often for humor, rapport, and familiarity. This area demands separate investigation and should be the subject of a future study.

NOTES

1. Arlene Matociños
2. The Philippine newspapers and periodicals analysed and the dates of the issues were as follows:

Title of Periodical	Date
Newspapers and other tabloids	
1. *Bulletin Today*	September 23, 1979
	September 24, 1979
	October 6, 1979
2. *Philippine Daily Express*	September 24, 1979
3. *The Times Journal*	September 24, 1979
	October 1, 1979
4. *The Daily Tribune*	October 6, 1979
5. *Evening Post*	October 9, 1979

(continued on p. 224)

(continued from p. 223)

Title of Periodical	Date
6. People's Journal	October 9, 1979
7. WE Forum	October 6–12, 1979
8. Sportsnews	October 12–18, 1979
9. Business Day	September 25, 1979
10. The Economic Monitor	October 8–14, 1979
11. Weekend	September 21, 1979

Magazines

1.	Philippine Panorama	June 3, 1979
		July 22, 1979
		August 26, 1979
		September 9, 1979
		September 23, 1979
		October 4, 1979
2.	Express Week	August 9, 1979
		September 20, 1979
		October 11, 1979
3.	Woman's Home Companion	August 30, 1979
		September 13, 1979
		October 11, 1979
		October 18, 1979
4.	MOD Filipina	August 10, 1979
		August 17, 1979
		October 5, 1979
5.	MR. & MS.	August 21, 1979
		October 2, 1979
6.	WHO	September 22, 1979
		October 20, 1979
7.	FOCUS	October 13, 1979
8.	Parade	August 3, 1979
		August 24, 1979
		September 23, 1979
9.	People	September 21, 1979
10.	Celebrity	February 15, 1979
11.	Manila Women's Wear	September 1979
12.	COED	October 1979
13.	Nation's Journal	October 18, 1979
14.	Kislap Magazine	October 4, 1979
15.	Sunburst	March 1979
16.	Manila Review	July–August 1979
17.	Yaman (for Filipino entrepeneurs)	August 1979
18.	HR (Magazine on Human Resources)	October 1979

Breakdown (in numbers) of

Editorials	9	Features	55
Columns (Regular)	32	Short Stories	1

3. Actually, *spread-eagle* used of the arms is a Filipinism (Llamzon, 1969) since an American would say "spread both arms."

4. *Ever since* is a Filipinism meaning *for a long time now.*

5. As part of the technical report for our research project, my research assistant and I counted the frequency of occurrence of these shifts:

Total number of articles		97
With style shifts	70	
	(72%)	
Without style shifts	27	
	(28%)	

Frequency of Shifts in Percentages

	Lexical Choices	*Collocations*	*Syntactic Features*
	Average Frequency in Running Text of Words	*Average Frequency in Running Text of Sentences*	
Formal to Informal Shifts	0.04%	0.9%	0.05%
Informal to Formal Shifts	0.4%	4.2%	0.7%

Occurrences of shifts were counted in this manner: For lexical choices, the number of occurrences was divided by the total number of running words in the text per article. The frequencies were then averaged for the articles and the percentage computed.

For collocations (phrases) and for syntactic features, the number of occurrences was divided by the total number of sentences (series of words separated by a period) in the text per article. The frequencies were then averaged for all the relevant articles and the percentage computed.

Note that the shifts are significantly more frequent from informal to formal, a clear indication of stylistic insecurity, in other words, of the Filipino's discomfort with the informal style and his tendency even when using the informal style to shift to the formal (composition) style.

REFERENCES

Andersen, Roger W. Expanding Schumann's pidginization hypothesis. *Language Learning.* 1979, 29, 1, 105–119.

Barrios, Mary Angela, SPC, Bautista, Lourdes S., Galang, Rose, Villamor, Esperanza, and Santos, Paulina. The greater Manila speech community: Bilingual and/or diglossic? Ateneo de Manila University–Philippine Normal College Consortium for a Ph.D. in Linguistics. Mimeographed, 1974.

Bautista, Ma. Lourdes S. The Filipino bilingual's competence: A model based on an analysis of Tagalog-English code-switching. Doctoral dissertation, Ateneo de Manila University–Philippine Normal College Consortium for a Ph.D. in Linguistics. Mimeographed, 1974.

Castillo, Emma S. Motivational variables in second language acquisition. *Philippine Journal of Linguistics.* 1972, 3, 2, 95–124.

Gonzalez, Andrew B. The language question: Language policy and national development in the Philippines. 1976. Contribution to Education Volume to be published by the Department of Public Information, Republic of the Philippines, for the forthcoming IMF Conference. In Press.

Gonzalez. Andrew B. Becoming bilingual in English in a Philippine setting: A partial report of a Manila sample. Paper presented to the Fourteenth Regional Seminar, SEAMEO Regional Language Centre, Singapore. April 16–21, 1979.

Gonzalez, Andrew B., and Alberca, Wilfredo. Philippine English of the mass media. Manila: Research Council, De La Salle University, 1978.

Llamzon, Teodoro A. *Standard Filipino English.* Manila: Ateneo de Manila University Press, 1969.

Marfil, Alice E., and Pasigna, Aida L. An analysis of shifts from Tagalog to English in printed materials. Unpublished M.A. thesis, Philippine Normal College, 1970.

Olonan, Zenaida. Language use in a multilingual community. Doctoral dissertation, University of Santo Tomas, Manila. Mimeographed, 1978.

Pascasio, Emy. Dynamics of code-switching in the business domain. *Philippine Journal of Linguistics.* 1978, 9, 1 & 2, 40–50.

Pascasio, Emy. *Language at Crossroads: English and Pilipino.* Quezon City: Ateneo de Manila University Press, 1979.

Riego de Dios, Maria Isabelita O. A composite dictionary of Philippine creole Spanish (PCS). Doctoral dissertation, Ateneo de Manila–Philippine Normal College Consortium for a Ph.D. in Linguistics. Mimeographed, 1976.

Sibayan, Bonifacio P. Languages and socioeconomic development: Resulting patterns of bilingualism/multilingualism. Paper presented to the Fourteenth Regional Seminar, SEAMEO Regional Language Centre, Singapore. April 16–21, 1979.

13 RHETORICAL AND COMMUNICATIVE STYLES IN THE NEW VARIETIES OF ENGLISH

Jack C. Richards

INTRODUCTION[1]

Recent years have witnessed changes in attitudes towards the new varieties of English which have emerged in multilingual countries where English has the status of a second language. The new varieties of English, described variously as "indigenous," "nativized," and "local" varieties of English by comparison with the established varieties of English in Britain, North America, and elsewhere, are now asserting their sociolinguistic legitimacy. Increasingly, linguists and educationists are forced to undertake a more serious examination of the linguistic, pedagogic, cultural, and societal variables involved (cf. Kachru, 1976b, 1978a, 1978b; Strevens, 1977; Llamzon, 1969; and Richards, 1974). On the one hand, the number of speakers of English involved, totalling as it does to probably as large a population of users of English as those within the "native" English-speaking countries, calls attention to a phenomenon of more than mere marginal or academic interest. On the other hand, the rapidity with which the new varieties of English have emerged and the distinctiveness of the new codes of English thus produced raise interesting questions of typology and linguistic change that call for adequate theoretical models and explanations. What is it that is common to the interplay of social, cultural, and linguistic factors in countries as diverse as Fiji, Singapore, Sri Lanka, Nigeria, and Jamaica, for example, that has led to the rapid emergence of new and relatively stable varieties of English in these countries? It is the investigation of questions such as this that constitutes the study of the new Englishes of Singapore, Fiji, India, and so on, a field of enquiry that is slowly emerging within linguistics and allied disciplines.

It is not only Anglicists who have had to revise their linguistic inventories. The speakers of these new varieties of English have themselves had to recognize the distinctiveness of their new speech patterns and to make attitudinal adjustments and decisions. It is not always the case that the new varieties of English receive recognition, even among those who speak them. There is an understandable sensitivity in some countries to investigation or acknowledgement of local norms for English usage, since there are both those who would not wish to see such linguistic phenomena legitimitized by the documentation and serious attention of linguistic scholars, and those who interpret such attentions as reflecting negative value judgments on the way English is spoken. Fortunately for those who are interested in the complex interplay of language with societal forces within multilingual societies, there are signs that such linguistic insecurity is beginning to fade, and there is a more receptive audience to serious accounts of the forms and functions of the new varieties of English. Scholars such as Kachru and Platt, for example, have initiated detailed empirical investigations of the linguistic phenomena involved in nativized varieties of English. Linguists such as DeCamp (1971) and Bickerton have developed new theoretical models which offer wider explanatory power when dealing with data from linguistic continua. Centers for linguistic research and professional meetings and conferences now include local varieties of English within their programmes of study and discussion. Thus the East-West Center held a two-week conference of invited specialists in April 1978, a major part of which was devoted to discussions of new varieties of English. A conference on English in Non-Native Contexts was held at the University of Illinois, Urbana-Champaign in June 1978, and an international conference on varieties of English was held at the Regional Language Centre, Singapore in 1981.

While there are encouraging signs of the increasing recognition of nativized or indigenized varieties of English within the disciplines of linguistics and applied linguistics, changed attitudes have yet to filter out to education officials, college lecturers, and classroom teachers in many countries, some of whom are concerned about the linguistic developments they encounter. They tend to attribute differences between the varieties of English in daily use and the varieties of English they regard as acceptable as resulting from poor teaching, poor learning, declining standards of English, and so on. This paper deals with a phenomenon that is common to a wide variety of situations in which English can be said to have become "indigenized," "nativized," or "localized," the fact of contrasting varieties of English usage in these settings, and tries to account for the diversity of language varieties that have emerged as a product of language nativization.

In speaking of the new varieties of English, I refer to countries in which English is used as a second language, that is, where English is widely used for societal interaction but where the variety of English used is no longer modeled on British or American English due to a transition to local English norms. Thus in Singapore, the Philippines, Nigeria, and so on, internal norms of phonology, lexicon, syntax, and speech acts are used for speech events in English, and the "parent" norms of British or American English are not necessarily accepted as legitimate for use in many contexts. The processes by which the target for language use and learning in such situations gradually moves from an external to an internal norm is what Kachru calls the *nativization* and Moag, Richards, and others, the *indigenization* of English (Kachru, 1978b; Moag and Moag, 1977; and Richards, 1978a). Nativization and indigenization of a language is an aspect of language change, and study of this phenomenon can be linked to a tradition of scholarly research into the norms of language use in bilingual or multilingual societies, and in particular to the effects of language migration on linguistic change. Such a tradition owes much to the work of Haugen, who was one of the first linguists to locate such phenomena within the domain of descriptive linguistics (Haugen, 1938, 1953). Thus in his studies of language ecology, particularly with reference to the gradual assimilation of Scandinavian immigrant communities into North America, Haugen documented the gradual divergence of the immigrants' linguistic norms from the language norms of the homelands. In their new sociocultural environment, new norms for language use emerged, and in a series of articles and books, Haugen set out to construct a typological account of the processes involved. *Code switching, interference,* and *borrowing* entered the terminology of bilingual studies at this time as phenomena of legitimate linguistic and descriptive interest. A similar interest is seen in Mackey's work on bilingual interference, motivated as it was by an attempt to establish code norms for bilinguals whose varieties of French or English displayed features that suggested a blending or integration of features from several different sources (Mackey, 1968, 1970). Haugen's descriptions of the changes that took place in the speech of Norwegian immigrants in America provide a theoretical and methodological starting point for an account of the linguistic characteristics and pragmatic functions of the new varieties of English. As Haugen remarks, "what has really taken place is a shift in structure . . . correlated to a shift in cultural and social form" (Haugen, 1938, p. 133). This double focus on both input and output is crucial to a study of the processes of indigenization and nativization. It entails a comparison of input factors—the social, cultural, and affective dimensions—with linguistic output, that is, the linguistic processes by which these dimensions are variously manifested in particular communities where English has been nativized.

INDIGENIZATION–NATIVIZATION OF ENGLISH

The terms "indigenization" and "nativization" have been used to describe the divergence of varieties of a language from a "parent" source (Kachru, 1978b, and Moag and Moag, 1977). Whinnom (1971) uses the term hybridization with similar meaning. Kachru describes Persianized Hindi and Indianized English as two instances of nativization. In a series of major articles Kachru has documented the linguistic processes which account for nativization of a language, with particular reference to the nativization of English in India; "during almost three hundred years of contact with Africa and Asia, English has completely been embedded in the local contexts and has slowly gone through the process of nativization" (Kachru, 1978b, p. 4). Nativization in this sense describes the emergence of linguistic features in new varieties of English that are *categorical*. It describes features of the code. It hence refers to permanent additions or modifications to the code of the language which reflect the force of cultural embedding. Thus, while acknowledging variation in Indian English according to region, ethnicity, and proficiency, Kachru has concentrated on describing the major categorical (that is, nonvariable) features of Indian English. The "Indianness" of Indian English is thus described in terms of linguistic manifestations at the level of phonology, lexis, grammar, and semantics, of distinct cultural, affective, and situational aspects of Indian society and culture. "The linguistic study of the following features of South Asian English has proved useful not only in understanding the formal features of the texts, but also in relating these to typically Indian contexts:

1. Register variation.
2. Style variation.
3. Collocational deviation.
4. Semantic shifts.
5. Lexical range" (Kachru, 1969, p. 656)

Kachru has documented the range of linguistic innovations found in both written and spoken Indian English, and has found a wide variety of linguistic evidence for nativization, some of the processes of which he refers to as contextualization, hybridization, and register extension.

CATEGORICAL AND VARIABLE FEATURES

Focussing on categorical features of varieties of English leads to the description of the linguistic features that characterize the speaker of both native and "nativized" varieties of English, enabling the identification of the "Canadianness" of Canadian English, the "Indianness" of Indian English, and so on. In addition to categorical features in the new varieties of English, however, there are also major *variable* features in Singapore English, Fiji English, Filipino English, and elsewhere, which are as significant as categorical features in contributing to the distinctiveness of these indigenized forms of English. In each of the speech communities mentioned, there is a wide variety of linguistic features which are observed to occur variably in the speech of individuals. In Manila, for example, in certain situations and with certain interlocutors a speaker may code-switch between Tagalog and English throughout the entire length of a speech event. In Singapore, speakers of English frequently switch effortlessly from a variety of English that is close to standard British English to a variety of English that is quite different from standard British. The different varieties of English in the Singapore English speaker's speech repertoire result from variable rules for major features of phonology and syntax. In a number of countries where nativized varieties of English are used we also observe variability at the lexical level. Thus, a word from a local language may temporarily displace an English word for certain types of speech events, the

English word reappearing for other speech events. Such manifestations of variable features in the speech of speakers of many nativized varieties of English I will refer to as *lect switching*. Lect switching hence describes the selection of a variable rather than a categorical feature from the speech code of the individual for particular types of speech event. Lect switching is a major and distinctive characteristic of many indigenized varieties of English. This paper seeks to illustrate and elucidate both the formal and functional dimensions of lect shifting with reference to indigenized varieties of English.

RHETORICAL AND COMMUNICATIVE STYLES

An adequate description of the processes of nativization that have led to the development of such varieties of English as Indian, Singapore or Filipino English, should include both the linguistic and the functional dimensions of language nativization. It would be inadequate to characterize the new English varieties as simply resulting from structural and phonological convergence of relevant linguistic features of English through contact with other languages. While such an approach might explain the formal linguistic characteristics of particular varieties of English, it would fail to explain the affective and social significance of the linguistic phenomena involved. What characterizes the development of new varieties of English is the functional motivation for the employment of new linguistic codes. Clearly, Indian English, Singapore English, Nigerian English, and so on would not gradually be achieving legitimacy if they did not have distinct functional uses and requirements that could not be met by imported varieties of English. To understand the significance of the processes of indigenization, we thus have to consider the functional values for the Singaporean, the Filipino, and the Indian, represented by the particular forms of English he or she employs.

Numerous approaches to the analysis of language use in functional terms have been proposed in recent years, and while serious problems present themselves when we attempt to interpret functional categories from linguistic data, the use of a functional approach would appear to be essential in accounting for language nativization. Haugen adopts a basically functional approach in discussing the divergence of American-Norwegian (the variety of Norwegian spoken among Norwegian migrants to America) from standard Norwegian (Haugen, 1977). Haugen makes a distinction between two contrasting norms for languages available to members of a community. One, the *rhetorical norm,* is the standardized variety of the language, codified in grammars and sanctioned by its use as a model for written language. It is thus the educated model of language, typically regarded as grammatically "correct" and used as a model for teaching in school. By contrast a different model of language is represented by what Haugen refers to as the *communicative norm,* which is the variety of language used in daily social interaction and which reflects the speaker's situational and communicative needs. In Haugen's example, the communicative norm of the Norwegian immigrants to America was a type of contact variety of Norwegian which had developed in America and which was much despised by purists. The rhetorical norm was the standard variety of Norwegian, particularly as it was spoken in Norway. Judged by the external norm, the new communicative norm for Norwegian was often denied linguistic legitimacy. "Those who cling categorically to the rhetorical norm either deride or deplore contact dialects and even go so far as to deny that there is any norm whatsoever in their usage" (Haugen, 1977, p. 94).

The concept of rhetorical and communicative norms provides a useful perspective on the processes of indigenization. Whereas in Haugen's case, the indigenization of Norwegian refers to *diachronic* changes in the language code as a result of which the source language norms came to be regarded as having rhetorical functions (and values) and the new contact variety of Norwegian as having communicative functions (and values); in the case of indigenized varieties of English the contrast between rhetorical and communicative exists at the synchronic level. It is hence a characteristic of *users* of the code. Consequently I will use the terms *rhetorical styles* and *communicative styles* to refer to contrasting styles of speaking within an individual's speech repertoire, and use the terms rhetorical and communicative norms to refer to the community's accepted norms for formal and informal speech.

Thus members of the English speaking communities in these countries can be said to possess variable linguistic rules to mark distinctions between rhetorical and communicative styles of speaking. The favoured speech variety for formal communication, the acrolect, can be regarded as the rhetorical norm of the community. The speech variety accepted for informal communication, the mesolect, can be regarded as the communicative norm of the community. *Lect shifting* refers to the use of variable linguistic rules to mark differences between rhetorical and communicative styles. All speech communities of course make use of lect shift rules, and distinctions between rhetorical and communicative styles are presumably universal. What calls for special comment in the case of indigenized varieties of English is the generation of new varieties of English markedly different from the source varieties of English, to meet the need for new rhetorical and communicative styles. Individual speakers have a command of contrasting speech styles, while within the community as a whole there is a continuum of speech varieties. The acrolect represents the idealized rhetorical norm for the community and the mesolect, the idealized communicative norm. The basilect may represent an actual communicative style but is scarcely recognized as a norm. Thus the speech varieties of a cross-section of the community represented by speakers A, B, C, D, and E, is shown in Figure 1. However, the situation is more complex in reality, in that an individual speaker may use an acrolectal speech variety as a rhetorical style and the mesolectal variety as a communicative style on some occasions, and on some occasions the same speaker may use a mesolectal variety as a rhetorical style and the basilectal variety as a communicative style, depending on speaker, role, and other situational variables. The speech repertoires X and Y of speakers E and A may be represented as in Figures 2 and 3.

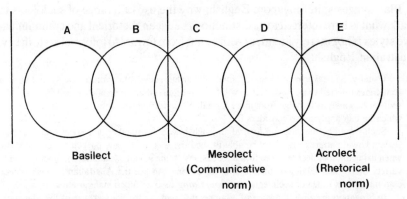

Figure 1 Speech varieties of a cross section of a community

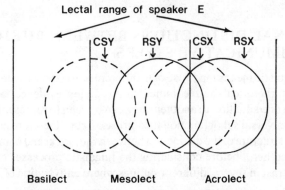

Figure 2 Speech repertoires — Speaker E

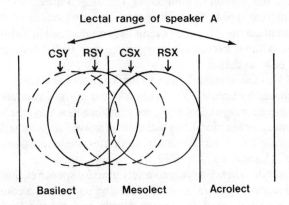

CS = Communicative style

RS = Rhetorical style

Figure 3 Speech repertoires—Speaker A

Platt suggests, in Singapore English, why the use of a range of sociolects to mark what is here referred to as distinctions between rhetorical and communicative styles is *not* merely identical with a shift from formal to informal style in say, Australian English:

> Usually, a speaker is not able to "shed" his or her sociolectal patterns easily and what is sometimes referred to as "sociolectal switching" is often rather a type of *style* switching, i.e., the speaker has a stylistic range from more formal to less formal speech *within* his own sociolect which he can apply as he considers fit.
>
> Such would be the case for Australian English where a speaker of a lower sociolect with certain vowel patterns would not be able to shed these easily on any particular occasion. But when using his sociolect on more formal occasions . . . he would use a different functional sub-variety than when talking to his workmates. So one can see the Australian English speech continuum as a range of sociolects each *containing* its own functional varieties.
>
> In Singapore English, the state of affairs is different . . . the whole range of the Singapore English speech continuum provides functional varieties for its speakers. (Platt, 1977a, p. 90)

FUNCTIONAL DISTINCTIONS BETWEEN RHETORICAL AND COMMUNICATIVE STYLES

While the linguistic means made use of in different nativized varieties of English to distinguish rhetorical and communicative styles evidence considerable diversity from one situation to another, they can be seen to represent a common and perhaps universal set of functional contrasts. Let us therefore consider first the functional structure of the distinction between rhetorical and communicative styles proposed here, before considering the linguistic processes employed to mark this contrast in several different settings where nativization of English has occurred.

The functional basis for distinguishing rhetorical and communicative styles depends on the recognition of contrasting values and differences in affective content for different types of speech events. Differing ranges of illocutionary force for different classes of speech events are summarized in Table 1 in sets of binary scales, without necessarily suggesting that such labels are mutually exclusive, or easy to define.

The use of variable linguistic rules to mark functional contrasts of this sort has been discussed by Labov: "We here make use of the distinction between a variable rule and an independent obligatory one in a new way: the variable rule has a communicative function—'stylistic,' 'expressive,' or 'emphatic' . . . while the invariant rule has none, it merely facilitates the expression of choices already made" (Labov, 1972, p. 237).

A rhetorical style is hence a speech variety used for speech events which have the functional status of *public, formal, high,* and so on, and a communicative style a speech variety used for speech events which have the contrasting functional status of *private, informal, low,* and so on. The defining characteristics of speech events giving them rhetorical versus communicative status depend in turn on characteristics that are related to speaker, role, settings, topic,

TABLE 1

Rhetorical Style	Communicative Style
Characteristics of the Speech event	
Public	Private
Formal	Informal
High	Low
Distant	Intimate
Impersonal	Personal
Careful	Casual
etc.	

and other variables. The distinction made here between rhetorical and communicative styles is thus an overarching distinction that subsumes a number of implicit contrasts within the ethnography of communication.

The processes by which English becomes nativized in a new cultural setting include the generation of new rhetorical *and* communicative speech varieties. Historically, indigenization takes place in situations in which there is a gradual shift for the functions of English within a society, as it becomes a language of personal interaction within a community and as it comes to take on more and more communicative functions. The nativization of English requires the development of new codes for both rhetorical and communicative functions and the existence of variable rules allows the functionally distinct contexts for language use to be formally marked.

In both instances the rhetorical and communicative styles are internal (local), rather than external (foreign) norms, though the rhetorical style will be closer to the source language rhetorical norms. The rejection of external rhetorical norms by speakers of Singapore and Filipino English and the use of internal rhetorical norms is related to the concept of Guiora et al. (1972) of language ego. Thus the personal and social identity of an individual is marked with reference to linguistic norms that define both personal and social boundaries. The use of a standard or informal variety of Singapore, Nigerian, or Filipino English is thus part of what it means to *be* a Singaporean, a Nigerian, or a Filipino. This is captured in the remark by Singapore's ambassador to the United Nations, quoted in the preface to Tongue's book: "When one is abroad, in a bus or train or aeroplane, and when one overhears someone speaking, one can immediately say this is someone from Malaysia or Singapore. And I should hope that when I'm speaking abroad my countrymen will have no problem recognizing that I am a Singaporean" (Tongue, 1974).

LINGUISTIC REALIZATION OF LECT-SHIFTS

A range of different linguistic resources is employed in nativized varieties of English to mark a shift from rhetorical to communicative styles. The following processes have been observed in Singapore English, Filipino English, Fijian English, and Indian English.

Phonological Shift

Variable phonological rules are perhaps the commonest marker of a shift from a rhetorical to a communicative style. Tay (1978) identifies a number of variable features in the pronunciation of speakers of Singapore English. For example:

1. *Decrease in aspiration*: Voiceless stops may be weakly aspirated or unaspirated in all positions.
2. *Simplication of consonant clusters*: Final consonant clusters in words like *went, just, ask* may be reduced to the first consonant of the cluster.
3. *Replacement of final stops*: Final stops may be replaced by glottals.

Other variable phonological features noted by Tay include changes in vowel and diphthong quality, stressing and intonation. Llamzon (1969) in his study of standard Filipino English likewise documents phonological variability in this variety of English with reference to vowel quality, diphthongs, consonants, stress, juncture, and intonation. Table 2 shows allophonic variation for formal conversational styles in Filipino English.

TABLE 2   *Allophonic Variation in Filipino English (from Llamzon, 1969, p. 37).*

Phonemes		Stressed		Unstressed			
				Formal, Semi-Formal		*Conversational*	
i	u	i	u	ə	ə	i	u
I	ʊ	I	ʊ	I	ʊ	I	ʊ
e ə o		e	o	ə ə ə		e a o	
æ a ɔ		æ a	ɔ	ə ə ə		a a o	

Grammatical Shift

A marked feature of many indigenized varieties of English is variable use of grammatical features to mark the shift from a rhetorical to a communicative style. This is sometimes referred to as lect shifting and an upper lect—the acrolect, a middle lect or mesolect, and a lower lect or basilect are sometimes referred to. Empirical studies of lectal variation in such settings as Guayana (Bickerton, 1975) and Singapore (Platt, 1975) suggest rather than three lects, a continuum of grammatical features, with different members of the community controlling different sections of the continuum as part of their speech repertoire. Bickerton compares the situation in Guayana with that found in Hawaii:

In Guayana, and probably in many other partially decreolized communities, there exist, among speakers of the absolute basilect, at least a few speakers who can hardly speak anything but the absolute basilect, alongside a considerably larger number who may speak the absolute basilect among their intimates but who command a varying number of higher lects for more formal purposes. Members of this class of monolectal speakers were always distinguished by the fact that they had never been to school. However, persons without schooling appear to be non-existent in Hawaii, and every native born speaker can shift lects to a greater or lesser degree. (Bickerton and Odo, 1976)

In Singapore, despite access to schooling for all children, monolectalism is more widespread than it would appear to be in Hawaii, thus there exists a significant number of speakers who are unable to vary their speech towards the rhetorical norm. For such speakers, rules employed variably by some members of the community, have categorical status.

Platt (1977a) identifies a number of variable grammatical features found in the mesolectal variety of Singapore English, including the following:

1. *Variable lack of marking for past tense*:
   My father bring my mother over.
   I atten(ed) night school.
   From there I pick(ed) up my English.
2. *Variable lack of realization of third person tense marking*:
   He mix a lot with them.
   My mother sleep in there.
3. *Deletion of it*:
   If by bus—is very convenient.
   You see—is compulsory.

Morpheme Addition

The English spoken by Singaporeans and by Filipinos in the Manila area displays other unique features which serve to mark a shift from rhetorical to communicative styles, one of the most distinctive of which is the variable employment of morphemes from local languages attached to English sentences to mark a communicative style. In Singapore English, a final sentence-particle *la,* probably of Hokkien origin, is extensively used when English is employed in informal settings and where the speech event calls for solidarity, rapport, and so on. In Manila, a Tagalog-based particle *na* likewise may enter the code of speakers of English when the speech event has communicative as opposed to rhetorical function. Examples of the *na* particle in Filipino English in Manila are:

> Let's go *na*!
> Come. Let's eat *na*!
> I'll go *na*.

The *la* particle in Singapore English is seen in the following examples:

> That depend on you *la,* if you want to take off one day, or your office give you, that up to you *la*.

Must go *la.*
I said no *la.*
Cannot *la.*   (Richards and Tay, 1977)

Lexical Shift

Lexical shift refers to the replacement of a known English word by a word from a local language when the speech event calls for a communicative style. This is thus distinct from *lexical borrowing,* which refers to terms from local languages that have entered the speech code but do not carry particular communicative or affective value and for which no English equivalent exists. In Singapore the word *satay,* taken from Malay, refers to a particular type of barbecued meat. Similarly in the Philippines the word *adobo* refers to a particular pork and chicken dish. In both cases, no English word exists for either of these popular foods. This is a case of lexical borrowing. This is a different situation however from the variable use of lexical items from local languages in many indigenized varieties of English. In Singapore English, for example, the Malay word *makan,* which refers to food and eating, may be used to replace the English words *food* or *eat* or *eating* when a communicative style is employed. Thus, *let's have something to eat* may become *let's go for makan* in the communicative style. The following examples of items subject to lexical shift illustrate that this phenomenon is found in Singapore English, Filipino English and Fiji English.

Rhetorical style	*Communicative style*	*Variety*
drunk	kasou	Fiji English
afraid	lamu	Fiji English
steal	talasi	Fiji English
ride	tumpang	Singapore English
"Good God!"	allama	Singapore English
a primitive place	an ulu place	Singapore English
busybody	kaypoh	Singapore English
to chat	to make kwento	Filipino English
ugly	pangit	Filipino English
handsome	pogi	Filipino English
arrogant	mayabang	Filipino English
later	mamaya	Filipino English

The choice of a word from a local language rather than the English word would appear to make the speech event more colloquial and informal or more virile and "genuine."

Code Switching

A further linguistic device employed in nativized varieties of English to signal a shift from rhetorical to communicative style is the use of rapid code switching. While code switching is a phenomenon found in many bilingual and multilingual communities, I am distinguishing the commonly described diglossic code switching from code switching as a special way of marking a communicative style, a phenomenon which is found in India, the Philippines, and in Singapore. In diglossic code switching "code alternation is largely of the situational type. Distinct varieties are employed in certain settings (such as home, school, work) associated with separate bounded kinds of activities (public speaking, formal negotiations, special ceremonies, verbal games, etc.) or spoken with different categories of speakers (friends, family members, strangers, social inferiors, government officials). Although speakers in diglossic situations must know more than one grammatical system to carry on their daily affairs, only one code is employed at any one time." (Gumperz, 1978, p. 3)

This is however a quite distinct type of code switching from a phenomenon that has emerged in a number of situations where English has become indigenized. In the Philippines, India, and Singapore, for example, a different type of code switching takes place in which speakers who are fluent in English-Tagalog, English-Hindi, and English-Hokkien, for example, and who regularly use both languages in the course of their daily routines, for particular types of speech events may use a mixed code based on alternate sections of English-Tagalog, in the case of Filipinos, and English-Hindi, in the case of Indians or English and a Chinese dialect, in the case of Singaporeans. Gumperz comments on the special features of this type of code switching.

> The exchange forms a single unitary interactional whole. Speakers communicate fluently, maintaining an even flow of talk. No hesitation pauses, changes in sentence rhythm, pitch or level of intonation contour mark the shift in code. There is nothing in the exchange as a whole to indicate that speakers don't understand each other. Apart from the alternation itself, the passages have all the earmarks of ordinary conversations in a single language. (Gumperz, 1978)

The variety of code-mixed English-Tagalog widely used in the Manila area of the Philippines is commonly known as Mix-Mix. The following examples of Mix-Mix are taken from a study by Bautista, and are extracts from conversations between the host of a popular radio show and his guests on a "talk-in" programme.

1. *Aside from this N.C.E.E. examination* ay naghihigpit na rin sila ngayon sapagka't *they won't worry about anymore* itong sinasabi nilang *decrease in enrolment* sapagka't magkakaroon na rin sila ng *technological, vocational* at saka *occupational courses so they cannot afford anymore to get in people who are not fit for college.*
2. *They're present in the reservations.* Pero sa ngayon po *we have actual counts in the reservations of about one hundred and forty-eight.*
3. *The farmer realizes that self-help will not only help him . . . his . . . socially or individually* kundi pwede *ring internationally.*

Kachru has documented the same phenomenon in India and gives the following example of English-Hindi Mix-Mix.

Mujhe is bat me bilkul *doubt* nahi, *rather I am sure* ki *this year B.Sc examination* ke *results* bahut kharab hai. Kuch to *examiners* ne *strictness* ki aur kuch *papers* bhi aise *out of way* aye ki *students to unexpected questions* ko *paper* me *set* dekh kar *hall* ki *ceiling* hi *watch* karte reh gaye. Itna *failure* to *last three or four years* me kabhi hua ni na tha abki *admission* me bhi *difficulty* uthani paregi. *Last year* bhi *in spite of all attempts* kuch *applicants* ke *admission almost impossible* ho gaye the. *After a great stir registrar* ki *move* kiya ja saka, jisse kuch *seats* ka *extra arrangement* kiya gaya. (Kachru, 1978b, p. 21)

While Bautista (1975) studies only the linguistic dimensions of the phenomenon, Gumperz (1978) gives a functional/semantic account of this type of code switching, and likewise attributes the motivation for it to the need for an effective communicative style. "It is this overtly marked separation between in- and out-group standards which perhaps best characterizes the bilingual experience. . . . What distinguishes the bilingual from his monolingual neighbour is the juxtaposition of styles: the awareness that his own mode of behaviour is one of several possible modes, that interpretation of what a speaker intends to communicate *depends on the style of communication*" (Gumperz, 1978, p. 6).

I hence regard code switching of the Mix-Mix type as part of a continuum of linguistic mechanisms that can be employed for the same communicative/functional effect. In this instance, the nonmixed English code is taken as a marker of a rhetorical style. Thus a Filipino informant reports: "If I go in to an office in Manila and try to get a clerk to do something for me, to get a document or some such thing, if I speak to the clerk in English, the situation becomes over formal; if I mix-mix the situation is easier to handle." Thus the code-switching has a 'softening' effect on the speech event. It signals the affective values associated with a communicative style. Again as Gumperz observes:

> Whenever a code or speech style is regularly associated with a certain class of activities, it comes to signify or connote them, so that its very use can signal the enactment of these activities even in the absence of other clear contextual clues. Component messages are then interpreted in terms of the norms and symbolic associations that apply to the signalled activity. (Gumperz, 1978)

LEARNING AND TEACHING

The emergence of contrasting rhetorical and communicative styles in nativized varieties of English raises several important questions concerning second language learning. I have argued here that the range of different linguistic devices and phenomena that contributes to the distinctiveness of new communicative styles for English in various countries reflects common functional values. They illustrate how changes in the functional roles of English generate changes in the linguistic code. In some instances, the rapidity of the changes creates puzzlement and bewilderment for those whose business is identified with the rhetorical style and for whom it represents the *true* and *grammatically correct* variety. Thus Sibayan comments: "I still remember the emotional difficulties and professional as well as personal concern that teachers, especially those teaching English in high schools and colleges, went through when English-

Tagalog code switching (hereafter mix-mix) started. The teachers were so concerned and they worried about what would happen to the English of their students. This became the subject of many seminars and conferences. But it was a losing battle they fought. Today—over radio, TV, and even in the highest government and social circles, mix-mix is the 'in' thing" (Sibayan, 1977). The same concern is voiced in Singapore, Fiji, and elsewhere, since what is *learned* appears to be in direct conflict with what is *taught*. What is the relationship between rhetorical and communicative norms in an educational context where English is used as a medium of instruction in the schools?

The link between rhetorical and communicative dimensions of language learning is best considered with reference to the social role of schools and their contribution to the socialization of the child through education. Holmes, in a detailed discussion of the acquisition of sociolinguistic competence in the classroom, points out that for the majority of children the first encounter with a formal variety of language comes through the school, and this is for social rather than pedagogic reasons. "The use of formal varieties in the school can be seen as a reflection of social features of the situation, non-linguistic constraints, which in turn reflect the values and beliefs of the society concerning education and the ways in which it is appropriately transmitted" (Holmes, 1978). With entry into school the child is thus exposed to a new set of values and corresponding language norms that are associated with those values. The contact with the school for the child is the first substantial encounter with the complex rules of social behaviour which relate the child to contexts and relationships outside his or her immediate family, and which initiate the child into public life and public roles. Likewise, within the school particular values associated with public life derive from the nature of institutionalized formal eduction. Some of these are:

1. Submission to authority
2. Control and organization of behaviour by others
3. Asymmetrical role relations
4. Social inequality of teachers and learners
5. Rule-governed rather than spontaneous speech

It is within the school that the basis for rhetorical styles of language use is established, since the type of language transmitted from teacher to students is different in both structure and function from the language the children have participated in up to this point in their lives. Children who come to school with some knowledge of English will have acquired communicative norms for child language within the home setting. Children from non-English-speaking homes will encounter both rhetorical and communicative varieties of English usage in the school, the former via the teacher and the latter through the gradual emergence of English as a language of peer-group interaction in the school. It has been shown in studies of child-child communication that even very young children are sensitive to difference in speech styles according to the age and role of the addressee (Sach and Devin, 1976). In addition, the school introduces the child to two new modes of language, the printed (reading) and the written (writing). Both of these modes of language require the acquisition of rules that are "external" to the child and that help to establish the reality of rhetorical as opposed to communicative styles. Thus language, through its rhetorical function in the school, is linked with the wider socializing function of education. As Mishler remarks:

As a primary socializing institution, the school has the task of instructing children about the content of their culture. A wide range of information is tranmitted from what things are called and how they are socially classified and organized, through basic adaptive and instrumental skills, to social values and codes of conduct (Mishler, 1972, p. 269).

The exposure to rhetorical varieties of language use at school and the addition of higher lects from the lectal continuum for specialized language functions in the community is a *normal,* rather than abnormal or unusual, situation. In many parts of Germany, for example, students arrive at school with a German dialect, and gradually acquire fluency in High German at school. This situation calls for no special comment or concern in the German context. Indeed, Fishman and Lueders-Salmon quote a German teachers' manual (Hildebrand) of 1903 to stress how ordinary and normal this situation has always been considered in Germany:

High German must not be taught as the opposite of the vernacular, but rather, the pupil must be brought to feel that it grows forth out of the vernaculars; High German must not be thought of as a substitute for and a displacement of the vernacular but as a refined form of it, like one's Sunday clothes alongside one's work clothes. (Fishman and Lueders-Salmon, 1972, p. 74)

Contrasting this attitude with that found in many English-speaking countries towards communicative varieties or vernaculars the authors go on to state:

American teachers are still largely innocent of this elementary fact of the sociology of language namely, that speech communities characteristically exhibit verbal repertoires and that the varieties in these repertoires are functionally differentiated—rather than merely linguistically so—in accord with societally established and reinforced norms of communicative appropriateness. Indeed, American teachers (and parents and administrators) are by and large still mesmerized by this fiction that there is only one proper kind of English for all purposes and that it alone should be allowed to cross the threshold of the classroom. (Fishman and Lueders-Salmon, 1972, p. 78).

It is not surprising perhaps therefore that teachers in India, Singapore, the Philippines, and Fiji are no different from their American counterparts in this respect.

Krashen's (1977) distinction between *learned* and *acquired* linguistic systems also offers a useful perspective on the functional relationship between *language learning* and *language acquisition.* The former refers to language learned in a formal situation, where the rules developed are the product of teaching and can be consciously employed. The latter refers to a subconscious process by which rules are internalized through informal learning procedures and where the linguistic system is the product of communication and interaction through language rather than through attention to linguistic form. Krashen goes on to suggest two rule systems may result: the rules acquired as a result of *language acquisition* (which we make use of in informal speech when we are concentrating on the *content* rather than the form of utterances), and the *learned* system (the set of rules we make use of when we are consciously paying attention to the forms of the utterance). Thus the learned rules may be used to monitor sentences generated from acquired rules. "Speech production is initiated in adult second language by an acquired system. When conditions allow, the consciously learned system can inspect and alter the syntactic shape of the utterance before it is spoken" (Krashen, 1977, p. 154). In the case of nativized varieties of English, the rhetorical variety corresponds to the *learned* system, and the communicative variety to the *acquired* system. It may also be the case that speech events that require a rhetorical style may involve monitoring, or suppression of the acquired system.

LITERARY STYLES

The linguistic and functional dimensions of speech varieties I have outlined so far have been discussed with reference to the spoken varieties of English found in various parts of the world where English has become indigenized. It is initially in the spoken language that the need for a distinct communicative code is felt and it is in the spoken English of Filipinos, Fijian, Indians, and others that evidence for distinctive communicative varieties is found. However, the indigenization of English also applies to the written mode, though with different manifestations than those observed in the spoken mode. The new functional and affective dimensions of English pose special problems for the creative writer—for the novelist in India, the Philippines, and West Africa, for example—who chooses English as a means of expressing himself in fiction. The problem for the creative writer in such situations is that the model of English that is widely employed in his or her country for written rhetorical functions—government reports, newspapers, learned journals, and other official purposes—is not necessarily felt to be a suitable mode for the natural expression of creative writing. The solution adopted is often the creation of new written norms for fiction and creative writing in English. This is not to suggest that there is a movement away from the employment of a standard rhetorical variety for writing in the direction of a nonstandard written variety for English; what is involved is on the contrary an employment of a special model of standard English for particular written communicative effects. Such a code may be referred to as a *written communicative style,* in contrast to the written norms employed for nonliterary writing in English.

Much of the linguistic innovation in Indian, Nigerian, and other literatures that has arisen in contexts where English is a second language results from the development of new written communicative styles appropriate for the expression of literature. "The imaginative, innovative function of English has resulted in different genres in different parts of the world. It is the use of English in creative contexts that has now resulted in a fast growing body of among others, Indian English literature, West African literature and Caribbean literature." (Kachru, 1978, p. 6) Kachru quotes Iyengar in this respect:

> Indian writing in English is but one of the voices in which India speaks. It is a new voice, no doubt, but it is as much Indian as others.

And referring to African literature, he quotes Achebe:

> If you take Nigeria as an example, the national literature, as I see it, is the literature written in English; and the ethnic literatures are in Hausa, Ibo, Yoruba, Effik, Edo, Ijaw, etc. (Kachru, 1978, p. 10)

This is not just a question, of course, of representing spoken communicative styles in writing, though this may too be required of the author. The contrast is not, as Crewe (1978) seems to suggest, between the use of standard English, and "the local dialect," but between a variety of written English accepted for rhetorical functions and for noncreative writing, and a variety of written English, which while grammatically still recognized as standard English, is capable of reflecting the communicative, innovative, and imaginative functions of language as literature. This is not merely a question of choice of subject matter but a choice of narrative and descriptive style. It is not surprising that a highly complex and creative literature in English has arisen in countries such as India and the Philippines, with a background of various literary and cultural traditions, each with their own literary styles and topic preferences. Kachru cites Raja Rao as illustrative. "A good example of extremely Indianized use of style variation may be found in Raja Rao's *Kanthapura,* both in the character types and the style *range* which is given to the characters." Pride quotes from the same writer:

> It may have been told of an evening, when as the dusk falls, and through the sudden quiet, lights leap up in house after house, and stretching her bedding on the verandah, a grandmother might have told you, newcomer, the sad tale of her village. (Pride, 1978)

The stylistic qualities of such writing may be quite different from those accepted in British or American literature, since it is through this stylistic creativity that the communicative function is realized. Achebe states:

> I feel that the English language will be able to carry the weight of my African experience. But it will have to be a new English, still in communion with its ancestral home but altered to suit its new African surroundings. (Kachru, 1978b, p. 14)

When this new breed of writers come to represent the spoken communicative style however, there is some degree of ambivalence. Kandiah, quoted by Pride, argues that in the Sri Lanka context, the use of habitual features of local English speech "would be greeted with embarrassment, hostility or derision." Ban and Lee reflect a similar sentiment when they comment:

> The desire to be 'up-to-date' has, indeed, been united with the search for identity. This has expressed itself in the deliberate use of a *local* idiomatic English, especially in recent years when variants of the English language outside Britain have been conferred respectable status. Not

only do themes and incidental remarks bear a direct Singapore or Malayan reference, but the language tries to convey these in terms immediately accessible to the reader from these countries, at times adopting colloquialism and local slang. (Ban and Lee, 1977, p. 142)

Bamgbose is similarly ambivalent towards the Nigerian novelist Amos Tutuola, and cites his novel *The Palm Wine Drinkard* as illustrative of a growing "folk-writing" tradition.

After a little we came from the farm to the house, but at the same time that he saw us, he left all the people with whom he was fighting and met us, so when we entered the house, he showed us to everybody in the house saying that these were his father and mother. But as he had eaten all the food which had been prepared against the night, then we began to cook other food, but when it was the time to put the food down from the fire, he put it down for himself and at the same time, he began to eat that again as it was very hot, before we could stop him, he had eaten all the food and we tried all our best to take it from him, but we could not do it at all. (Bamgbose, 1971, p. 39)

Other writers have skillfully exploited the resources of the local varieties of English, using the formal rhetorical style and the spoken colloquial style side by side, as in this passage from Achebe's novel *No Longer at Ease*:

'Good! See you later.' Joseph always put on an impressive manner when speaking on the telephone. He never spoke Igbo or pidgin English at such moments. When he hung up he told his colleagues: 'That na my brother. Just return from overseas. BA (Honours) Classics.' He always preferred the fiction of Classics to the truth of English. It sounded more impressive.
'What department he de work?'
'Secretary to the Scholarship Board.'
'E go make plenty money there. Every student who wan' go England do de see am for house.'
'E no be like dat,' said Joseph. 'Him na gentleman. No dit take bribe.'
'Na so,' said the other in disbelief. (Spencer, 1971, p. 6)

Singapore writer Catherine Lim exploits all three possibilities, the rhetorical style, a written literary communicative style, and a spoken communicative style. She makes use of the latter throughout the entire length of her story *The Taximan's Story,* an example of which is seen here:

Very Good, madam. Sure, will take you there in plenty good time for your meeting madam. This way better, less traffic, less car jams. Half hour should make it, madam, so not to worry.

What is it you say, madam? Yes, yes, ha, ha, been taximan for twenty years now, madam. Long time ago, Singapore not like this—so crowded so busy. Last time more peaceful, not so much taximen, or so much cars and buses.

Yes, Madam, can make a living. So so. What to do. Must work hard if wants to success in Singapore. People like us, no education, no capital for business, we must sweat to earn money for wife and children. (Lim, 1978)

Literary traditions in the new varieties of English thus offer evidence of two different kinds of style creation. First, there is the creation of a new communicative style for written English, which is distinct from the rhetorical style for written English as it is used in official, public, noncreative, or nonliterary functions. Second, there is the possibility of capturing the character of spoken communicative varieties in dialogue. Kachru has coined the term *contextualization* to describe many of the linguistic processes made use of by Indian writers of fiction in their creation of these new literary styles.

CONCLUSION

The emergence of nativized varieties of English demonstrates the relevance of a remark made by Fishman, Ferguson, and Das Gupta in the preface to *Language Problems of Developing Nations*: "Languages do not really exist except as part of a matrix of language varieties, language behaviors, and behaviors toward language. Any attempt to describe "a language" without recognizing its actual matrix position and any attempt to influence language learning or literacy without questioning what they signify for the language-and-behavior matrix of the prospective learners is to preserve or protect one's own ignorance in connection with those very matters towards which one's expertise would be directed." (Fishman et al., 1968, p. xi) Description of nativized varieties of English must hence include both the extent of linguistic variation *within* a particular variety of English, as well as attempt to understand and identify the social meaning of such variation. Such information is vital to both the planning of language teaching and for the interpretation of the results or effects of language instruction. The concept of rhetorical and communicative styles discussed here is an attempt to capture different values, statuses, and functions for speech varieties as reflected in the employment of variable linguistic rules within nativized varieties of English, and draws attention to the role of language in the expression and structuring of social meaning.

NOTE

1. Reprinted from *Language Learning,* Vol. 29, 1979, with the permission of J. C. Richards and *Language Learning.*

REFERENCES

Ban, Kah Choon, and Lee, Tzu Pheng. Only connect: guest and response in Singapore-Malayan poetry. In W. Crewe (ed.), *The English Language in Singapore.* Singapore: Eastern Universities Press, 1977.

Bamgbose, Ayo. The English language in Nigeria. In J. Spencer (ed.), *The English Language in West Africa.* London: Longman, 1971.

Bautista, Ma. Lourdes S. A model of bilingual competence based on an analysis of Tagalog-English code switching. *Philippine Journal of Linguistics.* 1975, 6, 1, 51–89.

Bickerton, Derek. *Dynamics of a Creole System.* London: Cambridge University Press, 1975.

Bickerton, Derek, and Odo, Carol. *Change and Variation in Hawaiian English* Vol. I. Honolulu: Social Sciences and Linguistics Institute, 1976.

Crewe, William (ed.). *The English Language in Singapore.* Singapore: Eastern Universities Press, 1977.

DeCamp, David. Toward a generative analysis of a post-creole speech continuum. In D. Hymes (ed.), *Pidginization and Creolization of Languages.* London: Cambridge University Press, 1971.

Fishman, Joshua, Ferguson, C., and Das Gupta, J. *Language Problems in Developing Nations.* New York: John Wiley & Sons, 1968.

Fishman, Joshua, and Lueders-Salmon, Erika. What has the sociology of language to say to the teacher? In C Cazden, V. John, and D. H. Hymes (eds.), *Functions of Language in the Classroom.* New York: Teacher's College Press, 1972.

Guiora, A. The effects of experimentally induced changes in ego states on pronounciation ability in a second language. *Comprehensive Psychiatry*. 1972, 13, 421–428.

Gumperz, John J. The sociolinguistic significance of conversational code-switching. *RELC Journal*. 1978, 8, 1–34.

Haugen, Einar. Language and immigration. 1938. Reprinted in A. Dil (ed.), *The Ecology of Language*. Stanford: Stanford University Press, 1972.

Haugen, Einar. *The Norwegian Language in America: A Study in Bilingual Behavior.* Philadelphia: University of Pennsylvania Press, 1953.

Haugen Einar. Norm and deviation in bilingual communities. In P. Hornby (ed.), *Bilingualism: Psychological, Stress, and Educational Implications*. New York: Academic Press, 1977.

Holmes, J. Sociolinguistic competence in the classroom. In J. Richards (ed.), *Understanding Second and Foreign Language Learning*. Rowley, Mass: Newbury House, 1978.

Kachru, Braj B. English in South Asia. In T. Sebeok (ed.), *Current Trend in Linguistics*. The Hague: Mouton and Co., 1969.

Kachru, Braj B. Indian English: A sociolinguitic profile of a transplanted language. *Studies in Language Learning*. 1976a, 1, 2, 1–49.

Kachru, Braj B. Models of English for the third world: White man's linguistic burden or language pragmatics? *TESOL Quarterly*. 1976b, 10, 2, 221–239.

Kachru, Braj B. Toward structuring code-mixing: an Indian perspective. In B. Kachru and S. Sridar (eds.), Aspects of sociolinguistics in South Asia. Special issue of *International Journal of the Sociology of Language*. 1978a.

Kachru, Braj B. The pragmatics of non-native varieties of English. Paper presented at the conference on English as an International Auxiliary Language. EWC Honolulu, 1978b.

Krashen, Stephen D. The monitor model for adult second language performance. In Burt et al. (eds.), *Viewpoints on English as a Second Language,* NY: Regents, 1977.

Labov, William. *Sociolinguistic Patterns*. Philadelphia: University of Pennsylvania Press, 1972.

Llamzon, Teodoro A. *Standard Filipino English.* Manila: Ateneo University Press, 1969.

Lim, Catherine. *Little Ironies: Stories of Singapore*. Singapore: Heinemann, 1978.

Mackey, William F. The description of bilingualism. In J. Fishman (ed.), *Readings in the Sociology of Language*. The Hague: Mouton and Co., 1968.

Mackey, William F. Interference, integration, and the synchronic fallacy. In J. Alatis (ed.), *Twenty-first Annual Round Table*. Washington, D.C.: Georgetown University Press, 1970.

Mishler, Elliot G. Implications of teacher strategies for language and cognition: Observations in first-grade classrooms. In C. Cazden, V. John, and D. H. Hymes (eds.), *Functions of Language in the Classroom*. New York: Teacher's College Press, 1972.

Moag, Rodney F., and Moag, Louisa B. English in Fiji: Some perspective and the need for language planning. *Fiji English Teacher's Journal*. 1977, 13, 2–26.

Platt, J. T. The Singapore English speech continuum and its basilect 'Singlish' as a 'creoloid.' *Anthropological Linguistics*. 1975, 17, 6, 363–375.

Platt, J. T. The sub-varieties of Singapore English: Their sociolectal and functional status. In W. Crewe (ed.), *The English Language in Singapore*. Singapore: Eastern Universities Press, 1977a.

Platt, J. T. A model of polyglossia and multilingualism with special reference to Singapore and Malaysia. *Language in Society*. 1977b, 6/3, 361–378.

Platt, J. T. The 'creoloid' as a special type of interlanguage. *Interlanguage Studies Bulletin*. 1977c, 2/3, 22–38.

Pride, John. Communicative needs in the learning and use of English. *Indian Journal of Applied Linguistics*. 1978, 4.

Richards, Jack. *Error Analysis: Perspectives on Second Language Acquisition*. London: Longmans, 1974.

Richards, Jack C. The dynamics of English as an international, foreign, second and auxiliary language. Paper presented at the conference on English as an International Auxiliary Language, EWC, Honolulu, 1978a.

Richards, Jack C. *Understanding Second and Foreign Language Learning: Issues and Approaches.* Rowley, Mass.: Newbury House, 1978b.

Richards, Jack C., and Tay, Mary W. J. The la-particle in Singapore English. In W. Crewe (ed.), *The English Language in Singapore.* Singapore: Eastern Universities Press, 1977.

Sach, S. J., and Devin, J. Young children's use of age-appropriate speech styles in social interaction and role playing. *Journal of Child Language.* 1976, 3, 1, 81–98.

Sibayan, Bonifacio. Language and identity. SEAMEO Regional Language Centre, Singapore: Twelfth Regional Seminar, 1977.

Spencer, John (ed.). *The English Language in West Africa.* London: Longman, 1971.

Strevens, Peter. *New Orientations in the Teaching of English.* London: Oxford University Press, 1977.

Tongue, R. K. *The English of Singapore and Malaysia.* Singapore, Eastern Universities Press, 1974.

Whinnom, Keith. Linguistic hybridization and the 'special case' of pidgins and creoles. In D. Hymes (ed.), *Pidginization and Creolization of Languages.* London: Cambridge University Press, 1971.

14 REGIONAL STANDARDS OF ENGLISH IN PENINSULAR MALAYSIA

John Augustin

INTRODUCTION

The impact of British rule and the influence of the English language in Malaysia began with the acquisition of Penang Island in 1786, at which time the population of peninsular Malaysia was predominantly Malay. As British influence and suzerainty gradually spread in the peninsular during the second half of the nineteenth century and early twentieth century the demographic pattern of the country changed. This came about with the immigration of Chinese to work the tin mines, and of South Indians (mainly Tamil speakers)

TABLE 1   *Population of Peninsular Malaysia (1911–1975)*

Year	Total	Malays	%	Chinese	%	Indians	%	Others	%
1911	2,339,000	1,370,000	58.6	693,000	29.62	239,000	10.2	37,000	1.6
1957	6,279,000	3,126,000	49.8	2,334,000	37.2	707,000	11.2	112,000	1.8
1969	9,010,000	4,561,164	50.6	3,272,000	36.3	994,000	11.0	193,000	2.1
1975*	10,500,000	5,596,650	53.3	3,706,500	35.3	1,113,000	10.6	84,000	0.8

* Estimated.

to work on the newly established rubber plantations. It will be noted (Table 1), that over a period of 60 years, the multiracial character of the country evolved and stabilised itself.

TABLE 2   *Rough Demographic/Linguistic Divisions of Peninsular Malaysia (current trends)*

ETHNIC GROUP	LOCALITY	PERCENTAGE POPULATION (estimated 1975)	L1	L2	LINGUA FRANCA
Malay	rural urban	46.5 6.8 — 53.3	Dialects: BM (e.g., Kedah or Kelantan Malay, Java, Rhio, Celebes, Acheh, Minangkabau).	BM and ME at primary/secondary school (bilingual)	Intragroup: L1 Intergroup: BM and/or ME
Chinese	rural urban	6.7 28.6 — 35.3	Various Chinese dialects: (e.g., Hokkein, Cantonese, Khek/(Hakka), Teochew, Hainanese Hock Chiew, Kwongsai, Henghua)	Mandarin and ME Mandarin BM and ME at primary/secondary school (bilingual/trilingual)	Intragroup: L1 Intergroup: BM (sub) or ME
Indian	rural urban	8.0 2.6 — 10.6	Indian dialects: (e.g., Tamil, Telegu, Malayali, Punjabi, Hindi)	Tamil, BM, and ME at primary/secondary school (bilingual/trilingual)	Intragroup: L1 Intergroup: BM (sub) or ME
Others	rural urban	– 0.8 — 0.8	Creole Portuguese/English	BM and ME at primary/secondary school (bilingual)	Intragroup: L1 or ME Intergroup: BM (sub) or ME

Notes: BM: Bahasa Malaysia = Standard Malay   ME: Malaysian English   BM (sub): Commonly called Bazaar Malay.
L2 refers to languages learned formally in the school curriculum.
Lingua Franca: BM (sub) is the dominant language for Intergroup communication in rural areas. BM (sub) and ME are commonly used for Intergroup communication in urban areas.

COMPLEXITY OF THE LANGUAGE SITUATION

In 1975 the population of peninsular Malaysia was estimated at 10.5 million, comprising 53.3 percent Malays, 35.3 percent Chinese, 10.6 percent Indians, and 0.8 percent others (Table 1). Within each major racial group there are several ethnic subgroups each speaking a language or dialect of its own. Table 2 outlines the rough demographic and linguistic division of West Malaysia.

THE STATUS OF ENGLISH: PRESENT AND FUTURE

Independence in 1957, and the implementation of the National Language Policy in 1967, have given prominence to Bahasa Malaysia and fulfilled an important psychological need of the newly independent country. The important role of English in science and technology and in international trade and commerce is recognised. English therefore is taught as a second language in primary and secondary schools to ensure that Malaysians are able to communicate in English for these purposes.

Nevertheless, the 1967 Language Policy prescribed a gradual phasing out of English as one of the media of instruction in secondary and tertiary education in the country. By 1980 this policy will have been completely implemented up to school leaving age (17+), and Bahasa Malaysia (the national language) will by then be the dominant language in the country. As a result the proficiency levels in English of Malaysians are expected to be lower than they are at present.

Today English is one of the four popular languages of the mass media. In 1976 (see Table 3) the total readership of the English Press was estimated at 633,900 (19.9 percent of the national dailies). Readership of the Malay Press was estimated at 1,206,400 (32.2 percent), the Chinese Press 1,701,000 (45.5 percent), and the Tamil Press 202,200 (5.4 percent).

Of TV programmes on both networks available to audiences in peninsular Malaysia at the beginning of 1978, English-medium broadcasts accounted for 58.4 percent of the weekly viewing time. Programmes in Bahasa Malaysia accounted for 32.3 percent while Chinese and Tamil media were each allocated an average of 4.65 percent of the total time per week.

The importance of English in the present Malaysian way of life is evidenced by the fact that from a total of 1.1 million who completed secondary education between the years 1956 and 1970, 69.8 percent had attended English-medium schools, 18.64 percent Malay-medium schools, 11.5 percent Chinese-medium schools, and 0.053 percent Tamil-medium schools (Table 4). This, in effect, means that the educated peninsular Malaysians now in the prime of life and who play leadership roles in government and trade are fairly competent in the use of English for intergroup communication. However, as has been pointed out earlier, this situation is expected to change with the implementation of the 1967 Language Policy.

TABLE 3   *Malaysian Newspapers and Readership (1976)* [*]

Language	Newspaper	Copies	Readership	
English	New Straits Times	140,000	(x 3)	
	Malay Mail	28,500		
	The Star	20,000		
	Straits Echo	12,000		
		211,300	633,900	16.9%
Bahasa Malaysia	Utusan Malaysia	73,000	(x 8)	
	Utusan Melayu	45,000		
	Berita Harian	30,800		
		150,800	1,206,400	32.2%
Chinese	Nanyang Siang Pau	82,000	(x 5)	
	Sin Chew Jit Poh	45,000		
	China Press	36,700		
	Malaya Thung Pau	75,400		
	Shin Min Daily News	101,100		
		340,200	1,701,000	45.5%
Tamil	Tamil Nesan	21,200	(x 6)	
	Tamil Malar	12,500		
		33,700	202,200	5.4%

*Source: P.T.M. Communications (Pte) Ltd. Design and Public Affairs
Consultants. 6th Floor, Oriental Plaza, Kuala Lumpur. (2 Sept.
1976).

Note: Figures in parentheses signify the numbers of readers per copy.

MALAYSIAN SPEAKERS OF ENGLISH

English is extensively used in urban areas for intergroup communication among English-educated peninsular Malaysians of all ethnic groups. It is estimated that approximately 25 percent (or 1 million) of the urban population use English in some form or other to communicate among themselves. By virtue of its being taught as a second language in schools, and its status as a second language in government, English is used in formal and semi-formal situations; a colloquial variety is used in informal or casual situations. Basically, the English of Malaysian speakers, as a group, spans a continuum ranging from near-British standard English (NBSE) to pidgin. Most English-educated peninsular Malaysians, however, are able to shift from one level to another with ease.

TABLE 4   *Secondary Education of Peninsular Malaysians (1956-1970)*

Current Age Group	Malay Medium	English Medium	Chinese Medium	Tamil Medium	Total
39-48 (Approx)	2,871	59,197	26,959	310	89,337
34-38	4,953	98,802	59,952	267	156,974
29-33	67,484	247,528	30,470	—	345,482
24-28	129,193	360,131	15,890	—	505,214
	204,501 (18.64%)	765,658 (69.79%)	126,271 11.511%)	577 (0.053%)	1,095,007

*Source: Education Statistics of Malaysia, 1930-1970 Ministry of Education.

VARIETIES OF MALAYSIAN ENGLISH

The main factors which have influenced the development of Malaysian English are:

1. The status of British Standard English (BSE).
2. English language acquisition through formal learning in primary and secondary English-medium schools in pre- and post-World War II.
3. Superimposed features of the main languages: Malay, Chinese and Tamil.
4. Influence of the mass media, bringing mainly American colloquial English through television and the cinema.

First then, BSE has been the model of Malaysian speakers of English and the goal towards which all English language teaching has been directed. For over a century British influence, especially through educational, administrative, and trade links, has consolidated this high regard for BSE. Consequently, English-educated Malaysians, currently over 19 years of age, tend to measure their English proficiency, and are measured, against this model.

Second, English teachers (originally from the United Kingdom) who taught English in the country, and the large numbers who were trained by them, became the "gate-keepers" of BSE for several generations of Malaysians educated through the English-medium schools.

Third, all children who have attended English-medium schools have come from different ethnic groups. As a result, features of the home languages or dialects have tended to interfere in their acquisition of English. The formal learning of English in the classroom, where BSE was the model, did not interfere persist in informal situations outside the classroom. The need to communicate in a commonly shared language gave rise to a complementary dialect of English in Malaysian schools for intergroup communication, characterised by features found in the home dialects of the pupils, especially those of the Malay, Chinese, and Indian groups. It is important to realise that this dialect became the major lingua franca for the multiracial school population and eventually for Malaysian adults with an English educational background.

Fourth, and finally, the advent of the cinema, and later TV, introduced the American variety of English against which the traditional gate-keepers were constantly on guard. The influence of American English, however, is minimal in formal contexts, although inroads are evident in colloquial speech.

These factors, which have operated at varying intensities at different times over a period of nearly 200 years, have created a distinctive Singapore-Malyasian variety of English, its salient features described by Tongue (1974), including a colloquial variety, Singlish, described by Platt (1975).

It is natural to assume that with the fading out of British influence, the BSE model will be increasingly difficult to attain. The major contributory factor will be the relegation of English to the status of a second language in the national educational system. This means, in effect, that by 1981, English will no longer be the medium of instruction in all primary and secondary schools in the country, and as a consequence, the overall level of English proficiency of educated Malaysians is expected to fall.

Because of the difficulty of assessing the relative influence of the above criteria on speech behaviour, the range over which a speaker can operate on the EME continuum is difficult to ascertain. An impressionistic assessment made by three lecturers in the Language Department of the Universiti Pertanian Malaysia (report on the status of English at the Agricultural University of Malaysia) shows how, on a four-point scale, speakers of EME tend to spread along the continuum. A random sample of 60 undergraduates (35 from English-medium schools and 25 from Malay-medium schools) showed that only 5 (8.3 percent) of the group could be classified as near-native BSE speakers. The remaining 55 were classified as EME speakers at varying proficiency levels (see Figure 1).

THE CONTINUUM OF MALAYSIAN ENGLISH

Four main varieties of Malaysian English are discernible:

1. Near-native BSE (NBSE) ⎫
2. English educated ME (EME) ⎬ Formal
3. Colloquial ME (CME) ⎫
4. Pidgin ⎬ Informal

NBSE: This is a variety with minimal deviations from BSE. It stands at the highest point of the continuum and is used in formal situations, such as lecturing, teaching, board meetings, and professional discussions. It is easily comprehensible by native speakers of English of any variety. It is estimated that about 10 percent of English-educated West Malaysians speak (or are capable of speaking) this variety.

EME: This is the more typical variety of ME. It too is readily comprehensible to native speakers of English of any variety. Speakers of this variety

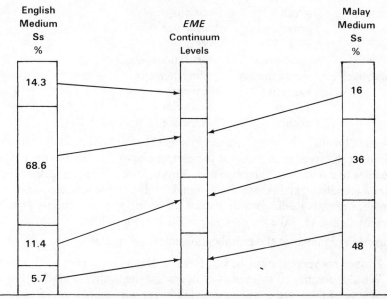

Figure 1   EME continuum (4-point scale) of students in Agricultural Universiti

understand BSE but, in performance, deviations from BSE are discernible that distinguish them from speakers of the NBSE variety. Its salient features are:

1. Deviations in the pronunciation of vowels, consonant clusters, and final consonants:

	RP	*ME*
river	[rivə]	[ribə]
after	[ɑ:ftə]	[ʌptə] or [ɑptə]
gate	[geit]	[get]
air	[ɛə]	[ɛ]
open	[oupən]	[opən]
coat	[kout]	[kot]
bottle	[bɔtl]	[bɔtɔl]
table	[teibl]	[tɛbəl]
think	[θiŋk]	[tiŋ]
looked	[lukt]	[lu:k]
correct	[kərɛkt]	[kɔrek]

2. Deviations in the accentuation of syllables in words of more than one syllable:

	RP	*ME*
Verbs	de*ve*lop	*de*velop
	re*fu*se	*re*fuse
	con*si*der	*con*sider
	*ad*vertise	ad*ver*tise

Nouns	*al*kali	al*ka*li
	*pro*vince	pro*vin*ce
	*vi*sit	vis*it*
	oper*at*ions	*ope*rations
Adjectives	simul*tan*eous	si*mul*taneous
	ex*ec*utive	exe*cut*ive
	edit*or*ial	*edi*torial
	*ac*curate	acc*u*rate

3. Erratic "breath" or "sense" pauses giving a staccato effect, caused by the failure of the speaker to pause at the correct places in order to convey the meaning of a sentence. This often occurs in situations where a speaker reads from a prepared text; his inability to immediately comprehend the sense of a sentence reveals itself when he pauses for breath at inappropriate places, thereby failing to make the meaning of the sentence clear.

4. Lapses in grammar at the morphophonemic level and in syntax:

> I myself not very happy in the way Heads of Departments conduct themself.
> We also committed to a policy of upgrading the quality of staff services.
> Mostly of them are intellectual and different with school where you are
>   being controlled.

CME: This is the variety spoken by educated Malaysians in urban areas in casual and intimate situations in intergroup communication. It incorporates many features from the major languages (or dialects) spoken in Malaysia. Because it is used mainly in casual and intimate situations, the style is basically colloquial. Influences from contact languages are consequently felt at this level. The standard forms of other languages have not, generally speaking, affected the evolution of CME because this variety is acquired very early in primary school when social interaction takes precedence over all other considerations.

The most salient features of CME are its intonation and rhythmic patterns. For casual and intimate communication the speaker is primarily motivated by a desire to express personal feelings and attitudes. In the Malaysian context the native languages and dialects rely very much on tones and rhythms to carry these sorts of meaning, hence the question in CME:

> How can man? is an echo of *mana boleh?* (Malay)
> (How can it be done?   *or*   How could you do it?)

Similarly, the frequent use of such items as *lah, ah,* or *man* in mid-statement or at the ends of statements constantly provide the additional syllable to carry the familiar rhythmic pattern:

> Yes we go *lah.* All sorts of things will come out *lah.*
> (Yes, we'll go. All sorts of things happen there.)

Again, a typical Bazaar Malay feature recurs in CME in the intonation patterns of yes/no questions. The Malay question marker *kah* is invariably contracted to *ah* and used in English questions:

Can 'ah? = *Boleh kah?* (Can it be done?)

Why 'ah? = *Sebab apa?* (Why is it so?)

Another salient feature that characterises CME is the consistent occurence of incomplete sentences giving one the impression that interlocutors communicate through fragments rather than in complete thoughts. There appear to be two basic reasons for this. Linguistically, the copula is nonexistent at surface level in Malay or Chinese. At the same time, in Malay mores the use of personal pronouns, particularly in subject position, is considered, on social grounds, bad form (Harun Deruah, personal communication):

Very shy to ask lah.—*Malu 'nak tanya.*
(I am too shy to ask you.)

No use to say more.—*Tidak guna cakap lagi.*
(It'll be of no use for you to say more.)

The variety of ways of asking questions in CME is another notable feature, brought about by linguistic rather than sociocultural interference. The tendency to translate from the mother tongue gives rise to such questions as:

What you want? (What do you want?)

You take my book what? (You have taken my book, haven't you?)

A further dimension involved in the comprehension of CME is that of lexis. The CME lexicon is derived mainly from BSE but at the phonetic and phonemic levels these lexical items deviate considerably from RP, occasionally with embarrassing results. The more common reasons have been mentioned already. Distinctions between *soap* and *soup, moral* and *morale*, and so on are examples of difficulties experienced by speakers and listeners of CME.

Certain words have taken on Malaysian contextual meanings through (1) literal translation or (2) coinage. The following examples are by no means exhaustive:

1. before (CME) = formerly (BSE)
   (Before I studied in a private school)
   after = or else
   (After you get cane)
   open = turn on, switch off
   (Open the light)

2. act = show off
   (Don't act too much)
   jack = to praise someone for an ulterior motive
   (He wants to jack the boss)
   angrified = to become angry
   (I was angrified with her)

Finally, a certain amount of "borrowing" from local languages or dialects has also taken place. Noun forms from the home language lexicon are freely used. Consequently, it is common practice for speakers to incorporate semantic components from a particular home language/dialect in a recognisably English sentence structure. It is observed, however, that only Malay verb forms tend to be used in predicate position. For example:

> Especially for us Chinese *ah* we go to P.J. *chuck fun* eighty cents. If you *tambah* ninety cents if you compare here you *tambah* only *ah*, at least one fifty (Chinese undergraduate).

Translation:

> If we Chinese go to Petaling Jaya (a suburb of Kuala Lumpur) *a plate of rice with assorted meat and vegetables* (Cantonese) will cost us eight cents. If you *take an extra helping of plain rice,* it will cost ninety cents. By comparison, an extra helping of rice here costs a dollar and fifty cents.

REFERENCES

Platt, John T. The Singapore English continuum and its basilect "Singlish" as a 'Creoloid.' *Anthropological Linguistics.* October 1975, 17, 7, 363–374.

Tongue, R. K. *The English of Singapore and Malaysia.* Singapore: Eastern Universities Press, 1974.

SECTION 5

A MODEL FOR THE THIRD WORLD?

15 NATIVE-SPEAKER ENGLISH FOR THE THIRD WORLD TODAY?

Irene Wong

INTRODUCTION

The title of this paper poses a question that must be asked now. The question would have been considered unnecessary in the past (and may still be considered unnecessary in some quarters today) as the answer was assumed to be emphatically and unquestioningly in the affirmative. No alternative was sought for and none was assumed to exist. The goal for excellence in language, it was believed, was acquiring a native-like command of the language. The realization that very few foreign learners ever managed to achieve this, except possibly in the case of immigrants who tried to assimilate themselves into their new environment, only served to increase efforts to make the goal more attainable by more people, not to a modification of the goal itself. This paper focuses on the correct choice of a model of English for the Third World today. It begins by questioning the commonly held assumption that native-speaker English should be the automatic choice as the goal for all English-speaking countries, whether the language be native or foreign to the country. It makes a case for considering possible alternatives in the context of the Third World, as opposed to those countries in which English is a native language. Each of these three models, native-speaker English and two viable alternatives in "Nuclear" English and "Utilitarian" English, is discussed in some detail as to its usefulness and suitability for the needs of the Third World.

THE CHANGING THIRD WORLD TODAY

English is now spoken not only by native speakers but also by nonnative speakers of the language. It has spread throughout the continents of the world, encompassing also the Third World. According to figures given by Gage and Ohannessian in 1977, approximately 275 million use English as their native language, while another approximately 115 million are studying it in schools as a second or foreign language. Of the latter, a substantial number are from the Third World, which would include India, Pakistan, Bangladesh, Sri Lanka, Malaysia, Indonesia, Thailand, Africa, and the Philippines. In each country, there will of course be variations in the functions of English and differing degrees of proficiency in the language However, there are also sufficient similarities in the situations of many of these Third World nations, as opposed to countries in which English is the native language, for the question that this paper asks to be posed of the region as a whole instead of each country individually.

Many of the countries of the Third World today had been colonized by native English-speaker countries, such as Britain and the United States. Thus English was in a position of prestige within each country. Moreover, there were sufficient numbers of native English-speakers in each country, sent there by the ruling nation to serve in positions of prestige and influence. Thus, native-speaker English was a potent force not only politically but also socially. However, the situation has now changed quite radically. The majority of these countries of the Third World have now gained their political independence from the ruling nation and have gone ahead to forge for themselves a linguistic independence as well, by establishing their own native national language to supplant English as the language of prestige and influence. Moreover, political independence also saw the gradual withdrawal of native English-speakers from their positions of influence and prominence as more and more local people became qualified to take over from them. This of course has led to the dwindling and fast diminishing numbers of native English-speakers in many Third World countries, a situation that has made it increasingly difficult to keep the flag of native-speaker English flying high in this region of the world. While English is retained in most of these newly independent nations, its function is mostly auxiliary in nature for purposes of wider communication at the international rather than the intranational level. Thus, in the Third World today, English is no longer looked upon as the prestigious language of the ruling class, but only as a functional auxiliary language. The prime motivation for its use, in most cases, is pragmatic rather than aesthetic. In other words, it is valued only in so far as it is found to be useful for international communication. Little emotional attachment to the language can be detected in many countries of the Third World, as they begin to assert their own existence and claims upon the rest of the world, not only in the political sphere but also in the linguistic realm, in both of which they are a potent and vocal force to be reckoned with.

It has taken some time for these Third World nations to assert their claims and make their existence felt in the linguistic realm. Until relatively recently, studies of English focused almost entirely on native-speaker English; whatever attention was paid to nonnative varieties was usually with the aim of pointing out their deviance from what was considered standard English, that is, native-speaker English. But nonnative varieties of English, many of which can be found in the Third World, are beginning to gain recognition and acceptance as valid standards in their own right and not merely as aberrant versions of standard English. For example, Kachru (1976) attempts to argue that the criteria which apply to English in native-speaker countries do not necessarily apply in nonnnative-speaker contexts too. He tries to establish a new and different viewpoint for the Third World, "to see the function of these varieties with reference to the country in which English is used, its roles in the sociocultural network and the dependency of the local variety on the native variety with special reference to interaction with native speakers" (1976, p. 234). Speaking particularly about Indian English, he says:

> We must accept two premises concerning Indian English, as we should about any other Third World variety of English. First, that the users of Indian English form a distinct speech community who use a variety of English which is by and large formally distinct because it performs functions which are different from the other varieties of English. Second, that Indian English functions in the Indian socio-cultural context in order to perform those roles which are relevant and appropriate to the social, educational and administrative network of India. (1976, p. 235)

In the conclusion of his paper, Kachru writes:

> It is obvious that in the Third World countries the choice of functions, uses and models of English has to be determined on a pragmatic basis, keeping in view the local conditions and needs. It will, therefore, be appropriate that the native speakers of English abandon the attitude of linguistic tolerance. The strength of the English language is in presenting the Americanness in its American variety, and the Englishness in its British variety. Let us, therefore, appreciate and encourage the Third World varieties of English too. The individuality of the Third World varieties, such as the Indianness of its Indian variety, is contributing to the linguistic mosaic which the speakers of the English language have created in the English speaking world. The attitude toward these varieties ought to be one of appreciation and understanding. (1976, p. 236)

Attempts such as Kachru's to argue for the acceptance of these Third World varieties of English, that is nonnative-speaker English, are not based on any claim that they are practically identical to native-speaker English. Rather, they acknowledge the fact that these Third World Englishes are different in various ways from native-speaker English, and justifiably and understandably so. With political independence, an upsurge of nationalism, and feelings of national identity, each country has gone ahead to forge for itself not only its own national language but also its own distinctive variety of English. The newly acquired dignity of these nonnative varieties of English arises from the realization that there ought to be no inherent reason why native-speaker standards for English should be imposed upon nonnative contexts. In other words, each country reserves to itself the right to use and mould English to its own requirements. Smith (1976) argues along the same lines when he says:

> English belongs to the world and every nation which uses it does so with different tone, color, and quality. English is an international auxiliary language. It is yours (no matter who you are) as much as it is mine (no matter who I am). We may use it for different purposes and for different lengths of time on different occasions, but nonetheless it belongs to all of us. English is one of the

languages of Japan, Korea, Micronesia, and the Philippines. It is one of the languages of the Republic of China, Thailand, and the United States. No one needs to become more like Americans, the British, the Australians, the Canadians or any other English speaker in order to lay claim on the language. (1976, p. 39)

If Smith's plea is taken to be valid, we are justified in questioning the continued acceptance of native-speaker English as the goal for the Third World, as if the requirements and needs of the Third World nations were identical with those of the native-speaker countries.

NATIVE-SPEAKER ENGLISH

Native-speaker English simply refers to the complete system of English in all its complexity and richness that is available to the native speaker, whether British, American, Canadian, Australian, or other. This is the variety of English found in native-speaker contexts all over the world, from Canada and the United States to Britain, Australia, and New Zealand. It is also the variety of English in which most scientific, technical, literary, and academic work is carried on. Obviously there is much to be said for the Third World also adopting the same native-speaker model of English for its own use.

However, desirable though this may be, assuming that the Third World nations give up this aspect of their linguistic independence and sovereignty, it is far from feasible. The fact remains that, even after decades of striving towards native-speaker English in the Third World, the rate of success has been trivial and incommensurate with the time, effort, money, and resources, which are never in plentiful supply in the Third World, expended in trying to attain this goal. Native-like command of the language is the possession of only a handful of speakers from each developing nation. These speakers form the elite of the English-speaking population, while the majority fall far short of the goals for English set up within each country.

The fact remains that, for the majority of its speakers, these Third World Englishes are different from native-speaker English. What seems to have happened is a gap of varying degrees between the goal (native-speaker English) and the actual level of achievement attained, for which a number of reasons can be advanced as causes. The crux of the matter perhaps lies in the fact that the English language teaching and learning situations in most Third World countries are less than ideal, to put it mildly, and far different from those in native-speaker English countries. Experts in language teaching have talked about "individualized instruction" or about other methods of teaching for classes of no more than 25 to 30 students each. This is hardly ever possible in the context of the Third World, where classes usually range from a minimum of 50 to a maximum of as many as 150 or even more. The amount of exposure to English, so very important a factor in the acquisition of a language, is also far different in the Third World from what is the case in native-speaker countries. The exposure may range from absolutely none (for example, in EFL countries) to merely adequate (for example, in ESL countries). However, it should be borne in mind that even in the case of adequate exposure to English, this exposure is usually to the localized indigenous variety of the language and not to native-speaker English. Added to these factors one could list the lack of funds for language teaching and learning equipment, the possibility of lack of motivation in the majority of students, who see little reason for studying English, the inadequate proficiency in native-speaker English of the teachers themselves, and so on, all of which are rampant in the Third World and form formidable obstacles towards the attainment of native-speaker English.

Faced with some of these very real problems, there have even been suggestions that, in the light of such depressing circumstances, we should not inflict English upon the masses, most of whom could very well do without it, but only teach it to the few who will require it for one reason or another, that is, the elite, thus freeing the majority from the unnecessary toil and travail which, for them, forms part and parcel of the unrewarding task of learning English. However, the problem, as has been recognized, is how to predict who will need English after the entire educational process is completed. Aptitude tests have been suggested, as have other procedures, but the death knell to all of them is usually provided by our modern-day ideas of democracy and justice, of equal opportunities for all and fairness to all, ideas that even the poorest countries try to cling to, at least in such areas as English language instruction.

The odds against the successful adoption of native-speaker English without paying too high a price, which the Third World can ill-afford, appear to be very great and perhaps even insurmountable. There are two possible ways out of this impasse. The first, up till now felt to be the only solution, is to continue to expend all available resources, even at the expense of other equally worthy causes, to find new and improved ways of achieving native-speaker English in Third World situations. However, this solution is now beginning to look less and less satisfactory against the growing strength of the nonnative varieties of English in the world today. The second avenue, which is worthy at least of consideration in the context of the Third World, is to look for some viable alternative to native-speaker English which would be more reachable and sufficiently adequate for the more restricted demands of these nonnative-speaker countries. That the first solution, that is, to find new and improved ways of achieving native-speaker English, is not workable in its totality, and even undesirable, has been officially recognised in Malaysia. The *Teachers' Handbook for the Primary School English Syllabus,* issued by the Ministry of Education in 1971, states the objective of English instruction in the schools is "international intelligibility." The handbook explains:

> It should however be stated that our aim of 'international intelligibility' does not imply that our pupils should speak exactly like Englishmen. There would not be sufficient time to achieve this nor is it necessary. What is aimed at is that they should be able to speak with acceptable rhythm and stress, and to produce the sounds of English sufficiently well for a listener to be able to distinguish between similar words. (1971, p. 3)

The Malaysian experience, more details of which will be given in the next section, thus lends more weight to the consideration of suitable alternatives to native-speaker English for the countries of the Third World.

ALTERNATIVES TO NATIVE-SPEAKER ENGLISH

Primarily two approaches have been recommended or adopted in TESL circles. One approach is termed the "integrative approach" and the other the "instrumental approach." According to the first, a learner wants "to identify with the members of the other linguistic-cultural group and be willing to take on very subtle aspects of their behavior such as their language *or even their style of speech*" (Prator, 1968, p. 474). On the other hand, the instrumental approach views language mainly as a tool to achieve desired ends, without any desire to identify with the culture of its speakers. Native-speaker English would be associated with the integrative approach, where the language is used to mark affirmation and or solidarity with another group, that is, the native-speaker of the language. The instrumental approach is seen in a number of models which exist today, where the language is used solely for the transmission of referential denotative information. This paper, however, limits its discussion to only two of such instrumental models of language, referred to respectively as Nuclear English and Utilitarian English in what follows, as constituting the most viable alternatives to native-speaker English for the Third World today. The goals in each are set lower than at native-like command of the language, but they would nevertheless suffice for the more limited demands made upon the language in these nonnative contexts.

Nuclear English

Nuclear English is the model proposed by Quirk (1978) to meet the world's need for an international auxiliary language. Based on the assumption that the possibility of a wholly new or artificially constructed language is not viable— witness, for example, the failure of attempt with Basic English, Esperanto, Novial, Occidental, Interlingua, and Volapuk— Quirk concludes that the only viable possibility for an international auxiliary language is either to adopt or to adapt an existing natural language, and English is at the moment the best candidate. It would not be difficult to see that, as part and parcel of its proposed role as an international auxiliary language, Nuclear English could possibly also function as the model of English for the Third World, which needs the language for its instrumental rather than for its integrative functions. Therefore what Quirk proposes for an international auxiliary language, his Nuclear English, could easily be applied to our problem at hand.

In introducing his concept of Nuclear English, Quirk assumes that the possiblity of adopting English as it exists in all its complexity for use as an international auxiliary language has been tried and found wanting. He says that "even in countries like India with a long-established policy of making English an auxiliary language, it can be argued that (because of its complexity and variety)

English has proved too expensive to be taught adequately on the wide scale required" (1978, p. 1). Planned simplification, he feels, is probably the best hope. Accordingly, his proposal for Nuclear English is predicated on the assumption that we are reduced to adapting English for international auxiliary use. To fulfil this role, he says, Nuclear English should be decidedly easier and faster to learn. Moreover, he adds, it must also be

(a) communicatively adequate, and hence a satisfactory end-product of an education system; and (b) amenable to extension in the course of further learning, if required. (1978, p. 1)

Quirk elaborates on these two criteria of communicative adequacy and amenability to extension thus:

In (a), communicative adequacy is to be understood as providing the learner with the means to express an indefinitely large number of communicative needs (in principle, all, however periphrastically, with the minimum ambiguity, the limit being imposed by his intellectual capacity, not by the capacity of the language. In (b), extensibility may be thought of in terms of 'English for Specific Purposes' modules (and hence imposes the requirement that the lexical and grammatical content of Nuclear English be made fully explicit, so that the 'fit' of additional modules may be exactly predicted); or in terms of less programmed skill-acquisition towards 'full' English (and this in turn imposes the requirement that, since nothing should have to be 'unlearned', the lexical and grammatical properties of Nuclear English must be a subset of the properties of full English and in no way be in defiance of them. (1978, p. 1)

Quirk gives an example of one type of structure that could be found in Nuclear English, the use of the question tag *is that so?* to substitute for the disproportionately burdensome English tag question, "with its requirement for reversed polarity, supply of tensed operator and congruent subject" (1978, p. 1). He supplies the following examples:

I'm late, *aren't I/am I not?*
She used to work here, *didn't she?*
They oughtn't to go, *ought they?*

and says:

For all of the italicised pieces, whose function as a response promoter is arguably worth retaining, we could achieve the same objective with *is that so?*, in full English a perfectly acceptable (if minority) form. (1978, pp. 1–2)

Another example he suggests is to dispense with the non-restrictive relative clauses, many of which he says "are in any case semantically inexplicit":

I chatted with the captain, who was later reprimanded.
I expressed my sympathy to the captain, who had been reprimanded. (1978, p. 2)

If these mean the following, he says,

I spoke to the captain and *as a result* he was (later) reprimanded.
I expressed my sympathy to the captain *because* he had been reprimanded.

it would do no harm to say so and at the same time rid us (in writing at least) of structures that could be misread as restrictive clauses. Nor need we retain in Nuclear English the option to construct noun clauses or restrictive relative clauses with 'zero' particle ('He was afraid she was hurt', 'The man she loves'). (1978, p. 2)

Quirk emphasises the fact that in all his examples, the solution does not lie in going beyond the rules of ordinary acceptable English. He also adds that his proposed solutions have no bearing at all upon frequency of occurrence in ordinary English. In fact, he even suggests that the most frequent items are those that are most to be avoided since they are the most polysemous. He says:

> Rather, the solution must lie in a principled mediation between (a) the grammatical structure of ordinary English and (b) a language-natural assessment of communicative needs. The order here is vital: the starting point must be (a), not (b). If we adopted the converse, we might for example seek a number system going beyond the existing two terms ('singular' and 'plural') to include a third ('dual') in view of the large number of items in human experience that go in two's (eyes, thumbs, feet, parents etc). An additional inflection (parent *sg*, parenten *dual*, parents *pl*) would enable us to avoid the ambiguity that is common in sentences like
> The permission of parents is required.
> (Does each child need to get permission from both parents or will the permission of only one be sufficient?) Needless to say, such a proposal would infringe one of the basic properties of Nuclear English (that it should contain nothing that had to be 'unlearned' by the user who proceeded to any extension beyond it) and would therefore be rejected. (1978, p. 2)

One of the major problems with Quirk's concept of Nuclear English is that, attractive though it may sound in theory, we do not as yet have a very clear idea of just what it entails. In his short paper (1978), he has just set forth the basic principles which he believes should underlie Nuclear English, but he concedes that "much research and experiment will be necessary to find out the extent to which these principles can be translated into a blueprint for describing the grammar of Nuclear English" (1978, p. 3). As such, it is extremely difficult to evaluate this model of English at the moment as a viable alternative to native-speaker English for the Third World.

At first glance, Nuclear English my appear to be most suitable as a model for the Third World, given the fact that native-speaker English is too costly and perhaps even unattainable. Nuclear English, as envisaged, would be simpler than native-speaker English and in this way more practical as a model for nonnative-speaker countries. Nevertheless, at the same time, it should provide the learner with the means "to express an indefinitely large number of communicative needs (*in principle, all*), however periphrastically, with the minimum ambiguity, the limit being imposed by his intellectual capacity not by the capacity of the language" [Quirk, 1978, p. 1 (emphasis mine)]. Moreover, Nuclear English would eventually lead to the complete system of native-speaker English, for Quirk describes it as being "amenable to extension in the course of further learning, if required" (1978, p. 1). One may perhaps question whether there is a contradiction of aims here. On the one hand, Nuclear English is seen to provide for a great range of communicative functions ("in principle, all") while on the other it is supposed to be the result of "planned simplification" of native-speaker English. If these two aims cannot both be achieved, as one would suspect, one of the most fundamental arguments for the use of Nuclear English would crumble.

This leads to the main objection against Nuclear English, which would very likely serve to disqualify it altogether as a viable alternative to native-speaker

English for the Third World. This is the fact that it is still a theoretical construct, as were the other artificially constructed languages proposed to meet the world's need for an international language, which Quirk mentions as having failed. No doubt Nuclear English is not a wholly new language, nor is it artificially constructed, being based as it is on the grammar of actual ordinary English. However, just because the starting point is grammar and not the communicative needs of the speakers, it would still take on the nature of an artificial construct, based as it is on theoretical considerations of grammar rather than on actual use. As such, there seems to be little hope that Nuclear English will succeed where the other languages like Esperanto, Interlingua, and Volapuk have failed. The crux of the matter is that there will be no native speakers of Nuclear English, a very important factor in ensuring the life of a language. As Quirk realizes, "Not only is the language to be learned by the non-native carefully and explicitly restricted: so equally must the language of the native speaker be constrained to a precisely corresponding extent when he is using Nuclear English as an international medium" (1978, p. 6). Quirk acknowledges that this is a tall order, but he considers it well worth the effort if the dream of an international language is to be achieved. The value of the goal of an international language cannot be questioned, nor the fact that it is well worth the effort. However, all this comes to nothing if it cannot be translated into practical terms. No doubt linguists are fully capable of developing a Nuclear English that would be admirably suited to the world's need for an international language. Though the notion is an appealing one on the theoretical level, in practical, realistic terms it obviously would be impossible to convince all the English-speaking countries, whether native-speaker or nonnative-speaker, to subscribe to Nuclear English, even though they may concede that the effort is worthwhile. The world has become more and more fragmented today, with each country, however tiny and poor, asserting its individual rights on the international scene. No one country, or group of countries, has any influence as far as the issue of language is concerned on the rest of the world. In such a context, the chances that Nuclear English can be imposed on all the English-speaking world are nonexistent. The world was not amenable to the earlier proposals of artificially constructed international languages and it is even less amenable today to the proposal to use Nuclear English, though it may be less artificial than, say, Esperanto or Interlingua. While far-reaching consensus has been achieved in other fields on the international scene, as evident for example in the changeover to the metric system in most parts of the world, in the field of language it has, for some reason or other, been unknown. Nuclear English, therefore, can be no more than a plaything for linguists to amuse themselves with. It has to be dismissed from consideration as a viable alternative to native-speaker English for the Third World today.

Utilitarian English

The term Utilitarian English, as used here, refers to a very functional variety of English that assumes that the communicative needs of its users will be far less than those of the users of native-speaker English or even of Nuclear English. This is the name given in this paper to the variety of English that, it is claimed here, is already spoken in many parts of the Third World, in regions where English has merely an auxiliary and instrumental role to play in nonnative-speaker contexts. For most of this section, specific reference will be made to the Malaysian situation in order to describe and explain this concept of Utilitarian English in greater detail.

Like many countries of the Third World, Malaysia (earlier known as Malaya) was a British colony and English was the key to higher education, better job opportunities and increased socioeconomic status. Prior to the days of independence in 1957 (and even in the initial years subsequent to it) there were substantial numbers of Britishers in the country, occupying positions that gave them a pervasive influence on the English of at least the upper classes of society. However, increasing Malaysianisation, in which locals gradually took over the jobs formerly held by expatriates, saw the loss of this native-speaker influence on the English used in the country. It became increasingly difficult to aim at standard British English, this not being too evident within the country. As Tongue notes, "In the new situation, the pressure to conform to a standard of the old colonial power eight thousand miles away is bound to be weakened" (1974, p. 4). This gained official recognition, as stated earlier, when the Ministry of Education issued its *Teachers' Handbook for the Primary School English Syllabus* in 1971, stating that no longer should teachers aim at producing pupils who could speak exactly like Englishmen. The target, as far as Malaysia was concerned, was the ability to speak with "acceptable rhythm and stress, and to produce the sounds of English sufficiently well for a listener to be able to distinguish between similar words." (1971, p. 3).

A distinctive variety of English had been emerging in the country, used mainly on informal occasions at the mesolectal and basilectal levels. When it became no longer possible (and even desirable) to conform as fully as possible to native-speaker English, this local variety of the language spread and developed more rapidly, supplemented by transfer features from the Malay, Chinese, and Indian speech communities in the country and reinforced by locally trained people in the same influential positions that Britishers once held. Malaysian English has now spread to the upper strata of society, especially on the colloquial level. Malaysians are now proud of their own individual brand of English and view it as one of the characteristics that mark one as being a Malaysian.

The year 1970 saw another radical change in the status of English in Malaysia. It began to be systematically replaced by the national language, Bahasa Malaysia, as the medium of instruction at school and tertiary level. Bahasa Malaysia is now the predominant language of the nation, with English being relegated to the status of a second and even a foreign language. Now, even more than before, the English of Malaysia is developing into the type of English referred to as Utilitarian English in this paper. With the role of English being reduced, the emphasis begins to be more and more on its utilitarian aspects, the stylistic and aesthetic features being deliberately ignored or neglected. This received official sanction in 1975 when the Ministry of Education brought out a new Communicational Syllabus, in line with the new and reduced role of English in the country, for the final two years of the secondary school system. To quote from it:

> This syllabus is concerned with the practical needs of the form five leaver. With the increasing use of Bahasa Malaysia in most areas of real-life communication, the need for the English language for general utility purposes diminishes. It does not, however, disappear altogether. Rather, it assumes an increasingly narrow, defined role and to a certain degree becomes specialised. (1975, p. 3)

The Communicational Syllabus focuses on a number of tasks; for example, relaying of information to others, making and receiving telephone calls, writing of various types of letters, describing and explaining of processes or procedures, and replying to or arguing against a viewpoint. It does not lay down the maximum or minimum level to be reached. The syllabus says, "For all practical purposes, the minimum level is simply where the communicational *intent* is successfully conveyed, irrespective of the linguistic finesse. The maximum level is, of course, native speaker ability" (1975, p. 4). For more and more students, the minimum level is now all they can aim for, given the situation of English in the country. All these factors have thus accelerated the development of a Utilitarian English in the country, something that would probably not have happened, at least not as quickly, if English had remained the dominant language of the country.

The situation in Malaysia today is similar to that of a number of countries in the Third World, as far as the role of English is concerned. Focusing on the Utilitarian English in Malaysia will therefore provide some idea of the type of Utilitarian English referred to in this paper. In one respect, though, Malaysia may have gone further ahead than the other Third World countries in that government policy, facing the realities of the situation and perhaps coming to grips with the inevitable, given the national education policy of putting Bahasa Malaysia as the first and primal language to suit national needs, appears to be backing the development of its own, simplified use of English. It is recognized that the aim of communication, never mind correct grammar, syntax, or style, will probably lead in the near future to a greatly simplified form of English used by the average Malaysian, but this is considered a small price to pay for the promotion of the national language. In the national education policy, English is now viewed and treated as a utilitarian language, a tool to be used instead of an object to be admired.

The minimum level required for communication purposes is marked, in the main, by simplification and reduction of native-speaker English, very evident on the levels of vocabulary, pronunciation, and grammar, with the last mentioned level possibly showing the most widespread examples of this. Simplification and reduction of target language forms is to be expected, as it is a normal process of second language acquisition, already well documented in the literature. The following three sections will now detail some of the simplifications and reductions that characterise the Utilitarian English as it is developing in Malaysia.

Vocabulary

The vocabulary of Utilitarian English in Malaysia is characteristically quite limited and thus devoid of the richness of synonyms, near-synonyms, and subtle distinctions of meaning prevalent in native-speaker English. As is evident, speakers of a language simplify it by reducing the number of words used. One consequence of this is that some of these words are overused, being made to serve a variety of functions which are normally performed by other words in native-speaker English. Thus these same words are given wide extensions of meaning not normal in native-speaker contexts. One notable example is the use of the verbs *open* and *close* to replace verb-particle constructions like *switch on* and *switch off*, *turn on* and *turn off*, as in the utterances:

open the light/fan/radio/tap/TV
close the TV/radio/light/fan/tap

In addition, the expression *open your shoes* is also not uncommon (though the converse, *close your shoes*, is never found), replacing the verb-particle construction *take off* (your shoes).

Another example of a word which has been given extensions of meaning is the verb *cut*, which is also used with the following meanings, in addition to the meanings of the word as used in native-speaker English:

overtake: "His car cut mine."
beat (someone), as in a competition: "He cut me by only one mark."
reduce, deduct: "He cut me five dollars."

The following list gives further examples of words found in Utilitarian English in Malaysia that have much wider applications of use and meaning than in native-speaker English. Only these extra meanings are indicated. These are in addition to the usual meanings of each word as they are normally found in native-speaker English.

1. The verb *call* is used with the following meanings:
    ask: "He called me to go out with him."
    invite: "I'll call Kok Cheng to come to the party."
    re-employ: "If you want to call me back, I'll be waiting."
    call out to, order: "Mother called them to stop shouting."
2. The verb *join* has the additional two meanings:
    take part in: "I joined the festivities that evening."
    attend: "He joined several extra-mural courses."
3. The verb *follow* is used with the additional meaning:
    go with, accompany: "Would you like to follow me?"

4. The verb *scrap* often has the additional meaning of:
   abolish or *cancel*: "Parking facilities have been scrapped in this building."
5. The verb *rear* is also used with the meaning of:
   breed: "He likes to rear fish."
6. The verb *keep* also has the meaning:
   put away: "I kept the empty box on top of the cupboard."
7. The verb *spoil* also has the meaning:
   to be out of order: "My telephone is spoilt" or "My radio is spoilt."
8. The verb *carry* may mean:
   to pull: "We carried him out of the wreck."
   to hold: "He carried a book in his hand."

It is perhaps significant that most of the more conspicuous examples of such wider applications of meanings are to be found in the verbs, rather than being roughly spread out among the four major form-classes of speech.

Another consequence of the simplification and reduction of native speaker English, as found in the Utilitarian English of Malaysia, is that many subtle distinctions between the meanings of near-synonyms are either completely lost or ignored. Again, it is in the area of the verbs that the most conspicuous examples of this are to be found. The differences of meaning between the following groups of verbs, for example, are extremely subtle, and thus very difficult for the nonnative-speaker of English to grasp and remember:

borrow/lend
come/go
bring/take/fetch/send
live/stay/put up
say/speak/talk

In a Utilitarian type of English, these distinctions are usually just ignored and the words in each group are used interchangeably, as if they had identical meanings. See the following examples, with the native-speaker equivalent of each verb used given within parentheses:

1. His father took him here. (brought)
2. I have to bring my son to see the dentist. (take)
3. I have to send Susan to school in the morning (take)
4. Can you come to Kok Seng's house tonight? (go)
5. Can I lend your book for a while? (borrow)
6. May I go to your room now? (come)
7. I stay in Kuala Lumpur. (live)
8. I put up with my brother. (live)

Yet another consequence of the simplification and reduction of native-speaker English is that words are sometimes used in other parts of speech in addition to their usual function. Sometimes these words may be given derivational suffixes to mark the change of function, but sometimes they are not. The noun *friend*, for example, has given rise to the verb *to friend* (someone), meaning *to be friends with*, as in the sentence very often heard among school children in Malaysia:

I don't want to friend him.

Another well-known example is the noun *school*, which has given rise to the verb *schooling* (with the *-ing* suffix), meaning *attending school*, as in the sentence:

Her children are still schooling.

This phenomenon of words being used in other functions and other parts of speech is very likely due to the fact that the total number of words in the vocabulary of Utilitarian English is quite restricted, so that some words have to serve in a number of new ways and contexts uncommon to native-speaker English.

Pronunciation

In the area of the pronunciation of Utilitarian English in Malaysia, simplification and reduction can be noticed in at least three areas: the simplification of consonant clusters, the simplification of 'difficult' sounds, and the simplification in stress. First, in the area of consonant clusters, many speakers of Utilitarian English find it extremely difficult to pronounce certain clusters of consonants, especially at the ends of words. This is understandable since most Asian languages seldom have two or more consonants pronounced together. The simplification and reduction of such difficult clusters is carried out in either one of two ways: (1) by dropping one or more of the consonants from the cluster, as can be seen in the following examples:

desks	becomes	*des*	*guests*	becomes	*guess*
tasks	"	*tas*	*prompts*	"	*proms*
risks	"	*ris*	*script*	"	*scrip*
depth	"	*dep*	*collect*	"	*collec*
clasps	"	*claps*			

(2) by inserting a vowel into the consonent cluster, thus breaking it up into two syllables, as in the following examples:

film	becomes	*filem*
little	"	*littel*
turtle	"	*turtel*

Incidentally, many English words borrowed into Bahasa Malaysia have undergone this second method of simplifying consonant clusters in the process of adaptation into the morphological structure of the borrowing language. The following list provides some examples of this:

stocking	becomes	setokin	padre	becomes	paderi
slipper	"	selipa	plan	"	pelan
cream	"	kerim	clinic	"	kelinik
critic	"	keritik	crisis	"	kerisis

Some of the sounds of native-speaker English are very difficult for the nonnative-speaker to pronounce. The strategy generally followed is to simplify these difficult sounds by substituting them with "simpler" equivalents. The most conspicuous example of this is the *th* sound, both voiced and unvoiced, which many Malaysians and even native-speakers find great difficulty with. The voiced *th* is usually replaced by *d* and the voiceless *th* by *t,* as in the following examples:

breadth	becomes	bred	that	becomes	dat
three	"	tree	this	"	dis
think	"	tink	clothes	"	clodz
thread	"	tread	bath	"	bat
thrill	"	trill	though	"	dough

Another sound that speakers of Utilitarian English in Malaysia find difficulty with is the *v* sound, especially in non-final position. This generally gets replaced with a sound rather similar to *w*, as indicated in the following examples:

| valley | becomes | walley | even | becomes | ewen |
| vow | " | wow | heaven | " | heawen |

However, it has been found that children can be taught quite easily to pronounce the *v* as in native-speaker English, once their attention is directed to it and the similarity between *v* and *f* is pointed out to them, but they, and therefore the majority of adult Malaysians, continue to experience great difficulty with both the *th* sounds throughout their lives.

The third type of simplification in the area of pronunciation is found in the stress placement of Utilitarian English. A large number of words in native-speaker English change the position of the stressed syllable according to the part of speech the word is found in. For example, the nouns *technology* and *technologist* are stressed on the second syllable but the adjective *technological* receives its primary stress on the third syllable instead. In Utilitarian English in Malaysia, the problem of where to put the stress, always an ever-present problem for the nonnative-speaker, is solved by keeping the primary stress on the same syllable, regardless of the change of form or function the word may undergo. This may be considered an instance of overgeneralisation, a common strategy for all language learners everywhere. Examples of the stress patterns in Utilitarian English follow:

| spec*ify* | spe*cific* | spe*cifically* |
| re*medy* | re*medial* | |

contri*bute*   contri*bu*tor   contri*bu*tion
ad*va*ntage   ad*va*ntageous
a*ca*demy   a*ca*demic
e*co*nomy   e*co*nomic   e*co*nomically

The placement of stress is therefore another area in which the tendency of Utilitarian English to simplify the native-speaker sound system can be seen, the simplification being the result of greater consistency in the placement of stress than is found in native-speaker English. Consistency and generalization are always simpler for the language learner than exceptions to rules, and thus it is not at all surprising to see this strategy in operation in the Utilitarian English of Malaysia.

Finally, in the area of pronunciation, mention should also be made of the tendency in Utilitarian English towards spelling pronunciations. While this is not strictly a simplification and reduction procedure, the rationale behind this tendency towards spelling pronunciations can be easily understood. In nonnative-speaker contexts such as Malaysia, where native-speaker English is seldom encountered by the average user of the language, the most convenient guide to pronunciation is the spelling, even for a language like English, which is notorious for its spelling inconsistencies. But the nonnative-speaker of the language has no better guide, even while admitting the inadequacies of the present English spelling system. Thus we have the following spelling pronunciations in Malaysia:

post-age   *Wednezday*
envis-age   *medicine*
waste-age   *plum-ber*
pur-chase   *sword*
re-cord (verb)   *haitch* (i.e., the letter *h*)
con-firm   *occasion*
fam-iliar (perhaps because of its apparent similarity with *family*)

In this connection too it should perhaps be mentioned that the tendency towards spelling pronunciations is also evident in at least one native-speaker country, that is the United States where the words *trait* and *draught* are often pronounced as they are spelled (*trate* and *draught*) rather than as *tray* and *draft*, respectively. This may be a consequence of the spread of English throughout the modern world today and the great influence and importance which the written word has, so much so that it is tending to guide rather than depict the pronunciations of words.

Grammar

It is in the area of grammar that the most widespread simplifications and reductions of native-speaker English may be seen. One could almost grade the variety of the language used according to the number of grammatical simplifications and reductions employed. The fewer they are, the nearer native-like ability the language is. This would therefore mark the acrolect in Malaysia, whose speakers would range between only five to ten percent. The mesolectal and basilectal varieties of the language would exhibit much more simplification and reduction, characteristic of the majority of Malaysians in the country. Only the more prominent simplifications will be pointed out in the following.

A. Simplification of the question tag:

The disproportionately burdensome English tag question has already been mentioned earlier in this paper, together with Quirk's proposal to regularize it to the one unchangeable form *is that so*? However, it is interesting to note that Utilitarian English users in Malaysia already have an invariant form to function as the question tag, the form *isn't it*?, regardless of the subject and auxiliary used in the main clause. Examples follow:

She was quite young, isn't it?
You're not doing anything now, isn't it?
Just flowers, isn't it?
He's a bore, isn't it?

B. Simplification of the noun system:

One important grammatical distinction in native-speaker English is that between countable and uncountable nouns. However, many nonnative-speakers of the language have great difficulty in remembering which nouns are countable and which are not, and which are the rules specific to each. Users of Utilitarian English tend to ignore this distinction between countable and uncountable nouns, thus simplifying the grammar of the language. They treat most nouns as countable, subjecting them to the same set of rules. This too can be considered a case of over-generalisation, again a common learning strategy in language learners. Thus, in Utilitarian English in Malaysia, we frequently meet with expressions such as the following:

Give me a chalk.
Pick up your chalks.
There are a lot of equipments in the shop there.
He likes to use a lot of jargons in his speech.
All the aircrafts there belong to the Air Force.
We saw beautiful sceneries all along the way. Women love to wear lots of
    jewelleries.
Let me give you an advice.
The mails come early in this part of the town.
I love to eat fruits.
Please put your luggages over there.

C. Simplification of the verb system:

The verb system of native-speaker English is extremely complex. It is not at all surprising, therefore, to find Utilitarian English simplifying this in several ways:

1. By using adverbial words and phrases which indicate time rather than inflecting the verb to show tense, for example:

He leave my house last night.
This evening we go shopping.
When we get there, he left already.
He say we must all be ready by five.

It is interesting to compare this with the other languages used in Malaysia which also do not inflect the verb to indicate tense but leave it rather to the context to do this.

2. By not inflecting the verb to show agreement with the number of its subject, for example:

He say it all the time.
Teacher don't let us do it.
My father work in a big office.
The breadman come everyday.

3. By not using some of the less common tense forms of native-speaker English, replacing them with just the simple present or the simple past tense. This thus effectively reduces the number of tenses that a speaker of Utilitarian English will have to deal with. For example, the conditional and the past perfect forms are usually dispensed with altogether, as in the following examples:

He called a cab by the time we arrived.
He mentioned this to me before.
Suppose you do it, and get into trouble, don't blame me.
When I saw him, he already bought the present.

D. Simplification of the modal auxiliary system:
The modal auxiliary system of native-speaker English is also extremely complex, and one which very few nonnative-speakers ever grasp fully. The modals are used to express notions of probability, possibility, certainty, permission, necessity (obligation and compulsion), inclination and ability. What further complicates matters is the fact that the same modal may be used to express more than one of these notions, with no overt markers of this. For example, the modal *can* may be used to express the notions of possibility, permission and ability, as in the following sentences:

He can be lying.	—	possibility
He can have five dollars.	—	permission
He can fix this for you.	—	ability

Similarly, the modal *may* is used to express both possibility and permission, as shown respectively in the two sentences:

He may bring something back.
You may leave the room.

This ambiguity of meaning occurs with some of the other modals, too. It is not surprising, therefore, that this causes great diffculties for nonnative-speakers of English.

Malaysian users of Utilitarian English have managed to develop a single, much simpler system of expressing notions which may well be expressed by the modal auxiliaries in native-speaker English. It is not possible within the scope of this paper to give a detailed account of the Malaysian system which, however, has been investigated in at least two unpublished dissertations (see Tan, 1980, and de Silva, forthcoming), the first dealing with the written norm and the second with the communicative norm. For one thing, Malaysians seldom bother to distinguish between the differing degrees of possibility, probability, virtual certainty, and certainty which Halliday says are expressed by the epistemic modals (1970). Often the initial phrase *I think* serves to introduce one notion, ranging from probability to certainty. If finer distinctions need to be drawn, Malaysians make do with just two, the first, possibility/probability, being expressed by *maybe* and the second, certainty, being expressed by *must be* or the adverb *surely*. Resorting to substitutes for the modal auxiliaries appears to be a simpler solution which users of Utilitarian English have discovered. The lexical items *possible/possibly/possibility, certain/certainly, sure/surely, presume/presumably, suppose, obvious/obviously, likely, perhaps*, for example, provide more overt markers to indicate the meaning intended. Hence the following sentences will be found in Utilitarian English:

I think he will be home.	— probability/possibility
Surely he will be home.	— certainty
Maybe he will be home.	— probability/possibility
Perhaps he will be home.	— probability/possibility
It is obvious that he will be home.	— certainty
It is likely that he will be home.	— probability/possibility
I am sure that he will be home.	— certainty

This appears to provide a simpler and more manageable system of expressing these notions of probability, possibility, and certainty, because some of the subtler distinctions are done away with and the remaining markers are overt ones, with meanings that are easily discernible.

E. Simplification of question structures:

The question structures of native-speaker English are also rather difficult for the nonnative-speaker. (The question tags were dealt with earlier.) Apart from these, native-speaker English has three other main ways of forming questions: by using *WH* words to form information questions, by either using the normal statement order but with rising intonation at the end or inverting the order of subject and auxiliary verb to form yes/no questions, and by using alternative structures with *or* to form alternative questions. Utilitarian English in Malaysia has these same three types of questions but the structures are simplified in each.

1. For the information questions, Utilitarian English uses the same set of question words, but often not inverting the order of the subject and the auxiliary verb where native-speaker English would. This can be viewed as a simplification strategy, since the same word order learned for the declarative sentences is largely retained for the interrogative sentences, too. (The inversion of subject and auxiliary in native-speaker *WH* questions gives a lot of trouble to the foreign language learner, who has not only to learn to invert the normal order (and thus also change the placement of tense and number agreement in the verb, for example, when the auxiliary *do/does/did* has to be created), but also to revert to the normal declarative order when the question is an indirect one.) The following question structures are quite typical of Utilitarian English in Malaysia:

> What you are doing?
> Who you buy that for?
> When you are leaving?
> Why you go now?
> Where you going?
> Which you buy for him?
> How you carry that?
> Why he must act like that?

2. Of the two methods employed in native-speaker English to form yes/no questions, that which retains the declarative word order pattern is preferred in Utilitarian English. This is understandable, since this pattern does not require the inversion of subject and auxiliary verb, something with which most foreign language learners have great difficulty. However, this type of structure in native-speaker English requires rising intonation at the end. Malaysians seem to prefer a less subtle way of indicating rising intonation (and thus an interrogative) by adding on a particle at the end, whose only function, it appears, is to provide a more overt marker for the rising intonation which signals a question to be attached to. This particle, in most cases, is something like *aa?* or *ah?* The following are some examples of this:

> You like this, ah?
> I get it for you, ah?
> You don't need this, ah?
> He gone out, ah?

It should be remarked in this connection that this particle, *ah?*, is also used with other types of question structures, for example the following:

Can you go with us, ah?
Why you are late, ah?
When you go, ah?
You want this or not, ah?

Any further discussion of the use of this particle must be tied in with the many other particles frequently used in Malaysian English, a topic that is not relevant to this paper.

3. Utilitarian English in Malaysia has simplified the alternative question structure by attaching the phrase *or not* to the preceding question, instead of providing two alternatives, one of which it is supposed is right, for the addressee to choose from, as in native-speaker English. Where a native-speaker would say,

Did you come by bus or by train?

a speaker of Utilitarian English would say,

You come by bus or not?

This type of structure is very useful, especially when the question does not really offer two alternatives apart from an affirmative or a negative answer, as in the following:

You like it or not?
You can do it or not?
He can come to my house or not?
You coming with me or not?

These are therefore not true alternative questions, as are those in native-speaker English, but rather function as yes/no questions. In fact, it may be useful to consider the phrase *or not* as one of those particles, like *ah?*, which are overtly used as markers of questions.

F. Miscellaneous simplifications:
Four other smaller areas of grammatical simplification and reduction, which cannot be grouped together in any other way, are discussed under the heading of miscellaneous simplifications. These are:

1. Omission of the copula.
The copula, with all its various forms, is possibly the most difficult verb in the English language. It is also possibly the verb with the least semantic content. When one bears in mind the fact that most Asian languages do not have a copula, at least not with the same extensive use as the English copula, it is not at all surprising to find it being omitted in Utilitarian English. Thus we have sentences such as:

That man my father.
He very tall.

She selfish.
He terribly afraid then.
You so silly lah.

2. Omission of the "dummy" auxiliary *do/does/did*.

This auxiliary is a purely grammatical construct, with no semantic content at all. Moreover, its placement confuses many nonnative-speakers of English. Speakers of Utilitarian English in Malaysia overcome this problem by omitting this auxiliary altogether, with no loss of meaning. Some examples of this have already been given in the examples of different question structures of Malaysian Utilitarian English. A few other examples of the omission of this auxiliary are:

How you get here?
What you buy?
Why you say that?
When you think you are free?

The examples of the omission of this auxiliary come mainly from the area of *WH* questions mainly becuase, with the lack of inversion in the yes/no questions, there is no reason for the use of *do/does/did* there. Incidentally, it is interesting to note in this connection that the auxiliary is retained for most negatives, for example:

He don't like it.
I don't think it will rain.
You don't want to come along, ah?

3. Omission of empty words.

English is a language in which words sometimes have to be used in order to fulfil the requirements of the grammar alone. In other words, these words are semantically empty, with no meaning of their own. One example is the word *it*, not to be identified with the third person singular pronoun of the same form, in native-speaker English sentences like:

a. It is raining.
b. I would appreciate it if you will let me know soon.
c. It is not permitted to dump rubbish here.
d. It is said that he may retire early.
e. It is true that I took your bicycle.

Speakers of Utilitarian English manage to avoid using the *it* by employing various strategies. Sometimes the word is omitted altogether, as in the Utilitarian versions of the preceding sentences (a) and (b):

Raining lah.
I would appreciate if you will let me know soon.

Sometimes it is by using some other structure which does not require the use of *it*, as in the following Utilitarian versions of sentences (c)–(e):

Don't dump your rubbish here.
People say that he may retire early.
Yes, I took your bicycle.

4.Refusal to invert word order after negative adverbs.

Negative adverbs like *neither, rarely, seldom, never,* and *not only* require an inversion of the normal subject and auxiliary verb order in native-speaker English, as in the following sentences:

Seldom did he meet with an accident.
Never have I met such stupidity before.
Rarely was he late for work.

Utilitarian English retains the normal word order in such contexts, since inversion is seldom ever carried out in this variety of the language, giving rise to sentences like:

Seldom he met with an accident.
Never I have met such stupidity before.
Rarely he was late for work.

UTILITARIAN ENGLISH FOR THE THIRD WORLD?

At first sight, the disadvantages of Utilitarian English appear to be enormous. Admittedly it would involve a lowering of sights from native-speaker English, and because of this the connotations of inferiority appear to be unavoidable. However, there are also strong arguments that can be put forward for the adoption of Utilitarian English by the Third World. After all, English is only *one* of the major languages of most countries in the Third World, and as such the demands on its use are necessarily more limited than those on the use of native-speaker English. It is not denied that there should still be room for an elite in each country, marked as such by native-like proficiency in English, whose need for the language will be greater; however, the model of language selected should not be geared towards them but rather to the average user of the language. If these arguments are accepted, then Nuclear English and Utilitarian English deserve thoughtful consideration as possible alternatives for the use of the Third World.

In this, Utilitarian English has an undeniable headstart over Nuclear English, in that some form of it is already in actual use in natural contexts in many parts of the Third World. Thus it is a natural language and not an artificial or a theoretical construct. It is a product of actual simplification and pidginization processes which show great areas of similarity across the geographical boundaries of the world. Not only this, but many of the simplification and reduction features of Utilitarian English are also evident in native-speaker children's speech (the difference, of course, being that these features are gradually eliminated in the process of the children acquiring adult speech, whereas in Utilitarian English these features are, as it were, fossilized). This would indicate that these simplification and reduction processes are based on some feature, though as yet not fully understood, which evidence would lead us to assume is present in the language acquisition device of all humans, regardless of actual linguistic context and geographical location.

This claim, however, needs empirical justification, and this is the task facing all who would agree with the choice of Utilitarian English for the Third World. We need descriptions of the local varieties of English in the countries of the Third World, so that across-the-board comparisons may be made and generalizations drawn. There are now encouraging signs of the increasing recognition of nativized or indigenized varieties of English within the disciplines of linguistics and applied linguistics. Serious accounts of the forms and functions of these new varieties of English have begun to emerge. However, most of these have not been carried out with Utilitarian English in view. As such, not all the descriptions are useful for the purpose at hand, and thus much more needs to be forthcoming. Chiefly, we need to distinguish, in these descriptions, between the features that can be attributed to simplification and reduction processes, and those that are due to interference features from the linguistic and social context. For the purposes of Utilitarian English, only the former would be relevant. Some of the pertinent simplification and reduction features of Malaysian English have been mentioned in the preceding section of this paper. It can reasonably be expected that many of these will likewise be found in the other Englishes of the Third World. For example, it is interesting to note that both Malaysian English and Indian English appear to have simplified and reduced the tag question to the invariant *isn't it?* form. If this were discovered to be the case in the majority of the other Third World Englishes, then it would be included as a feature of the "universal" Utilitarian English that is being proposed for the Third World. It is a demanding task, but perhaps not as demanding as aiming for native-speaker English in the Third World. Moreover, the chances of Utilitarian English succeeding are good, because similar versions of it have already developed in nonnative-speaker contexts, through learner strategies which appear to be identical, irrespective of linguistic or social context. Developing a universal Utilitarian English merely requires that the common feaatures be noted and encouraged, leaving room, at the same time, for regional differences to exist. In the end, there will not be just *one* Utilitarian English in use throughout the Third World, just as there isn't *one* model of native-speaker English used in native-speaker contexts today. However, on the lines of native-speaker English, the differences will not be so great as to impede intelligibility altogether. From the examples already provided, it will be noticed that very little loss of basic meaning ensues when the more complicated structures of native-speaker English get simplified and reduced into Utilitarian English. Utilitarian English is thus comprehensible to the native-speaker as it is to the nonnative-speaker; hence its suitability for use in international communication. Utilitarian English is thus yet another variety of English, which has its part to play in enriching the language and contributing to its linguistic mosaic.

It might well be asked why it is necessary to talk about actively choosing Utilitarian English for the Third World if it is already in existence in these countries today, even if only as a by-product of attempting to aim for native-speaker English. A happy compromise might seem to have been already reached in this, in that the learner of the language is allowed to go as far as he is able, linguistically, to reach even native-like command of the language if he has the capability for it, or to fall off by the way according to the degree of his linguistic capability. However, this compromise is an expensive one, in terms of the results it achieves, as has already been pointed out. Various forms of Utilitarian English have developed in the different regions of the Third World. Whether we like it or not, whether we encourage it or not, it seems the Utilitarian English will increase in use in the world today and in the near future. There is much in it that is attractive for the nonnative-speaker. Rejecting this and insisting on native-speaker English all this while has succeeded in doing no more than merely delaying the inevitable, the continued spread and increase of Utilitarian English on the world scene.

If we accept the fact that Utilitarian English is here to stay, working towards this rather than against it would be far less expensive, wasteful, and frustrating. Attempts to stop the development of Utilitarian English will not only prove futile, but are also undesirable from the linguistic point of view. Working towards Utilitarian English would entail, on the other hand, the recognition of communicative competence as the goal in the use of the language. The criterion should be *whether* a message is communicated, not *how well* it has been communicated in terms of style. The focus should be on what sorts of tasks the nonnative-speaker of English will conceivably be required to perform in English, and equipping the learner with the basics necessary to perform them. For example, one of the basics would be the normal declarative word order pattern in English. Deviations from this normal word order are merely secondary, as can be seen from the fact that Utilitarian English in Malaysia can retain the normal word order pattern unchanged, without exception, and yet remain intelligible to speakers of educated English everywhere. The singular plural distinction in countable nouns would also be regarded as basic, the uncountable nouns being the exceptions and therefore not emphasized. Focusing on basics, rather than on inessentials, which seem totally unmotivated from the point of view of the language learner, would lead to increased efficiency in language teaching in that it would allow the learner more time to come to grips with the essentials of the language, which he would also be motivated to grasp.

Native-speaker English appears to be on the way out in the Third World today, while Utilitarian English, in one form or another in the different regions of the Third World, is here to stay and grow from strength to strength. To ignore this and insist that nonnative-speaker contexts today would not only be unrealistic but also totally irresponsible. In conclusion, let us recognize and accept the existence of Utilitarian English in the Third World today, and adjust our goals and our attitudes towards it appropriately, as the Third World's choice of a satisfactory alternative to native-speaker English for its own ends.

REFERENCES

de Silva, E. Meaning and use of modality and modulation in the Malaysian English speech continuum. M.A. thesis. University of Malaya. Forthcoming.

Gage, W., and Ohannessian, S. ESOL enrollments throughout the world. *English Teaching Forum.* 1977, 15, 3, 19–21.

Halliday, M. A. K. Functional diversity in language as seen from a consideration of modality and mood in English. *Foundations of Language.* 1970, 6, 322–361.

Kachru, B. Models of English for the third world: White man's linguistic burden or language pragmatics? *TESOL Quarterly.* 1976, 10, 2, 221–239.

Ministry of Education, Malaysia. *Teachers' Handbook for the Post-1970 Primary School English Syllabus.* Kuala Lumpur, Malaysia. Dewan Bahasa dan Pustaka, 1971.

Ministry of Education, Malaysia. *English Language Syllabus in Malaysian Schools, Tingkatan 4–5.* Kuala Lumpur, Malaysia: Dewan Bahasa dan Pustaka, 1975.

Prator, C. The British heresy in TESL. In J. Fishman, C. A. Ferguson, and J. Das Gupta (eds.) *Language Problems in Developing Nations.* John Wiley & Sons, 1968, 459–476.

Quirk, R. On the grammar of 'Nuclear English.' Paper presented at the Conference on English as an International Auxiliary Language, East-West Center, Honolulu, 1978.

Smith, L. English as an international auxiliary language. *RELC Journal.* 1976, 7, 1, 38–42.

Tan, D. An analysis of the use of modal auxiliaries as indicators of modality and modulation in letters to the English language newspapers in Peninsular Malaysia, October 1976. M.A. thesis. University of Malaya, 1980.

Tongue, R. *The English of Singapore and Malaysia.* Singapore: Eastern Universities Press, 1974.